POLICY, OFFICE OR VOTES?

C000136939

Leaders of political parties often have to cho[...] such as influence on policy, control of the go[...] voters. This book examines the behavior of political parties in situations where they experience conflict between two or more important objectives. The volume offers a theoretical introduction and case studies of party leaders in Germany, Italy, France, and Spain, as well as six small European democracies. Each case focuses on the behavior of one or several parties in situations of goal conflict, such as the "Historic Compromise" in Italy, the 1982 *Wende* in West Germany, the making of the new Swedish constitution in the 1970s, and the termination of the Austrian "black-red" grand coalition. In their conclusions, the editors discuss how such leadership decisions can be understood and examine the causes of different choices among party leaders.

Wolfgang C. Müller is Associate Professor of Political Science at the University of Vienna. He has served as guest professor at the University of Mannheim, Humboldt University, Berlin, and the University of California, San Diego. He has published widely on Austrian politics and comparative politics. His articles have appeared in journals such as *Electoral Studies,* the *European Journal of Political Research,* the *Journal of Theoretical Politics, Legislative Studies Quarterly, Party Politics, Political Studies,* and *West European Politics.* His books (as coauthor and editor) include *Sozialpartnerschaft in der Krise: Möglichkeiten und Grenzen des Neokorporatismus in Österreich* (Vienna: Böhlau, 1985), *Politics in Austria: Still a Case of Consociationalism?* (London: Frank Cass, 1992), *The State in Western Europe: Retreat or Redefinition?* (London: Frank Cass, 1994), *Die Politiker* (Vienna: Manz, 1995), *Die Organisation der österreichischen Sozialdemokratie, 1889–1995* (Vienna: Löcker, 1996), *Handbuch des politischen Systems Österreichs* (Vienna: Manz, 1997), *Members of Parliament in Western Europe* (London: Frank Cass, 1997), and *Regierungskoalitionen in Westeuropa* (Vienna: Signum, 1997).

Kaare Strøm is Professor of Political Science at the University of California, San Diego. He is the author of *Minority Government and Majority Rule* (Cambridge University Press, 1990), for which he received the sixth UNESCO Stein Rokkan Prize in comparative social science research in 1994. He is coeditor of two other books, *Challenges to Political Parties: The Case of Norway* (Ann Arbor: University of Michigan Press, 1997) and *Regierungskoalitionen in Westeuropa* (Vienna: Signum, 1997). He has also published numerous articles in the *American Political Science Review,* the *American Journal of Political Science,* the *European Journal of Political Research,* and other leading journals. Strøm has also served on the editorial boards of the *American Political Science Review,* the *Journal of Politics,* the *European Journal of Political Research,* and *Legislative Studies Quarterly,* as well as on the Political Science Advisory Panel of the National Science Foundation.

CAMBRIDGE STUDIES IN COMPARATIVE POLITICS

General Editor
PETER LANGE Duke University

Associate Editors
ROBERT H. BATES Harvard University
ELLEN COMISSO University of California, San Diego
PETER HALL Harvard University
JOEL MIGDAL University of Washington
HELEN MILNER Columbia University
RONALD ROGOWSKI University of California, Los Angeles
SIDNEY TARROW Cornell University

OTHER BOOKS IN THE SERIES

Carles Boix, *Political Parties, Growth and Equality: Conservative and Social Democratic Economic Strategies in the World Economy*

Catherine Boone, *Merchant Capital and the Roots of State Power in Senegal, 1930–1985*

Michael Bratton and Nicolas van de Walle, *Democratic Experiments in Africa: Regime Transitions in Comparative Perspective*

Valerie Bunce, *Leaving Socialism and Leaving the State: The End of Yugoslavia, the Soviet Union, and Czechoslovakia*

Donatella della Porta, *Social Movements, Political Violence, and the State*

Roberto Franzosi, *The Puzzle of Strikes: Class and State Strategies in Postwar Italy*

Geoffrey Garrett, *Partisan Politics in the Global Economy*

Miriam Golden, *Heroic Defeats: The Politics of Job Loss*

Frances Hagopian, *Traditional Politics and Regime Change in Brazil*

J. Rogers Hollingsworth and Robert Boyer, eds., *Contemporary Capitalism: The Embeddedness of Institutions*

Ellen Immergut, *Health Politics: Interests and Institutions in Western Europe*

Thomas Janoski and Alexander M. Hicks, eds., *The Comparative Political Economy of the Welfare State*

Robert O. Keohane and Helen B. Milner, eds., *Internationalization and Domestic Politics*

Herbert Kitschelt, *The Transformation of European Social Democracy*

Herbert Kitschelt, Zdenka Mansfeldova, Radoslaw Markowski, and Gabor Toka, *Post-Communist Party Systems*

Herbert Kitschelt, Peter Lange, Gary Marks, and John D. Stephens, ed., *Continuity and Change in Contemporary Capitalism*

David Knoke, Franz Urban Pappi, Jeffrey Broadbent, and Yutaka Tsujinaka, eds., *Comparing Policy Networks*

Continued on page following index

POLICY, OFFICE, OR VOTES?

How Political Parties in Western Europe Make Hard Decisions

Edited by

WOLFGANG C. MÜLLER
KAARE STRØM

CAMBRIDGE
UNIVERSITY PRESS

PUBLISHED BY THE PRESS SYNDICATE OF THE UNIVERSITY OF CAMBRIDGE
The Pitt Building, Trumpington Street, Cambridge, United Kingdom

CAMBRIDGE UNIVERSITY PRESS
The Edinburgh Building, Cambridge CB2 2RU, UK   www.cup.cam.ac.uk
40 West 20th Street, New York, NY 10011-4211, USA   www.cup.org
10 Stamford Road, Oakleigh, Melbourne 3166, Australia
Ruiz de Alarcón 13, 28014 Madrid, Spain

First published 1999

Printed in the United States of America

Typeface Garmond #3, 10.5/12 pt.   *System* DeskTopPro$_{/UX}$® [BV]

A catalog record for this book is available from the British Library.

Library of Congress Cataloging-in-Publication Data
Policy, office, or votes? : how political parties in Western Europe
make hard decisions / [edited by] Wolfgang C. Müller, Kaare Strøm ;
[contributors, Torbjörn Bergman . . . et al.].
p.   cm. – (Cambridge studies in comparative politics)
Includes index.
ISBN 0-521-63135-1 (hardbound) ISBN 0-521-63723-6 (pbk)
1. Political parties – Europe, Western.   I. Müller, Wolfgang C., 1957– .
II. Strøm, Kaare.   III. Bergman, Torbjörn.
IV. Series.
JN94.A979P62   1999
324.24 – dc21   98-49530
                                                                    CIP

ISBN 0 521 63135 1 hardback
ISBN 0 521 63723 6 paperback

CONTENTS

FIGURES

TABLES

CONTRIBUTORS

Torbjörn Bergman, *University of Umeå*
Roberto D'Alimonte, *University of Florence*
Jørgen Elklit, *University of Aarhus*
Ron Hillebrand, *University of Leyden*
John D. Huber, *Columbia University*
Galen A. Irwin, *University of Leyden*
Michael Marsh, *Trinity College, Dublin*
Paul Mitchell, *Queen's University–Belfast*
Wolfgang C. Müller, *University of Vienna*
Thomas Poguntke, *University of Mannheim*
Donald Share, *University of Puget Sound*
Kaare Strøm, *University of California–San Diego and University of Bergen*

POLITICAL PARTIES AND HARD CHOICES

Kaare Strøm and Wolfgang C. Müller

Political leaders routinely make momentous decisions, but they cannot always get what they want. Very often their important choices feel both difficult and painful. This is sometimes because these leaders have to act on the basis of incomplete information or because they realize that their options are risky. But it could also be because they have to abandon one goal to attain another. Politicians feel the tug between conflicting options as much as anyone else. Even when making decisions does not mean choosing the lesser of two evils, there may well be severe and uncomfortable trade-offs between different goals they have set themselves. Leadership frequently means making hard choices.

In modern democracies, the leaders who make these choices are highly likely to be party politicians or indeed party leaders. Political parties are the most important organizations in modern politics. In the contemporary world, only a few states do without them. The reason that political parties are well-nigh ubiquitous is that they perform functions that are valuable to many political actors. Political parties play a major role in the recruitment of top politicians, on whom the momentous and painful political decisions often fall. With very few exceptions, political chief executives are elected on the slate of some established political party, and very often the head of government continues to serve as the head of the political party that propelled him or her into office. Democracy may be conceived as a process by which voters delegate policy-making authority to a set of representatives, and political parties are the main organizational vehicle by which such delegation takes place.

Therefore, government decisions and party decisions are often intimately linked. And if government leadership is difficult, so are the decisions that parties have to make. This book explores the latter. How do party leaders make decisions on behalf of their organizations? What trade-offs do they face, and how do they resolve them? What are the constraints under which party leaders operate, both within their parties and in their larger environments? These are the questions the contributors to this volume seek to address. Case studies of party leadership behavior in ten European democracies provide the evidence. To lay the foundations for our inquiry, however, we start by addressing the general role of political parties in modern democracies.

POLITICAL PARTIES AND DEMOCRATIC GOVERNANCE

Students of political parties commonly associate them with democracy itself. David Robertson, for example, claims that "to talk, today, about democracy, is to talk about a system of competitive political parties. Unless one chooses to reject the representative model that has been the staple of the theory and practice of democracy since the French Revolution, one must come to terms with political parties" (Robertson 1976: 1). Or, in the words of G. Bingham Powell, "the competitive electoral context, with several political parties organizing the alternatives that face the voters, is the identifying property of the contemporary democratic process" (Powell 1982: 3). Thus, representative democracy has long been associated with, and indeed equated with, party government. The vast scholarly literature on political parties reflects their real-life importance and has developed along with them. The early twentieth century represented the breakthrough of political parties as the democratic organization par excellence. Parties attained this position both because they were unrivaled in their representational functions and, in particular, because they were the vehicles of previously unenfranchised groups. Parties have taken on such functions *despite* the neglect or active resistance they have met among the framers of most older constitutions. The perceived "evils of faction" were such that political parties were rarely recognized and occasionally actively discouraged (see, e.g., Sartori 1976).

PARTY GOVERNMENT?

The significance of parties in modern democracies is such that observers in many countries have spoken of *partocracy*, or party government. In his studies of *The Future of Party Government*, Richard S. Katz (1986, 1987) defines party government as involving the following conditions:

(1) Government decisions are made by elected party officials or by those under their control.
(2) Government policy is decided within political parties.
(3) These parties then act cohesively to enact and implement this policy.
(4) Public officials are recruited through political parties.
(5) Public officials are held accountable through political parties.

In other words, under party government, parties serve to organize policy making in government (points 1, 2, and 3), they function as devices through which voters can make their voices heard (point 5), and they control the recruitment of political personnel (point 4). These functions remind us of V. O. Key's (1964) celebrated distinction between the party in government, the party in the electorate, and the party organization.

Two major works of recent vintage have made major strides toward accounting for the purposes of parties and demonstrating their continuing importance in U.S. politics. In *Legislative Leviathan*, Gary W. Cox and Mathew D. McCubbins (1993) argue that parties constitute rational responses by self-interested legislators to such "collective dilemmas" as coordination problems and collective action problems involved in their quest for reelection. Approaching American parties somewhat more broadly and historically, John H. Aldrich (1995) demonstrates the regulative role of parties in three fundamental democratic processes: the selection of candidates, the mobilization of voters, and the achievement of relatively stable legislative majorities. Like Cox and McCubbins, Aldrich identifies the roots of political parties and the functions they serve within the rational choice tradition and specifically in the "new institutionalism" (Shepsle 1986). Both Aldrich and Cox and McCubbins focus on party leaders as political entrepreneurs, a perspective shared by the contributors to this volume.

In recent years, this understanding of the functions of democratic political parties has come under serious attack, most notably among students of American parties. Doom-and-gloom treatises on political parties became a growth industry in the 1970s and 1980s (e.g., Broder 1972; Wattenberg 1990). The theme of party "decline" or "decay," which first appeared in the literature on American politics, has since, in various guises, made its way across the Atlantic. Yet, parties have played major parts in the recent democratization, or redemocratization, of Eastern Europe, Latin America, and parts of Asia and Africa. The alleged demise of political parties in the United States and Western Europe has in no way dissuaded elites in nascent democracies from developing such vehicles of representative mass politics. Even among students of American parties, dissenting voices insist that "the party goes on" (Kayden and Mahe 1985) or even that "the party's just begun" (Sabato 1988). Though political parties may no longer command the loyalties they once did, they are still critical to democratic government.

PARTY DEMOCRACY?

To the extent that parties still perform important political functions, what is their role in representative democracy? What conditions do parties have to meet to serve as useful vehicles of representation? According to the anti-elitist theories of democracy, true representative democracy requires, at the very least, internally democratic political parties. According to Alan Ware:

> There are two reasons why democrats who advocate the notion of popular choice might favour internally democratic parties. Such parties would extend the arena within the state in which citizens could be involved in making choices relating to the state's objectives; and, involving such people in the process of constructing policy programmes will make it less likely that unspecific and ambiguous statements will take the place of actual policies in the programmes presented to the voters. That is, democratic control of a party makes for both more democracy and acts as a mechanism to prevent distortions in the process of electoral choice. (Ware 1987: 25–6)

Party leaders must, in this view, be accountable to their rank and file and serve as their *delegates* rather than as *trustees*. That is to say, they should regard themselves as speaking for their constituents and voting as their constituents would have wanted. Democracy requires that citizens remain sovereign and capable of instructing their elected officials. In the view of some anti-elitists, true democracy may even require the absence of leadership and hierarchy. As Michels (1962: 364) puts it, "every system of leadership is incompatible with the most essential postulates of democracy." Representative democracy, then, is attainable only if "the iron law of oligarchy" within parties can be counteracted or at least contained.

This emphasis on intraparty democracy contrasts with a tradition in which *interparty* competition is considered sufficient for representative democracy. The classical formulation here is that of Schumpeter, who defines democracy as the "competitive struggle for the people's vote." The role of the people is simply to "produce a government" (Schumpeter 1943: 269), and Schumpeter shows no concern with the internal democracy of the organizations that guarantee popular rule. In Sartori's generally sympathetic interpretation, the Schumpeterian model implies that "large-scale democracy is not an enlargement or a sheer adding up of many 'little democracies' " (Sartori 1987: 152). William Riker, who essentially stands in the same tradition, argues that "the function of voting is to control officials, *and no more*" (Riker 1982: 9; emphasis in the original). In this *liberal* or *Madisonian* model of democracy, "the liberal remedy is the next election. That is all that is needed to protect liberty; so election and limited tenure are sufficient" (Riker 1982: 9).

These two traditions thus differ in the representational role they ascribe to democratic political parties. In the first ("populist" in Riker's terminology) tradition, parties should faithfully represent the policy preferences of their members and followers. In the second ("liberal") tradition, parties should maximize their opportunities to gain office, whether or not the positions they take correspond to the policy preferences of their members. Under certain circumstances, that might mean maximizing their expected number of votes. That brings us to the crux of this book, which is how party leaders choose between different objectives and how such decisions are constrained. Before we can address those issues, however, we need a more precise analytical framework in which to understand the functions of political parties and analyze the "goods" that they value.

PARTY GOALS AND BEHAVIORS

Scholars typically lament the previous lack of attention to their research topics of choice. One could hardly, in good faith, make such a complaint regarding political parties. The scholarly literature that examines political parties is enormous, and yet our systematic knowledge of party objectives and behavior is still quite modest. We have no general theory of the preferences and behavior of party leaders. Indeed, there is hardly even a commonly accepted vocabulary, and most theoretical efforts that have been made do not recognize the trade-offs that are our focus here. In recent years, however, the study of party behavior has increasingly been influenced by the rational choice tradition in political science. This literature has furnished us with some fruitful and elegant models of competitive party behavior, which assume that parties have a small and well-defined set of objectives. In the simplest terms, we can distinguish between (1) office-seeking, (2) policy-seeking, and (3) vote-seeking models of party behavior.[1]

1. *The Office-Seeking Party.* Office-seeking parties maximize their control over political office benefits, that is, private goods bestowed on recipients of politically discretionary governmental or subgovernmental appointments. The office-seeking party derives mainly from the study of government coalitions in parliamentary democracy (Leiserson 1968; Riker 1962). Riker distinguishes his position from the competing Downsian model in this way:

   Downs assumed that political parties (a kind of coalition) seek to maximize votes (membership). As against this, I shall attempt to show that they seek to maximize only up to the point of subjective certainty of winning (Riker 1962: 33)

   In Riker's view, what parties fundamentally seek is to win, and in parliamentary democracies, winning means controlling the executive branch, or as much of that branch as possible. Office-seeking behavior aims at such goods. As Laver and Schofield put it, "typically the yearning for office is seen, as it was seen by Riker, as the desire to control some sort of fixed prize, a prize captured by the winning coalition and divided among its members" (Laver and Schofield 1990: 40).

   While the idea that party leaders strive for office is well established, there is less agreement on their underlying motivations. Budge and Laver point out an ambiguity in the office-seeking model of party behavior:

We can defend in two ways the assumption that those involved in coalition bargaining are motivated by the desire to get into government. In the first place, the rewards of office may be valued intrinsically, in and for themselves. In the second place, office may be valued only instrumentally for the ability that it gives to influence policy outputs. The intrinsic and instrumental value of office have [sic] not traditionally been distinguished. (Budge and Laver 1986: 490)

We might add that party leaders could value office instrumentally for electoral reasons, too. Incumbency may be a help in future elections, and party leaders may seek office for that reason. In other words, a party might strive to capture executive office because its leaders simply want the spoils (perquisites), because they would like to use these levers to affect public policy, or because they think they can gain favor with the voters by exploiting the advantages of incumbency. Office can have an intrinsic value, or it can have an instrumental, electoral, or policy value. Although political office frequently does enhance policy effectiveness or future electoral success, the former may be more generally true than the latter. That is to say, for politicians who wish to affect public policy, it is almost always better to be in office than not. But although being in office is sometimes a help in future elections, this is far from always the case (see Rose and Mackie 1983). Incumbents gain recognition, which may help them with the voters, but they also get saddled with responsibilities, which may be much less electorally advantageous.

In many situations, it is beyond our capacity as analysts to identify the ultimate purpose for which office is sought. Yet, to explain different leadership choices, we need first of all to be able to differentiate clearly between them. We need to keep our operational definition of office-seeking behavior simple. When we try to identify office-seeking behavior, therefore, we "bracket" the more complex instrumentalities and simply ask, "Is this behavior aimed at increasing the party's control of executive office benefits, for whatever reason, even if it means sacrificing policy objectives or our prospects in the next election?"

The lure of office begins with the spoils that constitute cabinet portfolios. Students of executive coalitions commonly operationalize office benefits as shares of government portfolios. Empirical studies often treat these offices as if they were equally valued and interchangeable. Yet, there is no need to constrain our conception of office benefits to this extent (see Laver and Schofield 1990). Office benefits may include a huge number of subcabinet appointments, as in Belgium or in the Italian *sottogoverno*, and these lower-level benefits may indeed swamp the value of cabinet appointments. Occasionally, parties may share in subgovernmental spoils without participating in the cabinet coalition, as with the Italian Communist party (PCI) in the 1970s and 1980s. Office benefits also include government contracts, preferential treatment, and whatever other rents accrue to political parties because of their legislative bargaining power.

2. *The Policy-Seeking Party*. The second model of party behavior is that of the policy-seeking party, which seeks to maximize its impact on public policy. De Swaan, a leading proponent, puts the assumption this way: "considerations of policy are foremost in the minds of the actors . . . the parliamentary game is, in fact, about the determination of major government policy" (De Swaan 1973: 88). Like its office-seeking counterpart, the policy-seeking model of party behavior derives mainly from coalition theory. The policy-seeking model was developed in response to the "policy-blind" assumptions of the first generation of game theoretic studies of government formation. It specifically challenges the assumption that all parties are equally feasible coalition partners, that is to say, that parties are indiscriminate with respect to their coalition partners. Policy-based coalition theory instead assumes that coalitions are made by parties that are congenial in policy terms. If we represent policy positions along a single dimension on which we rank-order the parties, then policy-based theory suggests that successful coalitions should consist of parties that are spatially "connected" (or adjacent) (Axelrod 1970). Under more discriminating cardinal-level policy measures in one or several dimensions, the theory proposes that parties seek to minimize the *policy range* between themselves and their partners.[2]

Policy pursuit consists in taking positions on any number of issues or, more broadly, policy dimensions, related to public policy. A party's success in pursuing its policies depends on its ability to change public policy toward its most preferred positions or to prevent undesirable changes. However, parties may also experience policy sacrifices when they are asked to endorse policies that substantially deviate from the commitments they have previously made or from their most preferred policies. The latter type of policy sacrifice is one that often comes up in bargaining between political parties over cabinet or legislative coalitions.

The two meanings of policy pursuit may conflict, as when a party may secure an improvement over the status quo (e.g., a lower tax rate) through participation in a coalition, but where accepting this deal would mean compromising the party's ideal point or previous policy commitments (e.g., a major tax overhaul). Such an agreement may be construed as either a policy gain or a concession. The crucial question for our purposes concerns the view held by the party leaders themselves. Do they see such agreements as successes or failures in policy terms? Of course, the view of party leaders is, in turn, likely to be conditioned by the preferences of their supporters, or at least by the perceptions that the party leaders themselves have of these preferences. Most party leaders probably view their parties as allowing them discretion to make policy agreements within a certain range of options, which define their opportunities for policy gains or losses. Regardless of what these windows of opportunity are, or precisely how party leaders calculate their gains or losses, models of policy-seeking parties assume that party leaders can identify and differentiate between them.

At the heart of the policy-seeking model lies a belief in the reality and significance of the contest over public policy decisions that characterizes democracy. Citizens of democracies become politically engaged because these choices matter, and they support certain political parties over others because these parties make a difference. Politicians trade in promises of public policy, and the policy-seeking literature implicitly assumes that the ultimate outcomes that flow from such policies matter to them. But, like office, policy can have intrinsic or instrumental value. Party leaders may seek certain policy goals because they think they can benefit in other ways or because they sincerely believe in them.

Policy pursuit is typically presented as a supplement to, rather than a substitute for, office seeking. That is to say, policy-oriented coalition theory typically assumes, at least implicitly, that parties seek office, at least in part, for instrumental reasons, as a means toward policy influence. Thus, the literature portrays the policy-seeking party as one that seeks government portfolios as well as ideologically compatible coalition partners.[3] Since the possible trade-off between these objectives typically is not resolved, the policy-seeking party remains the least adequately developed model of competitive party behavior.

3. *The Vote-Seeking Party.* The third model is that of the vote-seeking party. In Downs's (1957) seminal work on electoral competition, parties are "teams of men" seeking to maximize their electoral support to control government. In Downs's famous formulation, "parties formulate policies in order to win elections, rather than win elections in order to formulate policies" (Downs 1957: 28). From this insight, Downs developed the argument that

> politicians . . . are motivated by the desire for power, prestige, and income . . . their primary objective is to be elected [to public office]. This in turn implies that each party seeks to receive more votes than any other. (Downs 1957: 30–1)

The attentive reader might observe that this assumption seems particularly applicable to two-party systems. Despite some recognition of the complexities of multiparty competition, however, Downs maintained the assumption of vote maximization even in the multiparty context:

> Yet the more votes a party wins, the more chance it has to enter a coalition, the more power it receives if it does enter one, and the more individuals in it hold office in the government coalition. Hence vote-maximizing is still the basic motive underlying the behavior of parties. . . . (Downs 1957: 159)

Thus, in Downs's own formulation, parties are not only vote seekers but also *vote maximizers.* The most preferred outcome for a party leader is one in which his or her party gets the greatest possible number of votes. Subsequent work in the Downsian tradition has amended the vote-maximizing assumption. If turnout is variable and vote-seeking ultimately serves office ambitions, then in a single district the rational candidate maximizes pluralities rather than votes

(Hinich and Ordeshook 1970). And in multidistrict contests, the rational party leader may maximize his or her probability of winning a majority of the contested seats (Robertson 1976). Yet these alternative models still belong to the family of *vote-seeking* parties. Their implications have been explored extensively in spatial models of electoral competition (Enelow and Hinich 1984; Ordeshook 1986).

Vote-seeking models of party behavior have had tremendous appeal to students of party and legislative behavior, particularly in the United States. Yet they are not totally persuasive as primitive assumptions. It makes little sense to assume that parties value votes for their own sake. Contrary to office or policy, votes can only plausibly be *instrumental* goals. Parties only seek votes to obtain either policy influence, the spoils of office, or both. Nevertheless, vote-seeking models can have great heuristic value. Note that Downs implicitly recognized the instrumentality of vote-seeking behavior (in the pursuit of office) but still insisted on the analytical simplicity of vote maximization.

TRADE-OFFS AND COMPROMISES

Party leaders rarely have the opportunity to realize all of their goals simultaneously. The same behavior that maximizes one of their objectives may not lead to the best possible outcome with respect to the others. In some cases, policy pursuit may conflict with a party's ability to capture office. When parties bargain over participation in a new government coalition, for example, they may often be asked to sacrifice some of their policy preferences in order to gain seats at the cabinet table. In order to find coalition partners, party leaders may need to dilute their policy commitments and thus potentially antagonize their own activists. During the lifetime of a coalition in which parties have had to make such compromises, policy conflicts may emerge time and again – for example, at the time of national party conferences, when delegates may seek to pressure party leaders into a renegotiation of coalition policies. As Marsh and Mitchell show in their chapter, the history of the Irish Labour Party is rife with such conflicts.

In other cases, the gains of participating in a cabinet coalition may be likely to carry a price in future elections, so that the trade-off is between office and future electoral performance. This trade-off between office and votes may be less frequently documented through vociferous intraparty exchanges, but it nevertheless exists. Examples may be seen where party leaders conclude that the electoral losses they have suffered are too heavy to justify continued government participation. The Austrian Social Democrats (in 1966) are an example explicitly cited in Müller's chapter, and Elklit makes the same point concerning their Danish "comrades." Similar cases would seem to include the Luxembourg Christian Democrats in 1974 and several of the smaller Italian parties, such as the Republicans (Strøm 1990: 168–74).

Finally, party leaders may find that insisting on particular policy preferences implies an electoral liability. This is often a trade-off party leaders face when they are drafting their electoral platform or manifesto. If this platform contains everything that the hard-core activists want, then it will probably cause the party to fare poorly among the regular voters. On the other hand, an electorally optimal platform may imply policy sacrifices that are hard for the party faithful to swallow. This dilemma is amply illustrated in the British Labour Party's long journey toward the eventual deletion of "Clause IV' (which demanded large-scale nationalization of British enterprise). Both Neil Kinnock and John Smith fought in vain to abolish this policy commitment before Tony Blair eventually succeeded. But even if party leaders manage to contain the claims of activists during the critical phase of the election campaign, such conflicts may reemerge once the party has made its way into government.

Occasionally, party leaders may find themselves in the fortunate situation that the strategies that maximize one of their objectives are also the best means to the others. Much more commonly, however, there are likely to be trade-offs between their different policy goals, and party leaders find that they have to compromise on some goals in order to reach others. Our interest in this volume lies precisely in such compromises: what forms do they take, and under what conditions are they made?

In order to discuss trade-offs and compromises between different party objectives, we have to consider the time horizons of party leaders. Electoral costs and benefits, for example, typically are not realized immediately. Typically, party leaders concern themselves with elections that lie a few months to a few years ahead. They seldom actively look beyond the next election in which they will be involved. Nevertheless, the time horizons of politicians may differ, as some take a more long-term perspective than others. Leaders of millenarian parties may be concerned with elections that lie far in the future and may, like Gramsci, anticipate a "long march through political institutions." Parties with younger supporters and leaders may have lower discount rates than parties populated by more senior citizens and leaders. Parties formed around a specific short-term issue may have little patience and their leader little flexibility to postpone the realization of their policy goals. Such differences in time horizons may, in turn, affect the trade-offs and compromises they are willing to make. Party leaders with a very short time horizon, for example, may be willing to incur more substantial electoral liabilities, particularly if the elections are likely to lie a few years down the road.

Finally, as noted earlier, politicians may be more or less instrumental in their pursuit of "goods" such as policy, office, or votes. As Budge and Laver (1986) have pointed out, party leaders may pursue policy goals either *intrinsically*, because they sincerely care about the policies in question, or *instrumentally*, as a means to the realization of some other goal, for example electoral support. The same distinction could be drawn, as Budge and Laver indeed do, with respect to office pursuits. Yet, electoral goals are different. It makes less sense to think of intrinsic electoral pursuit ("the pure thrill of winning") and more reasonable to assume that vote-seeking is normally instrumental. Votes are not valuable in themselves; they are simply a means by which other objectives, such as policy or power, may be realized.

If vote-seeking behavior is instrumental, then party leaders necessarily look forward to future benefits when they throw themselves into electoral contests, or when they "take positions" or "claim credit" for electoral purposes (Mayhew 1974). Since elections happen only at regular or irregular intervals, electoral pursuits typically mean forward-looking behavior. The degree to which party leaders are consumed with such anticipation and calculation is the best measure of their time horizons. This is particularly true when electoral pursuits conflict with more immediate policy or office gratification. The more party leaders value the future, the more willingly they defer other benefits in the hope of electoral success.

PARTY BEHAVIOR: A UNIFIED FRAMEWORK OF ANALYSIS

Let us then use these simple reflections as a basis for a unified framework in which to analyze the behavior of party leaders in situations of goal conflict. It is easy to fault each of the three simple models of party behavior, and each has often been found wanting empirically. Yet their simplicity and parsimony are virtues rather than reasons for summary dismissal. Their principal value lies in the powerful deductive results they generate in their respective applications. The challenge is to extend and integrate these models into a unified framework of analysis without losing all analytical traction. There have been only a few efforts to build formal models that recognize that party leaders pursue multiple payoffs (Austen-Smith and Banks 1988; Huber 1996; Sened 1995). This is not because rational choice theorists do not realize that such actors have complex objective functions, but rather because it is very difficult to incorporate such complexities in a tractable model.

Our objective here is less ambitious and more empirical. We are not in the business of constructing a deductive model of party behavior. Rather, we aim more modestly for a conceptual framework. This framework should serve three purposes. First, it should allow us analytically to describe different party objectives and relationships between them. Second, it should contain operationalizable terms that we can apply to concrete situations in which party leaders make their critical choices. Third, it should lend itself to more formal theoretical efforts by scholars who set themselves such goals.

In order to move toward such a framework, let us first examine each of the basic models we have just described. In its basic form, each model is *static*, which is to say that the simple models of party behavior seldom consider the instrumentalities we have just mentioned or the longer-term ramifications of different party choices. Second, each model treats parties as *unitary* actors, as if each party were a person (but see Laver and Schofield 1990: ch. 2; Robertson 1976). In reality, of course, most parties are complex organizations. We may get a much more adequate understanding of their behavior by disaggregating them analytically and looking inside these "black boxes." To understand their leaders' behavior, we need to look outside, as well as inside, political parties. Third, each model tends to view parties as *unconstrained* and ignores how the *institutional environment* may limit their options and bias their behavior (Laver and Schofield 1990; Strøm, Budge, and Laver 1994). Finally and relatedly, the simple models tend to imply that party behavior is entirely driven by demand, that is to say, by the preferences of politicians, rather than by the supply of political goods such as office benefits and policy-making opportunities. To understand these "supply-side" factors, we must examine the effects of political institutions, the "rules and roles" by which parties play their games.

To develop a more general behavioral account of competitive political parties, we retain the premise that party leaders may value all three goods discussed earlier: votes, office, and policy. They typically pursue all these goods. We can think of vote-seeking, office-seeking, and policy-seeking as three independent forms of behavior in which party leaders engage. The question is what sorts of trade-offs they make between these goods and under what circumstances.

Pure vote seekers, office seekers, or policy seekers are unlikely to exist, though each of the three basic assumptions can serve as an extreme case. In many situations (though not necessarily all), these pursuits conflict with one another. Our interest in this volume lies precisely in such situations. Figure 1.1 illustrates trade-offs between these different pursuits in a three-dimensional space in which each dimension represents one political good. This representation further assumes that there is some constraint on the total quantity of goods party leaders can obtain, so that they have to choose among their pursuits. The triangle allows us to represent the trade-offs party leaders are willing to make. For simplicity, this illustration assumes that we can think of these trade-offs in the form of weights that party leaders give to each pursuit, and that the sum of these weights is constant (for example, 1). We can thus locate any trade-off function in this three-dimensional space. Reality is obviously more complex, as we discuss throughout this volume, but our objective here is to come up with a simple and intuitive analytical tool.

Under these assumptions, all feasible trade-offs fall in the triangle ABC in Figure 1.1. A purely vote-seeking party, which is unwilling to sacrifice any votes for office or policy, would be at point A. A pure office seeker would be at B and a pure policy seeker at C. Parties that attach no value to any one of the three goods fall on one of the sides of the triangle. Thus, for example, parties that disregard votes fall somewhere on the line BC. Parties that value all three objectives fall somewhere in the triangle's interior. If, for example, a party places some value on votes and more on office than on policy, it falls inside the area ABD.

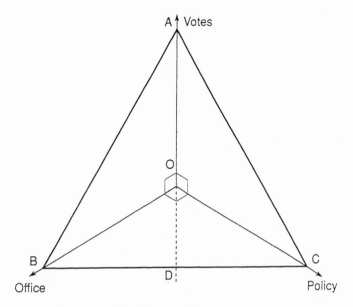

Figure 1.1 Range of feasible party behaviors.

This chapter examines the trade-offs party leaders make among votes, office, and policy. These are often difficult, painful, and consequential choices. They are made by small numbers of individuals in party leadership positions, but they are affected by many more political actors. We therefore focus on party leaders as entrepreneurs and propose some factors that systematically affect and constrain their goal priorities. These factors are organizational properties of political parties, particularly the constraints on their leaders, and the institutional environment and specific situations in which they operate. We use the spatial representation in Figure 1.1 as an illustrative device, but our object here is to develop a set of plausible and testable propositions rather than a formal deductive model.

LEADERSHIP AND PARTY ORGANIZATION

Since the time of Michels (1962), political scientists have been well aware of the oligarchical tendencies in political parties and of the critical role of party leaders. We may think of such leaders as *entrepreneurs*, who get into their business out of self-interest rather than altruism. That is to say, they become party leaders because they expect to benefit (Frohlich, Oppenheimer, and Young 1971). They are able to do so in large part because they help certain groups of citizens solve their collective action problems. They supply various types of political services, some of which may be public goods. Michael Laver (1997: 69) humorously likens them to the hired gun in Western movies: the "tough, fair, and ruggedly handsome stranger" that the townsfolk bring in "to run the villains out of town," that is, to solve their local collective action problem. In more prosaic and contemporary terms, party leaders organize political parties that structure legislative activity and supply public policies demanded by the electorate (Cox and McCubbins 1993). New entrepreneurs emerge through replacement of existing party leaders or through the creation of new parties.

THE OBJECTIVES OF PARTY LEADERS

What do party leaders want, and what are the consequences for their parties? Entrepreneurial party leaders primarily value office benefits, which they can convert into private goods. Votes have no intrinsic value to them, and the value they place on public policy outcomes is unlikely to suffice as a reward for their efforts in organizing political parties. Therefore, office benefits must figure prominently in the calculations of the individuals who become party leaders. Left to their own devices, then, party leaders should pursue office benefits rather than votes or policy (Laver 1997). The pure case of a party led by a dictatorial, unconstrained leader with no electoral competitors should be at B in Figure 1.1.

However, even hardened party leaders do not live by office benefits alone. After all, voters value policy, and there is no reason to believe that party leaders are *less* concerned with policy than ordinary voters. On the contrary, party leaders are typically more policy motivated than the average voter, since only policy-oriented individuals are likely to become leaders in the first place (Laver 1997: 84–5). This is in part because leaders are typically recruited from the ranks of officers and activists, who have self-selected themselves largely because they value policy.

Party leaders, moreover, are neither dictatorial nor unconstrained. Whatever their own preferences, leaders are bound by the organizational properties of their parties. That is to say, they have to consider the preferences of other individuals in their organizations. As Gregory Luebbert (1986: 46) argued, party leaders "are motivated above all by a desire to remain party leaders." To the extent that it is within the power of party members to dislodge their leaders, the latter must make a credible effort to act as a faithful agent of their supporters (see Laver 1997: ch. 4). This constrains the leaders' behavior to a greater or lesser extent. Their hands may also, to varying degrees, be tied by the institutional environment in which their parties operate.

THE ORGANIZATIONAL IMPERATIVE

Entrepreneurial politicians need extraparliamentary party organizations, since successful parties depend on extensive organizational capabilities and resources. Extraparliamentary party organizations commonly address four needs in partic- ular: (1) informational needs about the electorate and its preferences, (2) campaign mobilization of supporters, (3) party and campaign finance, and (4) development and implementation of party policy in various institutions to which it gains access. Party leaders therefore build and maintain organizations to help them compete electorally by acquiring information, mobilizing voters, raising funds, and implementing policy.

There are different ways of building such organizations. We can think of *capital* (e.g., survey and advertising technology) and *labor* (e.g., activists willing to go from door to door, make telephone calls, stuff envelopes, etc.) as the inputs that define the production function of political parties. To some extent, these inputs are mutually substitutable. Parties vary in their labor or capital intensiveness, and the relative efficiency of labor-intensive ("contagion from the left") versus capital-intensive ("contagion from the right") organizations is a matter of scholarly controversy (Duverger 1954; Epstein 1967). To the extent that party leaders are rational entrepreneurs, they build organizations up to the point where the expected marginal returns equal the marginal costs. They choose the ratio of labor to capital according to similar calculations.

ACTIVISTS

The costs of extraparliamentary party organization are very tangible. Competitive parties need considerable resources to compensate activists and professionals such as pollsters and advertising agencies. Campaign professionals generally require direct monetary compensation. Activists, on the other hand, are often happy with nonmonetary compensation such as public policy or spoils. In monetary terms, therefore, activists are cheap labor. However, activists may vary in their preferences for policy and office benefits. Party leaders are often financially strapped and prefer followers whose support is inexpensive. For most party leaders, therefore, the ideal activist is one who highly values promises of future public policy. In other words, party leaders prefer to offer activists *purposive incentives* (Wilson 1973).

However, policy compensation is not enough for activists performing demanding organizational tasks and professional services. Therefore, activists who provide such services, or a lot of services, are at least partly compensated by private benefits. Typically, public office generates most private benefits as well. The mix of office and policy influence benefits offered to party activists affects the balance between *amateur* and *professional* politicians recruited (Clark and Wilson 1961; Wilson 1962). The greater the proportion of office to policy influence benefits, the larger the ratio of professionals to amateurs.

INCENTIVE PROBLEMS

Party leaders commonly face the problem of motivating their activists to exert their best efforts on the party's behalf. A simple application of the "new economics of organization" can illuminate this problem (see Moe 1984). Because party resources typically depend so heavily on elective office, compensation tends to be *prospective*. Activists perform needed services in exchange for promises of future benefits to be delivered if and when the party wins office. At the time they are recruited, activists can have no assurance as to when (or if) they may be compensated. Their payoff, of course, depends on the choices of the voters and, perhaps, on the bargaining success of the party leaders.

Party organizations therefore face the problems of *nonsimultaneous exchange* (see Weingast and Marshall 1988). If activists provide their services before they are compensated, leaders have an incentive to renege on their promises. Recognizing this problem, activists may doubt that they will be appropriately rewarded. Hence, they may work less hard than they would if they knew they would get rewarded. This problem is particularly likely to arise in labor-intensive parties that are not frequently in office. Parties that rely on professional (capital-intensive) services are generally required to pay up front or enter into binding contracts. Therefore, they are less likely to be faced with this problem. Governing parties control larger resources and therefore have greater capacities for immediate compensation.

In many circumstances, the concern party leaders show for their reputations may mitigate this incentive problem (Kreps 1990). Party leaders anticipate future campaigns in which they will again need activists. Hence, they cannot afford to get a reputation for reneging on their promises. However, situations in which activists' performance is not *observable* or *verifiable* exacerbate the incentive problem (see Holmstrom and Tirole 1989). If leaders cannot truly know how well the activists perform, and if the activists have no way of demonstrating this, both groups have a problem, and the organization may suffer. Party leaders might then, without loss of reputation, renege and blame the activists for not delivering on their part of the deal. And the mere anticipation of such leadership behavior, in turn, might cause activists not to exert themselves as much as they otherwise would.

CREDIBLE COMPENSATION MECHANISMS

Leaders and activists therefore have a mutual interest in mechanisms that allow the former to make credible compensation commitments to the latter. Labor-intensive parties especially must seek to integrate their activists into the party. Party leaders thus seek to keep activists from shirking by giving them a stake (*equity*) in the party. One way for leaders to make their commitments more credible is by relinquishing their own control over *policy* or *office* decisions within the party. Three prominent strategies are (1) to decentralize intraparty policy decisions, (2) to restrict recruitment to party and government offices to existing activists and officers, and (3) to make leaders accountable to activists and members. Strategy 1 offers activists policy influence, whereas strategies 2 and 3 involve office concessions. Indirectly, the last two strategies may entail policy concessions as well. Each strategy imposes behavioral constraints on party leaders.

1. *Decentralization of policy decisions* (*intraparty democracy*) has particular appeal to policy-motivated activists (amateurs), who are more easily recruited if they are given a direct voice in policy decisions. Decentralization may consist in transferring decision-making authority from the party leadership or the parliamentary caucus to its annual conference or other broad extraparliamentary bodies. This strategy clearly has costs to party leaders. It may saddle the party with electorally undesirable policy platforms (as with the British Labour Party in 1983) or constrain its leaders in coalition bargaining (as with the Irish Labour Party, discussed by Marsh and Mitchell in this volume). The more leaders decentralize policy decision making, the more policy oriented the party is likely to become at the expense of office- and vote-seeking.

2. Party leaders may instead, or in addition, focus on internal office-related strategies, such as enhancing the prospects of upward organizational mobility for activists and officers or giving such members monopoly rights to higher ranks of the organization. They can accomplish both goals by creating *impermeable recruitment channels* (Putnam 1976). Such incentives are particularly likely to appeal to party professionals. Yet the main long-term effect of impermeability is to increase the policy orientation of party leaders. This may seem paradoxical since impermeable recruitment channels heighten the incentives for office seekers within the organization by enhancing their upward mobility. However, this rigidity in recruitment restricts the entrance of pure office seekers. Many such individuals will find a party career attractive only if they can enter at a high organizational level. If the organization bars such entry, only individuals who put a high value on policy rise to prominence in the party, since only such leaders come up through the activists' ranks. However, narrowly constrained promotion practices may leave a party with unattractive candidates for office, and the promotion of amateurs over professionals easily brings electoral costs (see Schlesinger 1965; Steel and Tsurutani 1986). Thus, impermeable recruitment channels will, in the long run, likely drive parties away from A and B and toward C in Figure 1.1.

3. *Leadership accountability* is a third factor that party leaders can manipulate to attract followers. *Accountability* refers to the ease with which activists and members can replace party officers on the grounds of performance in office. Amateurs are "vitally interested in mechanisms to ensure the intraparty accountability of officeholders and party leaders" (Wilson 1973: 107). An organization with a high degree of leadership accountability therefore attracts amateur activists at lower cost than an organization with less accountability. Party leaders, on the other hand, presumably offer accountability concessions only as a last resort. To the extent that party members have the authority to replace their superiors, they render party leaders vulnerable and threaten their

expected long-term surplus. Under these circumstances, leaders discount future benefits more heavily and show less concern about future elections. Where elites are vulnerable and expected turnover rates within the party high, such as in the Mexican Partido Revolucionario Institucional (PRI) and other Latin American legislatures under term limits (Carey 1996), leaders tend to "grab the money and run" (Putnam 1976: 67). Secondarily, leadership accountability may promote policy orientation at the expense of office benefits, since leaders must show greater concern for the policy preferences of their followers.

The preceding argument generates a number of testable propositions about the relationship between party organization and behavior. Subsequent chapters will examine the effects of some of these organizational features on party behavior in various national settings.

Does organizational decentralization in policy making affect the hard choices made by party leaders? For example, does organizational decentralization enhance the degree of policy pursuit at the expense of votes and office? To the extent that leaders in decentralized parties must share decision-making power with policy-oriented activists, we would expect to see a heightened emphasis on policy pursuits. Several chapters in this volume examine the effects of decentralized party policy making. Michael Marsh and Paul Mitchell study some pronounced effects of policy decentralization in the Irish Labour Party. Kaare Strøm compares the effects of policy-making rules in different Norwegian parties on coalition bargaining strategies. And Donald Share shows how policy centralization in the Spanish Socialist Party has contributed to the development of its strategies over time.

Leadership accountability could affect party behavior in several ways. Accountability may affect both the choices that party leaders make between different objectives and their time horizons. First, if Luebbert (1986) is correct in identifying retention of office as the overriding goal of party leaders, then the more accountable leaders are, the more likely they should be to accommodate the policy demands of their activists. Second, the vulnerability that leaders experience may affect how far they look ahead. If a high degree of accountability to the party organization makes a leader feel vulnerable, then he or she may tend to concentrate on short-term benefits and discount the longer term. To the extent that the vote-seeking propensity of political parties reflects their leaders' time horizons, accountable leaders may thus make for less vote-seeking parties. Are these expectations true? Do organizational features actually affect the trade-offs that party leaders are willing to make? Two of the chapters in this volume examine these questions in particular. Kaare Strøm examines the effects of Rolf Presthus's accountability to the Norwegian Conservative Party and finds in it the key to Presthus's otherwise puzzling behavior. Wolfgang Müller provides evidence of a striking correspondence between the personal career incentives of Austrian Social Democratic leaders and their positions on the grand coalition.

POLITICAL INSTITUTIONS

Political institutions also affect the behavior of party leaders. When we discuss these institutions, we have in mind broadly what Schlesinger (1991) calls the "structure of political opportunities," that is to say, the offices parties seek, the rules for attaining them, and the general patterns of behavior surrounding their attainment. Political institutions affect party behavior in two different ways. One influence is *direct* in that party leaders, regardless of the characteristics of their organizations, face different incentives in different institutional settings. For example, the same party leaders might make different trade-offs between policy, office, and votes after an electoral reform (as in France in the 1980s or in Italy in the 1990s) than they would have made before it. A second consequence is the *indirect* effect of institutions through different types of party organization. Again, electoral rules may affect party leadership decisions through their impact on party organization or candidate selection. We can identify indirect effects by examining the causes of such important organizational features as intraparty democracy, recruitment patterns, and leadership accountability. In this section, we focus on direct effects, but first, we briefly dwell on one especially important indirect link between institutions and party behavior. This factor is public financing of political parties.[4]

Since their inception in the 1950s, public subsidies have dramatically changed the environments of most democratic parties in Western Europe. Of course, public party finance comes in various forms, with differing consequences for party behavior: subsidies to parliamentary versus extraparliamentary parties, national versus local grants, free advertising or television time, support for auxiliary groups (e.g., youth organizations), and so on. Subsidies to legislative representatives and caucuses presumably have modest effects on extraparliamentary party behavior. Per capita voter or membership grants to local associations (as in Scandinavia) may even enhance labor intensiveness. But the most significant subsidies tend to support electoral campaigns. Free or easy access to media coverage, and financial aid to partisan media and publications, which are among the most important forms of subsidies, lessen constraints on party leaders.

Generous public subsidies thus should enhance the autonomy of party leaders, especially if these funds flow to central party organizations. Their primary effect is to reduce the cost to party leaders of different inputs. Specifically, public financing tends to subsidize *capital* inputs, for example, by facilitating media-focused campaigns. Also, direct financial subsidies are more fungible in capital-intensive campaigns. Consequently, party leaders may substitute capital for labor inputs. Consider the fact that over the last thirty years, public financing of political parties has become increasingly prevalent in the Western world (Alexander 1989; Katz and Mair 1992; Paltiel 1981; von Beyme 1985). This trend has coincided with a growing capitalization and professionalization of electoral campaigns. As parties become more capital intensive, the incentives

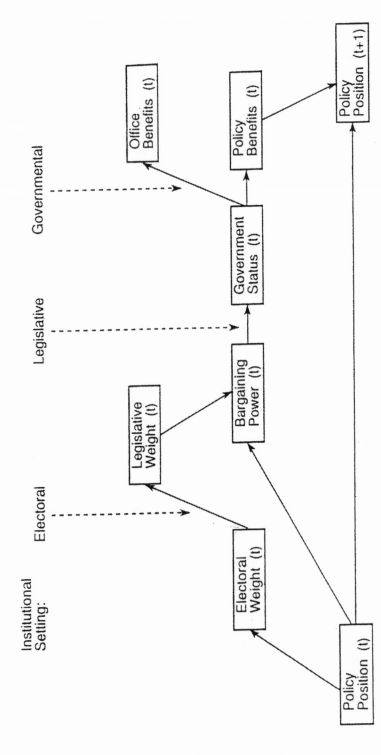

Institutional
Setting:

Electoral   Legislative   Governmental

Figure 1.2 The institutional framework of interparty competition in parliamentary democracies. Note: t and t+1 denote successive electoral terms.

for the previously discussed commitment strategies common in labor-intensive organizations may be diminished. Party leaders may no longer be so dependent on their activists, and they may not need to make the same policy concessions. Is there a causal connection here? Does public finance actually reduce the intensity of policy-seeking party behavior and increase parties' willingness to trade off policy against other objectives? Though we have no direct evidence, the argument is plausible.

However, our main focus here is on the *direct* effects of institutions on party behavior. For this purpose, we need to examine the conversion of votes into the goods party leaders intrinsically desire. Electoral exchange provides party leaders with votes, which they can cash in for policy or office benefits. Votes are the currency of democratic politics, but their use and value depend on the rules by which other goods may be purchased. A variety of political institutions shape the conversion of votes into spoils and policy influence. Figure 1.2 gives a schematic overview of these conversion processes in three institutional settings, here labeled (1) electoral, (2) legislative, and (3) governmental. Figure 1.2 illustrates the complexity of party competition and its dynamic character. Party behavior at one point in time affects future payoffs and is itself determined in light of these expectations.

Electoral competition is the process by which parties exchange benefits (or promises thereof) derived from their control of political institutions for electoral support. We assume for simplicity that the benefits parties provide for voters are policies. For one thing, policy promises are generally the least costly way for parties to secure electoral support.[5] Downs argues that electoral competition constrains parties to maintain consistent policy positions over time (Downs 1957: 103–9). Consequently, policy position in one election is determined partly by previous policy positions, including, for incumbents, government policy. Figure 1.2 illustrates the idea that voters base their choices on the past and present policy positions of the various parties.

Electoral competitiveness is the aggregate uncertainty of electoral contests as perceived by party leaders. Specifically, competitiveness is the degree to which electoral results *ex ante* are expected to vary across the set of feasible policy positions. The more electoral outcomes hinge on policy positions, the more competitive the election. Does the competitiveness of the election, in turn, affect party behavior? We might expect that the more competitive the election, the more keenly parties pursue votes. As Schlesinger (1965) notes, the greater the competitiveness, the more parties are forced to focus on fundamental objectives (electoral survival). But although electoral competitiveness may induce vote-seeking and thus a form of orientation toward the future, it may also condition a relatively short time horizon. Party leaders might always look toward the next election, but rarely beyond.

ELECTORAL INSTITUTIONS

If party leaders pursued votes for their intrinsic value, there would be no reason to extend this discussion of political institutions. But, of course, they do not. Votes are first converted into parliamentary seats (or *legislative weights*). Electoral laws define this purely mechanical process, which in most democracies yields strong positive correlations between electoral and legislative weights. However, this correlation is nowhere perfect, and distortions are often significant. Distortions are larger in single-member districts than in proportional representation systems. In the latter setting they further depend on district magnitude, electoral thresholds, the number of tiers of seat allocation, and the particular proportional representation formula applied (Cox 1997; Lijphart 1994; Taagepera and Shugart 1989).

In general, distortionary effects predictably favor large parties and disadvantage small ones. However, more perverse and unpredictable effects are not uncommon. In the 1951 British elections, the Conservatives trailed the Labour Party in the popular vote but won a majority in the House of Commons. Similarly, the New Zealand National Party in 1978 captured a comfortable majority of eleven seats in the House of Representatives despite running second to Labour among the voters. In the Irish elections of 1987, Fianna Fáil gained six seats and captured the government, despite slipping in first preference votes. In the Australian elections the same year, the Labour Party experienced a similar fortune. Similar examples abound.[6] Distortions produced by the electoral system can, at least in extreme cases, affect party behavior. The *predictability* of electoral system effects should be a key to their effects on party leadership behavior. The more unpredictable the effects of the electoral system are, the less incentive party leaders seem to have to maximize votes.

LEGISLATIVE INSTITUTIONS

Legislative weights are ultimately less interesting than legislative bargaining power, which, in turn, must be converted into governmental office. A variety of structural features may affect the latter process (see Laver and Schofield 1990). Constitutional provisions such as investiture requirements and the employment of *formateurs* or *informateurs* in coalition bargaining may favor certain parties or coalitions. In situations where no party has a majority, the process by which coalitions form and premiers are designated may make much or little of legislative pluralities. The partisan preferences of an influential head of state (e.g., until recently in Finland) may similarly bias the coalition formation process and the prospects of different parties. These are issues of *agenda control*, which deserve more attention than they have typically received in coalition-theoretic studies of government formation (but see Strøm et al. 1994).

However, our main concern is with the conversion of legislative representation into bargaining power. Except in pure two-party systems, bargaining power is no simple function of legislative weights. Whereas the translation of votes into seats is purely mechanical, their further conversion into bargaining power depends on the much more complex logic of strategic interparty behavior. In pure two-party systems, of course, majorities always emerge. As the number of political parties increases, the probability of single-party majorities dwindles and the complexities of strategic interaction multiply. The more strategic interaction enters into the picture, the less predictable the benefits of electoral strength. Policy considerations may further constrain the conversion of legislative numbers into executive power. If parties can only form coalitions with those who are adjacent in policy space, then centrist parties will be favored over parties at the extremes, whose bargaining power may be severely limited compared to their numerical strength. And the fewer the policy dimensions, the greater these distortions will be. But the less predictably votes transfer into bargaining power, the less single-mindedly we would expect party leaders to pursue them. Therefore, the value of votes should increase with the number of policy dimensions, that is, with the strength of the correlation between electoral results and bargaining power.

GOVERNMENTAL INSTITUTIONS

The third and final stage in the conversion of votes into office and policy benefits depends on control of elected office. Formal theories of party behavior typically assume that government incumbency is at least a necessary, and possibly a sufficient, condition for both policy and office payoffs. However, this assumption clearly oversimplifies reality. Parties not represented in government often have a significant impact on policy and may even share in office payoffs (Laver and Budge 1992; Strøm 1984). Of course, controlling the executive branch *does* help. Under most conceivable circumstances, governing parties have greater access to policy influence and office benefits than the opposition. But the degree to which institutions favor incumbents varies.

These differentials depend partly on the particular government and partly on the political system as a whole. Under otherwise identical circumstances, a minority government likely would have to share policy influence (and perhaps spoils) with the opposition to a greater extent than would a majority administration. There are also systematic cross-national differences in the distribution of these benefits. Some institutional arrangements favor governing parties more than others. Let us think of each polity as having a modal distribution of office and policy influence between government and opposition. Thus, we can speak of systemic *office benefit differentials* and *policy influence differentials* between governing and opposition parties. Office benefit differentials refer to the typical distribution of such goods (the perquisites of office) between government and opposition. In some democracies (e.g., Westminster systems), the governing parties essentially monopolize such payoffs, whereas in others (e.g., consociational ones), even parties that are formally in opposition may be cut in on many of these deals. The same holds with respect to policy benefit distributions. The office and policy benefit differentials, respectively, refer to the *ex ante* expectations among party leaders concerning the allocation of these goods. These two types of benefits may vary independently of each other, and both may effectively be constant-sum in the short term.[7] The greater the differential is with respect to each good, the greater the incentive for party leaders to pursue that objective. Thus, office pursuit should covary positively with office benefit differentials and policy pursuit correlate similarly with policy influence differentials.

In sum, institutions (or rather, party leaders' expectations concerning their effects) are likely to influence party behavior in a variety of ways. The more predictably votes translate into intrinsically valued goods such as policy influence or office, the more slavishly party leaders will follow their electoral incentives. As we have seen, this conversion depends on many political rules or institutions. And the relative availability of policy influence versus office benefits at the margin will determine the trade-offs party leaders make between these goods.

Most institutional variation, of course, exists *between* rather than *within* countries. Consequently, we generally have to look for differences and commonalities between the cases examined in the individual chapters in this volume to assess institutional effects on party behavior. The relevant institutional variables do vary in ways that can be captured within our set of cases. Public party finance, for example, is much more extensive in Germany, Austria, and most of the Scandinavian countries than it is in the other systems represented here. Electoral competitiveness can be captured through such indirect behavioral measures as electoral volatility, the closeness of elections, or alternation in power (Strøm 1989). Competitiveness has in recent years risen in most countries. Electoral system distortions are likely to be greater under single member district systems than under proportional representation. And the number of policy dimensions likewise varies in systematic ways, seemingly related to the effects of the electoral system. Although we can find variation in many of these institutional features, we cannot always measure them precisely. Moreover, in cross-national comparisons it becomes much more difficult to control for the myriad other potential determinants that may vary from one country to another. We are therefore in a less favorable position to examine systematically institutional (as opposed to organizational) determinants of party leader behavior.

SITUATIONAL DETERMINANTS

Organizations and institutions account for the most systematic sources of variation in the behavior of party leaders. Yet, we should hardly expect these variables to exhaust the range of factors that may help us understand such differences. Party leadership decisions are made in specific situations, and the nature of these situations may differ in important ways, even when institutions and organizations do not.

The same party leaders may have different trade-off functions in different situations. If general elections are impending, party leaders find it more difficult to ignore the electoral connection than if their encounter with the electorate is farther down the road. Parties that have previously been electorally successful but starved of office benefits, such as the Italian PCI in the 1970s, may be willing to swallow unusual compromises in order to gain representation at the cabinet table, whereas parties used to executive office may be more willing to wager such benefits in the hope of securing electoral gains, as did Norwegian Labor Prime Minister Thorbjørn Jagland in 1997. Party leaders who have staked their personal reputations on particular policy agendas, or on electoral success, may be less willing or able to sacrifice these goods. More senior party leaders, such as Ireland's Charles Haughey in the late 1980s, may make different decisions than freshly elected ones.

It is difficult to account systematically for all the situational determinants that may affect party behavior at any given time. What we can say is that such factors have to do in large part with (1) the set of parties involved in the relevant bargains and interactions; (2) the "endowments" of these parties in terms of office, votes, and policy; (3) their specific leaderships, histories, and expectations; (4) the constraints and expectations imposed by past events on the specific situation; and (5) the domestic and international context in which bargaining takes place. On several of these counts, there is little that can be said in any systematic way. Yet, on other counts, general observations may be in order.

ENDOGENOUS VERSUS EXOGENOUS DETERMINANTS

The first distinction to note is between endogenous and exogenous situational determinants. *Endogenous situational determinants* are those that the party leaders themselves are ultimately capable of affecting, even though there may be little they can do in the short run. They include such factors as personality characteristics and affinities, the timing of the bargaining situation relative to the electoral cycle or to intraparty events such as party congresses, the age and time horizon of individual party leaders, the existence or nonexistence of identifiable challengers in the various parties, and so on. We expect these things to matter, and sometimes in predictable ways. The more of a temporal buffer a party leader has, that is, the less he or she is faced with a competitive challenger, the more we expect that leader to be able to make policy concessions. And the more senior a leader is, the less concerned that person may be with future elections. Chapters in this volume show that such personal circumstances critically affected both Irish and Norwegian party decisions (and probably many more) in the 1980s.

Exogenous situational factors are those that are beyond the control of any of the party leaders. They may have to do with the prehistory of the bargaining situations, such as whether that situation was precipitated by a scandal, the death of a towering political figure, or the like. When bargaining in the wake of a scandal, politicians are likely to take special care not to make concessions that smack of the same kind of scandalous behavior. When bargaining is after the death of a beloved statesman, his successors may not be able to afford to compromise this person's legacy. Other exogenous factors may include social or economic events, such as riots, economic recessions, or events associated with powerful collective memories, all of which may curtail the set of feasible party behaviors.

BARGAINING COMPLEXITY

A slightly more concrete situational variable is the degree of bargaining complexity. Though such complexities do not follow strictly from the number of parties involved in the game, these two parameters tend to covary positively. In other words, all else equal, the greater the number of negotiating parties, the higher the level of bargaining complexity. But the latter may also be a function of a lack of unity on the part of the organizations involved or a lack of familiarity among the leaders of the relevant parties. The more disunited the parties, and the less of a track record they have with one another, the more complicated their bargaining is likely to be. Numerous, disunited, or unfamiliar parties are likely to give rise to information uncertainties among their partners in bargaining.

Bargaining complexity, then, is at least in part a function of the quality of information available to the relevant party leaders. The coarser their information about past events, potential payoffs, or player preferences, the more complex their calculations have to be. And the more uncertain party leaders are, the more consequential their risk attitudes are likely to be. Under many circumstances, party leaders tend to be risk averse, particularly those who have much to lose and little to gain politically. The more limited their information, the less likely risk-averse party leaders are to gamble on new coalition partners or on moves whose electoral implications are hard to foresee. Thus, in situations of highly imperfect or incomplete information, we may see fewer policy concessions and fewer unorthodox alliances than we might otherwise expect.

INITIAL ENDOWMENTS

Differences in *initial endowments* of policy, office, and votes may also account for variations in trade-offs across bargaining situations. In our initial discussion, for simplicity, we discussed trade-offs between these goods as if their relative "prices" were constant, at least for a given party and a given institutional environment. In other words, we discussed the matter as if, for example, the number of future votes a party would be willing to compromise to get a given share of cabinet portfolios would be constant. In reality, of course, this is a highly dubious assumption. How many votes a party leader is willing to give up is likely to depend heavily on how many he or she has. And what a set of additional cabinet portfolios is worth will probably depend significantly on how many the party already has or on how long it has been since the party was last able to reward its office claimants.

Briefly and roughly, the value of all three goods – policy, office, and votes – is likely to decline at the margins. The more votes or offices you already have, the less the marginal unit is worth. But several factors may complicate this seemingly simple relationship. For example, there may be critical values of any of these goods around which the marginal vote (office, policy concession) becomes particularly crucial. For votes, the threshold at which the party becomes a majority party, a plurality party, or falls below the threshold of representation may be such critical values. For embattled party leaders, it may be the point at which the electoral result shifts from a gain relative to the previous election to a loss, or vice versa. For office, it may be that critical portfolio that allows you to place all important ministerial aspirants. For policy, it may be that vital concession that determines whether your activists will rebel or not.

Thus, although it is difficult to account for them in systematic and comprehensive ways, we do expect situational factors to affect the choices that party leaders make between policy, office, and votes. Bargaining complexity is likely to matter, and so are the parties' existing shares of policy influence, office, and votes. And, finally, there may be myriad other endogenous or exogenous situational factors of greater or lesser import.

THE PLAN OF THE VOLUME

The aims of this book are to examine and explain the behavior of political parties in situations where they face hard choices, that is, conflict between two or more important objectives. The discussion in this chapter has sought to identify the trade-offs party leaders make when they encounter such difficult decisions. We have developed a framework in which such decisions can be analyzed and pointed to the organizational, institutional, and situational conditions that can help explain them. The contributors test the usefulness of our framework by applying it, in a broadly cross-national and historical fashion, to critical party decisions. The purposes are (1) to decide whether party behavior can be fruitfully analyzed in these terms, (2) to generate insight into the ways in which institutional, organizational, party system, and situational factors favor vote-seeking, office-seeking, or policy-seeking behavior, and (3) to assess the implications for the role of political parties as mechanisms of mass representation.

There are two main types of research design that allow us to examine the difficult choices party leaders face. The first involves the study of *natural experiments*. The ideal laboratory, if such a thing could be found, would be a case in which we could study the effects of small changes in well-defined parameters, be they organizational, institutional, or situational. Regrettably, such natural experiments are rare in the social sciences and particularly in the study of complex processes such as the ones before us. Case studies are typically the closest feasible approximation. Alternatively, we could proceed through *quasi-experimental* designs, in which, by statistical means, we attempt to estimate the effects of a range of specific variables while controlling for others. Unfortunately, such designs require precise observations of a large number of common parameters across a range of decision-making situations. Their success also depends on our ability to control for a host of other potential influences cross-nationally. Such information is rarely available to the scholar in this field.

At this stage in the development of the science of politics, the second approach seems to us fraught with more difficulties than the first. Besides the inherent complexities of the tasks, we are guided in this choice by the availability of scholarly talent. Professional expertise is still in large part country-specific, and our ability to make valid and reliable cross-national observations and comparisons is decidedly more limited. Therefore, the approach in this volume is tilted toward a more intensive, rather than an extensive, design. All of the studies in this volume are country-specific, and several approximate natural experiments in that they focus on the response of political parties to small but important changes in their environments.

Case studies and small-n comparative designs have much to offer at different stages of theoretical development, including the exploratory stage at which hypotheses are developed or put to initial tests (Eckstein 1975; Lijphart 1971). That is precisely the stage at which this research finds itself. Moreover, the case study method is particularly well suited for exploring complex phenomena, and many of the critical party leadership decisions we examine certainly fall under this rubric. To make sense out of case studies (beyond interesting tales), however, one needs at a minimum an analytical or theoretical framework, which we have sought to provide. And though case studies will not allow us to generalize *statistically*, their purpose is to help us do so *analytically* (Mohr 1996; Yin 1984).

Yet, a country-specific approach need not imply a highly intensive research design. Empirical studies of this kind could vary significantly in their design, and indeed the chapters in this book do. Scholars could adopt more extensive designs involving a large number of observations within a single country, either through studies of a single party at many different points in time or through studies of many parties in one or several choice situations. Both options would involve a large number of *observations*, although not necessarily *units* (see King, Keohane, and Verba 1994: 51–3). Intensive studies, on the other hand, would focus on a small number of observations, perhaps only a single one.

Though country-specific, the chapters in this book vary significantly in their extension. Some, such as the chapters on Denmark and Ireland, analyze a significant number of choice situations. Others, like the ones on Austria and Germany, are case studies in a strict sense: analyses of a single party in one particular choice situation. Extensive or intensive, the volume consists of studies in which the authors systematically apply the conceptual apparatus and analytical questions introduced earlier to their specific European democracies. Each case focuses on the behavior of one or several parties in situations of goal conflict. The cases we have selected had to satisfy two criteria. One is that the choices must have been hard or critical, which is to say, there must have been a perception among the actors that substantial fortunes were at stake and, preferably, that they might have to sacrifice some party goals for others. Secondarily, we have given priority to events that were objectively important in the politics of the country in question. Thus, our studies include the "historic compromise" in Italy, the 1982 *Wende* in West Germany, the making of the new Swedish constitution in the 1970s, and the termination of the Austrian "black-red" grand coalition.

Most, but not all, of the empirical cases thus concern the formation, maintenance, or termination of government coalitions. Theoretically, there is no reason that our study needs to confine itself to such questions, but they do offer salient and often well-documented cases for the analysis of party behavior. The dominance of such applications also gives additional coherence to the book and relates it to an ongoing stream of cross-national research in comparative politics.

Each empirical chapter raises three general questions: (1) To what extent did the leaders of the party or parties involved in each case perceive goal conflicts in terms similar to the ones developed in the introductory chapter? (2) What priorities, sacrifices, and trade-offs did these party leaders make in these situations of hard choices? (3) To what extent can their choices be explained by organizational, institutional, or situational factors?

The nature of the data analyzed varies from chapter to chapter. Some authors make use of original archival or interview data (e.g., Austria, France, and Sweden), whereas others rely more on secondary sources. Mostly, the evidence is a combination of "soft" (e.g., interviews, memoirs) and "hard" (e.g., electoral statistics) data. As editors, we have imposed on our study no data orthodoxy beyond the customary standards of good scholarship.

The case studies represent a broad range of European polities and parties. The empirical chapters include four major European countries (Germany, Italy, France, and Spain) and several studies of smaller European democracies. The volume begins with two of the latter, both of which provide a broad sweep of parties and time. In Chapter 2, Michael Marsh and Paul Mitchell examine a series of Irish coalition situations in the 1980s and identify important organizational differences between the various parties. They show that the decision-making process within the Irish Labour Party made it difficult for its leaders to pursue coalitions with the Fine Gael at the cost of policy compromise. Also, the personal incentives of the Fianna Fáil prime minister, Charles Haughey, played a major role in the party's unprecedented 1989 decision to forge a government coalition with the Progressive Democrats.

The next chapter is even more extensive in its design. Denmark experienced an uninterrupted series of minority governments between 1971 and 1993. Jørgen Elklit looks at five cases of government formation in the 1970s and 1980s and scrutinizes the motivations of the main actors. Again, Elklit finds significant differences between the various parties. Critical party decisions, we learn, reflect a combination of concerns in which the weight of each goal varies from party to party.

Next, we are treated to four single-party studies. The first two of these are longitudinal. Donald Share examines the dramatic transformation of the Spanish Socialist Party from an oppositional movement in an authoritarian state, through the status of a serious competitor and government alternative, to one of the most successful social democratic parties in Western Europe, and finally to corruption, electoral stagnation, and an eventual fall from grace. The different electoral fortunes went hand in hand with a behavioral transformation: from a policy-seeking party in the early 1980s to an office-seeking one a decade later. Lessened electoral competition, a hierarchical party organization, and a contractionary international economic environment facilitated this rapid and dramatic shift.

Ron Hillebrand and Galen Irwin analyze the shifting choices and fortunes of a social democratic party in their study of Dutch Labour Party decisions in 1981–2 and 1991 concerning coalitions with the Christian Democrats. The authors identify clear trade-offs faced by the party between policy concerns and electoral incentives, and they show why the Social Democrats in 1991 decided to enter this coalition despite policy compromises and drastic subsequent setbacks in the electorate.

The next single-party study, Roberto D'Alimonte's study of the PCI, focuses on a particularly critical political phase in postwar Italian politics: the Historic Compromise of 1976–9. D'Alimonte argues that the Communist leadership based their decision to seek policy influence through cooperation with the Christian Democrats on a misperception of the electoral costs and intraparty dissent involved. As these costs became clearer to the leadership, the PCI eventually abandoned the compromise.

Whereas D'Alimonte examines a stillborn coalition, the following chapter analyzes the end of a very long and successful period of interparty cooperation. In Austria, 1966 marked the end of the long period of the grand coalition. In his chapter, Wolfgang Müller discusses the controversial Socialist Party decision to end this agreement. The author shows that both electoral and policy concerns were prominent in the debate within the Socialist Party, and that the preferences of the various party leaders corresponded closely to their personal incentives.

The following chapter examines yet another case of an aborted coalition. Kaare Strøm discusses a spectacular case of Norwegian bargaining failure, the so-called Presthus Debacle, in which four nonsocialist parties failed to dislodge a minority Labor government. The author examines the critical decisions of three of these parties in detail and shows why the Progress Party gave priority to its electoral goals, the Center Party to its policies, and the Conservative Party to the prospect of gaining office.

As in the chapter on Austrian politics, the one on German politics discusses a historically momentous case of coalition termination. Thomas Poguntke examines the 1982 decision of the German Free Democrats to abandon their coalition with the Social Democrats and to opt instead for a coalition with the Christian Democrats. This was the critical decision that produced the German *Wende*. The author argues that despite the necessity of policy compromises, the Free Democrats ultimately benefited from a favorable constellation of electoral and office considerations.

The two final empirical chapters are less focused on cabinet coalition bargaining than most of the others. In Chapter 10, Torbjörn Bergman discusses the design of the new Swedish constitution in the early 1970s, and particularly the controversial status of the monarchy. Through an examination of the internal debate in the two largest parties, he shows how office, policy, and electoral considerations contributed to the eventual Torekov compromise. Through extensive scrutiny of primary sources, he shows significant internal disagreements over these trade-offs among the Conservatives as well as among the Social Democrats.

Finally, John Huber scrutinizes the budgetary process under minority government in France in 1988 and 1989. Through extensive interview data, he shows that the radically different courses these deliberations took were due in large part to the electoral calculations of the relevant parties.

Jointly, these chapters provide a rich and nuanced description of party leaders and their decision making in European democracies. They contain plenty of drama, and they illuminate a number of critical and controversial issues in the politics of the respective countries. We believe that they will also prove to be entertaining reading. But their main purpose is to bring us closer to the mind set of party leaders facing difficult trade-offs and to help us understand their decisions. In so doing, these studies show that elite political decisions are no mere reflection of social pressures. Nor can they be understood as the simpleminded pursuit of a single overriding political goal. Understanding the decisions of party leaders requires patience and some tolerance for complexity. Nonetheless, we think it is a worthy project that may even enhance our understanding of how and why the democratic process works.

NOTES

1. The literature sometimes posits other pursuits, such as internal party unity (Sjöblom 1968). In many cases, these goods seem implausible *intrinsic* goals and must

therefore be purely instrumental. If so, we can reduce this pursuit to whatever goal it serves (e.g., votes) and probably should do so in the interest of analytical parsimony. But, following this logic, why do we not similarly reduce vote-seeking behavior to the office or policy goals it serves? The answer, which is elaborated later, is that vote-seeking behavior allows us to gauge the time horizons (*temporal discounts*) of party leaders.

2. Early policy-based coalition theory often assumed a one-dimensional policy space. Generic *chaos* or instability problems make applications to multidimensional space much less tractable (for a good discussion, see Laver and Schofield 1990).

3. However, there is a smaller body of "purer" policy-seeking theory (Budge and Laver 1986; De Swaan 1973; Laver and Budge 1992).

4. Public party finance clearly is not the only institutional factor that may significantly affect party organization and thereby indirectly party behavior. Other factors, such as federalism, separation of powers, and franchise restrictions, may have similarly important ramifications. However, public party subsidies distinguish themselves by having consistent and observable effects, which lend themselves to fairly straightforward theoretical explanation.

5. Many political parties in clientelistic societies trade various private goods for votes. However, this form of exchange is clearly expensive for parties and depends on their ability to extract resources other than votes from their clients.

6. In the Irish and Australian cases, the results were at least partly due to their preferential voting systems, which reward party preferences beyond the first.

7. The latter assumption is eminently plausible for office benefits, perhaps somewhat less so for policy influence. In the long run, the sum of both types of benefits may change (most often increase). Indeed, in situations of low electoral competitiveness, rational political parties may collude in efforts to increase total benefits. Italian politics prior to the reforms of the 1990s appears singularly interpretable in such terms.

REFERENCES

Aldrich, John H. (1995). *Why Parties? The Origin and Transformation of Political Parties in America*. Chicago: University of Chicago Press.

Alexander, Herbert E. (ed.) (1989). *Comparative Political Finance in the 1980s*. Cambridge: Cambridge University Press.

Austen-Smith, David and Jeffrey Banks (1988). "Elections, Coalitions, and Legislative Outcomes." *American Political Science Review* 82, 2: 405–22.

Axelrod, Robert (1970). *Conflict of Interest*. Chicago: Markham.

Broder, David S. (1972). *The Party's Over: The Failure of Politics in America*. New York: Harper & Row.

Budge, Ian and Michael J. Laver (1986). "Office Seeking and Policy Pursuit in Coalition Theory." *Legislative Studies Quarterly* 11, 4: 485–506.

Carey, John M. (1996). *Term Limits and Legislative Representation*. Cambridge: Cambridge University Press.

Clark, Peter B. and James Q. Wilson (1961). "Incentive Systems: A Theory of Organizations." *Administrative Science Quarterly* 6, 2: 129–66.

Cox, Gary W. (1997). *Making Votes Count*. Cambridge: Cambridge University Press.
    and Mathew D. McCubbins (1993). *Legislative Leviathan: Parties and Committees in the U.S. House of Representatives*. Berkeley: University of California Press.
De Swaan, Abram (1973). *Coalition Theories and Cabinet Formation*. Amsterdam: Elsevier.
Downs, Anthony (1957). *An Economic Theory of Democracy*. New York: Harper & Row.
Duverger, Maurice (1954). *Political Parties*. London: Methuen.
Eckstein, Harry (1975). "Case Study and Theory in Political Science." In *Handbook of Political Science* (pp. 79–137), eds. Fred I. Greenstein and Nelson Polsby. Reading, MA: Addison Wesley. Volume 7.
Enelow, James M. and Melvin J. Hinich (1984). *The Spatial Theory of Voting: An Introduction*. Cambridge: Cambridge University Press.
Epstein, Leon D. (1967). *Political Parties in Western Democracies*. New York: Praeger.
Frohlich, Norman, Joe A. Oppenheimer, and Oran R. Young (1971). *Political Leadership and Collective Goods*. Princeton, NJ: Princeton University Press.
Hinich, Melvin J. and Peter C. Ordeshook (1970). "Plurality Maximization vs. Vote Maximization: A Spatial Analysis with Variable Participation." *American Political Science Review* 64, 3: 772–91.
Holmstrom, Bengt R. and Jean Tirole (1989). "The Theory of the Firm." In *Handbook of Industrial Organization* (pp. 61–133), eds. Richard Schmalensee and Robert D. Willig. Amsterdam: North-Holland.
Huber, John D. (1996). *Rationalizing Parliament*. Cambridge: Cambridge University Press.
Katz, Richard S. (1986). "Party Government: A Rationalistic Conception." In *Visions and Realities of Party Government* (pp. 31–71), eds. Francis G. Castles and Rudolf Wildenmann. Berlin: Walter de Gruyter.
    (ed.) (1987). *Party Governments: European and American Experiences*. Berlin: Walter de Gruyter.
    and Peter Mair (eds.) (1992). *Party Organizations: A Data Handbook*. London: Sage.
Kayden, Xandra and Eddie Mahe, Jr. (1985). *The Party Goes On: The Persistence of the Two-Party System in the United States*. New York: Basic Books.
Key, V. O. (1964). *Politics, Parties, and Pressure Groups*. Fifth edition. New York: Crowell.
King, Gary, Robert O. Keohane, and Sidney Verba. (1994). *Designing Social Inquiry: Scientific Inference in Qualititative Research*. Princeton, NJ: Princeton University Press.
Kreps, David M. (1990). "Corporate Culture and Economic Theory." In *Perspectives on Positive Political Economy* (pp. 90–143), eds. James E. Alt and Kenneth A. Shepsle. Cambridge: Cambridge University Press.
Laver, Michael J. (1989). "Party Competition and Party System Change." *Journal of Theoretical Politics* 1, 3: 301–24.
    (1997). *Private Desires, Political Action*. London: Sage Publications.
    and Ian Budge (eds.) (1992). *Party Policy and Governmental Coalitions*. London: Macmillan.
    and Norman Schofield (1990). *Multiparty Government: The Politics of Coalition in Europe*. Oxford: Oxford University Press.

Leiserson, Michael (1968). "Factions and Coalitions in One-Party Japan." *American Political Science Review* 62, 3: 770–87.

Lijphart, Arend (1971). "Comparative Politics and the Comparative Method." *American Political Science Review* 65, 3: 682–93.

(1994). *Electoral Systems and Party Systems: A Study of Twenty-Seven Democracies, 1945–1990.* Oxford: Oxford University Press.

Luebbert, Gregory M. (1986). *Comparative Democracy: Policymaking and Governing Coalitions in Europe and Israel.* New York: Columbia University Press.

Mayhew, David R. (1974). *Congress: The Electoral Connection.* New Haven, CT: Yale University Press.

Michels, Robert (1962). *Political Parties.* New York: The Free Press. First edition 1915.

Moe, Terry M. (1984). "The New Economics of Organization." *American Journal of Political Science* 28, 4: 739–77.

Mohr, Lawrence B. (1996). *The Causes of Human Behavior.* Ann Arbor: University of Michigan Press.

Ordeshook, Peter C. (1986). *Game Theory and Political Theory.* Cambridge: Cambridge University Press.

Paltiel, Khayyam Zev (1981). "Campaign Finance: Contrasting Practices and Reforms." In *Democracy at the Polls* (pp. 138–72), eds. David Butler, Howard R. Penniman, and Austin Ranney. Washington, DC: American Enterprise Institute.

Powell, G. Bingham, Jr. (1982). *Contemporary Democracies.* Cambridge, MA: Harvard University Press.

Putnam, Robert D. (1976). *The Comparative Study of Political Elites.* Englewood Cliffs, NJ: Prentice-Hall.

Riker, William H. (1962). *The Theory of Political Coalitions.* New Haven CT: Yale University Press.

(1982). *Liberalism Against Populism: A Confrontation Between the Theory of Democracy and the Theory of Social Choice.* San Francisco: W. H. Freeman.

Robertson, David (1976). *A Theory of Party Competition.* London: John Wiley.

Rose, Richard and Thomas T. Mackie (1983). "Incumbency in Government: Asset or Liability?" In *Western European Party Systems: Continuity and Change* (pp. 115–37), eds. Hans Daalder and Peter Mair. London: Sage Publications.

Sabato, Larry J. (1988). *The Party's Just Begun: Shaping Political Parties for America's Future.* Glenview, IL: Scott, Foresman.

Sartori, Giovanni (1976). *Parties and Party Systems.* Cambridge: Cambridge University Press.

(1987). *The Theory of Democracy Revisited.* Chatham, NJ: Chatham House.

Schlesinger, Joseph A. (1965). "Political Party Organization." In *Handbook of Organizations* (pp. 764–801), ed. James G. March. Chicago: Rand McNally.

(1991). *Political Parties and the Winning of Office.* Ann Arbor: University of Michigan Press.

Schumpeter, Joseph A. (1943). *Capitalism, Socialism, and Democracy.* New York: Harper.

Sened, Itai (1995). "A Model of Coalition Formation: Theory and Evidence." *Journal of Politics* 58, 2: 350–72.

Shepsle, Kenneth A. (1986). "Institutional Equilibrium and Equilibrium Institutions." In *Political Science: The Science of Politics* (pp. 51–81), ed. Herbert F. Weisberg. New York: Agathon Press.

Sjöblom, Gunnar (1968). *Party Strategies in a Multiparty System*. Lund: Studentlitteratur.

Steel, Brent and Taketsugu Tsurutani (1986). "From Consensus to Dissensus: A Note on Postindustrial Political Parties." *Comparative Politics* 18, 2: 235–48.

Strøm, Kaare (1984). "Minority Governments in Parliamentary Democracies: The Rationality of Nonwinning Cabinet Solutions." *Comparative Political Studies* 17, 2: 199–227.

(1989). "Inter-Party Competition in Advanced Democracies." *Journal of Theoretical Politics* 1, 3: 277–300.

(1990). *Minority Government and Majority Rule*. Cambridge: Cambridge University Press.

Ian Budge, and Michael J. Laver (1994). "Constraints on Cabinet Formation in Parliamentary Democracies." *American Journal of Political Science* 38, 2: 303–35.

Taagepera, Rein and Matthew S. Shugart (1989). *Seats and Votes: The Effects and Determinants of Electoral Systems*. New Haven, CT: Yale University Press.

Von Beyme, Klaus (1985). *Political Parties in Western Democracies*. New York: St. Martin's Press.

Ware, Alan J. (1987). *Citizens, Parties and the State: A Reappraisal*. Princeton, NJ: Princeton University Press.

Wattenberg, Martin P. (1990). *The Decline of American Political Parties: 1952–1988*. Cambridge, MA: Harvard University Press.

Weingast, Barry R. and William J. Marshall (1988). "The Industrial Organization of Congress; or, Why Legislatures, Like Firms, Are Not Organized as Markets." *Journal of Political Economy* 96, 1: 132–63.

Wilson, James Q. (1962). *The Amateur Democrat*. Chicago: University of Chicago Press.

(1973). *Political Organizations*. New York: Basic Books.

Yin, Robert K. (1984). *Case Study Research: Design and Methods*. Beverly Hills, CA: Sage Publications.

2

OFFICE, VOTES, AND THEN POLICY: HARD CHOICES FOR POLITICAL PARTIES IN THE REPUBLIC OF IRELAND, 1981–1992

Michael Marsh and Paul Mitchell

INTRODUCTION

In comparison with some other West European countries, the Irish party system has always seemed to stand out as an example of the competitive office-seeking model of party behaviour. In a system of government formation in which the bargaining environment was always constrained to a choice between single-party Fianna Fáil governments or a coalition of almost the entire opposition, it seemed clear that office motivations would tend to prevail over considerations of policy compatibility. Since for most of the period Fianna Fáil was assumed to be centrist on the key socioeconomic policy dimension, any potential coalition was by definition spatially unconnected. Gallagher observes that "Fianna Fáil and Fine Gael had been catch-all parties while the phrase was still a glint in Kirchheimer's eye" (1981: 271), and Farrell sums up the prevailing opportunistic thesis when he says that "in the main, Fine Gael and Labour have at best accepted coalition as a necessary evil, the essential price for replacing Fianna Fáil in government" (1983: 257).

That said, Irish political parties have had to face strategic choices that have had quite dramatic effects on their electoral success, coalition alliances, government incumbency, and, not to forget, the longevity of their leaders as leaders. Since we can only evaluate the choices made in terms of those available, the first section of this chapter sets out in a relatively brief manner the broad strategic context in which Irish political parties have operated. It concentrates on the main institutional and behavioural constraints that are likely to have been important in shaping the parties' trade-offs between votes, office, and policy.

The following three sections then move away from such general features to focus on a sample of five hard choices made by Irish parties. The second section Deals with the party system as it was between 1973 and 1987, when only a coalition of Fine Gael and the Labour Party could displace Fianna Fáil from office. During this period, most of the hard choices had to be made by the Labour Party, and this section deals with the conflict over Labour's varying coalition stances, examining three cases in which Labour decided between government and opposition. The following two sections, which cover the period from 1987 to 1992, deal with a radically altered strategic context in that Ireland shifted much more clearly to a five-party system. The range of options was thus different. The third section outlines the adoption of a seemingly deviant strategy by Fine Gael when that party (until then "catch-all" office seeker) offered ongoing "responsible opposition" to their archrival Fianna Fáil's minority government in return for nothing more than the pursuit of a general budgetary strategy. The fourth section examines the dramatic events surrounding the installation of the first ever Fianna Fáil–led coalition, its motivation, and the possible consequences for the leader, the organisation, and its prospects for the future.

STRATEGIC CONTEXT

Much of the incentive for Irish political parties to be first and foremost office seekers rests at the general institutional level, in that Ireland has a Westminster-type system in which office is a prerequisite for policy influence. In fact, the opportunities for the opposition to have policy influence in parliament are even more curtailed than in Westminster itself. The Irish Dáil (lower house) meets relatively infrequently and is poorly attended; its committees lack status, resources, and authority. Parliament, then, is simply a forum for the extension of party political electoral competition. In these circumstances, there are strong incentives for political parties to govern, irrespective of whether parties are primarily office or policy seekers (Strøm 1990: 588). Add to this an available electorate (Mair 1987) – one that has relatively weak ties to any party – and a relatively proportional electoral system, and we have a perfect recipe for office-seeking underpinned by hard electoral competition. Vote-seeking may be hampered by this strong office-seeking motivation. As we shall see, parties have usually paid for their years in office at the subsequent election, losing votes, seats, and usually office too. The need to construct the alliances necessary to gain office may also have immediate electoral costs for a party, restricting the field of competition and constraining certain types of electoral appeal.

At least until 1989 the overriding behavioural feature of the system had been the refusal of the largest party, Fianna Fáil, to join any coalitions. It is debatable whether this was a point of principle or an electoral strategy. This refusal was particularly important given the party's historic electoral strength. Since 1948 it had collected between 42 per cent and 51 per cent of the popular vote, with an average of about 46 per cent. The proportional electoral system in Ireland, however, meant that the only party with a realistic chance of winning an overall Dáil majority, Fianna Fáil, in fact did so on only four occasions (1957, 1965, 1969, and 1977). Given the party's refusal to enter a coalition, it is not surprising that minority governments were fairly frequent in Ireland.

Minoritarian solutions accounted for one-third of government duration in Ireland. Strøm (1990: 61) found that most (almost two-thirds) minority cabinets are not coalitions. This was also the case in Ireland, where 70.5 per cent of minority cabinets were single-party Fianna Fáil governments. This said, majority single-party governments have been common enough in Ireland to encourage vote-seeking, both by Fianna Fáil, which has generally come close to an overall majority, and by the other parties to prevent Fianna Fáil from doing so.

Of course, if Irish political parties were pure office seekers, then we would not expect any minority governments, since it would always be in the interests of the other parties to combine and defeat Fianna Fáil. Since this has not always happened, it must be assumed that there are policy and/or electoral costs that prevent the opposition from doing so. Laver has put the point well:

> What is clear is that, until 1989, the party composition of the coalition that could displace Fianna Fáil was pretty much fixed. The impact of party policy, therefore, was in determining how difficult it was for Fianna Fáil's opponents to go into government together. (Laver 1992: 48)

Before delving into case studies of critical choices, we shall briefly examine the electoral costs of incumbency and the responses of the parties to these costs. It is central to the notion of a trade-off between office-seeking and vote maximization that government incumbency may have subsequent electoral costs. After all, if this is not the case, then parties can maximize both goals simultaneously: there would not be a hard choice. Whether or not incumbency in government is an asset or a liability was studied by Rose and Mackie (1983) for all Western countries. Table 2.1 is based on the techniques used by Rose and Mackie and shows the figures for Ireland only.

A record in government has generally been an electoral liability in Ireland. In nine of the fourteen governments in office during the period 1948–92, all government parties lost votes at the next election, with a net government average of −3.5 per cent. Rose and Mackie (1983: 127) also drew attention to the fact that "coalition parties are more likely to jostle each other than to share a common fate." Although by 1992 there were only six cases of completed coalitions, it does seem that the electoral record of Irish coalitions has been almost uniformly disastrous for the parties concerned. Where coalition has taken place, jostling has been little more than nominal, and, taken as a whole, coalition governments have fared much worse at subsequent elections than

Table 2.1. *Electoral fate of Irish governments, 1922–1992*

	1922–48		1948–92		1922–92	
	N	%	N	%	N	%
All government par- ties gain votes	5	50	2	17	7	32
Some gain, some lose	0	0	3	21	3	13
All parties lose votes	5	50	9	64	14	58
Net average government vote change (%)	−0.58		−3.5		−2.5	

single-party governments.[1] Thus, being in government in Ireland is indeed likely to be costly in terms of votes lost at the next election, and this vote loss is likely to be translated into loss of the reins of power.[2] Parties have failed to maximise their vote and office payoffs simultaneously. Rather, being in office now prejudices their potential office payoff after the next electoral cycle. This is quite evident in Tables 2.2 and 2.3, which show the pattern of election results over the last thirty years and the parties in government.

Of course, to say that office holding incurs an electoral cost is not to say that parties are unwilling to pay it. As noted earlier, the institutional structure in Ireland provides strong incentives for office-seeking behaviour. Fianna Fáil, which sees itself as the natural party of government, has in fact always gone into government when it could, irrespective of electoral considerations. So, in that sense, there is no conscious trade-off between votes and office for Fianna Fáil. Put crudely, the office motivation always wins. There is nevertheless one fundamental qualification to all of this. In a minority situation (every election since 1977) it is conceivable that Fianna Fáil could have bought its way to power by agreeing to a coalition deal. It did not do this until 1989. To be sure, Fianna Fáil has often accepted external support and has occasionally even negotiated it. Nevertheless, single-party government is (or rather was) a core party value, as well as a significant part of the party's unique electoral appeal. The party always claimed that it alone could provide single-party government and that coalition governments do not work. In vote-seeking terms, sharing of-fice was a poor option for Fianna Fáil. The qualification, then, is that Fianna Fáil periodically gave up some immediate office payoffs in the knowledge that it would return after the next election and claim all of the prizes.

The second largest party, Fine Gael, is also essentially an office-seeking party, but its vote is both smaller and more volatile than Fianna Fáil's. Since 1948 its vote has oscillated between 20 per cent and 39 per cent with an av-

Table 2.2. *Dáil seats and votes (in parentheses), 1973–1997*

Election	Fianna Fáil	Progressive Democrats	Fine Gael	Labour	Other	Total
1973	69	—	54	19	2	144
	(46.2)		(35.1)	(13.7)	(5.0)	
1977	84	—	43	17	4	148
	(50.6)		(30.5)	(11.6)	(7.3)	
1981	78	—	65	15	8	166
	(45.3)		(36.5)	(9.9)	(8.3)	
1982 (Feb)	81	—	63	15	7	166
	(47.3)		(37.3)	(9.1)	(6.3)	
1982 (Nov)	75	—	70	16	5	166
	(45.2)		(39.2)	(9.4)	(6.2)	
1987	81	14	51	12	8	
	(44.1)	(11.9)	(27.1)	(6.5)	(10.4)	166
1989	77	6	55	15	13	166
	(44.1)	(5.5)	(29.3)	(9.5)	(11.6)	
1992	68	10	45	33	10	166
	(39.1)	(4.7)	(24.5)	(19.3)	(12.4)	
1997	77	4	54	17	14	166
	(39.5)	(4.7)	(27.9)	(10.4)	(17.5)	

erage of 31 per cent. The third party, Labour, has always been smaller than the other two, oscillating between 6 per cent and 19 per cent, with an average of 12 per cent. Fine Gael always tried to go into government if it could. Its success in doing so depended solely on the attitude of the Labour Party and, in particular, the latter's willingness to make the policy compromises necessary to facilitate a coalition deal. The following section looks primarily at the varying coalition stances of the Labour Party, the factor that was crucial in determining whether or not there would be any government alternation during the 1973–87 period.

LABOUR'S COALITION STANCES: 1981–1987

LABOUR INTO GOVERNMENT IN 1981

The three episodes discussed in this section deal with the electoral alliances and governing coalitions between Labour and Fine Gael in the 1980s and show the impact of an additional element in party-to-party relationships: the role of the extraparliamentary organisation. As is evident from Tables 2.2 and 2.3, it was a time when the strength of Fianna Fáil and Fine Gael and Labour combined was delicately balanced, so much so that there were three elections between June

Table 2.3. *Patterns of government formation, 1973–1997*

Period	Type of government	Percentage of Dáil seats	Parties involved in government	Duration in months
1973–77	Majority coalition	50.7	Fine Gael, Labour	51
1977–81	Majority single party	56.8	Fianna Fáil	48
1981–82	Minority coalition	48.2	Fine Gael Labour	8
1982 (Mar–Dec)	Minority single party	48.8	Fianna Fáil	9
1982–87	Majority coalition	51.8	Fine Gael, Labour	49
1987 (Jan–Mar)	Minority single party	41.8	Fine Gael	2
1987–89	Minority single party	48.8	Fianna Fáil	28
1989–92	Majority coalition	50.0	Fianna Fáil, Progressive Democrats	40
1993–94	Majority coalition	60.8	Fianna Fáil, Labour	22
1994–97	Majority coalition	50.6	Fine Gael, Labour, Democratic Left	30
1997–	Minority coalition	48.8	Fianna Fáil, Progressive Democrats	na

Source: Adapted from Mair 1987: 37.

1981 and November 1982. Whether Fianna Fáil could be replaced in government in 1981 and again in November 1982 depended on the result of the election, but also on the ability of Fine Gael and Labour to agree to terms on which to renew the alliance that put them into government for four years in the mid-1970s. The various parts of this section trace the stormy relationship between the two parties. The marriage of political convenience that was entered into in 1981 endured, despite a trial separation, until 1987, when Labour walked out for good (or at least until 1994). The third section, covering the period 1987–9 then deals with some of the hard choices made in the new context created, in part, by this divorce. We start with the runup to the 1981 election, dealing first with the strategic manoeuvres prior to the election and then with the deal struck afterwards.

Stage 1: Votes versus Policy

At the start of the 1981 campaign, an alternative government seemed a slight possibility even without a coalition, but this presented Fine Gael with a problem.

The challenge facing Fine Gael was to maximise its vote without jeopardising its relations with Labour, whose future support, passive or active, it would certainly need, at best in a minority government or more likely as a future coalition partner. (O'Malley 1987: 37)

Private market research conducted for Fine Gael indicated that there was an unprecedented opportunity to attract votes away from Fianna Fáil, partly due to the (in some circles) unpopular accession of Charles Haughey to the leadership of Fianna Fáil. The Fine Gael general secretary, Peter Prendergast, concluded that Fine Gael standing on its own (that is, with no pre-ballot pact) could beat Fianna Fáil. Yet it soon became apparent that there was no serious prospect of this materialising and that only a coalition could displace Fianna Fáil. During the campaign, Fine Gael, of course, maintained a rhetorically tough stance. When the media actively began to float the prospect of coalition, Garret Fitz-Gerald (the Fine Gael party leader) retorted firmly:

> I give an unqualified assurance that the programme which we implement in government will be the Fine Gael programme. . . . Fine Gael are prepared to forego office rather than compromise on the fundamental elements in our programme which we have put forward. . . . Despite what Fianna Fáil might suggest, there will be no reintroduction of rates, no resurrection of the wealth tax. (*Irish Times*, June 5, 1981: 1)

Reports suggest that senior Labour Party members were not unduly perturbed by the speech, even finding encouragement in FitzGerald's declaration that there would be no compromise on "fundamental" issues, judging this to be merely an "understandable bargaining position" (*Irish Times*, June 5, 1981: 1). The media, however, were on to a story. Would such an explicit rejection of a wealth tax preclude a coalition arrangement with Labour? Or, more to the point, could Labour compromise on such a fundamentally totemic item of policy as the wealth tax?

In fact, however, despite its importance as a policy that, perhaps more than any other, signalled the independence of Labour's appeal as a distinctly socialist party, the wealth tax was not going to be allowed to be the rock on which all attempts at coalition formation would founder. The Labour position on a wealth tax became progressively more vague as the prospect of having to negotiate with Fine Gael approached (the opinion polls strongly indicated the likelihood of a hung Dáil). Back in February 1980, Frank Cluskey (the Labour Leader) had forthrightly promised that "If Fianna Fáil do not legislate for an effective wealth tax, as seems likely, we will contest the next election with a programme which will include a commitment to its reintroduction. That commitment will not be negotiable in any conceivable circumstance" (Gallagher 1982: 233). At the press conference launching Labour's election manifesto, Cluskey again affirmed that the wealth tax was nonnegotiable. When pushed on the issue, however, he equivocated. Was he then, after all, flexible on a wealth tax in the event of a possible coalition deal? Cluskey began his reply by saying, "It depends. . . ." (*Magill*, May 31–June 6, 1981: 37). He complained that people get "hung up on jargon" and clarified his position by saying that what Labour sought was "a genuine redistribution of wealth through the tax code" (*Irish Press*, May 26, 1981: 1). Hence, not necessarily a wealth tax.

Labour had, therefore, tacitly indicated during the election campaign that they would be prepared to concede ground in this area in the event of realistic negotiations with Fine Gael. This is just one small example of the way in which the *prospect* of a likely coalition deal constrained the parties' electoral policy positions, and in turn, the electoral strategies adopted, and thus increased the *probability* of a subsequent Fine Gael–Labour coalition.

Stage 2: Policy versus Office

In the period after the election, it was clear that party policy did not play an important role in defining the party *composition* of the government since the bargaining environment was restricted to only one possible coalition. However, policy was vital to the *content* of the coalition agreement, and the primary reason for this was the new organisational arrangement adopted by the Labour Party since the fall of the 1973–7 coalition.

Strøm has suggested that party leaders may attempt to give activists a stake in the party by offering them "whole or partial control over policy or office decisions within the party" (1990: 577). Obviously, this may have substantial costs for the party leadership in that such "compensation mechanisms" tend to result in the party's becoming more policy oriented at the expense of office- and vote-seeking goals (see Chapter 1 of this volume). Such a strategy led the Labour Party to what became known as the *Killarney compromise*, and eventually to office-seeking taking third place to policy and electoral concerns.

Controversy over whether the party should rule out any further participation in government sharply divided the party after the electoral defeat of the 1973–7 Fine Gael–Labour coalition. A particular point of contention concerned who should decide whether or not a coalition was in the best interests of the party. The then leader, Frank Cluskey, devised a compromise at the 1979 party conference held in Killarney. This removed the power of the party leader (and parliamentary party) to take the party into coalition. The idea was that the leader would negotiate with other parties and then submit the results obtained to the Special Conference for a decision on participation in government.

Activists at a postelection Special Delegate Conference thus directly decided whether or not the policy package negotiated was sufficient to warrant the "costs" – electoral and policy (that is, movement away from the party's ideal policy position) – of participation in government. Clearly, this meant that the party's inner leadership's office motivations were now organizationally constrained in a direct manner by the wider party. Not surprisingly, the party leadership attempted to get around this constraint by negotiating a good policy package during coalition negotiations. The full implications of this innovation for coalition politics can perhaps best be illustrated with a short description of what happened when this procedure was first used in 1981 (a very similar pattern emerged at the 1982 formation).

It is clear from the 1981 government formation that the Joint Programme for Government was consciously designed to have enough Labour input to ensure ratification at the Labour Party Special Delegate Conference (Mitchell 1996). Michael O'Leary (the new Labour leader) was staking his personal leadership on securing conference endorsement, and this, combined with the general aversion to another general election (which Labour in particular could not afford), secured a procoalition vote by a majority of 260 votes out of 1,250 (roughly 3:2). The importance of the delegate conference for the coalition game was quite evident. As Farrell says: "While this was in some measure a response to a desire among party activists to restrict the power of the leader and parliamentary party, it could also be argued that it strengthened the leader's hand in conducting negotiations with the more powerful coalition partner" (1987: 139). However, having outlined this possibility, Farrell then goes on to deny its importance during the 1981 formation period. He says that "the special delegate conference was largely confined to a liturgical function; it had no effective role in government formation" (139).

However, this account substantially underestimates the importance of the Labour Special Delegate Conference. While it is true that both O'Leary (Labour leader) and FitzGerald (Fine Gael leader) were committed to the view that, a priori, they should form a coalition, FitzGerald could be sure of his own party's support in a way that O'Leary never could. The institutional rules of the bargaining process had thus been altered significantly. The Labour Party leader could no longer strike deals autonomously with other parties precisely because the Labour Special Delegate Conference could refuse to accept their leaders' recommendation to enter coalition. Moreover, they might well do so (Horgan 1986: 145).

Therefore, by 1981, it was not just about two leadership teams bargaining about a deal mutually acceptable to themselves. In addition, both sets of leaders had to have an eye on the mood of the wider Labour Party. Specifically, the policy basis of the coalition contract had to have enough in it to appeal to a majority of the Labour delegates (who, after all, receive no office payoff from the coalition and hence are assumed to be primarily policy motivated). Clearly, the bargaining game had become much more complex, largely because we could no longer treat the Labour Party as a unitary actor without doing great violence to reality.

This need conditioned the coalition bargaining process. Contrary to Farrell's statement that the Special Delegate Conference "had no appreciable effect" (1987: 139) on coalition formation, the effect was that the increasing clamour of anticoalition voices aided O'Leary's task in securing generous concessions from Fine Gael at the negotiating table. As *Magill* magazine put it,

> the negotiations were extraordinary because it was not a question of two sides hammering out a joint agreement, rather it was of two sides trying to

estimate what the Labour conference would buy. Throughout the negotiations Garret FitzGerald was worried about O'Leary's capacity to anticipate what the conference would agree to. (Browne 1981: 26)

It seems, therefore, that intraparty factors were crucial in the negotiations. To take just one example, Fine Gael's industrial relations policy going into the election included items such as the introduction of restrictions on unofficial strikes and the imposition of cooling-off periods. Yet during coalition negotiations these policies were readily dropped, ostensibly on the grounds that "Labour couldn't possibly 'sell' that to its conference" (*Magill*, July 1981: 26). The admittedly limited evidence suggests that Fine Gael were more than willing to make policy concessions to Labour in order to get into government. Laver's manifesto analysis shows that "for two cases in which we can draw firm conclusions [1981, 1982 (November)], Labour did best out of the coalition policy package and Fine Gael actually did worse than Fianna Fail, the opposition party" (Laver 1992: 51).

"FOLLOW THY LEADER": LABOUR OUT OF GOVERNMENT DURING 1982

We have seen how the Labour Party leadership decentralised control over the office–policy trade-off in an attempt to hold the party together. This next episode shows how difficult it can be to reverse that process, particularly when the extraparliamentary party does not put such a high value on office as does the leadership. The coalition government collapsed when it could not ensure the support of Independent deputies for a budget that promised to eliminate the deficit in four years and began by cutting a number of subsidies and imposing new taxes on such sensitive items as children's shoes. The election itself produced little change. Fine Gael slightly increased their vote but lost two seats, Labour lost 0.8 per cent but retained fifteen seats, and Fianna Fáil gained 2 per cent and three seats.

The collapse of the 1981–2 coalition government provided the catalyst for a reintensification of hostilities between the pro- and anticoalition wings of the Labour Party. The Left of the party had become increasingly dismayed at the performance of the government, with the party's Administrative Council (AC) even voting at the end of October 1981 to censure the Labour ministers for exceeding their mandate from the June 1981 Special Conference when they agreed to the details of the July 1981 supplementary budget.

Now, however, party leader Michael O'Leary appeared to be trying to commit the Labour Party unilaterally to a new coalition after the February 1982 election. The Fine Gael and Labour leaders gave a joint press conference in the Burlington Hotel to launch the government's campaign. O'Leary declared: "It was a tough Budget, but it was a fair Budget. We are not trying to wriggle out from under the amount of tax we had to impose" (*Irish Times*, February 1, 1982: 1). The day before this press conference, O'Leary and other Parliamentary Labour Party (PLP) members had to battle hard at a meeting of the AC to prevent a further coalition being ruled out a priori. Eventually a compromise statement was passed that declared the party's resolve to contest the election, on the basis of its own policies. After the election, the leader was to consult with the AC and PLP to ensure the pursuit of these policies, and any developments would be put before a delegate conference (*Irish Times*, February 5, 1982). O'Leary, however, had argued that "It would be absurd to run an independent election campaign, and at the same time remain in government with Fine Gael until the new Dáil meets on March 9" (O'Byrnes 1986: 139). Despite the clear instruction of the AC that the party would fight an independent electoral campaign, O'Leary proceeded to behave as if there were a pre-ballot pact between the parties. In an attempt to make such a pact possible, the Labour ministers argued strongly in the cabinet for some changes to be made in the budget. With the support of some Fine Gael ministers, it was decided to drop the controversial 18 per cent value-added tax (VAT) on children's shoes and clothes. This in itself was a somewhat extraordinary decision, since it was the government's refusal to compromise on this issue that had led to the budget defeat two days before.

By this stage, many members of the AC were incensed by O'Leary's assertion that an electoral alliance existed between the parties. Party Chairman Michael D. Higgins explicitly denied that the party's AC had agreed to any such alliance. In fact, he claimed that there was a majority against coalition but that the meeting had agreed on the compromise statement for the sake of preelectoral unity. The agreed-upon statement, however, said nothing about any alliance or coalition arrangement.

After the election the AC, in a surprising move, instructed the leader to negotiate with all other parties and to report back on March 2, when the AC would make a decision on participation in government (*Irish Times*, February 25, 1982: 1). It is not clear why the leader and the parliamentary party agreed to such a practice, since they must have realised that they had a better chance of getting a coalition deal endorsed at a Special Delegate Conference than at an AC meeting. Nevertheless, O'Leary had indicated at the outset of the campaign that he did not believe that a Delegate Conference would be necessary (*Irish Times*, February 1, 1982: 1). He clearly hoped to get the endorsement of both the PLP and the AC. O'Leary then proceeded to negotiate a new coalition deal with FitzGerald that eliminated most of the unpleasant items in the budget. Food subsidies were retained in full, the VAT on children's clothes disappeared, and the school entry age was revised. However, despite the evident success of the leader's negotiations with Fine Gael, after six hours of debate the AC rejected any participation in government during the twenty-third Dáil on the casting vote of the party chairman, Michael D. Higgins. The decision by the

AC led to much bitterness and many recriminations, especially since twelve of the fourteen PLP members who were entitled to vote supported the leader (one Dáil deputy and one senator voted against coalition) (*Irish Times*, March 10, 1982: 7). Much debate followed about whether the parliamentary party was bound by the decision of the AC, but this was never put to the test since Fianna Fáil managed to form a minority administration when the Dáil assembled on March 8, 1982. Nevertheless, this round was clearly won by the anticoalitionists.

While the authority of the Labour Party leader was weakened by the revolt of the AC, his leadership as such was not under immediate threat since he was elected solely by the parliamentary party, which remained very supportive. The recriminations against the party chairman at the next PLP meeting were reportedly so severe that he left the meeting. The deputy leader of the party, Barry Desmond, described the chairman's casting vote against coalition as "an incredible piece of dilettantism" (*Irish Times*, March 10, 1982: 7) Such statements reveal the extent to which the party was openly divided on the coalition question and the profound sense of humiliation felt by the PLP at the fact that twelve of their fourteen voting members had been overruled by the party's AC.

These were the first shots in the run-up to the party's annual conference in October, at which the PLP hoped to have the no-coalition decision reversed. Under party standing orders, matters decided at conference cannot be raised again for three years. For questions of electoral strategy this rule is rigidly adhered to, and electoral strategy was due to be discussed at the 1982 conference.

The Party Conference met in Galway on October 23. It was agreed unanimously that the party should fight all future elections on its own independent policies. Then came the crucial business of postelectoral strategy. The motion endorsing the decision of the AC that Labour should not enter coalition government with Fine Gael was defeated by 657 votes to 523 (deputies Higgins and Taylor voting in favour) (*Irish Times*, October 25, 1982: 1). However, despite the defeat of the motion ruling out future coalitions a priori, the party leader was still very unhappy with the high "cost" of the accountability entailed in the Killarney compromise. He therefore pushed a motion to withdraw conference's control over the coalition (office) decision and recentralise it to a joint meeting of the PLP and the AC. Such an arrangement would be likely to have an in-built majority for the views of the party leadership. Not surprisingly, the annual conference was less than enthusiastic and voted against. The status quo was maintained.

The immediate result of all of this was that within days O'Leary resigned both from the leadership and from the party, and soon joined Labour's prospective coalition partner, Fine Gael. What seems clear from this is that the wider Labour Party did not value office as highly as the leadership did and that the leader himself valued it more than his own leadership.

THE WITHDRAWAL FROM COALITION

These upheavals in the Labour Party probably appeared as merely minor squabbles to an electorate that had been entertained, if that is the word, by a set of "grotesque, unprecedented, bizarre and unbelievable" occurrences in the short life of the 1982 Fianna Fáil government. The words are those of the prime minister, Mr. Haughey, and were used by a columnist to coin the acronym GUBU, which is now used to describe the scandals of the period. When the tiny Workers' Party finally pulled the plug by voting against the Fianna Fáil minority government, sufficient electoral support drained away to give the combined Labour and Fine Gael deputies a significant overall majority at the November 1982 election. The new Labour leader, Dick Spring, and Garret FitzGerald lost no time in drawing up a programme that was endorsed by a relatively handsome majority at Labour's Special Conference (846 to 522). Thus began the third Fine Gael–Labour coalition government. Initially, it offered the promise of clean government, but the economic difficulties that had brought down the previous coalition were no less severe eleven months later, and to them were added a host of other problems ranging from abortion and divorce to the national question.

The perennial dilemma of the Labour Party is the unpalatable choice between perpetual "socialist opposition" and loss of its identity within a coalition. The identity problem is a severe one for a small party in alliance with a larger one. Mair has observed that

> the logic of voting for Labour *rather than for Fine Gael* proved difficult to sustain; since a vote for Labour was a vote for a Fine Gael–dominated coalition, then in many ways it makes more sense simply to vote for Fine Gael *per se*. Of course, this logic might not hold true if Labour were seen to have a discernible and independent impact on the policies of the coalition. (Mair 1987: 56–7; emphasis in the original)

What was evident from about 1984 on was that the longer the party remained in government, the faster its electoral identity dwindled. The party's 9.4 per cent vote at the November 1982 election declined to opinion poll ratings of 7–8 per cent throughout 1983–4 to only 4 per cent by 1986.

In the face of increasing pressure from within the party to withdraw from government, the Labour ministers attempted to toughen their bargaining position with the aim of scoring identifiable policy victories. There were some successes. For example, in the social welfare area the government met most of its promises made in the initial joint programme for government. Indeed, given the severe recession and the pressure for spending cuts, the government increased social welfare payments in line with and in some cases above the inflation rate. This was largely due to Labour pressure. Nevertheless, given the increasingly monetarist tone of Fine Gael economic policy (especially in the face of new electoral competition from the Progressive Democrats [PD] party, founded late in 1985), many of Labour's "successes" seemed somewhat reactive in nature, in the sense that they were presented more as curbing the worst excesses of Fine Gael financial policy than as implementing distinctly Labour policies. The problem for Labour was that an electoral appeal based on the essentially counterfactual claim that "it would be much worse if we were not in cabinet" is less likely to translate into votes than are identifiable Labour Party policy successes.[3]

The Labour Party does seem to have suffered from several aspects of what we might call the politics of joint policy programmes. On the one hand, the party is pressured to negotiate a package that includes specific commitments to Labour policies. This, after all, is essential in order to secure the endorsement of the Special Delegate Conference. Given Fine Gael's strong desire to form a government, the necessary policy concessions have been forthcoming without too much trouble. The problem for Labour has been the actual enactment of its policy commitments in a time of recession. The party's attempts to get tough (during the 1982–7 government) were hampered by at least three factors. First, collective cabinet responsibility was usually adhered to despite periodic public showdowns between the Fine Gael finance minister and the Labour leader. This meant either that Labour successes went largely unnoticed or that the coalition as a whole benefited rather than the Labour Party specifically. Second, given that Labour had no other prospective coalition partners, it could use its ultimate sanction, the threat to withdraw, only occasionally. Third, the party could be outvoted directly in cabinet. This in fact happened at a crucial cabinet meeting on October 16, 1986, when majority voting procedures were used to push through a Fine Gael target for the budget deficit.

Having failed to increase its popularity from within the government, the Labour leadership came under increasing pressure to withdraw (see Mitchell 1996: 264–92). A Labour Party electoral commission that had been set up to advise the party on future strategy reported in September 1986. The commission identified participation in coalition as the single biggest cause of the party's decline and argued that "it follows logically that renewal of growth can only come in opposition." The alternative, if participation in government were continued, "may be no party at all" (Labour Party, 1986: 32). By this time, then, the party itself regarded the office–vote-seeking trade-off as a zero sum game, especially given the difficulties of policy implementation when in government.

Even so, the party stopped short of ruling out further coalitions in all conceivable circumstances. Under pressure from the leadership, the electoral commission left the door open for future coalitions by setting out a list of "fundamental" policies that would constitute Labour's nonnegotiable minimum demands for participation in government, although these were generally either vague or fairly unremarkable. For example, potentially the most far-reaching of these "conditions" is "the commencement of a process of drawing up a new, secular Constitution."[4] While this might be a laudable aim, in its vagueness it hardly constitutes much of a coalition condition. After all, even Fianna Fáil, the most conservative Irish party on such matters, might well agree to "commence a process" if it was involved in serious coalition negotiations. Other items, principally in the economic area, are more specific. For example, the party would demand an increase in capital taxation over three years from the present level of 4 per cent of total tax returns to 12 per cent. Even this only constitutes a return to the position that prevailed in 1974. Significantly, the commission rejected a proposal that the party should refrain from joining any government until a threshold of twenty-five Dáil seats was reached (*Irish Times*, September 4, 1986: 1).

While the leadership still wanted to leave the door open to coalition (the party was, after all, still in government at this point), the anticoalitionists within the party were now strong enough to kick it shut. The party leader was forced to retract his initial interpretation of the electoral commission's report, which he saw as favouring further coalition deals, albeit with tougher policy bargaining. A front-page story in the *Irish Times* argued that this "embarrassing and politically damaging volte-face was forced on Mr. Spring because of fierce internal criticism of his initial interpretation of the report by the Commission on Electoral Strategy in which he indicated that participation in coalition was a realistic short-term option and that a set of key party demands could be negotiable" (September 8, 1986: 1). In an attempt to forestall a challenge to his leadership, Mr. Spring's revised position was that he "looked forward to being the first Labour party leader to recommend to the party that we don't participate in government and that we pursue an independent role" (*Irish Times*, September 8, 1986:1).

Four months later, the Labour ministers resigned from the government over proposed cuts in social welfare, health, and education. This provided them with a policy platform to fight the subsequent election but only four weeks to reestablish an independent identity. Given the historically unparalleled unpopularity of the 1982–7 government, the Labour Party ran a successful damage limitation exercise, recovering to 6.4 per cent (from opinion poll ratings of 4 per cent) and losing only four seats. Further, in the 1989 election, after more than two years of an oppositional strategy, the party vote rose to 9.5 per cent. Therefore, the Labour Party again seemed to be faced with the same strategic dilemma of choosing between relatively long-term opposition, compensated by "policy purity" and gradual electoral growth (without reaching majority status), and occasional raids into government as a junior partner in a conservative coalition, with all the negative effects that this would entail for the party's identity and electoral appeal.

FINE GAEL'S "TALLAGHT STRATEGY"

This section deals with a unilateral decision by Labour's erstwhile coalition partner, Fine Gael, to support a Fianna Fáil government. Fine Gael received nothing from Fianna Fáil in exchange; in particular, there were no office benefits, and while certain policy objectives were achieved, they paid a high cost. In some respects, the actors in this tale play the opposite roles to those in the stories of the Labour Party just related. The leader put policy above electoral advantage and got little credit in his party for doing so.

The decision by the Labour Party to opt out of possible coalition, together with the dramatic rise of the right-wing PD party and the continued growth of the left-wing Workers' Party, made government formation much more difficult after the 1987 election. The result was inconclusive. Fianna Fáil failed by three seats to win an overall majority, and the opposition was much too fragmented to form an alternative government. On a previous occasion, in 1982, Fianna Fáil had concocted a notorious deal with an Independent candidate to ensure his support. This time they said there would be no deals and dared the opposition to prevent a Fianna Fáil government from forming, threatening another election. Fianna Fáil won a dramatic Dáil vote by attracting the support of some independents and by choosing another sympathetic Independent as speaker (*Ceann Comhairle*). His casting vote made Charles Haughey Taoiseach.

The new government was insecure and was further imperiled by a difficult political agenda. With the national finances in a critical state there were hard decisions to be taken. In an almost total contradiction of their somewhat expansionist election rhetoric, the Fianna Fáil government introduced the budget drawn up by Fine Gael and delayed by the sudden general election. Their only modifications were to cut the public borrowing requirement still further, and they continued to implement a draconian policy of fiscal rectitude. This was certainly not to the liking of all of their members, let alone those outside. Another election never seemed far away, despite the fragmentation of the opposition. There was more than one false alarm, most notably in June 1987, when Fine Gael threatened to vote against unpopular health cuts unless certain conditions were met. The concessions they obtained were widely seen to be no more than nominal.[5] The *Irish Times* leader had asked, "Who will blink?" It was clear to all that the new Fine Gael leader had done so.

Alan Dukes had been elected by his party (Fine Gael) to replace Garret FitzGerald when the latter stood down following the election of the Fianna Fáil government. FitzGerald had been eleven years in the job and had led his party to unprecedented electoral successes in the early 1980s. Although the 1987 election was disastrous for FitzGerald and his party, his was a hard act to follow. The episode of the health cuts was a bad one for the new Fine Gael leader. Three months later, in September 1987, he made a speech containing a clear and strong commitment to support the next Fianna Fáil budget as long as Fianna Fáil continued to follow a sound economic programme. This became known as the *Tallaght Strategy* (the name derives from the place where the speech was made), which virtually insulated Fianna Fáil from the possibility of defeat on any major economic issue.[6] In justification Dukes emphasised the national interest. The country needed these policies to save it from bankruptcy, and without some basis of stable support, Fianna Fáil would find it increasingly difficult to push them through. An election would not be helpful; it would merely increase the uncertainty. However laudable its motives, and whatever the benefits to the national finances, the strategy brought little obvious reward for the Fine Gael party. It created considerable discontent internally, and its lack of electoral benefit undermined the position of the party's new leader, who was later forced to resign – an unprecedented event in Irish politics – after only three and a half years in the job.

Dukes's offer of support for Fianna Fáil was not completely novel, which may explain the lack of impact initially made by the speech. When the new government had been installed, Garret FitzGerald declared Fine Gael's support in the Dáil for the new Fianna Fáil government if it pursued sound economic policies. Fine Gael's general support for the 1987 budget was in accordance with this, although that did not prevent the threat of defeat on the health cuts. Dukes warned on June 21 that Fine Gael was not offering "blanket support," saying, "for the good of the country we have not opposed this year's budget. 1988 is another matter. If the 1988 budget does not conform to Fine Gael objectives we will oppose it" (Irish Times, June 22, 1987: 1). What distinguished the Tallaght Strategy was rather its scope and its explicitness, which became much more apparent as time went on. It is significant that when the party chairman at a press conference the following week claimed that the government could still be defeated on specifics, Dukes corrected him, saying that this would be very unlikely if the broad lines of the budget were okay.

Fianna Fáil and Fine Gael whips worked together fairly successfully to spot and head off potential difficulties, and Fianna Fáil remained in office for almost another two years, in which significant improvements were made in the national finances, economic growth increased dramatically, and the rise in unemployment began to level off. However, these achievements did little for Fine Gael. There was severe internal opposition to the strategy and criticism of the departure from the highly adversarial style of political conflict that Fianna Fáil had used to particularly good effect in the years 1982–7. Normal "Dáil warfare" was suspended, and Fine Gael found itself supporting unpopular policies while its rivals, also in opposition, were able to vote against them, secure in the knowledge that to do so would not precipitate an election. The opportunities for electoral advantage were not being taken. One backbencher suggested bitterly that the leader was the sort of person who would go out with a fork when it was raining soup. In the summer of 1988 there was a front bench reshuffle. Dukes dropped some senior members in an attempt to cement control over his team, but opposition rumbled on. Particularly serious from Fine Gael's viewpoint was that the government later became increasingly popular but Fine Gael did not. Rather, support continued to decline for another six months and never clearly exceeded its 1987 election level. Out of office, Fine Gael might well have expected to pick up support. Standing still could be seen as going backwards. Dukes's personal poll ratings were relatively high, but only because many Fianna Fáil voters approved his stance. Fine Gael voters were much more critical.

The government eventually resigned simply in a misguided attempt to capitalise on its popularity in the opinion polls and win an overall majority, something it failed to do. Following the 1989 election Fianna Fáil went into coalition with the PDs, at which point the Tallaght Strategy was abandoned. It was argued that its purpose had been achieved, and anyway, the government no longer needed the reassurance of Fine Gael support.

On the face of it, then, this was a strategy that could be seen to bring about real policy gains but carry very high costs in terms of organisational morale – a key electoral resource – and no benefits in terms of public support. There were certainly no office benefits. Yet as we have shown earlier, Irish parties, including Fine Gael, are usually seen to emphasise office rather than policy. So: why the Tallaght Strategy?

There are a number of possible explanations. The first is that advanced by Fine Gael and Dukes himself: the national interest required it. Such was the depth of the crisis that normal politics had to be suspended. The problem with this notion is that it can easily become an escape clause whenever models are faced with untidy reality. It also raises the question: why did the other parties not do the same thing, in particular the PDs, whose policy objectives were very similar. More critically, would Fianna Fáil have done the same thing, and if not, why not?

The second explanation is that Dukes was actually buying time. His party was unprepared for an election. The coffers were empty, with almost all constituency associations in debt after the 1987 election (D. Farrell 1990). The party needed time to fill them, time to adjust to the new challenge of the PDs, and time to allow the electorate to forget the depths of its dissatisfaction with the previous Fine Gael government. On this interpretation, there was a policy gain, and also the advantage that the party could build up electoral resources to retrieve lost votes.

Neither explanation is really sufficient. The PDs were in a similar financial position, and they too approved the general style of policies being followed. Why did Fine Gael choose this tactic? Moreover, why was it so explicit? The gains, in terms of policy and time, could have been achieved simply by acting pragmatically and supporting the government when necessary without making such an open-ended commitment. In this way, Fine Gael might have been able to make capital out of attacking Fianna Fáil without bringing down the government. This is essentially what was done before September 1987, and it is what the PDs went on doing afterwards. The volte face on the health cuts revealed some of the problems of such an approach (and also underlined Fine Gael's unreadiness to face the electorate), but such embarrassment seems slight compared with the enduring problems of the Tallaght Strategy.

There can be no understanding of the decision without taking the nature of the party leader into account. The decision was strongly identified with him, and although it was said to have been cleared by the front bench in advance, there were cracks in the façade of unity, as the disagreement between party

leader and party chairman previously described demonstrates. Dukes was a
relatively new deputy, elected in 1982. He had spent no time in opposition and
was certainly not socialized into the style of political warfare that had passed for
constructive opposition in recent years. An economist by background, he was
uncomfortable with the idea of opposing something with which he fundamentally agreed. The Tallaght Strategy was a sensible, statesmanlike means of
dealing with the crisis, and was perceived as such generally by economic and
business commentators. It is hard to imagine a different leader, such as Dukes's
successor, John Bruton, doing the same thing in the same way, even though he
supported the strategy. In addition, it is possible that the decision was a case of
poor (party) political judgement. Dukes claimed that Fine Gael would get
electoral credit for its strategy. In his speech to the party's 1987 Annual
Conference (*ard fheis*) he argued that Fine Gael would reap electoral rewards,
saying that "Ireland will put Fine Gael first because we put Ireland first" (*Irish
Times*, November 2, 1987: 1). Many commentators at the time thought this was
naive, and time appeared to prove them right.

The very cool response of the party organisation is interesting, given the
manifest policy gains. After all, rank-and-file members are supposedly motivated
by a stronger concern for policy. Of course, the policy provoked criticism when
it proved electorally ineffective, but it also produced discontent because it was
a deviation from party norms. Fianna Fáil were the party's opponents and had
always been so, a fact that the lack of policy difference may have served to
increase rather than decrease. Defending Fianna Fáil's actions without even
having any direct control over those actions put members in a very difficult
position and one with which they had little experience. The 1987 annual
conference was said to "lack lustre," and Dukes's defence of his strategy, while
not challenged, evoked a very unenthusiastic response from the delegates, who
seemed concerned about the party's "identity" (*Irish Times*, November 2, 1987).
This concern was then amplified by the party's poor showing in the polls and
gave rise later to much more explicit criticisms of the leadership.

More generally, it does seem to be the case that alleged policy gains do not
translate automatically into electoral payoff for supporting parties, whether they
are outside the cabinet, like Fine Gael here, or the Labour Party as a junior
coalition member in the earlier examples cited. Rather, if there are electoral
gains from policy implementation, the credit seems to go quite disproportionately to the party leading the government.

FIANNA FÁIL BECOMES "COALITIONABLE"

This last case study is of the decision by Fianna Fáil to enter into a formal
coalition with the PDs following the 1989 election. As mentioned, the overriding behavioural feature of the party system had been the refusal of Fianna
Fáil to join any coalitions, so this decision meant the abandonment of what had

been one of the basic parameters of Irish politics. There are some similarities with the previous episode, in particular the possible damage to vote-seeking of the decision, the importance of the party leader, and the strong opposition generated within the party organisation, that cannot be attributable to policy costs. However, the main parallels are with the Labour cases outlined earlier, despite the different institutional arrangements in Fianna Fáil. The leader wanted office, and the character of the negotiations reflected the need to bring his party with him.

The election result left Fianna Fáil with 77 seats out of 166. If the speaker remained in place, Fianna Fáil required at least six extra votes to form a government, and these were not available from Independents. No coalition that did not include Fianna Fáil was at all likely. The Fine Gael–PD alternative coalition that had been offered to the electors totalled only sixty-one seats. The left-wing parties, Labour and the Workers' Party, wanted what they labelled "the parties of the right" to form a government, leaving them free to oppose and promote a more clearly structured left–right cleavage in the Irish party system. Labour was not interested in dealing with Fianna Fáil, and Fine Gael's terms were unacceptable: Dukes demanded half of the cabinet posts and a rotation of Taoiseach between the two party leaders (he had moved a long way from the Tallaght Strategy). For a time it appeared that the only way to resolve the impasse was to call a new election. Polls suggested, however, that such an election would not help matters, that Fianna Fáil could actually lose votes, and that the parties would still have to make some kind of deal afterwards.

Negotiations lasted for twenty-eight days, an unprecedented amount of time in a country where the shape of the government is normally known once the votes are counted.[7] The election result was known on June 17, and the Fianna Fáil leader was given the go-ahead by the Fianna Fáil cabinet to talk to other party leaders on June 20. The PDs were an obvious target, and they were offered a policy deal and a say in government through committees of the Dáil (lower house of parliament). They rejected this and decided to consult their grass-roots supporters before making further decisions. Following this process, they offered talks with Fianna Fáil on the condition that nothing was ruled in or out in advance. This meant coalition, but the "unconditional condition" was too much for some in Fianna Fáil. At the subsequent meeting of the Fianna Fáil parliamentary party, a few maverick backbenchers suggested that the party drop its objections to coalition, but the leadership, bolstered by the sense of the meeting, stayed with the idea of a minority government. The meeting approved what had been done so far and authorised more talks. These took place between the PD and Fianna Fáil leaders on July 4 but again broke down over coalition. A senior minister announced after a subsequent cabinet meeting that the cabinet was unanimously against coalition, and that all sections of the party had insisted that "no coalition" was a core value that could not be compromised. In fact the cabinet was far from unanimous, and it seems that Haughey himself had decided that this value could be jettisoned. He rang O'Malley (the leader of the PDs) to initiate new talks the next day, when, perhaps coincidentally, a new poll showed 71 per cent of voters to be against another election. The two leaders then made a joint statement to say that coalition could be discussed, and the meeting of the Fianna Fáil parliamentary party on July 6 gave Haughey authority to negotiate what he called a "political alliance." Discussions started on the afternoon of July 6 but were not concluded until July 12, with the *number* of cabinet seats now proving to be the major stumbling block. The PDs wanted two seats (O'Malley did not want to be the only PD in the cabinet), and Fianna Fáil offered one. Again the Fianna Fáil parliamentary party met and gave their leader carte blanche to do whatever was necessary to form a government. The next day, Fianna Fáil made a deal. General principles of a joint policy programme were quickly agreed on, and the PDs got two cabinet posts and one junior ministerial position. The six seats of the PDs gave the new government a bare majority.

It was a minimal winning coalition, in itself, like the Tallaght Strategy, unexceptional. However, several features made it remarkable. As we have said, Fianna Fáil has always made much of its unique ability to provide single-party government, claiming that it alone can provide stability and strength of purpose. Its current leader was on record even after the election as saying that "coalitions don't work."

A second feature is that the PDs were a party formed as a breakaway from Fianna Fáil by those who were strongly opposed to the Fianna Fáil leader, his style of leadership, and his policies. Most of its senior figures are former Fianna Fáil deputies. Initial suggestions by one PD Dáil deputy on June 18 that the PDs might have to enter coalition with Fianna Fáil were met with some grassroots protest and provoked another PD deputy to say that no deal could be done under the present Fianna Fáil leader.

What explains Fianna Fáil's decision? The most obvious benefit was immediate office. The coalition put Fianna Fáil back in government. Moreover, future office benefits were arguably increased by this move. Mair (1990), for instance, argued that now that it was "coalitionable," Fianna Fáil should stay in government for the foreseeable future, at least as long as the party system remained so fragmented and polarised. What about the costs? Policy costs were incurred to the extent that the Joint Programme for Government, agreed to between Fianna Fáil and the PDs, differed from Fianna Fáil policy (or from other potential coalitions). Few would see any such differences as either salient or significant (this is not to say that the parties did not have policy differences, only that such differences, for instance on tax policy or church–state differences, even inasmuch as they were in some way resolved in the Joint Programme, were not responsible for Fianna Fáil protests[8]). It was cabinet seats that caused the difficulties in the negotiations, not policy. The office costs for Fianna Fáil were two cabinet seats and a junior minister's position, although again, these may have been greater under any other arrangement. More important might appear to be the consequences for electoral support in future and the response of the party organisation. Fianna Fáil's argument that it alone could provide single-party government has arguably won it votes over the years and has contributed to its dominance of Irish politics. The coalition deal relinquished this unique electoral pitch. Only by knocking the PD–Fianna Fáil government could Fianna Fáil claim that "coalitions don't work." The "core value" was surrendered in 1989 and cannot be recaptured. This could weaken its electoral appeal in future.[9]

Most accounts have seen the position of the Fianna Fáil party leader as crucial to understanding what took place. Stephen Collins, for instance, emphasises Haughey's central role in the process, asserting that the leader claimed that only he could have pulled it off, and that he did so, if not in defiance of the cabinet, at least without their knowledge (Collins 1992). Laver and Arkins have argued that in simple game theoretic terms, Fianna Fáil need not have done any deal. However, they suggest that holding out until the other parties conceded defeat could have taken a long time and could have involved the removal of Haughey as leader:

> We will never really know whether Fianna Fáil could have governed alone. What seems likely is that they could not have done so without jeopardizing the political future of their leader. (Laver and Arkins 1990: 206)

Since it was the leader who directed operations, this was a crucial element in the decision. Brian Farrell suggests that both Haughey and the PD leader, O'Malley, saw a Fianna Fáil–PD alliance as the only realistic option very early in the process. What requires explanation is why the negotiations took so long. Farrell argues that this was because each saw it as a difficult thing to sell to their own parliamentary party and rank and file. This difficulty was not a matter of policy or office or votes but essentially what Farrell calls the "emotional stumbling blocks" to an agreement (B. Farrell 1990: 187). This analysis directs attention again to the solidaristic basis for activism that needs reinforcement by the maintenance of certain symbolic aspects of party identity rather than by policies per se. The episode also illustrates the reality of intraparty constraints on coalition negotiations.

Even while talks were taking place, Fianna Fáil protesters were holding anticoalition meetings in various constituencies around the country: Galway, Limerick, Dublin, and Meath. Discontent was particularly marked where electoral competition between Fianna Fáil and the PDs was most significant. Fianna Fáil deputies and local members may feel that the costs of coalition are particularly severe when these costs reduce their chances of an extra seat: it could be argued that they carry the burden of the office costs. Some of the opposition in meetings of the parliamentary party came from such quarters. But to explain the discontent fully, it is also necessary to consider less rational aspects of party life. Fianna Fáil considered itself to be more than a party and unlike any other. Coalition removed its badge of distinctiveness. Coalition with the PDs was especially hurtful since the PD leaders featured prominently in Fianna Fáil demonology in the period after the split of 1985.

Haughey's position as party leader following his party's "historic compromise" was closely tied to the success of the coalition. When the coalition policy agreement was renegotiated in the autumn of 1991, Haughey's commitment to the continuance of the arrangement was clear, and in marked contrast to the position of some of those aspiring to succeed him as leader. His poll ratings in 1990 initially suggested that he had successfully avoided any lasting unpopularity within the party on account of his role in creating the coalition, but once his ratings and those of his government began, for a number of reasons, to fall, coalition once again became a stick with which his opponents in the party could beat him. Following the successful renegotiation of the agreement, he fought off a challenge to his position in November 1991, but his tenure of the office still remained uncertain, particularly since he had to sack two senior cabinet members, including his minister for finance, Albert Reynolds, in order to hold on to power. In January 1992 an allegation by a former Haughey loyalist and minister for justice that Haughey, as the then Taoiseach, had known the details of a 1982 phone tapping scandal, despite his denials, led directly to an ultimatum from the PDs. They would give Haughey a few days to resign so that Fianna Fáil could elect a new leader; otherwise, they would bring down the government. Haughey, already extremely low in the polls, had no stomach for a general election, and finally did the decent thing and resigned quietly. Ironically, Reynolds, the finance minister Haughey had sacked, who had been a leading opponent of Fianna Fáil's entering coalition in the first place, was elected as the new leader, on the clear understanding that this would facilitate the continuation of the coalition.

CONCLUSIONS

We have suggested in our title that the normal hierarchy of party goals in Ireland is office, votes, and then policy. These episodes all show how parties encountered problems in trying to pursue the several goals of office, policy, and votes. They also show that there is at times a very clear trade-off between them, and that different sectors of each party can attach different weights to each of the goals. The history of Labour and coalition in the 1980s testifies to the clear trade-off between office and votes. The leadership always wanted to choose the immediate benefits of office, and moved from this position only when the bills were due and Labour faced electoral catastrophe after their participation in the 1982–7 government. For the rank and file, votes and policy always came ahead of office. The existence of an effective membership veto on coalition may have helped the party minimise policy sacrifices as far as the coalition agreement was concerned, although such agreements do not guarantee that policies will be enacted and implemented. By the closing months of the 1982–7 government, however, all sectors of the party seemed agreed that the bottom line was votes. Without a degree of electoral success nothing could be achieved, hence the withdrawal from government in the hope of salvaging something from the ruins.

The experience of Fine Gael in 1987 showed a leader apparently putting policy first. This may have been a strategic error in that he hoped his actions would also win votes. What is most interesting is the response of the membership, who, although upset when the votes and office did not materialise, seemed equally upset by the break with the traditional adversarial relationship with Fianna Fáil. Fine Gael members certainly showed no signs of rating policy above the other goals, and Alan Dukes's short reign as party leader suggests that few in the party shared his priorities.

Fianna Fáil have always appeared to place office at the top of their list of priorities, but subject to the proviso that the party would not share power. Fianna Fáil activists and many senior party figures were upset when their leader apparently put office ahead, if not of policy then of their "core value" against coalition government. Clearly, there may have been office costs in this for constituency parties, and there may in future be electoral ones too, but criticism and opposition to Haughey's deal with the PDs also sprang from the break it made with Fianna Fáil's claim to be a party unlike the others. In both of these cases, there were few signs of member concerns over any policy implications that might follow these decisions.

These episodes also emphasise the role and priorities of the party leader. The decisions of Haughey and those of the Labour leadership are in line with the common generalisation that, unless party leaders are heavily constrained, their primary motivation will be to get into office. Indeed, Luebbert has suggested:

> It is normally the case that party leaders choose very carefully indeed those issues on which participation in government will depend. Many other issues will certainly play a role in negotiations: they can be used as inexpensive concessions, bartered, brought to the fore to demonstrate concern for a party faction. But, as a rule . . . coalition bargaining is substantive and pragmatic, despite the presence of much ideological rhetoric. (Luebbert 1986: 51)

The evidence presented in this chapter sustains this contention in the Irish context. As we might expect, the general attitude of the party leaders as regards the a priori desirability of forming a coalition government, irrespective of the actual policy content of the agreement, is of crucial importance. During the formation of both the 1981–2 and 1982–7 Fine Gael–Labour Party coalitions, both leadership teams were predisposed to form a government. On the whole, the negotiations appear to have been marked by considerable pragmatism engendered by a strong desire to reach a successful conclusion and hence form a government. In 1989 it can be argued that both leaders wanted to form a government. The pragmatic bargaining, when it finally took place in earnest, was mainly about how many offices the PDs would get.

That said, even office-seeking parties will have to be at least instrumentally concerned with the policy content of their agreement to govern for fear of being punished at the next election by their (allegedly) more policy-oriented followers. Luebbert has stressed the importance of intraparty constraints on coalition formation. One comment is worth quoting at length:

> What makes talks so long, difficult and complex is generally not the lack of goodwill among the elites, but the fact that negotiations must appear the way they do in order to satisfy the members whose orientations are still largely attuned to the vocal, symbolic, and ideological aspects characteristic of each respective political culture. It is wrong to assume that, because interparty negotiations take a long time, much is being negotiated among the parties. Most negotiation in cases of protracted government formation takes place between leaders and their followers and among rival factions within parties. (Luebbert 1986: 52; see also Laver and Schofield 1990: 107–9)

Intraparty pressures have constrained the ability of the Labour Party's leader to trade away policies during coalition negotiations. This was especially so in the 1980s, when the extraparliamentary party generally exercised a veto power over coalition agreements. Leaders therefore cannot enter office unless, as it were, they take their followers in with them. However, we would also suggest that the vocal, symbolic and ideological aspects of party culture go beyond mere policy and explain the difficulties some leaders have encountered in doing deals, however reasonable their motivations in doing so. In the final analysis, leaders must be conscious too of their own tenure in their party office, not least for its instrumental value in opening up the possibility of a cabinet position. The desire of leaders to remain leaders, then, may explain aspects of wider party strategy, although they are, of course, not always successful. Alan Dukes's failure to mobilise his party behind his strategy ultimately cost him his job, and Charles Haughey had difficulty overcoming his rejection of party norms. Michael O'Leary solved his personal strategic problem in a quite different way. If the wider Labour Party did not value office as highly as he did, O'Leary himself valued it more than his own leadership. Even more ironically, Charles Haughey's very success in forming a coalition eventually cost him his job. Haughey had a long and impressive record of controlling dissent within his own party, but his erstwhile colleagues, now in the PDs, could no longer be treated in the same fashion.

NOTES

1. The average net coalition loss (1948–92) was 6.9%. The only party in a coalition that has substantially improved its vote is Fine Gael on two occasions: first during the interparty government (1948–51) when the party gained 6% at the 1951 general election and more recently after the 1994–7 government, when the party

gained 3.4% at the 1997 election. The average net coalition loss for the entire period (eight completed elections) is −7.1%.

2. Indeed, no government has been returned to power following an election since 1969. In addition, all government resignations since that date have led to partisan alternation in office.

3. The claim is counterfactual because we will never know "what Fine Gael would have done had it been able to govern without Labour, so we can never really evaluate the impact of Labour participation on coalition policy in Ireland" (Laver and Schofield 1990: 57).

4. Labour Party, Report of the Commission on Electoral Strategy, 1986: 29–30.

5. There is some irony in this, as one of Fianna Fáil's more potent electoral slogans in 1987 was "Health cuts hurt the old, the poor and the sick."

6. The government in fact suffered several defeats, the last of them over its refusal to compensate haemophiliacs who had become infected with AIDS, but none of these defeats were on any issues central to the government's economic policy.

7. What follows is taken from the accounts in Collins (1992), Brian Farrell (1990), and Farrelly (1990).

8. Collins (1992: 167) claims that only Northern Ireland policy proved a stumbling block in the policy deal between the two parties, with Haughey refusing to make a commitment to devolved government in the province.

9. So far this could be seen as having been the case, as at both elections in the 1990s, Fianna Fáil won only 39% of the vote compared with an average of 45% in five elections in the 1980s.

REFERENCES

Browne, Vincent (1981). "The Making of the Government. The Inside Story." *Magill* (July), 18–29.

Collins, Stephen (1992). *The Haughey File: The Unprecedented Career and Last Years of the Boss.* Dublin: O'Brien Press.

Farrell, Brian (1983). "Coalitions and Political Institutions: The Irish Experience." In *Coalition Governments in Western Europe* (pp. 248–62), ed. Vernon Bogdanor. London: Heinemann.

   (1987). "Government Formation and Ministerial Selection." In *Ireland at the Polls 1981, 1982 and 1987* (pp. 131–55), eds. Howard R. Penniman and Brian Farrell. Washington, DC: American Enterprise Institute.

   (1990). "Forming the Government." In *How Ireland Voted 1989* (pp. 171–99), eds. Michael Gallagher and Richard Sinnott. Galway: Galway University Press and PSAI Press.

Farrell, David (1990). "Campaign Strategies and Media Coverage." In *How Ireland Voted 1989* (pp. 23–43), eds. Michael Gallagher and Richard Sinnott. Galway: Galway University Press and PSAI Press.

Farrelly, J. (1990). *Who's Who in Irish Politics: The Top 500.* Dublin: Blackwater Press. Revised edition.

Gallagher, Michael (1981). "Societal Change and Party Adaptation in the Republic of Ireland 1960–1981." *European Journal of Political Research* 9, 3: 269–85.

(1982). *The Irish Labour Party in Transition 1957–82*. Manchester: Manchester University Press.

Horgan, John (1986). *Labour: The Price of Power*. Dublin: Gill and Macmillan.

Labour Party (1986). *Report of the Commission on Electoral Strategy*. Dublin: The Labour Party, September 1986.

Laver, Michael (1992) "Coalition and Party Policy in Ireland." In *Party Policy and Government Coalitions* (pp. 41–61), eds. Michael Laver and Ian Budge. London: Macmillan.

and Audrey Arkins (1990). "Coalition and Fianna Fáil." In *How Ireland Voted 1989* (pp. 192–207), eds. Michael Gallagher and Richard Sinnott. Galway: Galway University Press and PSAI Press.

and Norman Schofield (1990). *Multiparty Government: The Politics of Coalition in Europe*. Oxford: Oxford University Press.

Luebbert, Gregory (1986). *Comparative Democracy: Policy Making and Coalitions in Europe and Israel*. New York: Columbia University Press

Mair, Peter (1987). *The Changing Irish Party System*. London: Francis Pinter.

(1990). "The Irish Party System into the 1990s." In *How Ireland Voted 1989* (pp. 208–20), eds. Michael Gallagher and Richard Sinnott. Galway: Galway University Press and PSAI Press.

Mitchell, Paul (1996). The Life and Times of Coalition Governments: Coalition Maintenance by Event Management. Florence: PhD dissertation, European University Institute.

O'Byrnes, Stephen (1986). *Hiding Behind a Face: Fine Gael Under FitzGerald*. Dublin: Gill and Macmillan.

O'Malley, J. (1987). "Campaigns, Manifestos, and Party Finances." In *Ireland at the Polls 1981, 1982 and 1987* (pp. 31–56), eds. Howard R. Penniman and Brian Farrell. Washington, DC: American Enterprise Institute.

Rose, Richard and Thomas T. Mackie (1983). "Incumbency in Government: Asset or Liability." In *Western European Party Systems: Continuity and Change* (pp. 115–37), eds. Hans Daalder and Peter Mair. London: Sage Publications.

Strøm, Kaare (1990). "A Behavioural Theory of Competitive Political Parties." *American Journal of Political Science* 34, 3: 565–98

3

PARTY BEHAVIOUR AND THE FORMATION OF MINORITY COALITION GOVERNMENTS: DANISH EXPERIENCES FROM THE 1970s AND 1980s

Jørgen Elklit

For more than two decades, all Danish governments were minority governments. Seven out of thirteen minority cabinets in the period from October 1971 to January 1993 – the period under scrutiny here – consisted of one party only, while six were minority coalition governments.

If we count the months these governments were in office, we get an almost identical picture: 47 per cent of the months saw a single-party minority government and 53 per cent a minority coalition government. During these many years, Denmark could be seen as a polity where both kinds of minority governments did occur to almost the same degree, the single-party variant being dominant during the 1970s and minority coalitions during the 1980s. The four-party majority coalition installed in January 1993 commanded only 50.3 per cent of the seats in parliament, and this only was a temporary deviation from the dominant pattern.

Thus, Denmark is obviously a case in point when Kaare Strøm challenges the conventional political science view of minority government and the formation of such governments. One of Strøm's conclusions in his book on minority government and majority rule reads:

Conventional explanations associate minority cabinets with political instability, fractionalization, polarization, and long and difficult formation processes. My results offer little support for these propositions. In fact, in some cases the data show the exact opposite to be true. My alternative explanation sees minority governments as consequences of rational party behavior under conditions of competition rather than conflict. On the whole, the data have given considerable support to this theory. (Strøm 1990a: 89)

In Strøm's study, which covers fifteen Western parliamentary democracies between the end of World War II and 1987, minority governments account for 35 per cent of all cabinets formed. Denmark is looked upon as the extreme case, since only three of the twenty-five governments during this period were *not* minority cabinets (Strøm 1990a: 59). Since the time of Strøm's analysis, Denmark has had four more minority cabinets (and one majority cabinet), changing the number to four of thirty cabinets during the period 1945–97. The minority government proportion is thus an impressive 87 per cent.

This prevalence of minority governments makes Strøm's study – and the general explanations he offers – particularly interesting in a Danish context, since it provides a convincing understanding of a well-known phenomenon (see also Strøm 1986). It also makes Denmark an obvious test case for general propositions about minority government formation and functioning. This is even more true if we consider the composition and size of the various minority governments, for which the relevant data are given in Table 3.1.

Strøm argues that the study of government coalition formation would benefit considerably if the stress on structural factors that has dominated the field up to now is complemented by an analysis of behaviourial factors. Only by taking into account the intraparty organizational explanations of differences in party objectives and party behaviour – aptly summarized under the headings of office-seeking, vote-seeking, and policy pursuit – will it be possible to reach a comprehensive understanding of government formation processes (Strøm 1990a: 242–43; Laver and Shepsle 1990b).[1] Even though less optimistic, the reasoning in von Beyme (1983) points in the same direction.

Before 1973, the Danish party system was a traditional unidimensional Scandinavian party system with a large Social Democratic Party, one or two small Communist or Socialist parties to the left of it, and three centre-right parties to the right of it. The general election of December 1973 – often referred to as the *earthquake* election – changed this situation by adding entirely new elements to the party system, by changing its overall configuration, and by gradually letting the parties – new and old – find their places in either the central or peripheral parts of the party system (Pedersen 1987: 16–17).

The selection of cases to be included in this discussion of minority government formation in Denmark rests on four criteria: (1) data availability, (2) intersituational variation in regard to the parties included in the government formation attempts, as well as the kind of government attempted (single-party or coalition government), (3) inclusion of cases that are critical because the parties involved were unable to fulfill all three general party objectives (office-seeking, vote-seeking, and policy pursuit), and (4) recentness, that is,

Table 3.1. *Party composition of Danish governments since 1968*

Period	Parties (seats)[a]	Per cent of seats in parliament held by parties in government[b]
Jan. 1968–Oct. 1971	Social Liberals (27)	55
	Conservatives (37)	
	Liberals (34)	
Oct. 1971–Oct. 1972	Social Democrats (70)	39
Oct. 1972–Dec. 1973	Social Democrats (70)	39
Dec. 1973–Feb. 1975	Liberals (22)	12
Feb. 1975–Feb. 1977	Social Democrats (53)	30
Feb. 1977–Aug. 1978	Social Democrats (65)	36
Aug. 1978–Oct. 1979	Social Democrats (65)	48
	Liberals (21)	
Oct. 1979–Dec. 1981	Social Democrats (68)	38
Dec. 1981–Sep. 1982	Social Democrats (59)	33
Sep. 1982–Jan. 1984	Conservatives (26)	36
	Liberals (20)	
	Centre Democrats (15)	
	Christian People's Party (4)	
Jan. 1984–Sep. 1987	Conservatives (42)	43
	Liberals (22)	
	Centre Democrats (8)	
	Christian People's Party (5)	
Sep. 1987–June 1988	Conservatives (38)	39
	Liberals (19)	
	Centre Democrats (9)	
	Christian People's Party (4)	
June 1988–Dec. 1990	Conservatives (35)	37
	Liberals (22)	
	Social Liberals (10)	
Dec. 1990–Jan. 1993	Conservatives (30)	33
	Liberals (29)	
Jan. 1993–Sept. 1994	Social Democrats (71)	50[c]
	Centre Democrats (8)	
	Social Liberals (7)	
	Christian People's Party (4)	
Sept. 1994–Dec. 1996	Social Democrats (63)	42
	Centre Democrats (5)	
	Social Liberals (8)	
Dec. 1996–	Social Democrats (63)	40
	Social Liberals (8)	

[a] The prime minister's party is named first in the case of coalition governments.
[b] Percentages are calculated on the basis of all 179 members of the Folketing, i.e. including two from Greenland and two from the Faeroe Islands.
[c] 50.28 to be more precise.

no cases older than the early 1970s (Elklit, Willemoes Jensen, and Prehn 1993).

This introduction is followed by a short section on the formal rules of government formation in Denmark. Then follow, in consecutive order, sections on the four government formation situations selected (1973, 1975, 1982, and 1988), describing and interpreting these cases and the differences between them. The final section discusses the possibility of drawing general conclusions, as well as the restrictions on such an undertaking.

GOVERNMENT FORMATION IN DENMARK

The Danish Constitution does not say much on the government formation process, since the gradual development of Danish parliamentarism since 1901, with its negatively formulated confidence requirement – formally in the Constitution only since 1953 – has not made detailed constitutional rules on government formation a necessity. The central passage is Section 15 (2), which reads: "If the Folketing [the Danish unicameral parliament] passes a vote of no confidence to the Prime Minister, he must hand in his resignation, unless a general election is called."

The brevity of this constitutional provision is generally considered instrumental in securing minority government formation and survival, since it, firstly, "allows governments to seek their support from different quarters for different issues" (Pesonen and Thomas 1983: 83) and, secondly, does not require the government or the premier-designate at any point in time to command a positive majority in parliament – as long as a majority against the government (or the premier-designate) has not been registered.

In a parliament as fragmented as the Folketing – at least since the early 1970s (Elklit 1993: 48) – this leaves ample room for manœuvring, and there is no doubt that this constitutional arrangement contributes substantially to the ability of Danish minority governments to survive – and not only to survive, but also to build legislative majority coalitions.

Constitutional practice has developed not only since the latest constitutional changes in 1953, but since 1901, when parliamentarism was accepted by the crown; another essential element is the gradual development of a set of informal rules, which has filled out the vacuum left by the Constitution. The present set of informal rules has been summarized by Damgaard on the basis of Kaarsted's work (Damgaard 1990a: 19; 1992; Kaarsted 1988: 12ff., 91). Six such rules – which can also make the government formation process rather complicated – can be identified:

(1) If uncertainty about the appointment of a new government arises, each party will have to give its advice to the crown.
(2) If the advice of the parties unambiguously points towards a majority

government – or a minority government supported by a majority – the
crown has to follow this advice.

(3) If no majority can be found, the most viable minority must be found.

(4) The interpretation of the advice of the parties is the responsibility of the
acting prime minister, not the crown.[2]

(5) During the opening phases of the process, a royal *informateur* may be
appointed.[3]

(6) The advice given by the parties is not subject to specific rules or norms
in regard to its framing or wording.

A recent paper by Damgaard (1994) has approached the study of Danish
government coalitions from the opposite end, that is, the termination of such
governments.

FOUR CASES OF GOVERNMENT FORMATION IN DENMARK

The selection of the four cases for analysis is, as mentioned previously, based on
a set of criteria, among which are data availability as well as intersituational
variation in regard to the parties included in the government formation attempts
and the kind of government attempted (single-party versus coalition government).

The cases have been selected in order to ensure the inclusion of those critical
to the parties. *Critical cases* is the expression used for difficult decision-making
situations in which two or three of the party objectives discussed throughout
this volume (office-seeking, vote maximization, and policy pursuit) conflict with
one another. Special attention should be given to cases where a conflict between
office-seeking and policy pursuit is suspected to exist. This means that no a
priori assumption about parties being *only* policy pursuers or *only* office seekers
has been made, since such assumptions would restrict the empirical relevance of
the analysis of party behaviour (Budge and Laver 1986).

Strøm's advocacy for an integrated theory of competitive party behaviour
represents a fascinating step in the pursuit of a relaxation of the previously
mentioned assumption (Strøm 1990b; see also Chapter 1 in this volume). Vote
maximization certainly is a party objective that differs from office-seeking and
policy pursuit, primarily because of its genuinely instrumental character but
also because of its temporal (future-oriented) dimension.

THE CASE OF 1973

The December 1973 earthquake election paved the way to the Folketing for five
parties not represented in the previous legislative, while those five parties, which
had been represented in parliament before the election, all suffered heavy losses

(see Table 3.2). Anker Jørgensen, the Social Democratic prime minister, imme-diately resigned, but because parties representing a plurality of seats named him in their advice to the crown, he was appointed formateur.

The parliamentary situation was chaotic, as can be seen in Table 3.2., which also gives an indication of the parties' positions from left to right and of their centrality, in the party system – and thus of their bargaining power.

The Social Democrats wanted to abandon government responsibilities, which was not surprising, considering (1) the reactions of the electorate, which had left the party organization as well as the entire political system in a state of shock, (2) the oil crisis, and (3) the very austere general economic prospects. Many Social Democrats – party elite and ordinary members as well – did prefer a nonsocialist government in order to give their own party a much needed chance to recover electorally, while others argued that a situation might arise in which the party could not avoid accepting responsibility for forming a new government or participating in some coalition (Jørgensen 1989a: 204–6).

This internal discussion does not challenge the assumption of party unity – and not only because the various groups did not argue in public. But the definition of the issues – and the weight accorded to various combinations of objectives, that is, value complexity – was definitely influenced by these discus-sions. In this respect, intraparty politics matters. This conclusion also follows from the analysis of other parties in other government formation situations, such as the Social Liberals or the Centre Democrats in 1975 (see the later section entitled "The Case of 1975").

Most Social Democrats in 1973 obviously had a preference for deferred gratification as compared to immediate portfolios or the kind of influence on policies that follows from cabinet participation. Even though Danish Social Democrats consider their party an obvious candidate for cabinet participation – which also (at least as they see it, since their party is bigger than the other parties) includes the right to prime ministership – the situation in December 1973 was considered so problematic that both the party leadership and the ordinary members did prefer electoral recovery to offices and policy concessions immediately – if that option had been available.

Why did Anker Jørgensen accept the position as formateur if the party did not want to participate in any government? The explanation is twofold: (1) despite its losses, the party still had more seats than any other party, and (2) even though the party did not want – or foresee – government participation, it was still interested in the result of the government formation process. It was, of course, important which government would eventually be formed, and in this respect the position of formateur could prove helpful. There really was no reason why the party should decline this position during the first round of negotiations.

It soon became evident that Anker Jørgensen could not solve the problems of forming a new government, and therefore a new formateur was needed; the leader of the second largest party, the new Progress Party, was Mr. Mogens Glistrup. The party (i.e., Mr. Glistrup) recommended to the crown that he

Table 3.2. *Party composition of the Folketing, 1971–1997*[a]

	Sep. 1971	Dec. 1973	Jan. 1975	Feb. 1977	Oct. 1979	Dec. 1981	Jan. 1984	Sep. 1987	May 1988	Dec. 1990	Sep. 1994
Unity List	•	•	•	•	•	•	•	•	•	•	6
Left Socialists	—	—	4	5	6	5	5	—	—	•	•
Communists	—	6	7	7	—	—	—	—	—	•	•
Common Course	•	•	•	•	•	•	•	4	•	•	•
Socialist People's Party	17	11	9	7	11	21	21	27	24	15	13
Social Democrats	70	46	53	65	68	59	56	54	55	69	62
Justice Party	—	5	—	6	5	—	—	—	—	—	•
Social Liberals	27	20	13	6	10	9	10	11	10	7	8
Centre Democrats	•	14	4	11	6	15	8	9	9	9[b]	5
Christian People's Party	—	7	9	6	5	4	5	4	4	4	—
Conservatives	31	16	10	15	22	26	42	38	35	30	27
Liberals	30	22	42	21	22	20	22	19	22	29	42
Progress Party	•	28	24	26	20	16	6	9	16	12	11
Independents	—	—	—	—	—	—	—	—	—	—	7
Total	175	175	175	175	175	175	175	175	175	175	175

Note: The dot means that the party did not contest this election.

[a] Not including the four members of parliament elected on Greenland and the Faeroe Islands.

[b] One Centre Democratic member of parliament defected during the government formation negotiations in January 1993; this explains the difference between Tables 3.1 and 3.2.

should be appointed prime minister "today or tomorrow," but he did not get the support of any other party. The parliamentary leader and chairman of the Liberals, Mr. Poul Hartling, then won the support of five bourgeois and centre parties, and he was therefore appointed formateur after Anker Jørgensen.

From 1968 to 1971 a bourgeois majority coalition of Liberals, Conservatives, and Social Liberals had governed Denmark. After the 1973 election, the three parties together commanded only 32 per cent of the seats, and it soon became evident that the Liberals had no interest in a new government coalition. The three former partners would have to include either the Social Democrats (who would claim the premiership) or the Progress Party plus one other party (and that was not politically viable) or at least four of the small parties to form a majority. The formation of the various protocoalitions is discussed more theoretically by Grofman (1982: 83–5).

In this situation, Poul Hartling realized that no majority government coalition could be formed. Furthermore, he was convinced that it would be preferable – with an extremely fragmented Folketing – to have a minority government consisting of only one party, namely, his own (Hartling 1983: 68–72; Kaarsted 1988: 40ff.). The official reason for preferring a one-party government was that it, because of internal policy agreement, would have more manœuvrability than any possible coalition.

Mr. Hartling's memoirs, as well as other available evidence, support the interpretation that it was his prime objective to form a single-party government – much to the regret of the Conservatives, one of his former coalition government partners. The Social Liberals acquiesced more readily.

Mr. Hartling soon established that a Liberal minority government would not receive a vote of no confidence in the Folketing, so he could go ahead and form such a government; a few days later, he could present his "slim" government with only twelve cabinet members, based on a mere twelve per cent of the seats in parliament. Obviously, he could rely on a broader support coalition in parliament (Grofman 1982), even though the theoretical protocoalition formation steps counted by Grofman lack empirical counterparts.

What were the main objectives of Mr. Hartling and the Liberals in this situation, and were these objectives incompatible, so that we can talk of a "critical" situation? The situation definitely was difficult, since the party had lost a quarter of its seats, but one could argue that electoral recovery would be easier after a visible effort in government, even though it is commonly acknowledged by politicians that government participation costs – especially in difficult times. Furthermore, the relations between the former bourgeois coalition partners were tense – the positive relations from the time of the tripartite government had no endurance – so it could also be argued that both office-seeking and policy pursuit according to the Liberals' platform and party manifesto would be easier if the party exploited the situation alone, not in some government coalition.

If a majority coalition government was not feasible, policy pursuit would require manœvrability in parliament, and therefore a one-party government – no matter how few seats were behind it – would be preferable. So, the question remains: even though it was not decisive for the Liberals' behaviour were Mr. Hartling's objectives primarily office-seeking, policy pursuit, or a combination of the two? And to what degree did his personal objectives coincide with those of his party?[4]

The available evidence suggests that the Liberals in this situation were office seekers. In his memoirs, Mr. Hartling denies that he was driven by personal ambition (Hartling 1983: 77), but what else could he say? At any rate, there are no visible traces of discussion of policies, which could be pursued more successfully from a government than from an opposition position.[5] Since Mr. Hartling is concerned about his public image and reputation, it is remarkable that he does not mention specific policy objectives, which could be achieved through the possession of governmental power. Such objectives could have functioned as excuses for the lust for power and portfolios that other political actors and observers noticed in the behaviour of Mr. Hartling and the Liberals.

One question remains, however. The available evidence – primarily newspaper articles and memoirs – about these government formation discussions and attempts includes a great variety of names and all possible and impossible combinations of parties, which were considered, or maybe just mentioned in passing, during the various phases of the process. Is this a characteristic feature of government formation deliberations or was it more evident than usual in December 1973 due to the dramatic shifts in the Folketing, which offered – at least theoretically – more coalition combinations than previously, even though many theoretically possible combinations were not politically viable? The answer to this question will appear during the study of later government formations attempts.

The year 1973 thus saw two government formation attempts, one less serious by Anker Jørgensen and one much more serious by Poul Hartling.[6] The two parties also behaved rather differently, the Social Democrats being future-oriented vote maximizers (votes being instrumental for future policy pursuit and office-seeking), the Liberals short-term office seekers. Seemingly, none of them cared much about policies. It should, however, be remembered (1) that vote-seeking is often instrumental in the attainment of positions allowing the pursuit of policy objectives and (2) that the possession of cabinet posts can be instrumental in the pursuit of policy objectives.

This observation reflects a general problem in studying party objectives. If these two observations are correct – and most parties will say so, if asked – then it becomes extremely difficult to determine the true motives of Mr. Hartling and the Liberal Party elite. The absence of records of policy discussions between the parties during the government formation process is remarkable.

The Liberal minority government had a difficult time, with a large number of parties in parliament, with no external support agreements, and with a number of severe economic difficulties on the agenda (Nannestad 1991: 134–

56). Nevertheless, it succeeded in establishing some formalized legislative agree-
ments that brought together different combinations of parties (Rasmussen and
Rüdiger 1990: 480); thus, it was able to survive for twelve months. Mr.
Hartling then called a general election, to take place in January 1975.

THE CASE OF 1975

In this early 1975 election the Liberals' seats almost doubled in number, from
twenty-two to forty-two. Their success was achieved, however, at the expense of
the Social Liberals, the Conservatives, the Centre Democrats, the Progress Party,
and the Justice Party, the overall result being that the nonsocialist parties
dropped from a total of 112 to 102 seats.

Parliamentary fractionalization declined slightly but was still high, above
.8 (Pedersen 1987: 5), and the government's viability had not changed. The
government wanted to remain in office; since it had not resigned, it could do so
because it had not received a vote of no confidence.

Mr. Hartling immediately started on what were to become long and tedious
rounds of government negotiations (Hartling 1983: 132–53; Kaarsted 1988:
53ff.). The objective was to find out if a majority in parliament wanted him to
resign or – to put it differently – if he and his party could stay in office.
Hartling's conclusion after the first round of negotiations was that since only
the socialist parties (with a total of seventy-three seats) had recommended that
he resign, and since a clear majority, that is, all remaining parties (commanding
a total of 102 members) had given no such advice, he could remain in office.

The next round of negotiations took place in order to find out if a majority
(of Liberals and Social Democrats) or a broader minority government was feasible
(Hartling 1983: 134–6). As it turned out, neither of these two possibilities was
feasible, though Hartling's diary entries are difficult to interpret. Was the offer
to the Social Democrats only formal, since it required the party to accept an
agreement of September 1974 between the bourgeois and centre parties on tax
and budget cuts – a condition that was clearly unacceptable to the Social
Democrats? Some newspaper articles, however, imply that the negotiations were
serious (see examples in Teaching Material 1976), but the Social Liberals did
not see any point in entering a minority coalition, which would be in no better
position than the present government to have its policies accepted by the
Folketing. The Christians followed suit.

Mr. Hartling would probably argue that he was seriously trying to form a
government, which, better than the previous one, could carry out the economic
policy proposals needed to solve the problems of the country, that is, that his –
and his party's – main objective was to form a government with the best
possible chances of pursuing the necessary economic policies. Others argue that
his main objective was to continue in office as long as possible, and that he
deliberately used the negotiations to pursue primarily this latter objective.

It is not possible to tell which interpretation is more correct. Office possession might, of course, be seen as instrumental for the pursuit of the policy objectives of the party, but the insistence on these policies could also be instrumental in keeping the Social Democrats out of office, either in a majority coalition or in a new single-party minority government, formally or informally supported by the Social Liberals (and maybe other parties as well). Most non-Liberal observers got the impression that Mr. Hartling wanted to stay in office, which is also Tage Kaarsted's conclusion in the only scholarly analysis of the event (Kaarsted 1988). A former Liberal minister of defense agrees with this interpretation (Brøndum 1988). Even though there is no definite proof of the correctness of this interpretation, which shows conclusively that Mr. Hartling (and his few advisors in the party elite, including the general secretary of the party organization) were primarily office seekers in January 1975, it appears to be a more obvious interpretation than seeing their behaviour as being primarily motivated by policy concerns.

What options were available to the Social Democrats? They did not want to join any majority coalition with the Liberals because that would presuppose their support of the economic policies of the Liberal government, as well as of the September 1974 agreement between the bourgeois and centre parties on tax and budget cuts. And if they supported a vote of no confidence, they might themselves end up as a minority government – facing a number of difficult problems, which they would have even greater difficulty handling than Mr. Hartling and the Liberals (or a bourgeois–centre coalition) – and with the foreseeable consequences that electoral recovery would be even further postponed.

Obviously, the Social Democrats did not know what to do. They could not submit to the Liberals' economic policies, and it was too dangerous electorally to take on government responsibility given the composition of the Folketing and the many complicated problems ahead. So, it was considered better to keep a low profile during the government formation negotiations, hoping that the result of the next general elections might solve the party's problems. Thus, the Social Democrats' primary objective, once again, was future-oriented vote seeking.

However, neither the Liberals nor the Social Democrats were free to define the situation themselves. Both the Social Liberals and the Socialist People's Party were preparing motions of no confidence for the first meeting of the Folketing (Kaarsted 1988: 68–9); private – and separate – negotiations between these two parties and the Social Democrats had the surprising result that the Social Democrats proposed a motion of no confidence, stressing that the prime minister should resign in order to allow "free" negotiations with the purpose of forming a "broad" majority government. Some introductory words on the need for economic policies that would be beneficial to the unemployed and to industrial development were primarily frosting on the cake.

Why did the Social Democrats engage in this undertaking if they had no intention of taking on government responsibility themselves, as argued earlier?

The explanation put forward by Kaarsted (1988: 68) is quite convincing: The rhetoric of the party, as the main opposition party, required it to vote in favour of motions of no confidence, and in order to control the situation, it was better to have some influence on the wording of the motion than to leave this to the other parties. Therefore, the Social Democratic motion should not be interpreted as meaning that the positive conclusion concerning the vote-seeking objective discussed earlier cannot be retained. Eventually, the motion was accepted, with 86 votes in favour and 85 against; 5 abstentions and 3 absences bring the total to 179.

Mr. Hartling immediately announced that he would hand over his resignation to her majesty the queen. This outcome was definitely not his original intention, and again we must ask for the reasons behind his seeming dislike for opening negotiations, which could have prevented it. Kaarsted explains it by his fatigue after thirteen months of stressful and thankless service in an under-sized government (Kaarsted 1988: 70–1), combined with the political impossibility of resigning immediately after an impressive electoral victory. Maybe, but this argument does not fit in with the government formation process that followed after Mr. Hartling's resignation. If fatigue explains his behaviour before the meeting of the Folketing, why did he then engage wholeheartedly in the process of forming a new government (see also Brøndum 1988)?

It is just as arguable that Mr. Hartling and his party, after the electoral victory, were still interested in staying in power (even with a fragmented parliament), just as they were interested in avoiding implementation of the Social Democrats' policy proposals. The situation then escaped Mr. Hartling's control, primarily because he was unable – or unwilling? – to understand the reactions of his two 1968–71 coalition partners, the Conservatives and the Social Liberals. They both felt that Mr. Hartling and their voters had slighted them, the voters – for the second or third time in a row – preferred better alternatives, leaving them with fewer seats than at the previous elections.

The speaker of the house, Mr. Karl Skytte, was appointed informateur – not because anybody believed that he could possibly form a broad majority coalition (which task was his formal obligation), but because this could be a period in which the parties could perform some mating dances, which might prove important in later rounds of negotiation, when a minority coalition was expected to be the object of discussion (Kaarsted 1988: 78ff.; Jørgensen 1989b: 42ff.).

The mention of a majority coalition in the motion of no confidence was instrumental in bringing the slight majority together, forcing Mr. Hartling to resign; therefore, it had to be the formal topic of the first round of negotiations. Since the Social Liberals, positioned in the middle of the political spectrum, might be central in later negotiations, the Social Democrats had no problem with letting Mr. Skytte – who was not only speaker of the house, but also a highly respected Social Liberal leader – act as informateur.

The negotiations proved unsuccessful, both when conducted collectively under the chairmanship of Mr. Skytte and when bi- or multilateral. The main discussion themes were keeping the September 1974 agreement on cuts and the premiership, especially when the Liberals and the Social Democrats were having talks. The atmosphere during these talks was reportedly not very agreeable. Soon Mr. Skytte realized that no majority coalition (broad or otherwise) was possible.

In the next advisory round to the crown, a slight majority of eighty-six, consisting of the leftist parties, the Social Democrats, and the Social Liberals (as against eighty-five), pointed to Anker Jørgensen. But since the Social Liberals, both for internal reasons and for political-strategic reasons, had narrowed their advice by recommending that the Social Democratic Party (i.e., not necessarily the party leader) should form a majority coalition of five parties (Social Democrats, Conservatives, and the three centre parties), which the Social Democrats had mentioned during the negotiations, Mr. Jørgensen's mandate was restricted accordingly. He accepted the task, but was not optimistic about his chances of succeeding (Jørgensen 1989b: 56ff.).

It soon turned out that this majority[7] coalition could not be formed, partly due to differences regarding policies and partly because at least two of the small parties could not accept Anker Jørgensen as prime minister. Jørgensen himself gives no indication of the reasons for stressing the question of the premiership so emphatically during the first meeting of the five parties,[8] but Kaarsted reports – based on internal sources – that this was part of the Social Democratic strategy, aiming at a quick collapse of this round, which was considered only an interlude on the way to the solution (Kaarsted 1988: 94).

A new advisory round took place the following day; the result was that parties representing eighty-nine seats advised the queen to appoint the acting prime minister (Mr. Hartling) as formateur, and since the Social Liberals declared that they would not support a vote of no confidence against a minority government, Mr. Hartling could safely advise the queen to ask him to form the new government. This was the third formation attempt.

A month had elapsed since the election, and so many negotiations had been carried out that what can be seen as the first serious government formation attempt could take place without further delay. Apparently, Mr. Hartling could form his second government – a minority coalition consisting of his own Liberals, the Conservatives, the Christians, and the Centre Democrats – after a short meeting in which agreement on major political issues was reached.

Everything was ready for the installation of the government when Mr. Hartling realized that some statements by Mr. Glistrup of the Progress Party should not be taken too lightly. Mr. Hartling had taken the parliamentary support of the Progress Party for granted because the party had supported him as formateur. But his failure to take their striving for political power and recognition seriously turned into a boomerang. Since they were not considered reliable – and since the Social Democrats, when asked directly, would not guarantee not to vote against the government in a vote of no confidence – Mr.

Hartling's government-to-be ran the risk of being met with a vote of no confidence. Therefore, he could not – as acting prime minister and following the rules of the game – advise her majesty to appoint him and his new minority coalition. Furthermore, he probably felt it beneath his dignity to engage in negotiations with Mr. Glistrup or other representatives of the Progress Party.

A fourth advisory round thus had to take place. This time Anker Jørgensen got more support than Mr. Hartling (seventy-five compared to sixty-five votes), since the Social Liberals passed again (because only some members of the parliamentary party wanted to support Anker Jørgensen and because there was internal agreement that Mr. Hartling should not be supported), and since Mr. Glistrup's very specific and very complicated advice was not acceptable to Mr. Hartling (with the consequence that the seats of the Progress Party were not included in the count).

This time the commission of Anker Jørgensen was not restricted, and the final government formation attempt could start. It is difficult to tell if this outcome was the intention of the Social Democrats throughout – probably not, as argued earlier, but most of the core party elite[9] had realized, at least during the course of events, that the process might achieve this result. Even though the Circle was well aware of the economic and employment problems ahead, they now preferred a Social Democratic single-party minority government to most other possibilities. But is this only a euphemism for their continuous interest in taking over again after the Liberal interlude? Is it a slip of the tongue when Anker Jørgensen on February 11, 1975, writes in his diary: "Nevertheless a certain pleasure. I am the winner of this game, which has been going on for so long" (1989b: 65)? Wryly, Mr. Hartling wrote in *his* diary that he got the impression that the result corresponded to old plans of the Social Democratic leadership (Hartling 1983: 149).

It nevertheless appears that Anker Jørgensen would have preferred a minority coalition with the Social Liberals (Jørgensen 1989b: 23ff.).[10] This point of view also had some support among the trade unions.[11] Anker Jørgensen asked Mr. Hartling if he and his party would be interested in joining a government under Social Democratic leadership, but after a short round of negotiations – in which general policy questions were also raised – the Liberals declined. It can be argued that these negotiations were primarily a show. It might have been the intention of Anker Jørgensen to demonstrate to the Social Liberals, whom he was to see immediately afterwards, that he had done his utmost to form the broadest possible coalition – thereby both obeying the wording of the motion of no confidence and demonstrating his good intentions to the Social Liberals, who previously often had formed government or legislative coalitions with the Social Democrats. The Social Liberals nevertheless declined the offer, due to electoral fears or policy reasons, or both (Kaarsted 1988: 112).

One conclusion appears to be that neither in 1973 nor in 1975 did the Social Democrats – as individuals or as a unified party – engage in simple, unidimensional value maximization (or optimization). Instead, their positions were characterized by value complexity, very much in accordance with the assumptions made by Peterson and De Ridder (1986: 566–7). Furthermore, the evidence conveys the impression of a certain development over time regarding which party objectives were given highest priority.

Apparently, value complexity was also the case with the Liberals, even though office-seeking seemed most important to them. On the basis of observable party behaviour, one can probably more easily characterise the Social Liberals and the Centre Democrats as policy pursuers than as office-seekers, while the Conservatives were office seekers more than policy pursuers.

THE CASE OF 1982

Anker Jørgensen managed to stay in office from 1975 to 1982. Four of five governments during this period were single-party minority governments, while the fifth, from August 1978, was a Social Democratic–Liberal coalition. Since its opposition was bilateral, it came close to being an acting majority government. But the two parties were strange bedfellows, and their split, in the autumn of 1979, was only a matter of time (Damgaard 1989, 1994).

Anker Jørgensen formed what was to be his last government after the 1981 electoral defeat, despite internal disagreement as to the wisdom of continuing in office (Hansen 1982; Rasmussen and Rüdiger 1990: 293). The economic prospects were poor, and so were the government's prospects of forming legislative coalitions that could cope with the economic problems, unemployment, and so on. In September 1982, the Social Democrats left office without calling an election (Damgaard 1989: 76; Jørgensen 1990: 541 ff). Anker Jørgensen's resignation paved the way for a bourgeois minority coalition headed by the Conservative leader, Poul Schlüter, who managed to stay in office for more than ten years, even though the composition of his various coalitions changed on several occasions (Table 3.1).

The 1982 government formation is interesting for two reasons. One is that Anker Jørgensen tried to form another government before resigning. The other reason is the formation of the bourgeois minority coalition: What motives did the four parties have, and what objectives were behind the Social Liberals' decision to support this government on some issues?

Negotiations between the Social Democrats, the Socialist People's Party, and the Social Liberals after the December 1981 elections had been unsuccessful, both regarding the inclusion of the two smaller parties in a coalition government and regarding an agreement on cooperation in parliament (Hansen 1982: 102; Rasmussen and Rüdiger 1990: 293). It appears that the main problem was disagreement over income policies, but the Social Liberals also preferred a coalition that included one or more of the bourgeois parties.

During the spring of 1982, the government succeeded in establishing a legislative coalition, which carried through an agreement on unemployment policies, but it also became evident that economic problems were growing beyond the government's control. At the same time, the centre and bourgeois parties – including the Social Liberals – were becoming less and less interested in forming legislative coalitions with the Social Democratic government. In this situation, Anker Jørgensen once again tried to broaden his government's parliamentary basis by including the Social Liberals, but they also declined his offer this time.

Why did Anker Jørgensen, or at least the other leading Social Democrats (Kaarsted 1988: 11), try to stay in office? The evidence gives the impression that the main reason was to be able to influence policies, which objective could best – at least as seen by the leading Social Democrats – be pursued in a coalition government with a centre–bourgeois party, functioning as intermediary between the Social Democrats themselves and the bourgeois parties, in particular the Liberals and the Conservatives. The harsh policy measures foreseen do not point to vote maximization as a prime objective, and one gets the impression that office-seeking (possession) was not of crucial importance – but that, of course, is the very impression politicians want to generate.

The Social Liberals declined Anker Jørgensen's offer for policy reasons. Portfolios were easily available, but the Social Liberal leadership, now headed by Niels Helveg Petersen, insisted on preceding agreements on income policies, which were unacceptable to the government. Internal discussions among Social Liberal left- and right-wingers also played a role, and probably so did Mr. Helveg Petersen's expectations about a future bourgeois coalition, with or without participation of his party (Teaching Material 1984).

In early September 1982 Anker Jørgensen resigned, and the Conservative leader, Mr. Schlüter, was appointed formateur. After several rounds of negotiation, primarily between the bourgeois parties, Mr. Schlüter became prime minister in a four-party minority coalition consisting of his own Conservative Party, the Liberals, the Christian People's Party, and the Centre Democrats. The government was soon termed the *four-leaf clover*.[12]

The 1982 government formation has not been analyzed in any depth, but the impression at the time was that the distribution of portfolios between the parties was a more interesting subject than the policy discussions. The parties were eager to take over, and they knew that they agreed on a number of issues. Therefore, it was less important to discuss in any detail the policies to be pursued by the new government. They also knew the sizes of the party groups in the Folketing, and since neither the Social Democrats nor the Progress Party were prospective participants, the government by necessity would be a minority government. Therefore, no policy concessions could turn it into a majority coalition.

The Social Liberals decided against joining the government. Their inclusion would bring about a majority government only if the Progress Party also came on board, and that was unacceptable – at least to the Social Liberals, but probably also to other prospective participants. So once again, the Social Liberals did not join a government, arguing that their policy influence would be greater outside government than inside. This argument was based on the party's self-image as being close to the centre of the party system. And, once again, the objectives of the Social Liberals appeared to be closer to the policy-seeking model of party behaviour than to the two other models discussed in this volume.

THE CASE OF 1988

The four-leaf clover government managed to stay in power for almost six years, much longer than most Social Democrats had expected. The declared main objective of the four parties was to make the Danish economy recover after many years of Social Democratic mismanagement, but it has also been argued convincingly that their paramount objective was to stay in power (Damgaard 1988: 6; Damgaard and Svensson 1989: 734).

The Social Liberals and the Progress Party both accepted the primacy of the economic policy objective. Therefore, the government could survive numerous legislative defeats concerning foreign policy, environmental issues, public spending for cultural purposes, judiciary reform proposals, and so on. In such matters, the Social Liberals joined forces with the opposition to the left – a legislative coalition termed the *alternative majority*. This unorthodox parliamentary pattern has been extensively analyzed and described by Damgaard (1989, 1990a, 1990b, 1992; Damgaard and Svensson 1989; see also Hansen 1988a; Petersen and Svensson 1989; Strøm 1990a: 105–8).

Following another defeat on a foreign policy and defence issue in April 1988, the government called a sudden election. As a results of the election, the four coalition partners together commanded the same number of seats as before, but the general situation in parliament had destabilized because the Progress Party had almost doubled its standing. However, the alternative majority was still a majority, even if reduced (see Table 3.2).

On election night, the Social Liberals required that Mr. Schlüter tender his resignation and that real[13] government formation negotiations take place – perhaps with Mr. Niels Helveg Petersen, the Social Liberal leader, as formateur. Mr. Schlüter did submit his resignation, and a protracted government formation process – which eventually produced a different minority coalition – started (Damgaard 1988; Hansen 1988b).

Four advisory rounds can be counted. First, the Social Democrats took everybody by surprise by proposing that the speaker of the Folketing – who happened to be a Social Democrat – should find out if a governmental pro-gramme supported by a broad majority in parliament could be put together. He failed, one reason being that the parties of the four-leaf clover government did not engage seriously in the talks.

The Social Democrats kept the initiative by proposing that Mr. Helveg Petersen, as informateur, should – according to newspaper reports – investigate the possibilities for the construction of a programme for a government supported by a majority in the Folketing. It was no surprise that he did not succeed either.

The third attempt was made by the acting prime minister, Mr. Schlüter. His mandate was restricted because the advice of the Social Liberals stressed the need for policy agreement entailing government formation and broad cooperation in the Folketing. The negotiations actually did produce a programme, which was not immediately rejected by a majority of the parties.

In the fourth advisory round, it became evident that Mr. Schlüter was more acceptable to the Social Liberals as formateur than the Social Democratic leader, Svend Auken. It remains an open question if this outcome – and the ensuing minority coalition of Conservatives, Liberals, and Social Liberals – was intended by the Social Liberals, and perhaps also Mr. Schlüter, all along.

Evidently, the Social Liberal Party was the central party during these negotiations. It is equally evident that the major parties took the Social Liberals' point of view very seriously – concerning both the conduct of the government formation negotiations and the third-round proposal of putting together a policy programme.

Some Social Liberals objected to the party's joining a government coalition with the Conservatives and the Liberals, thereby at the same time giving up the party's traditional bridging role between the socialist and nonsocialist camps and risking the possibility of working for the party's key issues, some of which were also key issues of the socialist parties. This discussion among the Social Liberal leadership and groups of party activists demonstrates that the party was not totally united, even though the unitary actor assumption is not violated. But since the party leadership maintained that economic policy influence was the major concern – and since government participation in this party is the decision of the parliamentary group only – no true obstacle to government participation existed. The official Social Liberal argument for government participation was thus policy concern. Many political commentators and observers, however, got the impression that office-seeking in 1988 had also become a prime objective, at least as important as policy pursuit.

The gains of the two major parties that remained in office, the Conservatives and the Liberals, were obvious: they stayed in power and, perhaps even more important, they succeeded in destroying the alternative majority, especially in foreign policy issues (Petersen and Svensson 1989: 49), thereby removing a parliamentary irritant. And the two small government partners could probably still be counted on as members of legislative majorities behind government proposals. The government formation negotiations obviously had a positive effect on subsequent party behaviour in parliament and on the formation of ad hoc legislative coalitions. One explanation is that the negotiations on the programme proposal had made the parties' policy stands on a number of issues more or less public knowledge.[14]

CONCLUSION: A VICIOUS CIRCLE OF INSTRUMENTALITIES?

This discussion of the behaviour of Danish political parties in four cases of government formation during the 1970s and 1980s has aimed to subject the idea of rational party behaviour and rational models of party behaviour to critical tests, using types of evidence that are not normally used in such tests. The general expectations behind the exercise have been the following:

(1) The use of models of competitive party behaviour of the rational choice tradition (vote maximization, office-seeking, and policy pursuit) is most rewarding when the models are not treated in isolation from one another.
(2) An integrative model of party behaviour would presumably be an important advance in the understanding of party behaviour and the constraints on such behaviour, especially in parliamentary contexts.
(3) Previous empirical analyses have indicated that policy pursuit might be an important party objective (e.g., Peterson and De Ridder 1986; Strøm and Leipart 1993). Basic assumptions in recent theoretical analyses point in the same direction (Laver and Shepsle 1990a).

Between 1971 and 1993, that is, for more than two decades, all Danish governments were minority governments. Within this empirical framework, this analysis has aimed at testing the relevance of the preceding expectations for more general analyses of Danish party behaviour, using government formation negotiations and party behaviour in critical situations as test cases.

Within the limits of the available qualitative evidence – a kind of evidence that has been used purposely – a complicated picture has emerged: no definite answer about the primacy of any of the three party objectives can be given, since they all have proved important determinants of party behaviour in some of the situations under scrutiny – especially when a temporal/dynamic dimension is also taken into consideration.

Vote-seeking at future elections has been an important objective for some parties on some occasions, most obviously the Social Democrats in 1973 (and in 1975 for some members of the party leadership). The instrumental character of vote maximization (or satisficing) for either policy pursuit or office-seeking (or both) has been manifest. This observation fits in very well with some of the points made in Chapter 1 of this volume, as well as with Strøm's conclusions about the significance of competitive elections and increased electoral volatility for the prevalence of minority governments (Strøm 1990b). This is especially so since aggregate electoral volatility was higher in the 1970s than in previous and later decades (Elklit 1991: 67; Pedersen 1983). One problem with the vote-seeking motive is that it is self-evident to such a degree that it is not always mentioned. This obviously means that one cannot argue on the basis of its absence in party debates, either internal or external.

Office-seeking has been an essential, evident, and frequent party objective in the government formation processes studied here. This is especially so when the behaviour of the Liberals in 1973 and 1975, as well as the behaviour of parties in the bourgeois coalitions in the 1980s – especially the two major coalition partners, the Conservatives and the Liberals – is considered. The behaviour of the Social Democrats after 1982 has also revealed a growing lust for office. The length of the period as parliamentary opposition is one evident explanatory factor behind this objective and the ensuing party behaviour.

In a study of policy concerns and party behaviour in Norway, Strøm (1994) argues that office-seeking to a considerable degree is instrumental to, and therefore also compatible with, the pursuit of specific policies via the possession of specific portfolios. It appears that office-seeking as such cannot be as easily dismissed in the Danish case as in Strøm's study of Norwegian party behaviour. This observation does not deny the possible instrumentality of office-seeking for the pursuit of policies – also among the parties studied here – but it certainly demonstrates the need for caution when trying to separate the different party objectives in empirical studies.

The available evidence for the qualitative study of government formation processes – newspaper articles, memoirs, personal interviews, and so on – includes abundant references to party combinations, individuals, and portfolio allocations. Strøm argues that a focus on postelectoral negotiations may exaggerate the importance of portfolio concerns to Norwegian parties, obviously an argument in favour of his previously mentioned conclusion about policy pursuit (Strøm and Leipart 1993). To some degree, this might also be the case in Denmark, but certainly not to a extent that dismisses office-seeking as an important independent motive behind party behaviour in many of the cases studied here.

Policy pursuit is the party objective identified most often and most regularly when the public party evidence and statements from politicians are taken into account. There are at least three reasons for this:

(1) Policy pursuit *is* evidently an important party objective.
(2) Vote-seeking and office-seeking are less defensible in public – at least in a Danish context, but this is probably a general phenomenon. Therefore, parties will be tempted to paraphrase these two objectives, using references to policies as explanations of party behaviour, which is caused by vote- or office-seeking motives.
(3) Policy pursuit might *in itself* be instrumental to vote-seeking (e.g., among the social groups from which the parties originally emerged or which they now claim to represent) as well as to office-seeking.

Earlier, it was mentioned that another conclusion is that it is also paramount that one's research design allows one to control both the temporal dimension and the political-parliamentary framework within which party behaviour takes place. An example might illustrate this point. The situation of the Social Democrats was very different in 1973, 1975, 1982, and 1988. The party objectives identified reflect recent electoral fate and future prospects; government position and success (or the lack of it); if in opposition, the length of time since the latest government possession; and general economic prospects of the country – and policy interests were never absent!

In 1973 and 1975, the party apparently was most interested in electoral recovery – of course, with the intention of making a strong comeback that, in due time, would bring about both office *and* policy influence. The situation in 1982 is less clear regarding the balance between policy influence and office continuation objectives. The situation in 1988 is also difficult to interpret clearly. Vote-seeking was primarily instrumental for other purposes, but was the apparent lust for office genuine – as it seems – or was it also considered instrumental for pursuing specific policy objectives? The fulfilment of some of these latter objectives could then, in due time, be instrumental for staying in office.

It might be hypothesized that the apparent goal differences (and ensuing party behaviour) between major Danish parties are to be explained, at least partly, by organizational factors, as is also argued in Chapter 1 of this volume. It is thus plausible that relevant Social Democratic bodies had more de facto influence than corresponding bodies in the two major bourgeois parties on matters relevant to government formation and participation, at least in regard to the insistence on policy matters. A test of such a hypothesis would not only have to identify such differences between the parties, but would also have to strike a delicate balance between accepting the unitary actor assumption and taking intraparty processes and value complexity into consideration.

The conclusion, then, is that all three party objectives have been clearly identified in the cases under scrutiny – but with different weights in different situations, both within and between parties. The parties studied have not included all Danish parties of the 1970s and the 1980s, but only those that were most directly engaged in government formation and therefore offer the most interesting critical cases to study, that is, cases focusing on the conflict between office-seeking, vote-seeking, and policy pursuit. It has also been argued – and it is evident in all the cases studied – that vote-seeking, office-seeking, and policy pursuit might be seen as instrumental to the fulfilment of at least one of the other two party objectives.

Hence, the three party objectives are closely – and causally – connected, offering a case of multicollinearity, so that it is extremely difficult to separate the effects of the various independent variables. The consequences are intriguing, for the following reasons:

(1) It may be necessary for even more complicated functions to handle the theoretical models than those presented, for example, by Strøm (1990b).

(2) High standards of empirical evidence, both quantitative and qualitative, are required. So, the observational model to be used is also influenced. Yet, the question of static versus dynamic models is only part of the problem.

It thus remains extremely difficult to determine the precise character of the interrelationships between vote-seeking, office-seeking, and policy pursuit objectives, on the one hand, and between these objectives and party behaviour, on the other. This is due to both theoretical and observational problems. Some pertinent research problems, which are relevant beyond the Belgian or Danish cases, are succinctly described by Peterson and De Ridder (1986: 567) in their discussion of government formation as a specific policy arena:

(1) Intraparty bargaining and negotiation might be at least as important as interparty bargaining and negotiation. This underlines – again – that party type and party organization are important analytical elements. Peterson and De Ridder assume that actors in government formations are not monolithic or unitary, but this observation is important even if one does not dismiss the validity of the unitary actor assumption,

(2) Value maximization might be extremely difficult due to value complexity; the interplay of competing values becomes particularly important under the assumption that actors are not monolithic, but value complexity might also – as demonstrated earlier – complicate government formation under the unitary actor assumption.

(3) The government formation process is iterative.

The interplay between these three problems and the two problems mentioned earlier, concerning the character of the theoretical models and the problems of evidence, might be the reason why the overall picture of the objectives behind party behaviour in the cases studied here remains somewhat obscure.

Some tendencies are, however, clear. In the four government formation cases studied, office has been an important objective for the two major bourgeois parties, both when in opposition and when in government. This is not to deny the importance of policy considerations – also in the form of keeping the Social Democrats out of office – but there certainly is no reason to dismiss the office-seeking objective for these two parties. And Social Democratic behaviour after 1982 has repeatedly demonstrated the significance of this objective, which has both intrinsic and instrumental policy value.

The cases selected do not include government formation processes or party behaviour determined by office-seeking objectives after the December 1990 election and later events.[15] It is, however, worth mentioning that the three major parties have continued to act as if office possession is precious, not only as a party objective per se, but also in order to be in a better position to set the political agenda and to influence the formulation and implementation of policy proposals – thereby also keeping the policy influence of one's political adversaries at a minimum.

NOTES

1. This does not necessarily imply a relaxation of the traditional coalition theory unitary actor assumption, even though this is advocated by Peterson and De Ridder (1986); however, Laver and Schofield (1990: 14–35) argue rather convincingly that this assumption remains valid – at least in the coalition formation situations they analyze – due to the discipline of most European parties. See also the discussion in von Beyme (1983).
2. Thus, it is inadequate when Schou (1988: 169) claims that "the role of the monarch is not insignificant in the process of government formation."
3. An *informateur* is a person, typically a respected politician, who will open negotiations on who the *formateur* should be and report back to the monarch.
4. It has been argued that Mr. Hartling also had personal motives, since in 1968 he did not have the influence on the formation of the bourgeois majority coalition to which he felt entitled.
5. Obviously, such an argument in itself does not allow us to argue that policy objectives played no role in the thinking of Mr. Hartling and his few party elite advisors, since it would be a classical *argumentum e silentio.*
6. Based on *Keesing's Contemporary Archives,* Strøm has counted four government formation attempts (Strøm 1990a: 249). With only two formateurs, two of these attempts must be explained by changes in the *intended party composition* of the government to be formed, a factor also included by Strøm (1990a: 67). But Anker Jørgensen probably never intended to form a majority coalition (since he thought it impossible), and Mr. Hartling probably never thought of anything but his single-party Liberal government. The inclusion of changes in intentions when establishing counting rules only makes the entire effort more dubious. Are we to look primarily for public statements about intentions (which might be dishonest in order to hide true motives) or are we also to consider the sincere objectives of the political actors? And how can we separate a sincere intention from a stepping stone towards some other combination of parties?
7. The five parties together had only eighty-nine seats, but two of the four seats from Greenland and the Faeroe Islands could also be relied on.
8. It appears that Anker Jørgensen's diaries suffer from the same problem as other diaries and memoirs, including Mr. Hartling's: They report the position on various issues of a number of people, but if the question is a delicate one, the author does not reveal his own point of view or he says something like "NN shared my views on this very important or crucial matter."
9. The so-called Circle, advisors with whom Anker Jørgensen conferred at least once a day.
10. This observation also points the talks in 1982, to be discussed later.
11. See, e.g., the editorial in the weekly newspaper of the semiskilled workers' union, *Fagbladet,* 25 January 1975. The editorial is reprinted in a collection of material (Teaching Material, 1976) on government formation in 1975.

12. Strøm counts two formation attempts (1990a: 250), while Rasmussen and Rü-
    diger (1990: 118) point to no less than four different intended coalitions, which
    were negotiated one after the other.
13. As opposed to the pretended negotiations after the 1987 election.
14. References to some of these agreements are found in Rasmussen and Rüdiger
    (1990: 483).
15. Primarily the Social Democratic coup in April 1992, when the then party chair-
    man, Svend Auken, was ousted because he was held responsible for being unable
    to bring the party back into government position and the formation in January
    1993 of a government majority coalition under the new Social Democratic chair-
    man, Poul Nyrup Rasmussen.

REFERENCES

Brøndum, Erling (1988). "Firkløver-regering, der aldrig blev til." *Fyens Stiftstidende*,
    4 October.
Budge, Ian and Michael Laver (1986). "Office Seeking and Policy Pursuit in Coalition
    Theory." *Legislative Studies Quarterly* 11, 4: 485–506.
Damgaard, Erik (1988). "Den radikale regeringsdannelse." *Administrativ Debat* 2: 6–
    7.
    (1989). "Crisis Politics in Denmark 1974–1987." In *The Politics of Economic
    Crisis. Lessons from Western Europe* (pp. 70–88), eds. Erik Damgaard, Peter
    Gerlich, and Jeremy J. Richardson. Aldershot: Avebury.
    (1990a). "Parlamentarismens danske tilstande." In *Parlamentarisk forandring i
    Norden* (pp. 14–44), ed. Erik Damgaard. Oslo: Universitetsforlaget.
    (1990b). "Danmarks nye Folketing." In *Parlamenten i Norden* (pp. 1–22), ed.
    Krister Ståhlberg. Åbo: Åbo Academy.
    (1992). "Denmark: Experiments in Parliamentary Government." In *Parliamen-
    tary Change in the Nordic Countries* (pp. 19–49), ed. Erik Damgaard. Oslo:
    Scandinavian University Press.
    (1994). "Termination of Danish Government Coalitions: Theoretical and Em-
    pirical Aspects." *Scandinavian Political Studies* 17, 3: 193–211.
    and Palle Svensson (1989). "Who Governs? Parties and Policies in Denmark."
    European Journal of Political Research 17, 6: 731–45.
Elklit, Jørgen (1991). "Faldet i medlemstal i danske politiske partier. Nogle mulige
    årsager." *Politica* 23, 1: 60–83.
    (1993). "Simpler Than Its Reputation: The Electoral System in Denmark Since
    1920." *Electoral Studies* 12, 1: 41–57.
    Gorm Willemoes Jensen, and Karen Prehn (1993). *Danske politiske partier 1970–
    92. En bibliografi.* Aarhus: Department of Political Science, University of
    Aarhus.
Grofman, Bernard (1982). "A Dynamic Model of Protocoalition Formation in Ideo-
    logical N-Space." *Behavioral Science* 27, 1: 77–90.
Hansen, Holger (1982). "Regeringsdannelsen 1981." *Juristen* 64: 96–103.
    (1988a). "Regeringsdannelsen september 1987." *Juristen* 70, 1: 1–5.
    (1988b). "Regeringsdannelsen efter folketingsvalget d. 10. maj 1988." *Juristen*
    70, 8: 337–49.

Hartling, Poul (1983). *Godt vejr og dårligt vejr, Erindringer 1971–1978*. Copenhagen: Gyldendal.

Jørgensen, Anker (1989a). *Bølgegang. Fra mine dagbøger 1972–1975*, Vol. 1. Copenhagen: Fremad.

(1989b). *I smult vande. Fra mine dagbøger 1975–1977*, Vol. 2. Copenhagen: Fremad.

(1990). *Brændingen. Fra mine dagbøger 1978–1982*, Vol. 3. Copenhagen: Fremad.

Kaarsted, Tage (1988). *Regeringen, vi aldrig fik. Regeringsdannelsen i 1975 og dens baggrund*. Odense: Odense University Press.

Laver, Michael and Norman Schofield (1990). *Multiparty Government. The Politics of Coalition in Europe*. Oxford: Oxford University Press.

and Kenneth A. Shepsle (1990a). "Coalitions and Cabinet Government." *American Political Science Review* 84, 3: 873–90.

(1990b). "Government Coalitions and Intraparty Politics." *British Journal of Political Science* 20, 4: 489–507.

Nannestad, Peter (1991). *Danish Design or British Disease? Danish Economic Crisis Policy 1974–1979 in Comparative Perspective*. Aarhus: Aarhus University Press.

Pedersen, Mogens N. (1983). "Changing Patterns of Electoral Volatility in European Party Systems, 1948–1977: Explorations in Explanation." In *Western European Party Systems. Continuity and Change* (pp. 29–66), eds. Hans Daalder and Peter Mair. London: Sage.

(1987). "The Danish 'Working Multiparty System': Breakdown or Adaptation?" In *Party Systems in Denmark, Austria, Switzerland, the Netherlands, and Belgium* (pp. 1–60), ed. Hans Daalder. London: Francis Pinter.

Pesonen, Pertti and Alastair Thomas (1983). "Coalition Formation in Scandinavia." In *Coalition Government in Western Europe* (pp. 59–96), ed. Vernon Bogdanor. London: Heinemann.

Petersen, Nikolaj and Palle Svensson (1989). "Valgenes politiske sammenhæng." In *To folketingsvalg. Vælgerholdninger og vælgeradfærd i 1987 og 1988* (pp. 22–51), eds. Jørgen Elklit and Ole Tonsgaard. Aarhus: Politica.

Peterson, Robert L. and Martine M. De Ridder (1986). "Government Formation as a Policy-Making Arena." *Legislative Studies Quarterly* 9, 4: 565–81.

Rasmussen, Hanne and Mogens Rüdiger (1990). *Tiden efter 1945*, Vol. 8. In *Danmarks historie*, ed. Søren Mørch. Copenhagen: Gyldendal.

Schou, Tove Lise (1988). "Denmark." In *Cabinets in Western Europe* (pp. 167–82), eds. Jean Blondel and Ferdinand Müller-Rommel. London: Macmillan.

Strøm, Kaare (1986). "Deferred Gratification and Minority Governments in Scandinavia." *Legislative Studies Quarterly* 9, 4: 583–605.

(1990a). *Minority Government and Majority Rule*. Cambridge: Cambridge University Press.

(1990b). "A Behavioral Theory of Competitive Political Parties." *American Journal of Political Science* 34, 2: 565–98.

(1994). "The Presthus Debacle: Intraparty Politics and Bargaining Failure in Norway." *American Political Science Review* 88, 1: 112–27.

and Jørn Leipart (1993). "Policy, Institutions, and Coalition Avoidance: Norwegian Governments, 1945–1990." *American Political Science Review* 87, 4: 870–87.

Teaching Material (1976). *Teaching Material on the 1975 Government Formation Nego-*
tiations. Aarhus: Department of Political Science, University of Aarhus.
    (1984). *Teaching Material on the August 1982 Government Formation Negotiations.*
Aarhus: Department of Political Science, University of Aarhus.
Von Beyme, Klaus (1983). "Governments, Parliaments and the Structure of Power
in Political Parties." In *Western European Party Systems. Continuity and Change*
(pp. 341–67), eds. Hans Daalder and Peter Mair. London: Sage.

4

FROM POLICY-SEEKING TO OFFICE-SEEKING: THE METAMORPHOSIS OF THE SPANISH SOCIALIST WORKERS PARTY

Donald Share

INTRODUCTION

> *From being a party of militants, who in theory at least were expected to be disciplined, thoroughly committed, active, and schooled in the theory and practice of socialism, the PSOE went a long way towards an alternative electoralist model in which the role of the militant was relegated and party leaders sought direct communication with an electoral clientele by means of mass media and marketing techniques.*
>
> GILLESPIE (1989a: 300)

This chapter attempts to explain the Spanish Socialist Worker's Party's (PSOE) rapid shift from a policy-seeking party (as late as 1978) to an office-seeking party (by 1982). The PSOE emerged from the transition to democracy as a classic policy-seeking party: Its radical agenda was aimed more at party activists than at the electorate. After a loss in the 1979 general elections, the party moderated its image to enhance its electability, thus becoming more of a vote-seeking party. This strategy paid off in the 1982 elections, but the party entered government with some vestiges of a policy-seeking party. The Socialist leadership quickly eliminated these traits after the 1982 elections, and the PSOE subsequently became a largely office-seeking party. A new emphasis on economic modernization, efficient administration, and the desire to create "Things Well Done" (the PSOE campaign theme for the June 1987 elections) replaced the old concern for equality and participatory democracy (*autogestión*). The PSOE adopted a new image, based on its technocratic-administrative capability and the charisma of its leader, Felipe González, and it rapidly shed its social democratic skin.

Several scholars (e.g., Gunther 1986; Share 1989) have tried to explain this metamorphosis, but this chapter attempts to do so using the framework of political party behavior outlined by Strøm and Müller in Chapter 1 of this volume. Their model stresses the importance of a set of internal *organizational* variables and systemic *institutional* variables when explaining political party behavior. Organizational variables include the degree to which party organizations are labor or capital intensive, the degree of intraparty democracy, the amount of control over recruitment to leadership positions, and the nature of leadership accountability. Institutional variables include the amount of public financing of political parties, the nature of electoral institutions, the manner in which governments are formed, and the ability of parties to influence policy.

I argue that these two sets of variables were important, but they were not primary causes of the PSOE's change of behavior. The Strøm–Müller model is useful because many of the organizational and institutional variables – especially the former – encouraged and facilitated the PSOE's shift to an almost exclusively office-seeking party. However, a more complete explanation of this case requires consideration of three factors that are not part of their model: First, the role of organizational leadership was crucial in Spain, just as it appears to have been accentuated in other new Southern European democracies. Second, the "transactive" or negotiated nature of the democratic transition itself entailed a set of informal norms and "rules of the game" that shaped and constrained the behavior of party elites far more than organizational or institutional variables. Third, the international context formed an important political economic backdrop against which the behavior of PSOE leaders must be analyzed. Prevailing conditions in the international political economy encouraged PSOE leaders to pursue policies that directly contradicted past positions and that encouraged a shift to the office-seeking model.

After a cursory historical overview of the PSOE, this chapter explains the metamorphosis of the party, focusing first on the internal *organizational* and *institutional* variables described in Chapter 1. The additional variables noted earlier are then considered.

THE PSOE'S AMBIGUOUS HISTORICAL LEGACY

The PSOE has been one of Spain's most important political parties for over a century, but until 1982 it had held political power only briefly.[1] The PSOE collaborated briefly with the ill-fated Primo de Rivera dictatorship in the 1920s, a decision that split the party's ranks. During the short-lived Second Republic (1931–6), the PSOE was the largest and best-organized Spanish political party, but it did not formally participate in the pact that created the new regime (Contreras 1981). The PSOE leadership was never able to heal a complex set of ideological, tactical, and personal schisms that wracked the party. These divisions were caused by a rapid growth in PSOE membership and a dramatic surge in popular mobilization.

Faced with growing political polarization, the inability of the Republic to deliver on promised economic reforms, and the rightist government of 1934–6, some PSOE leaders adopted what Juan Linz (1978: 142–215) has called "semiloyal" positions vis-à-vis the democratic regime, even though much of the party remained loyal to bourgeois democracy. PSOE involvement in the ill-fated Asturian revolution of 1934 split the party further, weakened the republican regime, and antagonized the right. According to one historian of the period (Juliá 1986: 231), "Union and Party, which had been unified behind the project of consolidating and upholding the Republican regime, had become divided, unable to formulate a policy, and torn between supporting the Republic and undertaking a definitive assault against it."

In 1936 the last democratic elections prior to the Spanish Civil War (1936–9) once again gave the PSOE a legislative plurality (37 percent), but the "victory" did not stem the internal disintegration of the PSOE. The party's left dominated the parliamentary party and refused to collaborate with centrist forces. The bitter tactical, ideological, and personal struggles within the PSOE turned violent and continued even after the outbreak of the Civil War.

During the thirty-six-year dictatorship of Francisco Franco, the PSOE was virtually eliminated as a political force within Spain, despite repeated efforts to regroup.[2] As a relatively open mass party, the PSOE was less able to adapt to a clandestine existence than its much smaller rival, the Spanish Communist Party (PCE). Franquist repression forced PSOE members into a party largely of exiles and turned its leaders into what Gillespie (1989a: 135) calls "men without names." Thousands of them were executed, and six consecutive PSOE Executive Committees were arrested between 1939 and 1953. In addition to the severe repression, continued internal divisions hampered a revival of the PSOE during franquism. By the early 1950s the PSOE had become a small, embittered group of political exiles whose activity was increasingly irrelevant to Spanish politics. Indeed, the only unifying theme within the exiled PSOE was its militant anticommunism, which prevented it from forging effective antifranquist alliances with forces inside Spain.

Despite the atrophy of the PSOE in exile, by the mid-1950s a number of disconnected socialist movements were emerging inside Spain, separate from or only loosely connected to the exiled leadership. The stubborn refusal of the exiled leadership to acknowledge and integrate these groups created yet another division within the PSOE between internal and exiled forces.[3] It was not until the early 1970s that the socialist forces of the interior were able to wrest control of the PSOE away from the exiled old guard, and it was not until 1974, a year before Franco's death, that the party was led by a new generation of PSOE militants from inside Spain. In that year, Felipe González, a young Sevillian, was elected general secretary of the PSOE.

For the purposes of this chapter, it is useful to divide the discussion of PSOE's evolution after González's rise to power within the PSOE into four periods. In the first, from October 1975 to June 1977, the PSOE adapted to semilegality and struggled to react to the franquist regime's various attempts at reform. In the second period, from July 1977 to March 1979, the PSOE became a loyal opposition party within the new regime, participated in the construction of the new democracy, and consolidated its position within the left. In the third period, from March 1979 to October 1982, the PSOE focused on the centralization of power within the party and the elimination of the party's left. The final period, after the PSOE assumed power in October 1982, was characterized by a dramatic reversal of key party policies and the pursuit of neoliberal political economic strategies, with continued authoritarian tendencies inside the PSOE.

EMERGING FROM CLANDESTINITY

After the death of Francisco Franco, the PSOE faced a number of important political challenges in an atmosphere of extreme uncertainty (Share 1989: Ch. 3). Political mobilization and labor unrest were on the rise, but political power remained firmly in the hands of Franco's heirs. Without the dictator, the postfranquist authoritarian leadership oscillated between reform and reaction, creating a confusing political scenario for the inexperienced PSOE. The sudden resurgence of political activity after years of repression also gave rise to numerous leftist competitors, including Enrique Tierno Galván's Popular Socialist Party and the rump old guard PSOE–Historical Sector.

The PSOE maintained a largely skeptical and hostile posture toward the internal reform attempts of the postfranquist leadership, even after Adolfo Suárez assumed the prime ministership in July 1976. The PSOE continued to press for a democratic clean break induced by pressure from below, even though the objective conditions within Spain (weak political organizations, low levels of mobilization, continued widespread support for the franquist regime, and the still intact authoritarian repressive apparatus) did not favor such an outcome. In part, the PSOE's rigid posture was caused by the failure of political reform within the franquist regime before Suárez's appointment, but in large part it reflected the crude Marxist ideology that was popular among the PSOE's young new leadership. While there had always been an active left wing in the PSOE (most notably during the later years of the Second Republic), the revolutionary rhetoric espoused by the party in the 1970s was largely superficial and was the result of special circumstances within the PSOE and within Spain.

Only Suárez's remarkable record of rapid political reform between July 1976 and June 1977 persuaded the recalcitrant PSOE leadership to support his strategy of "transactive transition" (Share 1986). Suárez was able to convince the franquist Cortes to approve a political hara kiri and then quickly obtained popular approval for a broad political reform law in a December 1976 referendum. In early 1977, Suárez prepared for general elections by legalizing most political parties and dismantling pillars of the authoritarian political structure. His shocking decisions to legalize the Communist Party and abolish the franquist National Movement in April 1977 convinced all but the most skeptical within the PSOE that Suárez's democratic reforms were real.

The rapid pace of Suárez's democratic reform and the political situation within the PSOE could not have been more out of sync. After years of franquist repression and clandestine politics, a young, politically inexperienced leadership and a rapidly growing party membership responded to newly obtained freedoms with radical political rhetoric. The PSOE's first Party Congress inside Spain since the Civil War proclaimed the party to be "mass, Marxist, and democratic" and rejected "any attempt to accommodate capitalism, or any simple reform of the system" (PSOE 1977). The party's program advocated extensive nationalization and officially rejected the Suárez reform. Gunther (1986: 11) has argued that this radical posture reflected the weakness of the PSOE vis-à-vis an uncertain political situation in the predemocratic period. After thirty-six years of political impotence, the PSOE leadership had no way of gauging how the party would fare in competition against other socialist parties and, after April 1977, against the better-organized Communists. Given this uncertainty about electoral prospects, the PSOE publicly deemphasized elections and instead behaved more like a classic mass party, with an emphasis on mobilization and pressure from below. The PSOE's confrontational approach reflected a logical distrust of the Suárez reform and of the emerging democratic politics in general.

Nevertheless, as the PSOE turned its energy toward the June 1977 elections, thus implicitly accepting the Suárez reform, its combative rhetoric softened somewhat. The PSOE's electoral campaign, engineered and funded with support from Western European socialist parties, downplayed the party's radicalism and emphasized the figure of Felipe González. While PSOE leaders continued to project a radical party image to activists at party rallies, its electoral propaganda presented a milder social democratic image. Even the last-minute candidacy of Adolfo Suárez at the helm of the Union of the Democratic Center (UCD) could not provoke the PSOE to attack the prime minister's reform program.

BECOMING A LOYAL DEMOCRATIC OPPOSITION

The June 1977 elections were a watershed in the PSOE's political trajectory. Despite its second-place finish, the PSOE's strong showing (28.5 percent of the vote and 33.7 percent of the lower house seats) gave it a moral victory.

As the young leaders consolidated their control over the party, and as it became apparent that the Suárez strategy had indeed produced a democratic regime, the PSOE's radical party platform became increasingly awkward. While as late as 1977 party leaders continued to make surprisingly radical statements on political, economic, and foreign policy matters, by 1978 González had decided that a substantial ideological overhaul was necessary.

There were two major reasons why González and the PSOE leadership sought a substantial moderation of the party ideology and platform. The first and most important reason was electoral. Public opinion specialists linked to the PSOE (Maravall 1979; Tezanos 1983) presented well-documented arguments that only through a more moderate electoral appeal could the PSOE hope to gain a majority in the legislature. Survey data consistently demonstrated that the average Spanish voter was only slightly to the left of the political center. In the 1977 and 1979 general elections the PSOE was still viewed by many voters as too radical, a weakness adeptly exploited by Suárez in both campaigns. Party leaders increasingly felt that the PSOE had to broaden its appeal to include the vast middle classes and to encompass traditionally shunned sectors of the electorate (e.g., the Church, small farmers, and entrepreneurs). José Félix Tezanos (1983: 57), the party's leading pollster, argued in 1979 as follows:

> An incorrect definition of the class nature of the PSOE that fails to take into account new social realities, or that looks down at or ignores the importance of these new social sectors, could not only lead to a dangerous isolation, preventing the achievement of an electoral majority, but could also cause serious political setbacks.

Second, PSOE leaders were genuinely concerned about threats to the consolidation of democratic rule. Since the beginning of the transition, the PSOE had reestablished itself as the major force on the Spanish left, and it had recovered a great deal of legitimacy. It had absorbed competing socialist parties and built a stronger political machine. Its general secretary was among the most charismatic leaders in the country. In short, the PSOE had been handed a huge stake in the new democracy. Its leaders increasingly harbored real fears about the fragility of democratic politics, concerns that were compounded by persistent terrorism and by the attempted coup of February 1981.

Moreover, the slow and agonizing self-destruction of Suárez's governing centrist party, UCD, created the potential for a dangerous political polarization. As early as 1979, PSOE leaders were fearing the destruction of UCD, or its turn to the right, and a resulting polarization between an anachronistic and questionably democratic neofranquist right and a radicalized PSOE left. For González and his supporters in the party leadership, this scenario was too reminiscent of the disastrous Second Republic. The types of reforms contemplated in the 1977 party platform would logically antagonize powerful sectors in Spanish society, but given the fragility of democracy, the PSOE leadership was not willing to initiate such a confrontation: the stakes were simply too high.

Finally, as noted later in this chapter, the PSOE's organization was too weak to advocate a radical democratic socialist platform: The PSOE was a minuscule party, and while it enjoyed close links with the General Confederation of Workers (UGT), the UGT was only one of several competing unions within an extremely weak trade union movement. Moreover, the PSOE leadership was completely inexperienced in government. Even if a party with such a democratic socialist platform could get elected, and even if the taking of power by such a party did not destroy the fragile democracy, the idea of initiating a transition to socialism while occupying the decrepit franquist state seemed out of the question.

The PSOE's leadership's belief that it must moderate the party program for electoral reasons, and in order to help consolidate democracy, was nicely summarized by González's statements in early 1979: "The Party has to represent the desire for social change of many social sectors that are not identified with one class, contrary to the analysis at the start of the century. Secondly, the Party has an obligation, in this historic moment, to be a source of tranquillity for society, transcending the boundaries of the Party itself. And it has this obligation because this role can be played only by the Socialist Party. And that is contradictory for a party based on change. This is the whole drama of the PSOE" (quoted in Claudín 1979: 11–13). Thus, in mid-1978 González shocked many PSOE members by suggesting publicly that the party should drop its Marxist label. The party campaign platform for the March 1979 general elections was far more moderate than the 1977 version and directly contradicted the more radical statement of party goals developed at the December 1976 twenty-seventh Congress.

DEMOCRACY OUTSIDE THE PSOE, AUTHORITARIANISM INSIDE THE PSOE

In the period between the 1977 and 1979 elections the PSOE uneasily straddled the "mass-mobilization" and "catch-all" party models (Gunther 1986: 11–13). Party elites widely interpreted the failure to defeat Suárez's centrists in the 1979 elections as proof that only through a catch-all strategy could the PSOE win future elections. The ability of UCD campaign strategists to harp on radical aspects of the PSOE platform, raising fear among voters, was certainly a factor motivating González and Deputy Party Leader Alfonso Guerra to take action in order to move the party toward a mass mobilization model.[4]

At the PSOE's Twenty-eighth Congress (May 1979), González formally attempted to remove this source of confusion by proposing an end to the Marxist definition of the party, a move that was defeated by the delegates but later approved at a Special Congress in September. While a full description of these measures is beyond the scope of this chapter, it is important to note that the PSOE leadership snuffed out the last serious source of internal discord at this congress (Gillespie 1989a: 354; Share 1989: Ch. 3). Some rank and file leftist opponents, loosely called *críticos,* were able to stop the leadership's plan to water down the PSOE's Marxist image and rhetoric, but the leadership won less publicized but far more important organizational and policy battles. The Congress ended in deadlock, and a Special Congress was convened several months later to resolve these issues. Felipe González, furious over the resistance of the rank and file, refused to present himself for reelection to the PSOE leadership.[5]

Faced with González's resignation, the PSOE's left opposition disintegrated and opposition members were unable to form an opposition slate to replace him. Gillespie (1989a: 347–8) notes:

> Most delegates wanted the impossible: radical resolutions without losing González as a leader. . . . There was genuine affection for him, as well as an accurate appraisal of how the party's fortunes had become identified with those of its leader. . . . The left fell victim to the strength of *felipismo*, which at this time cut across left and right. They criticized the star marketing of the *superlíder* . . . but they naively tried to challenge this without counter-organization.

Delegates to the Special Congress were then elected under a new set of party rules that implemented an indirect, strictly majoritarian, winner-take-all electoral system. The new system virtually eliminated internal opposition by filtering out minority views at each level of the indirect delegate selection process.[6] During the Congress itself, new procedures required delegations to vote in blocs. Voting during Congresses was now conducted by the heads of sixty-eight delegations, facilitating the leadership's control over the entire process. Alfonso Guerra, González's lieutenant, was now able to single-handedly control the entire Andalusian delegation, about one quarter of the total delegates. The newly elected delegates included far more PSOE professionals and far fewer workers and students (Tezanos 1983: 143).[7] In short, by centralizing power in the hands of provincial and regional PSOE organizations, the leadership became less beholden to party members on policy issues. The new party rules included strong sanctions and even expulsion for public criticism of the PSOE, and they even required party members to get permission to attend rallies or meetings not sponsored by the party (Gillespie 1989a: 346–7).

By the time of the Twenty-ninth Party Congress (October 1981), the social democratization of the party ideology and program was complete, Marxism was relegated to the role of a purely analytical tool, and there were no longer calls for nationalization of industries or *autogestión* in the workplace.

THE PSOE IN GOVERNMENT: BECOMING AN OFFICE-SEEKING PARTY

The PSOE came to power after winning an absolute majority in the October 1982 legislative elections. Its Party Program called for a typically Keynesian stimulation of the economy in order to create 800,000 new jobs, thereby reducing Spain's alarming unemployment rate (over 16 percent in 1982). While eschewing nationalization of industry, the PSOE did call for a significant redistribution of income and vastly increased social expenditures. The party advocated Spain's withdrawal from NATO and promised a referendum on the issue.

Once in power, the PSOE abandoned each of these commitments. The government almost immediately embarked on a harsh economic austerity program and instituted a severe industrial streamlining plan. By 1987 over 3 million Spaniards (over 21 percent of the labor force, over 40 percent among twenty- to twenty-four-year-olds) were unemployed, the highest rate of any developed country. The PSOE had banked on an economic recovery that, coupled with lower inflation and increased foreign and domestic investment, would create jobs, but the dramatic economic recovery never reduced unemployment to the extent expected. During the "hot spring" of 1988 and the general strike of December 1988, many sectors of Spanish society protested the government's political economic policies, and Spain experienced the highest level of mass protest and mobilization in years. As early as 1984, the government had also changed its position on NATO membership, and in 1986 the government held a referendum in which the PSOE successfully persuaded a majority of voters to approve Spain's continued membership in the Atlantic Alliance. By early 1984 one scholar was calling the PSOE "Spain's new centrist party" (Serfaty 1984: 492).

Despite its blatant abandonment of the 1982 electoral pledges, the PSOE continued to chalk up political victories. The party scored its most stunning victory in the March 1986 NATO referendum, despite the fact that a substantial and remarkably stable majority of Spanish voters supported the withdrawal from NATO up until the day of the referendum (Gunther 1986: 25). The PSOE won a second absolute majority in the June 1986 general elections, and, though weakened somewhat, continued its political hegemony in the June 1987 municipal, regional, and European Parliament elections. The party barely retained its majority in the October 1989 general elections, but it still remained far and away the largest party in the Spanish parliament. Only after a long series of corruption scandals in the early 1990s was the continuation of the PSOE government called into question, but the party was able to hold power until 1996.

EXPLAINING THE METAMORPHOSIS OF THE PSOE

INTERNAL ORGANIZATION

The behavior of party leadership is constrained by party organization. In order to carry out party goals, leaders need to gather information about the electorate, mobilize supporters in campaigns, and implement party policy if elected to office. Many traditional labor-intensive parties have given way to modern capital-intensive political parties (Strøm 1990: 575), and this is especially true of southern European socialist parties over the last two decades (Pridham 1990: 116). Capital-intensive parties are more able to depend on high-tech media campaigns and highly paid professionals in order to lure voters. They are far less dependent on their mass memberships to spread the word during campaigns and are less beholden to amateurs. Capital-intensive parties are thus less likely than labor-intensive ones to be constrained by policy preferences of their membership. They are also far more likely to renege on promises to party activists after elections, since they can more easily afford the cost, in angry or disillusioned cadres, than labor-intensive parties.

Since 1975 the PSOE has become the increasingly capital-intensive party described by Strøm and Müller. To begin with, the party has never had a sizable membership. Party membership did not even reach 75,000 until 1936 (at a time when the PSOE won 16 percent of the votes). Membership during the long Franco dictatorship never totaled more than several thousand. With the transition to democracy the PSOE experienced a rapid growth in party membership, peaking at about 215,000 in 1988.[8] Despite the euphoria of the transition and the electoral success of the PSOE in 1982, its membership figures were below those of socialist parties in smaller European countries like Austria or Belgium.[9] According to the PSOE's own data, the party had a smaller voter-to-member ratio than any of its European socialist counterparts (Del Castillo 1989: 186). All contemporary Spanish political parties have notoriously small memberships, in large part due to forty years of authoritarian rule, but by the 1980s the PSOE had fewer members and a lower member-to-voter ratio than the conservative opposition party, the Popular Alliance.

Not only was the PSOE not beholden to party activists, but in the early 1980s over half of its members were paid party professionals (López Guerra 1984: 132). By 1988, a staggering 70 percent of PSOE Congress delegates held elective office or posts in government administration (Padgett and Paterson 1990: 103). The tiny membership of the PSOE, and the fact that much of that membership depended directly on the party leadership for their livelihoods, gave the leadership an unusual amount of insulation from its rank and file. These factors made it highly unlikely that the membership would take the PSOE leadership to task for straying from official party policy once in office.

A party's dependence on amateurs or professionals is determined in part by the mix of policy influence benefits versus office benefits (spoils) a party can deliver since "[t]he greater the proportion of office to policy influence benefits, the larger the ratio of professionals to amateurs" (Strøm 1990: 756). This relationship is nicely illustrated in the case of the PSOE after 1982. On the one hand, as described earlier, the PSOE rank and file were unwilling and/or unable to influence many of the policies taken by the new Socialist government, even when these policies openly contradicted official party policy. On the other hand, the new PSOE administration represented the first genuine opportunity for broad administrative turnover in forty years. While in opposition, the PSOE had criticized the *patrimonialismo* of UCD governments, and it pledged in 1982 to make only 4,000 political appointments. Once in office, the PSOE abandoned this pledge and made about 25,000 appointments between 1984 and 1987 alone (Gillespie 1990: 132). What the PSOE was unwilling to deliver to its supporters in policy influence benefits it more than compensated for with the spoils of office, leading one observer to lament the "hemorrhage of cadres

destined for public office" and to note that the PSOE "lacks sufficient membership or cadres to continue as a socially rooted party, especially after thousands
of its supporters were recruited by the state apparatus" (*El País*, December 10,
1984: 10). The growing influence of party professionals and the decreasing
dependence of the PSOE on party volunteers to win elections in 1986 and 1992
helped the party to ignore campaign pledges, internal discord, and other forms
of pressure from below.

Secondly, Strøm (1990: 577) argues that "[T]he more policy decisions are
decentralized, the more policy oriented the party becomes at the expense of
office and vote seeking." As noted earlier, from the party's reemergence in the
mid-1970s to its electoral success in 1982, the PSOE's organizational structures
became more centralized, majoritarian, and authoritarian. As López Guerra
(1984: 138) notes, the party's electoral success after 1982 was in large part a
reflection of the fact that it alone remained a unified and coherent party.

Socialist leaders' views of intraparty democracy were strongly influenced by
both distant events and recent history. Some analysts (Linz 1978: 142–215)
have argued that the PSOE's internal discord was a contributing factor in the
breakdown of Spanish democracy during the Second Republic. Many PSOE
leaders learned the historical lesson that internal ideological and tactical bick-
ering during the Republic had helped sabotage the regime. More recent history
seemed to confirm this lesson. The spectacular collapses of the UCD and the
Spanish Communist Party (PCE), the two parties that flanked the PSOE in the
Spanish party system, were both directly caused by internal discord. The leadership of the PSOE had solid historical reasons to desire a strict limit on party
democracy and dissent.

Despite the fact that the "new" PSOE was born in 1974 out of an open act
of rebellion by the faction led by Felipe González and Alfonso Guerra, the two
soon implemented strong measures to restrict intraparty democracy. In short,
most students of the Spanish socialists see 1979 as a watershed: "It saw the
consolidation of the personal authority of Felipe González in the party, as well
as decisive moves to transform the PSOE from being a party of militants into
an electoral party" (Gillespie 1989a: 337). Strengthened by new party rules, the
leadership began to intimidate internal critics by removing them from electoral
lists (or demoting them) and by applying tough party sanctions. These rule
changes were so effective in preventing a repeat of the 28th Congress turmoil
that observers at the next two party congresses criticized the eerie unanimity
and lack of debate, comparing the atmosphere with that of the franquist and
Soviet legislatures.

During the 1980s there emerged serious concern about the lack of party
democracy, even by those who supported the leadership on most policy issues.
A new set of party rules adopted in 1984 officially tolerated "currents" within
the party but seriously proscribed all organizational attributes. The leadership
was aware that its effort to unify the party and avoid internal fragmentation
seriously threatened party democracy, and it consequently called for a renewed

internal debate on a wide range of issues. However, after crushing most internal dissent and breaking the back of its major opposition during the NATO controversy, the leadership's new concern for party democracy appeared to many as both belated and somewhat hollow.[10] Only after the PSOE's defeat in the 1996 elections did significant internal party reform take place.

The PSOE's leadership recruitment policy increasingly gravitated away from the promotion of activists, facilitating the overall shift toward office-seeking behavior. Since many of the most loyal party members found themselves in the internal party opposition (the party left), and since this opposition was defeated in 1979, the party leadership has tapped a number of individuals who lacked much history of party militancy or even affiliation. The PSOE absorbed members and integrated many leaders from the plethora of leftist parties that were weeded out during the first two general elections, further minimizing the importance of activist loyalty. After 1982 the PSOE frequently chose non-PSOE persons and technocrats to fill important government posts.[11]

Thus, organizational features are important in explaining the PSOE's evolution from a policy-seeking party to an office-seeking one. The PSOE was a small party with few activists to constrain party leadership. Its internal political structures were increasingly authoritarian (at least until the late 1980s). The PSOE became a highly capital-intensive party. Office benefits clearly outweighed policy benefits since stated policy objectives were consistently ignored or contradicted (the NATO about-face and the reversal of political economic policies are the best examples). With a permeable leadership structure and no policy content, the party became little more than a vehicle for careerism and personal advancement. In the words of one expert (Gillespie 1989b: 67), "the party gained a new image of middle-class careerism, not exempt from 'yuppie' insinuations. Socialist designs seemed to some to have been replaced by designer socialism." The spectacular series of corruption scandals that plagued the PSOE in the 1990s is perhaps best understood in this context.

INSTITUTIONAL VARIABLES

I now consider four sets of institutional variables that may help explain party behavior: public financing of parties, electoral institutions, legislative institutions, and government institutions.

Even before the first democratic elections in Spain, political parties were heavily dependent on public finance and public campaign subsidies.[12] In terms of electoral financing, Spanish law provides for compensation of parties per vote won only in districts in which the party obtained at least one seat. Parties get an additional subsidy per seat obtained in the legislature. In short, Spanish law favors successful parties and penalizes marginal ones. The discrimination against extraparliamentary parties is enhanced further by the fact that Spain's lower house electoral law (proportional representation using the D'Hondt allocation method) already favors large parties. The weakness of most Spanish political parties and the fact that, in comparative perspective, Spanish campaigns tend to be among the most costly increase the importance of the discriminatory nature of Spanish campaign financing laws.

Spanish law also provides for the public funding of the normal operating expenses of political parties. The criterion for allocating these funds is similar to those employed for campaign financing. However, rather than fixing an amount of compensation per vote (pegged to inflation) or seat, acting governments establish levels of compensation in their annual budgets. These provisions thus not only discriminate against extraparliamentary and smaller parliamentary parties, they also give the governing party the power to increase its own spoils.

Since the first elections in 1977, most major political parties have become heavily dependent on the state for both their campaign and day-to-day financing, and this is especially the case for the PSOE. Del Castillo (1989: 189) reports that 92 percent of PSOE revenue obtained from 1981 to 1984 came from state subsidies. Membership dues contributed only 3 percent of the total, and this figure consisted mostly of the mandatory 10 percent contribution from PSOE employees' salaries. The economic importance of the PSOE membership has therefore been minimal. Trade union financial support, so crucial to parties of the left in many countries, is negligible in Spain, where unions suffer the same organizational and economic weaknesses as political parties (Del Castillo 1989: 190). Del Castillo (1989: 195) concluded that "The group which has been receiving the greatest amount of state support due to its excellent electoral results, PSOE, has been the least successful in obtaining economic resources from its members and sympathetic social sectors."

Other institutional aspects of the Spanish political system have favored office-seeking behavior by the PSOE. From 1982 to 1989, the presence of strong majority governments and the absence to date of governing coalitions raised the value of both winning votes and holding office. Spain's legislative institutions follow the Westminster model, which gives parties a strong incentive to occupy government. Indeed, it is fair to say that for the first decade of PSOE government, opposition parties in the Spanish system have not been able to influence government policy or obtain government spoils.[13] Gillespie (1990: 133) argues that "a 'winner-takes-all' attitude has prevailed among the Socialist leaders, and the prestige of the Cortes has suffered as a result." The PSOE leadership also centralized its power by altering the prevailing pattern of legislative–executive relations. Using strict party discipline to centralize control over legislative activity in the hands of the cabinet (and especially in the hands of Deputy Prime Minister Guerra), the PSOE government effectively abandoned the consociational model of decision making that had characterized the five years of weak and fragmented UCD government. As a result, during the first four years of PSOE government, the percentage of laws resulting from parliamentary initiative, including PSOE backbenchers, plummeted.[14] Due in large part to the PSOE's imposition of tight party discipline and strong centralized leadership, the Spanish Cortes – like Parliament in the United Kingdom – has been widely assailed as a mere rubber stamp and debate forum (Capo Giol, García Cotarelo, López Garrido, and Subirats 1990: 93–130).

Greater electoral competitiveness (and greater electoral uncertainty) encourages parties to value votes over office-holding. From the PSOE's point of view, Spain's party system between 1982 and 1993 was not highly competitive, despite the fact that the PSOE's electoral strength steadily diminished after 1982 (see Table 4.1). The 1982 electoral results were an unexpected windfall for the PSOE. Not only did the party win a large absolute majority in parliament (57.7 percent of lower house seats and a plurality of votes in forty-one of fifty-two provinces), followed by equally impressive victories at the local level in 1983, but the PSOE's two major competitors (the centrist UCD and the communist PCE) were virtually destroyed in the election. The governing UCD declined from 168 to 12 seats and did not win a single constituency, while the PCE dropped from 23 seats to only 4. Moreover, both parties further self-destructed after their respective electoral debacles, with the UCD disappearing altogether and the PCE splitting in two. After the 1982 elections the only serious parliamentary opposition was the conservative Popular Alliance (30 percent of the seats), a party also in turmoil that, according to all electoral analyses, was simply too far right to win a parliamentary majority.

After the June 1986 elections, the situation was roughly the same. The PSOE continued to have a parliamentary majority, though slightly reduced, and there was still no serious competition to the left or right. The renaissance of the center under Adolfo Suárez was remarkable, but his new party, Centro Democrático y Social (CDS), captured only 5 percent of the seats, and the Popular Alliance still controlled only 30 percent. While the PSOE came close to losing its majority in the October 1989 elections, the opposition remained equally fragmented (thanks in part to the steady success of a plethora of regional parties), and the PSOE retained its political dominance. Only with the electoral setback of June 1993 was the minority PSOE government obliged to compromise with parties of the opposition (mainly the Catalan nationalists).

Ironically, the major consequence of the destruction of the PCE and the UCD was to provide the PSOE with an electorally cost-free opportunity to occupy center ground in the political system. The PSOE was free to pursue neoliberal economic policies without fearing punishment by a Communist left. The party was confident that, barring the unlikely rebirth of the center, it could replenish the small number of lost votes on the left with the mass of party-less voters in the center. The destruction of a powerful centrist opposition, the crumbling of the PCE, the repeated failure of new political forces to take their place, and the inability of the Popular Alliance to take advantage of the PSOE's electoral decline have given the PSOE over a decade of relative electoral comfort. Indeed, the steady decline of votes for the PSOE has had little if any impact on party policy or electoral strategy.

Table 4.1. *Congress of Deputies seats won in Spanish general elections, 1977–1996*

	1977	1979	1982	1986	1989	1993	1996
AP/CP/PP	16	9	106	105	106	141	157
UCD/CDS	166	168	12	19	14	0	—
PSOE	118	121	202	184	176	159	140
PCE/IU	20	23	4	7	17	18	21
CIU	2	8	12	18	18	17	16
PNV	2	7	8	6	5	5	5
Others		14	4	11	14	10	11

Source: Anuario El Pais (various years) and *El Pais Internacional.*

THE ROLE OF THE TRANSITION TO DEMOCRACY

It should be clear from the preceding discussion that internal organizational and institutional variables were important in explaining the PSOE's rapid shift toward office-seeking party behavior. However, three other factors are necessary to explain this outcome: the role of the transition to democracy, the international context, and leadership.

The PSOE's metamorphosis occurred within the context of the transition to democracy. As I have argued elsewhere (Share 1986, 1987: 525–48), the transition was based on intraelite negotiation in which party masses were utterly ignored. As Pridham (1990: 116) points out, "In Spain, the parties have certainly tended to develop far more as institutional than as social actors, partly because of historical patterns, also because their élites devoted more attention to the first role in managing the transition and that seems to have had some effects on later party development." Opposition party leaders negotiated terms of the transition with the outgoing authoritarian leaders. This arrangement entailed a number of dilemmas and contradictions, most notably the agreement by the opposition parties to allow (at least initially) the authoritarian leadership to control the pace and extent of reform. This *consensus model* institutionalized elite behavior in all parties that downplayed internal democracy, mass membership, or policy considerations. Like all Spanish political parties, the PSOE therefore "renounced the goals of mobilizing and revitalizing civil society, accepting 'provisional democracy' rather than risking destabilization" (Caciagli 1986: 210). According to Gunther, Sani, and Shabad (1988: 117):

> A . . . crucial feature of the politics of consensus was that negotiations took place in private, and not in public arenas. Privacy shields party representatives from the scrutiny of their respective supporters and electoral clienteles, and thus facilitates the making of concessions central to compromise agreements. Deliberations in public forums provide incentives toward dem-

agogic posturing and reduce the willingness of political elites to make embarrassing concessions.

Despite some real sacrifices, the PSOE leadership viewed transactive democratization as a complete success. The party emerged from the transition process as one of the two largest vote getters, easily defeating its rivals on the left. Its strong showings in 1977 and 1979 and its electoral victory in 1982 were evidence that the negotiated transition had paid off for the PSOE more than for any other party: The UCD, the other great beneficiary of the transition, had disintegrated, while the PCE was in disarray and the Popular Alliance was saddled with its connection to the franquist regime. The success of the Spanish transition model for the PSOE contrasted markedly with the party's experience during the ill-fated Second Republic. Internal division and ideological polarization had been replaced with an almost haunting intramural unity and an ideological homogeneity. Instead of competing leaders battling for party power, there was now a single, unassailable socialist leader. Instead of a party of activists with links to trade unions and mass movements, the party was now made up mostly of professionals and paid staff. Instead of a party platform aimed at fundamental change of the system, the PSOE now had a vague ideology aimed mostly at integrating Spain into European capitalism. Instead of forty years in political exile, the PSOE enjoyed the spoils of power only five years after the first democratic elections in 1977. Viewed in this context, many PSOE leaders were more than willing to abandon traditional policies and guide the party toward an office-seeking posture.

This logic became even more pronounced after the failed coup of February 1981. If before that date PSOE references to the need to preserve democracy contained a large element of rhetoric, after the coup attempt few in the party doubted the need for political moderation and internal party discipline. The coup was widely interpreted as a reaction to the internal discord and resulting powerlessness of the beleaguered UCD government, and PSOE leaders at the time took note.

THE INTERNATIONAL CONTEXT

The international context of the PSOE's metamorphosis is also crucial. Felipe González and his Seville faction gained control of the party in 1974, only a year after the Pinochet coup in Chile and the same year as the Portuguese Revolution. These events were followed closely by Spanish socialists, and interviews with PSOE leaders made it clear that they formed important reference points for many party elites.[15] Both experiences seemed to point to the dangers of premature mass mobilization and the futility of implementing political economic policies that contradicted prevailing international trends.

On a global level, the late 1970s and early 1980s was a time of contraction in the international capitalist political economy. Implementation of a policy of job creation through government spending, as called for in PSOE platforms as late as 1982, would require bucking the internal trend of fiscal austerity (Merkel 1989: 25). It is important to remember that the context within which the PSOE operated was "that of a relatively isolated European country democratizing late, during a period of economic downturn, and immediately being faced with a need for expeditious 'modernization' if it were to do well in a more integrated Europe where most of its partners were more developed" (Gillespie 1989b: 62). On a regional level, the PSOE leadership watched with horror as the French Socialist Party (PS) tried unsuccessfully to implement just such a policy (under far more favorable conditions). The PS paid a heavy price for its inability to contravene trends in the international capitalist political economy. In short, the international climate made commitment to policy change appear futile.

Finally, it is worth noting that the PSOE received important financial and technical support from its German and Swedish counterparts (Del Castillo 1989: 180). Such influential figures as Willy Brandt were strongly opposed to the radical party platform and incendiary rhetoric of the PSOE's Twenty-seventh Congress in late 1976 (De la Cierva 1983: 250–1). These connections enhanced the power of the central party leadership and encouraged PSOE leaders to abandon their more radical policy orientations (Gillespie and Gallagher 1989: 178).

LEADERSHIP AS A CRUCIAL VARIABLE

While the organizational variables discussed earlier help explain why the PSOE leadership was able to behave with few intramural constraints, they fail to take into consideration the specific nature of political leadership. As I have argued elsewhere (Share 1986), the Spanish transition to democracy enhanced the role of party leaders while diminishing the importance of party activists. Indeed, a common outcome of Southern European transitions to democracy has been the enhanced role of political leaders. According to Gianfranco Pasquino (1990: 42), "party leaders enjoy an unusual amount of political visibility, strategic flexibility, and tactical discretion in the phases both of transition and [of] consolidation." Important conditions of the transition and whole sections of the Spanish constitution were hammered out between political elites, with little or no consultation from party members.

Within the PSOE, authoritarian political structures helped González retain his hegemony within the party, but the absence of charismatic contenders for power within the PSOE was equally important. The importance of personal charisma at a national level, so crucial in a new democracy that follows a long period of authoritarian rule, worked within political parties as well. González's ability to defeat the PSOE old guard in 1974 gave his image within the PSOE almost mythical proportions (Calvo Hernando 1987; Chamorro 1980). His daring confrontation with the PSOE left in 1979 only served to enhance this image. Even his ability to finesse what were essentially complete policy reversals gained him respect both within and outside the party. During the Thirtieth Congress (December 1984), González once again drew on his popularity within the party to gain acceptance for the NATO policy reversal, despite strong opposition within the party. In the words of one internal PSOE critic, at key points González convinced party members and voters that the choice was between "Felipe or chaos."

González's youthful image, disarming sense of humor, and ability to relate to common folk – his ability to turn on his Andalusian accent and charm was remarkable – were immensely important in weakening potential critics. González was also fortunate to have a loyal and highly skilled number two man, Alfonso Guerra, to deflect much criticism. Guerra was widely perceived as doing much of the dirty work, especially in maintaining party discipline.

However, González's good fortune to have presided over a period of stunning political successes was most important in bolstering his charisma and creating a myth of an invincible *Felipismo*. After decades of political stagnation, González took hold of the PSOE in 1974 and quickly guided it through a difficult transition and a short period of political opposition before leading the party to over ten years in office. During that time Spain became a member of the European Community, and its economy boomed despite lingering problems with unemployment.

González's adaptability as a leader added to the durability of his image, which evolved rather quickly from that of a fiery leftist orator in the mid-1970s to a sage and somewhat aloof head of government in the 1990s. Ironically, questions about experience and maturity that long haunted the PSOE plagued opposition leaders once the PSOE was in government. The historical figures of the opposition (Suárez, Fraga Iribarne, Carrillo) faded away, leaving González as the only national leader with experience and a record. His increasing interest and participation in international affairs helped insulate him from the seemingly unending series of corruption scandals that rocked the party during the 1980s and early 1990s. By 1994 these political disasters had badly eroded the popularity of the governing PSOE, but polls showed the González's image fared somewhat better than that of his party. Even after the PSOE lost power in 1996, González continued to be rated as Spain's most popular politician.

In short, González built a charismatic image that has facilitated his iron control over the PSOE and greatly facilitated the shift from policy-seeking to office-seeking behavior. According to Gillespie (1989a: 299), "[i]f the party that formed a government in 1982, not long after celebrating its centenary, was recognizable to outsiders as that which had renovated itself a decade earlier, this was mainly because the image of the party leader had become synonymous with the party initials." His image translated directly into political capital that was expended in crucial situations, such as the party crisis of 1979 or the NATO referendum of 1986.

The PSOE's dependence on the leadership of González was part of a general trend in Southern European socialism toward increased personalization of party leadership. Padgett and Paterson (1990: 102) observe that "[T]his historic dichotomy of strong leadership/pliant membership in northern Europe and weak leadership/assertive factionalized membership in southern Europe has largely been reversed in the 1980s." Gillespie and Gallagher (1989: 184) note that "for southern Europe as a whole, the years 1983–1985 represented a period of maximum socialist conformity around personalist leadership." This trend is in large part explained by the enhanced role of political elites in transitions to democracy throughout the region.[16]

CONCLUSION

A number of variables explain the PSOE's rapid and dramatic shift from a policy-oriented party to an office-seeking party. Foremost among them was the willingness of the PSOE leadership to accept the rules of political compromise inherent in Spanish democratization. Of secondary but still crucial importance was the ability of the leadership to impose such a compromise on a rapidly growing and undisciplined party membership during the period 1977–9. Organizational and institutional variables were clearly important in the PSOE's transformation, but they are best viewed as indirect environmental factors, not as direct causes. Indeed, the organizational and institutional contexts within which the change occurred were very much the conscious creation of party elites, who sought to create political institutions and intraparty organizational structures that would facilitate concrete political outcomes. The electoral system and party finance laws, for example, were designed to favor a majoritarian system of government. Likewise, PSOE elites were clearly aware of the need to centralize authority and create discipline within the party in order to assume the role of a moderate catch-all political force capable of governing and capable of integrating Spain into the Western European political economy. Gunther et al. (1988: 395) conclude that

> the behavior of political elites was by far the most important factor in the emergence of the new party system. Electoral and party financing laws were the product of conscious deliberations and negotiations among party leaders. Elites were the driving force behind the creation or expansion of party organizational infrastructures. Their electoral strategies determined the ideological stance, and overall image they would present to the voters. Moreover, in the role of electoral strategists political elites determined how organizational resources would be deployed.

Once established by political elites, intraparty organizational and institutional variables clearly help to explain the PSOE's continued office-seeking behavior, even if they were not the primary causes of it. The PSOE's weak membership, centralized leadership, and permeable recruitment structures greatly facilitated the shift to more office-seeking behavior. The PSOE's ability to procure state funds, the electoral system, the noncompetitive party system, and the lack of opposition party access to spoils also encouraged office-seeking behavior.

In addition to the role of leadership, the nature of the transition, and intraparty organization and institutional variables, the international context formed an important backdrop for the PSOE's evolution. Implementing the PSOE's radical party platform would have entailed bucking prevailing international trends. Only a policy-oriented party with broad popular support and a strong organizational base could have attempted such a confrontational strategy, and even then the odds for success would have been low. The international context thus created a strong incentive for party leaders to abandon official party policy, to deemphasize intramural democracy, and to direct party policy toward office holding and away from original policy objectives.

NOTES

1. The best historical overview of the PSOE in English, with a telling title, is Gillespie (1989a). Some other fine works include Padilla Bolívar (1977), de la Cierva (1983), and Moral Sandoval (1979).
2. On the PSOE during the franquist regime, see Preston (1986).
3. An overview of the divisions within PSOE during the late franquist regime is Caro (1980).
4. As Gunther (1986) and others have noted, it is unclear whether González was originally predisposed to a strategy of mass mobilization. Some view his radical rhetoric of the 1974–7 period as purely opportunistic. Others argue that González underwent a genuine ideological and tactical conversion due in part to the evolution of political events between 1977 and 1979.
5. González complained that Spain "cannot wait ten years for the Party to mature. The Party cannot afford the luxury of immaturity." Quoted in Claudín (1979: 8).
6. For a full description of these rule changes, see Nash (1983: 46–7). She estimates that despite the support of about 40 percent of the PSOE membership, the left opposition received only about 10 percent of the delegates to the Special Congress.
7. There were widespread reports that the PSOE leadership urged only González supporters to pay their dues and later excluded all those who failed to do so from the delegate selection process. It has also been alleged that the German Social Democratic Party threatened to withold financial aid if González was not re-elected to the party leadership. See De la Cierva (1983: 263).
8. The figure was quoted by PSOE Secretary of Organization Txiki Benegas in *Cambio 16* (January 18, 1988: 23). The number is almost certainly too high. Del Castillo (1989: 187) estimates the PSOE membership at 160,000 in 1985.
9. Useful data on Spanish party membership in comparative perspective can be found in *El País* (October 14, 1988: 18). See also Caciagli (1986: 224).
10. In 1989 the Spanish socialists officially initiated a working group within the

PSOE, called "Program 2000," to begin such a discussion of a long-term political vision. The fact that the group was dominated by the party leadership and completely excluded all members of the PSOE left did not augur well for the enterprise. See *El País* International Edition (March 5, 1990: 12–13). A key author of the document, Manuel Escudero, admitted that past PSOE governments have "paid too much attention to only one school of experts, the monetarists." Escudero argued that the party must take on environmental issues and must reach out to "environmentalists, feminists, Christians and intellectuals." See Guerra et al. (1986: 18). These bold announcements coincided with the party's decision to dissolve "Democratic Socialism," a dissident party faction, and to expel its leader, Ricardo García Damborenea.

11. Examples abound, but the most prominent case was the appointment of Francisco Fernández Ordóñez as foreign minister in July 1985. Fernández Ordóñez had been a UCD cabinet minister, and he replaced Fernando Morán, a party loyalist widely identified with the PSOE left.

12. On Spanish financing of political parties, see Del Castillo (1989: 179–99). The following discussion draws heavily on that excellent work.

13. This is true only at the national level, since opposition parties in Spain are able to wield considerable influence and enjoy spoils of office though regional and local government. After the June 1993 elections the PSOE became especially responsive to and dependent on the Catalan nationalists.

14. Between 1979 and 1982, 13.4 percent of laws were initiated by parliament, compared with only 6.4 percent between 1982 and 1986. See Capo Giol et al. (1990: 111).

15. Interviews with PSOE elites were conducted by me in 1982 as part of my research for *Dilemmas of Social Democracy: The Socialist Workers Party in the 1980s*.

16. For an excellent overview see Higley and Gunther (1992).

REFERENCES

Caciagli, Mario (1986). *Elecciones y partidos en la transición española*. Madrid: Centro de Investigaciones Sociológicas.

Calvo Hernando, Pedro (1987). *Todos me dicen Felipe*. Barcelona: Plaza & Janes.

Capo Giol, Jordi, Ramón García Cotarelo, Diego López Garrido, and Joan Subirats. (1990) "By Consociationalism to a Majoritarian Parliamentary System: The Rise and Decline of the Spanish Cortes." In *Parliament and Democratic Consolidation in Southern Europe* (pp. 92–130), eds. Ulrike Liebert and Maurrizio Cotta. London: Pinter.

Caro, Miguel Peydro (1980). *Las esciciones del PSOE*. Barcelona: Plaza & Janes.

Chamorro, Eduardo (1980). *Felipe González. Un hombre a la espera*. Barcelona: Planeta.

Claudín, Fernando (1979). "Interview with Felipe González." *Zona Abierta* 20: 6–12.

Contreras, Manuel (1981). *El PSOE en la II República: Organización e Ideología*. Madrid: Centro de Investigaciones Sociológicas.

De la Cierva, Ricardo (1983). *Historia del socialismo en España, 1879–1983*. Barcelona: Planeta.

Del Castillo, Pilar (1989). "Financing of Spanish Political Parties." In *Comparative Political Finance in the 1980s* (pp. 172–99), ed. Herbert E. Alexander. Cambridge: Cambridge University Press.

Gillespie, Richard (1989a). *The Spanish Socialist Party: A History of Factionalism*. Oxford: Clarendon Press.

   (1989b). Spanish Socialism in the 1980s." In *Southern European Socialism: Parties, Elections and the Challenge of Government* (pp. 59–85), eds. Tom Gallagher and Allan M. Williams. Manchester: Manchester University Press.

   (1990). "Regime Consolidation in Spain: Party, State, and Society." In *Securing Democracy: Political Parties and Democratic Consolidation in Southern Europe* (pp. 126–46), ed. Geoffrey Pridham. London: Routledge.

   and Tom Gallagher (1989). "Democracy and Authority in the Socialist Parties of Southern Europe." In *Southern European Socialism: Parties, Elections and the Challenge of Government* (pp. 163–88), eds. Tom Gallagher and Allan M. Williams. Manchester: Manchester University Press.

Guerra, Alfonso, Andrés de Blas, Virgilio Zapatero, Manuel Escudero, José Félix Tezanos, Ramón García Cotarelo, Emilio Menéndez del Valle, and Francisco Laporta. (1986). *El Futuro del socialismo*. Madrid: Editorial Sistema.

Gunther, Richard (1986). "The Spanish Socialist Party: From Clandestine Opposition to Party of Government." In *The Politics of Democratic Spain*, ed. Stanley Payne. Chicago: Chicago Council on Foreign Relations.

   Giacomo Sani, and Goldie Shabad (1988). *Spain After Franco: The Making of a Competitive Party System*. Berkeley: University of California Press.

Higley, John and Richard Gunther (eds.) (1992). *Elites and Democratic Consolidation in Latin America and Southern Europe*. Cambridge: Cambridge University Press.

Juliá, Santos (1986). "República, revolución y luchas internas." In *El socialismo en España* (pp. 231–54), ed. Santos Juliá. Madrid: Editorial Pablo Iglesias.

Linz, Juan J. (1978). "From Great Hopes to Civil War: The Breakdown of Democracy in Spain." In *The Breakdown of Democratic Regime* (pp. 142–215), eds. Juan J. Linz and Alfred Stepan. Baltimore: Johns Hopkins University Press.

López Guerra, Luis (1984). "Partidos Políticos en España: Evolución y perspectivas." In *España: Un presente para el futuro* (pp. 132–84), ed. E. García de Enterría. Madrid: Instituto de Estudios Económicas.

Marvall, José María (1979). "Del Milenio a la práctica política: el socialismo como reformismo radical." *Zona Abierta* 20: 89–97.

Merkel, Wolfgang (1989). "After the Golden Age: A Decline of Social Democratic Policies in Western Europe During the 1980s?" Working Papers, Center for European Studies, Harvard University.

Moral Sandoval, Enrique (ed.) (1979). *Cién años para el socialismo. Historia del PSOE (1879–1979)*. Madird: Editorial Pablo Iglesias.

Nash, Elizabeth (1983). "The Spanish Socialist Party since Franco: From Clandestinity to Government: 1976–1982." In *Democratic Politics in Spain: Spanish Politics after Franco* (pp. 29–62), ed. David S. Bell. New York: St. Martins Press.

Padgett, Stephen and William E. Paterson (1990). *A History of Social Democracy in Postwar Europe*. New York: Longman.

Padilla Bolívar, Antonio (1977). *El movimiento Socialista Español*. Barcelona: Planeta.

Pasquino, Gianfranco (1990). "Party Elites and Democratic Consolidation: Cross-national Comparison of Southern European Experience." In *Securing Democracy: Political Parties and Democratic Consolidation in Southern Europe* (pp. 42–61), ed. Geoffrey Pridham. London: Routledge.

Preston, Paul (1986). "Decadencia y resurgimiento del PSOE durante el régimen franquista." In *El socialismo en España*, ed. Juliá Santos. Madrid: Editorial Pablo Iglesias.

Pridham, Geoffrey (1990). "Political Actors, Linkages and Interactions: Democratic Consolidation in Southern Europe." *West European Politics* 13, 4: 103–14.

PSOE (1977) *XXVII Congreso del Partido Socialista Obrero Español*. Barcelona: Avance.

Serfaty, Maier (1984). "Spain's Socialists: A New Center Party?" *Current History* 49, 2: 164–81.

Share, Donald (1986). *The Making of Spanish Democracy*. New York: Praeger.

(1987). "Transitions to Democracy and Transitions Through Transaction." *Comparative Political Studies* 19, 4: 525–48.

(1989). *Dilemmas of Social Democracy: The Socialist Workers Party in the 1980s*. Westport, CT: Greenwood Press.

Strøm, Kaare (1990). "A Behavioral Theory of Comparative Political Parties." *American Journal of Political Science* 34, 2: 565–98.

Tezanos, José Félix (1979). "El espacio y sociológico del socialismo español." *Sistema* 32: 51–75.

(1983). *Sociología del Socialismo Español*. Madrid: Tecnos.

5

CHANGING STRATEGIES: THE DILEMMA OF THE DUTCH LABOUR PARTY

Ron Hillebrand and Galen A. Irwin

Not all political parties in the Netherlands have had to make the same hard choices that are analyzed in this book, at least not to the same degree. For example, the Catholic Party and its successor, the Christian Democratic Appeal (CDA), participated in every government coalition between 1917 and 1994. Its Protestant colleagues, who joined in forming the CDA in 1979, were also hardly ever absent. For these parties office was simply taken for granted, not as something about which decisions had to be made. They could rely upon a solid base of support that hardly wavered, whatever policies were agreed upon with their coalition partners. Even after electoral support began to decline in the 1960s, the Christian Democrats controlled enough seats in Parliament so that, given the structure of the party space, no government could be formed without them until the 1990s. It is one of the few parties that for a substantial period really had it all – votes, office, and policy.

Because of the domination of the Christian Democratic parties, most of the other parties were also not faced with difficult choices. Since the introduction of universal suffrage, support for the Liberal Party (or sometimes parties) fell at times to less than 10 per cent of the vote, and the party became content with obtaining office whenever invited by the Christian Democrats to join a coalition. The choices were seldom hard. The numerous smaller parties in the Netherlands have seldom had the opportunity to make decisions concerning office. Aside from Democrats '66 (D66), in only two instances (Democratic Socialists '70 in 1971 and the Radical Party in 1972) have such smaller parties ever been included in government coalitions, and both of these parties no longer exist.

But if many parties in the Netherlands have never had to force such hard choices, this is surely made up for by the dilemma of the Labour Party (and its predecessor, the Social Democratic Workers Party). The Socialists were first asked to join a coalition in 1913 but refused, hoping that universal suffrage would bring them majority status. When this status did not arrive, the party was forced to develop strategies that would try to maximize policy, votes, and office. Throughout this century the party has wrestled with the problem of finding a satisfactory balance between these goals. It has changed strategies numerous times but has never found one that produced an optimal solution.

The case studies to be examined in this chapter have been chosen to illustrate how such hard choices have been made and what factors have influenced the choice of strategy. Although many cases from the past could have been chosen to illustrate an almost perpetual dilemma, the two selected are from the most recent decades. The first involves health benefits, jobs, and financial problems in 1981 and 1982. The second relates to proposed cuts in employment disability in 1991. One reason for the selection of these two cases is that although the circumstances that surround them show considerable similarity, the decisions reached were quite different. Thus, by comparison and contrast, we can better understand the calculations that parties must make.

THE INSTITUTIONAL ENVIRONMENT

It is the contention of the *unified model of party behaviour* that the question of whether a party will focus upon vote-seeking, policy-seeking, or office-seeking is dependent upon the institutional environment in which the party operates. In Chapter 1 of this volume, the editors argue that "we must examine the effects of political institutions, the 'rules and roles' by which parties play their games." These "rules and roles" of the institutional environment relate not only to the electoral and political system in which the party must operate, but also to the internal rules by which the party is organized and carries out its functions. Before proceeding to the case studies themselves, it is thus necessary to examine the most important characteristics of the environment in which the Labour Party functions.

THE EXTERNAL ENVIRONMENT

The first characteristic of importance is that the Netherlands has a multiparty system. Political parties began to arise in the nineteenth century around the four dominant groups within society – Catholics, Protestants, liberals, and socialists. The political parties were, to a greater or lesser degree, the political arms of what have been called the *pillars* of Dutch society.

Although the multiparty system developed under a system of election by electoral district, the introduction of proportional representation in 1917 certainly buttressed this system. The Dutch system of proportional representation is one of the most proportional in the world and produces only minimal distortion between votes and seats in the Second Chamber of Parliament. However, because of the nature of the electorate, it has also guaranteed that no single party has ever achieved a majority of either the vote or parliamentary seats.

Since no party has ever held a majority, government has always been by coalition. Being a part of this coalition is virtually essential if a party is to have any substantial influence upon policy. Virtually all legislation is introduced by the governing coalition, which relies upon its parliamentary majority to ensure adoption. Opposition parties can attempt to influence matters through debate within Parliament and discussions outside Parliament. It is also true that the Dutch system is, to an extent, based upon a search for consensus, and a majority may be reluctant to force a policy upon a minority for whom it is completely unacceptable, but in the final analysis, opposition parties can have only limited and indirect influence upon policy.

Because they were most often the largest party, and because they controlled the centre of the party space, the Catholic Party (i.e. the Roman Catholic State Party before the Second World War and the Catholic People's Party after the war) controlled the coalition formation process. Although together with the Protestants they often held a majority of seats, they generally chose also to involve either the liberals or the socialists in a coalition. The choice of which way to turn was perhaps the hardest choice that the party was forced to make. In what seems to be a strategy of shifting the blame as much as sharing the power, the Christian Democrats formed governments with both the left and right.

The Christian Democrats could maintain this control over the cabinet formation process in part because of the nature of the political party system. It can be argued that the party space is two-dimensional, with a religious–secular dimension in addition to the more usual socioeconomic dimension. However, until 1994 all coalitions were formed along the latter dimension. On this dimension the Christian Democrats can be placed in the centre with the socialists to the left and the liberals to the right. After an early postwar attempt to include liberals and socialists in a coalition, the liberals initially and the socialists in reaction excluded any future collaboration. This mutual exclusion meant that for decades no cabinet could be formed without the Christian Democrats.

From the introduction of universal suffrage and proportional representation in 1917 until the mid-1960s, the support for the major parties was extremely stable, and very few parliamentary seats changed hands after elections. This aspect of the external environment was important for the choices the parties had to make, since it meant that, whereas parties gained freedom of movement to pursue office and policy goals on the one hand, on the other hand, extra votes could hardly be won with good policies or outstanding performances in office. During the 1960s voters began to become more mobile, and the number of voters switching parties between elections rose substantially (Andeweg 1982).

Rather than relying almost exclusively upon their position in society to determine their vote, the voters began to take issues and other factors into account
more often. The substantial losses by the Catholic People's Party and the
Christian-Historical Union helped revive hopes among socialists for a socialist,
or at least a progressive majority and greatly influenced their choice of strategy.

THE INTERNAL ENVIRONMENT

In Chapter 1, various internal characteristics of political parties that may influence party choices were discussed. The case studies to be presented in this
chapter will illustrate many of these points, but several important general
aspects of the Dutch Labour Party should be mentioned here before proceeding.

First of all, it is crucial to note that the Labour Party has had a decentralized
organizational structure in which the party leaders are subjected to a great deal
of accountability by the rank-and-file members. The party council and party
congress have at times played decisive roles in determining which strategy was
chosen. At times in the past, the call for accountability was so great that
provisions for the recall of party office holders were called for. The party also
has a tradition of discussing its problems openly and publicly so that not only
members but also outsiders can follow the debate.

Second, the Labour Party is a party with a high proportion of amateurs.
These amateurs fulfil an important role in the mobilization efforts of the party,
but often they also wish to play a role in the party's internal functioning and in
the determination of the strategy to be followed. Many of these amateurs are
motivated by a strong commitment to a socialist or social-democratic ideology.
To the extent that they can still be called amateurs, many hold elected office on
municipal and provincial councils, often viewing this as a stepping stone to
obtaining a full-time career political position. As such they are particularly
sensitive to the effects of decisions made at the national level upon their electoral
prospects. The recruitment for elected offices is fully controlled by the political
parties in the Netherlands, which submit lists of candidates for elections. However, many appointive positions, such as mayors, queen's commissioners, and
even higher-level civil service positions, are also distributed, often proportion-
ally, among the parties. Although talent and experience may be determining
factors, party service and loyalty may nevertheless be an asset.

Third, the Labour Party, like all Dutch parties, receives no direct governmental subsidy to help fund party expenses. The only governmental subsidies
are earmarked for specific activities, such as scientific research, education, and
training. Party leaders thus do not have this source of support that might allow
them more freedom of movement. In the Labour Party more than 80 per cent
of the operating costs of the party are met from membership dues (Koole 1992:
191).

BACKGROUND: STRATEGIES OF THE PAST

This brief review of some important aspects of the external and internal environments within which the Labour Party operates will help to demonstrate how the party reached decisions in the two case studies presented. In addition, it is important to understand some of the problems the party faced in the past in making choices between votes, office, and policy. These choices of the past have also influenced the choices in the case studies.

First of all, there is the recurring dream of the Socialists of achieving a socialist, or at least a progressive, electoral majority. The drive for universal suffrage was motivated by the belief, or at least hope, that an electoral majority would ensue. The disappointment at receiving only slightly more than one-fifth of the vote was great. After the period of German occupation (1940–5), the sparks of hope for a majority were rekindled. The Social Democratic Workers Party merged with a radical liberal party to form the new Labour Party in the hope of producing a breakthrough in Dutch politics. Many of the Marxist trappings of the former party were dropped in an attempt to appeal to workers with a Catholic or Calvinist identification. Again the hopes were doused as the party received only between 25 and 30 per cent of the vote. The electoral instability of the 1960s fanned the fires again, as the party hoped to win votes that were being lost by the Catholic People's Party and the Christian-Historical Union. A new, aggressive vote-seeking strategy was adopted, which emphasized polarizing politics and the electorate. The strategy was to (1) protect the purity of the party programme, (2) attract more votes, and (3) assume governmental responsibility based upon an electoral majority of the left-wing parties on the basis of a preelection agreement. The shortcomings of a pure vote-seeking strategy were shown glaringly when in 1977 Labour received an all-time high percentage of the vote, but after months of difficult negotiations, the gap with the religious parties could not be bridged and the latter formed a coalition with the Liberals.

Lacking a majority, the Labour Party can participate in government only by joining a coalition. This has not been easy. In 1913 an invitation to join a coalition was refused in the hope of achieving a majority position after universal suffrage was introduced. Following the First World War, a call for revolution by one of the party leaders led the other parties to react by excluding the Socialists from office until the eve of the next world war. Thus, only since the Second World War has participation in government become a true option. A major difference with the interbellum period was that the other parties could see the advantage of sharing power with the Labour Party during the period of reconstruction and later in laying the foundations of the welfare state. During the period 1948–58 the Catholics and Labour cooperated under the prime ministership of the Socialist Willem Drees. Between 1958 and the period of our first case study, the Labour Party was part of the government coalition only in

1966–7 and 1973–7. The fact that during this period the Catholics showed a preference for governing with the Liberals caused considerable frustration in the Labour Party and led the Dutch political scientist Hans Daudt (1980) to formulate the theory of "only as a last resort." According to this theory, the Labour Party is included in a governmental coalition only if no other option appears viable. Others, such as Koole (1987), are more inclined to blame the Socialists themselves for their inability to gain access to office, in part perhaps because of their frustration due to dependence upon the Christian Democrats.

THE SECOND VAN AGT CABINET 1981–1982[1]

THE ELECTIONS OF 1981

As part of its *polarization strategy* for winning additional votes, the Labour Party in 1977 declared that if it were to continue in government, a number of points in the party programme could not be compromised. When the lengthy cabinet formation attempt failed and the Labour Party was forced into the opposition, many critics placed the blame on this uncompromising attitude. Thus, in preparing for the 1981 elections, the party was faced with the choice of whether to maintain the polarization strategy and formulate tough demands for its participation in government or adopt a more flexible position in order to increase the chances of acceptance as a coalition partner. Former prime minister (in 1973–7) and party leader Joop Den Uyl argued for a more moderate party programme that would make a return to power more likely. In this way he attempted to help his well-known statement, "The second Den Uyl Cabinet will be formed in any case," to become reality (Table 5.1).

The primary source of conflict between those pressing for an uncompromising position and those favouring a flexible position was the responsibilities of the Netherlands within the nuclear weapons strategy of NATO. At the time, six nuclear weapons systems were operational in the Netherlands. A battle quickly developed between Den Uyl and rank-and-file party members. For a time it appeared that the party would adopt the position of the Inter Church Conference (IKV) of "Rid the world of nuclear weapons, beginning in the Netherlands." Den Uyl announced that he was unwilling to lead the party at the upcoming elections if it should choose to renounce all Dutch nuclear weapons responsibilities. In preparing the draft of the party programme, the party executive opted for a compromise position in which the six nuclear responsibilities would be reduced to a maximum of two; which two those would be played virtually no role in the discussion. This compromise was acceptable to Den Uyl. The debate within the party over this compromise position was extensive and at times quite heated. At the party congress, supporters of the atomic pacifist position made an emotional appeal to Den Uyl to revise his stand. He refused and was thenceforth known in some circles as Joop Atomic.

In the end it was the party that gave way. A large majority of the delegates

Table 5.1. *Dutch parliamentary parties, 1981–1982*

	1981 election	
Party	Votes	Seats
Christian Democratic Appeal (CDA)	30.8	48
Labour Party (PvdA)	28.3	44
Liberal Party (VVD)	17.3	26
Democrats '66 (D66)	11.1	17
Communist Party (CPN)	2.1	3
Pacifist Socialist Party (PSP)	2.1	3
Political Party Radicals (PPR)	2.0	3
Political Reformed Party (SGP)	2.0	3
Reformed Political Union (GPV)	0.8	1
Reformed Political Federation (RPF)	1.2	2
Other	2.4	
Total	100.1	150

at the party congress accepted the compromise position. Some of the party faithful did so in recognition of the very likely possibility that refusal of any nuclear responsibilities would make Labour totally unacceptable to the Christian Democrats as a coalition partner, whatever the election results might be. Others, less concerned about office-seeking motivations, supported the compromise because they saw no possibility for choosing a successor to Den Uyl so close to the upcoming elections. To switch leaders at such a late date would certainly lead to electoral losses. In the end, the party congress determined that the renunciation of at least four nuclear responsibilities would be a requirement for participation in a coalition.

In addition to the question of nuclear responsibilities, the party formulated five other positions that were of central importance, including a job plan to provide for the creation of 300,000 jobs. In contrast to 1977, these positions were not viewed as immutable, but rather as starting points for discussions and negotiations with potential coalition partners. The results of any negotiations would be measured against these standards. The congress also registered a preference for a coalition with other progressive parties; a coalition with the Christian Democrats was clearly a second choice.

The Labour Party lost heavily at the 1981 elections, falling from fifty-three to forty-four seats in Parliament. In public discussions, this electoral defeat was interpreted as punishment for the fact that the party had failed to form a coalition four years previously, despite the gain of ten parliamentary seats. Following this line of reasoning, the dogmatic and uncompromising position of the party in 1977 was seen as responsible for loss of both office and votes. Was it therefore any wonder that the party leadership wished to do everything possible to return to power?

THE CABINET FORMATION

Despite the electoral losses, the possibility of a return to government was certainly present. The coalition of Christian Democrats and Liberals lost three seats (going from seventy-seven to seventy-four) and thereby its parliamentary majority. Continuation of the coalition was thus viewed as impossible. Although D66 was the major winner at the elections and now held seventeen seats, this party had announced prior to the elections that it would not lend its support to a continuation of the Christian Democratic–Liberal coalition, but preferred to join a cabinet with Labour and the Christian Democrats. Lacking the possibility of continued D66 support of the former coalition, the Christian Democrats had the choice of resorting to (implicit) support by the small religious parties or a coalition with Labour, with or without D66.

When it became clear that D66 would not reverse its preelection position, negotiations began between Labour, the Christian Democrats, and D66. The party council of the Labour Party met and, despite attempts by a radical group, placed no restrictions on the negotiations. Difficulties did arise, however, between the principal participants. Christian Democratic leader Dries Van Agt had been minister of justice in the Den Uyl Cabinet, and for various reasons had become quite unpopular in socialist circles. In the meantime, Van Agt had himself been prime minister for four years, so a major question of the negotiations was whether he or Den Uyl would lead the new government. Not only were there ideological differences between the two men, their personalities clashed as well.

The substantive differences in the Cabinet formation centred on social-economic policy and nuclear weapons. In addition to the question of which and how many nuclear responsibilities within NATO the Netherlands would maintain, a new matter arose – whether or not the country would accept deployment of cruise missiles. None of these questions was really resolved during the Cabinet formation process, and the parties decided upon an "agreement to disagree." The Labour Party did, however, make absolutely clear that acceptance of the cruise missiles was unthinkable and that any decision to accept deployment would lead to their immediate departure from the coalition. Thus a time bomb was placed under the new Cabinet. However, other problems would lead to the dissolution of the coalition before the bomb could explode.

The chasm between the parties on issues of social-economic policy that developed during the Cabinet formation process was never fully bridged. The Netherlands was facing rapidly rising unemployment at a time when the tax burden and the level of governmental borrowing had also reached record heights. The financing deficit (the difference between governmental income and outlay, diminished by payments for long-term loans) had grown from slightly more than approximately 4 per cent in the years 1975–8 to 7.6 per cent in 1980 and was still rising. The public sector portion of the economy would reach 70 per cent in 1981. The Christian Democrats felt that in both cases maxima had been reached and that governmental policies should be aimed at stimulating the economy and creating jobs by reducing the financing deficit and not allowing the public sector to increase beyond the 70 per cent level. The Labour Party, on the other hand, gave absolute priority to creating jobs and to the protection of purchasing power, not only for those still working, but in particular for those receiving governmental benefits. Of utmost importance for the party were the so-called social minima, those with the lowest incomes, who deserved the most protection.

The battle over the governmental programme became intertwined with the question of whether the Labour Party would accept Van Agt as prime minister in the new Cabinet. The Christian Democrats had the stronger claim to the office by virtue of their larger number of seats. The leaders of the parliamentary Labour Party were divided among themselves over whether Van Agt could be accepted and, if so, under what conditions. In the end, Van Agt was accepted only after a solution was found for the position of Den Uyl and concessions were made on other points, such as allowing the Labour Party to fill the post of minister of education. Den Uyl became minister of social affairs, but this position was given more than usual responsibilities, such as project minister for employment and coordinating minister for social and economic policy. The leader of the opposition referred to Den Uyl as a "superminister," almost more important than the prime minister.

The Cabinet formation process was completed with a compromise on government policy that both parties agreed to, in part, it would later appear, because they placed different interpretations on its content. The difference of opinion centred on the level of budgetary cuts that were to be reached in the 1982 governmental budget. During the coalition negotiations the Christian Democrats had demanded a package of measures that would have amounted to cuts of 4.5 billion guilders. This figure had been unacceptable to the Labour Party. Thus the document that stated the new governmental policies was silent on both the level of the cuts and how they would be achieved. Such ambiguity quickly led to disagreements within the Cabinet. Despite the ambiguities and unresolved problems, however, on September 11, 1981, the new Cabinet was installed by the queen.

Before the Cabinet could present its policies to Parliament, tensions within the new coalition reached a boiling point. The interim government had made the necessary preparations for presentation of the 1982 budget, but now the new Cabinet would have to complete the process and make any desired revisions. The Den Uyl plan for increasing employment was estimated to cost 4 billion guilders. The Cabinet was faced with the virtually impossible task of finding this amount of money to stimulate jobs while also attempting to reduce borrowing to the agreed-upon level. The task was further complicated by a number of financial setbacks that quickly appeared. The interim Cabinet had failed to find sufficient income to cover all the posts in the budget, and to make matters even worse, revenues for the sale of natural gas were proving lower than had been projected. The Christian Democrats and D66 were willing to make no more than 300 million guilders available in order for Den Uyl to implement his plan for job creation. This was unacceptable to the Labour Party, and on October 16 the Cabinet offered its resignation to the queen.

The resignation, however, was not accepted, and two professors of economics were appointed to attempt to patch up the break. After three weeks of work, in which attempts were made to clarify some of the most ambiguous issues left over from the Cabinet formation period, the Cabinet withdrew its resignation. Nevertheless, the amount of time was insufficient and the positions of the parties were so different that complete clarity was not possible. A number of conflicting goals remained, and for a number of problems, even if broad goals could be defined, specification of the content of the policies that would be necessary to reach the goals was left to a later date. Inevitable disagreements were merely being postponed.

POLICY VERSUS OFFICE

The matter of funding Den Uyl's job creation plan was not resolved, since the amount of money to be made available still had not been agreed upon. Fundamental differences thus continued on questions of social-economic policy and financial policy. To make matters even worse, every new financial report brought bad news for the Cabinet. Government revenues were continually falling behind projections. Since the Cabinet had agreed to reduce the amount of borrowing and not increase taxes and social insurance premiums, spending cuts would have to be even greater than had been anticipated. At the same time, the Labour Party, and Den Uyl in particular, continued to demand funds for the creation of jobs. In order to find the necessary funds, proposals were made to substantially reduce expenditures for social insurance programs and to reduce the salaries of government workers. Such measures would disproportionately affect two ministries that were held by the Labour Party: Social Affairs and Internal Affairs, the latter headed by Den Uyl's Labour colleague Ed Van Thijn. The fact that Labour ministers had accepted such proposals made them even more infuriating to many of the party faithful.

In order for the government's financial policy to succeed, the coalition partners agreed that wages would have to be held down. However, neither the employers nor the unions were willing to cooperate. The employers demanded even greater budget cuts, tax relief for business, a ceiling on price compensation in the new contracts, and differential increases between wages and social benefits. The unions were unwilling to moderate their demands as long as it was not clear what was to happen to Den Uyl's job creation plans. As a result, no agreement between the employers and unions could be reached, and Den Uyl was forced to take unilateral measures and impose a contract upon both parties, something that the Labour Party had always rejected when they were in opposition. The measures were popular with neither the employers nor the unions. The latter were particularly upset over the necessity of breaking existing agreements, and they threatened with legal action and strikes.

Such differences between the Labour Party and the trade unions could hardly fail to affect potential electoral support for Labour. Public opinion polls showed that support for the party had dropped considerably since its 1981 election level, which itself had been seen as an electoral defeat. It appeared that support might even have fallen below that for the Liberals. Moreover, the leader of D66, Jan Terlouw, was receiving heavy criticism as minister of economic affairs, so that both parties of the left in the centre–left Cabinet appeared to be in trouble. Polls are only polls, but in March 1982 elections were held for the provincial legislatures. The results for Labour were catastrophic. The party received almost 6.5 per cent fewer votes than at the parliamentary elections the previous year, while the Liberals indeed surpassed the Labour percentage (22.2 per cent against 21.8 per cent). D66 fell from 11.0 per cent in 1981 to 8.3 per cent. Although provincial elections have no direct impact upon the number of seats held in Parliament, they have always been viewed as an indication of the level of support for the national parties. In any case, such poor results weakened the position of the Labour and D66 members of the Cabinet.

As time passed, it became more difficult to postpone the decisions the Cabinet would eventually have to take concerning specific budgetary measures. The Cabinet was scheduled to announce its plans in its spring budget message. The Christian Democratic parliamentary leader, Ruud Lubbers, had demanded that this message be published before March 1. Although Prime Minister Van Agt denied that the announcement was delayed intentionally, he certainly had no regrets that it was postponed until after the provincial elections, as the other parties were now in a much weaker position.

Governmental finances were also weaker, and agreements that had been reached only weeks or months previously were no longer sufficient. After two weeks of negotiations, a compromise was reached. Among the proposals were these: governmental expenditures would be cut by 3 billion guilders; purchasing power would decrease, although some relief would be found for the most needy; business would receive some relief; the level of borrowing would not be reduced; 300 million extra guilders would be made available for job creation.

THE CABINET FALLS

For some, the compromise proposals were shocking. Without consulting either members of Parliament or his own party executive, Labour Party Chairman Max Van den Berg declared that the proposals were unacceptable. The loss of purchasing power for persons with the lowest incomes was greater than had been agreed upon earlier, and the relief provided for business was greater than the amount available for new jobs. Van den Berg called for a meeting of the party council, which, in his view, should force the Labour ministers to resign. In his view, office holding was having too little impact upon policy. Lengthy discussions within the party elite did little to improve the relations between the party chairman and the party leader, as Den Uyl felt personally insulted by the opposition of his own party chairman.

The Labour Party members of Parliament were also critical of provisions of the compromise, so that the Labour ministers were forced to attempt to renegotiate portions of the package. Despite the obvious difficulties, some progress toward a new agreement with the Christian Democrats was reached. However, this was achieved during the absence of Prime Minister Van Agt, who was visiting the United States. Upon his return he felt betrayed by Den Uyl. Any hope for cooperation between the coalition partners was now gone, and on May 12 the Cabinet submitted its resignation.

THE LUBBERS–KOK CABINET, 1989–1994

PRELIMINARIES: THE 1982 AND 1986 CABINETS

Following the fall of the Van Agt Cabinet, new elections were held in the fall of 1982. The losses for the Labour Party were less than projected based upon the provincial elections. The party received almost 8.6 per cent more of the vote than at the provincial elections and gained a total of forty-three seats in the Second Chamber, a loss of only one seat. There was nevertheless no possibility for a return to office, as the Christian Democrats turned to the Liberals to form a new government. Van Agt withdrew from national politics and was succeeded by Ruud Lubbers. The Labour Party was forced to the opposition benches, where it would remain for seven years. After his first four years as prime minister, Lubbers had attained considerable popularity, and in 1986 his party entered the election campaign with the slogan "Let Lubbers finish the job." The Christian Democrats broke with long-standing tradition and announced *prior* to the elections that if the results made it possible, they would prefer to continue their coalition with the Liberals. By virtually eliminating the possibility of a coalition with Labour, the latter had little hope of gaining office despite the fact that the party booked one of its best electoral results ever by gaining nine seats to reach a total of fifty-two. The Christian Democrats and Liberals controlled 81 of the 150 seats in the Second Chamber and in a relatively short period were able to reach agreement on the continuation of their coalition.

In ensuing years, however, the relationship between the coalition partners eventually began to deteriorate. The Liberals became increasingly irritated by the fact that, in their eyes, the Christian Democrats attempted to dominate the formulation of policy. Lubbers had matured in his role and dominated the Cabinet in a way few Dutch prime ministers have been able to do. He was able to do so in part because his party was considerably larger than the Liberal Party. The latter began to suffer from a sort of inferiority complex, and irritations grew to such proportions that the Liberal members of Parliament took the unusual step of bringing down a government. The issue at stake – a cabinet proposal to eliminate the tax deduction for workers travelling long distances between home and work – seems almost minor in comparison with the action taken, but tensions had simply reached the breaking point. On May 2, 1989, the Cabinet fell and new elections were called for the following September.

LABOUR'S NEW PRAGMATISM
AND OFFICE-SEEKING

This break in the coalition suddenly opened the door again for the Labour Party. Even those who believed that the Christian Democrats would accept the Socialists only as a last resort could see that this was an ideal opportunity. Some in the Labour Party went even further in their analysis and saw this as a do-or-die situation. The desire and pressure for office were greater than at any time in recent memory. If Labour could not obtain governmental responsibility now, it might never again do so. If, under these circumstances, the party, as the second largest party in the country, could not show that it was capable of being an acceptable coalition partner and a responsible governing party, it would lose all credibility with the voters.

After leading the party for twenty years, Joop Den Uyl had retired to the back benches following the 1986 elections. He was succeeded by Wim Kok, who had for a number of years headed the largest trade union federation. Ironically, it was Kok who had been one of the strongest opponents of Den Uyl in the 1982 controversy described in the preceding case study. The second Den Uyl Cabinet had never formed, so now it was up to Kok to bring the party back to office. Between 1986 and 1989, under Kok's leadership, the Labour Party had gone through a long period of soul searching. The need to restore party self-confidence was great, and a regeneration of commitment and a new vision were called for. Three separate internal party commissions produced reports intended to revive and rejuvenate the party (*Schuivende Panelen* 1987; Commissie C 1987; *Bewogen beweging* 1988). They argued that changes in policies and programmes were needed, as well as changes in party structure and organization. Finally, changes were needed in how the party viewed itself and its relation to other parties and social organizations in the country. A result of these internal discussions was to push the party toward a more pragmatic orientation. In terms of the three models of party behaviour discussed here, it can be argued that the party attempted to lower its policy-seeking commitment in order to make it more acceptable as a coalition partner. By changing its course ever so slightly, the party hoped to become more attractive to the Christian Democrats.

Although this course change was quite limited, it was unacceptable to a number of party members to the left of the ideological spectrum. In the spring of 1989, some even went so far as to found a "project group socialism 2000." The internal discussions were still continuing when the Liberal ministers were forced out of the Cabinet and early elections were called.

In accordance with its new and more pragmatic course, the election programme of the Labour Party was a moderate document. Yet the new course was no guarantee of success and the party lost three parliamentary seats, falling to forty-nine. The Christian Democrats held their fifty-four seats, but the Liberals suffered a loss and fell to only twenty-two. (In the Netherlands, the saying is, "He who breaks pays.") D66 won three seats and raised its total to twelve. In fact, the coalition of Christian Democrats and Liberals still held the slimmest of parliamentary majorities (seventy-six seats) and could have revived their coalition, but many felt this margin was too narrow (Table 5.2).

The Christian Democratic members of Parliament were divided in their coalition preferences. Some felt it improper and/or undesirable to revive a coalition with the Liberals, who had abandoned the previous government; these individuals preferred attempting to form a government with Labour. The more right-wing branch of the parliamentary party was, however, not yet in favour of this centre–left solution. The compromise that was reached in the parliamentary party gave first preference to a coalition with the Liberals, but with expansion to include D66. The second choice was a coalition with the Labour Party, but without D66. This combination of preferences had some advantages for the Christian Democrats. First of all, they hoped thereby to woo D66 away from its alliance with Labour. During the campaign, D66 had often repeated that it would not provide the seats necessary for the Christian Democrats and Liberals to achieve a majority. By offering D66 ministerial posts in a centre–right coalition but not in a centre–left one, the Christian Democrats hoped that D66 could be weaned away from its campaign promise. Within a coalition with D66 to their left and the Liberals to their right, but with themselves holding a numerical majority, the Christian Democrats would retain a pivotal position. On the other hand, if D66 were to be included in a coalition with Labour, the Christian Democrats would be in a minority position, and a majority of ministerial positions would have to be given to the coalition partners. Although votes are seldom taken in a Dutch cabinet, both the Christian Democrats and Labour would nevertheless prefer to hold a majority of the ministerial portfolios.

D66 rejected the advances of the Christian Democrats and remained true to its campaign promise. Labour, however, demanded that D66 be included in any negotiations regarding a centre–left coalition. The Christian Democrats countered with the proposal that this was agreeable, but that any ministerial posts allocated to D66 would have to come out of the Labour allocation. The Christian Democrats demanded seven of the fourteen positions, whether D66 was represented or not.

In the past, such a demand would have been rejected outright by Labour negotiators. In previous Cabinet formations they had placed their own demands on the number of posts they felt they should have. Now they were being asked

Table 5.2. *Dutch parliamentary parties 1989–1994*

| | 1989 election | |
Party	Votes	Seats
Christian Democratic Appeal (CDA)	35.3	54
Labour Party (PvdA)	31.9	49
Liberal Party (VVD)	14.6	22
Democrats '66 (D66)	7.9	12
Green Left	4.1	6
Political Reformed Party (SGP)	1.9	3
Reformed Political Union (GPV)	1.2	2
Reformed Political Federation (RPF)	1.0	1
List Janmaat/Centre Democrats (CD)	0.9	1
Other	1.2	
Total	100.0	150

to accept a less than proportional share. Out of their overwhelming desire to return to power and out of fear that a Christian Democratic–Liberal coalition, with or without D66, might yet be arranged, Labour submitted to the demand. Thus, to their own dissatisfaction, the Christian Democrats had no choice but to accept D66 in the talks to form a new government.

Acceptance at the negotiating table, however, did not mean that they had accepted D66 into the new government. The next move of the Christian Democrats was to demand that the first question to be resolved was the policy of the new coalition toward euthanasia. D66 had actively campaigned for a policy that would make it possible, under closely specified conditions, for doctors to assist patients in terminating of their lives. This policy was supported, albeit less strongly, by the Labour Party, but was seen by most Christian Democrats as being contradictory to biblical teaching and thus completely unacceptable. The D66 members of Parliament saw this attempt to manipulate the agenda of negotiations as a direct attack on their party and announced their withdrawal from the bargaining table. If they had hoped that the Labour Party would support them and similarly withdraw, they were quickly disappointed. Labour was honestly disappointed by the decision, but in order not to put its own position in danger, it agreed to continue the negotiations with the Christian Democrats. D66 joined the Liberals on the opposition benches.

LABOUR POLICY DESIRES

By Dutch standards, the discussions over the policies and programmes of the new government went quite quickly and smoothly, especially given the two partners involved. On October 26 the members of Parliament of the two parties accepted the results of the work of the party negotiators. In keeping with its party customs, the Labour Party held a party congress on November 6 to discuss the participation of the party in a government based upon the programme that had been agreed upon. In the electoral campaign, Labour had put forward proposals for new policies in areas such as education, health care, the environment, and improvement of the deteriorating areas of the large cities. The governmental pact allowed room for new initiatives in line with Labour's wishes but placed strict conditions on the allocation of funds for the financing of such new policies. For example, the total level of taxes and social insurance premiums would not be allowed to rise, and the financing deficit in the budget was to be decreased in strictly designated yearly steps. Another policy of central concern to the Labour Party, the coupling of the level of social welfare benefits with the level of wages in the private sector, was dependent upon the financial passages of the agreement.

Labour leader Kok defended the agreement with full conviction. In addition to the commitment to fulfill a number of the wishes of the Labour Party, the new Cabinet would shoulder the responsibility of improving the financial position of the treasury. In order to achieve this, Kok would himself take the position of minister of finance. Within the Labour Party there was disagreement concerning the wisdom of this decision. Kok seemed to be emphasizing the importance of holding this office in order to help counteract the popular image of the Labour party as "spendthrifty," unable to keep inflation down, and unable to provide for a sound economy. Opponents, however, were motivated more by policy concerns. They feared that in his zeal to guard governmental finances, Kok would be placed in a position of refusing to allot funds for the implementation of Labour policies. This would present a contradictory picture to potential voters. They therefore preferred to have Kok take the position of minister of social affairs, as Den Uyl had done in 1981.

THE CHOICE FOR OFFICE

Despite the fact that there was considerable lack of clarity concerning the financial passages in the coalition agreement and whether the financial conditions would allow for implementation of specific policies desired by Labour, the party congress was eager not to follow the disastrous example of 1977 and seized the opportunity to govern again. Kok made it quite clear to the party congress that because of the limited financial possibilities, the new Cabinet would be forced to make some extremely difficult decisions. He reasoned, however, that the party should not be blinded by unrealistic policy desires and should not avoid the responsibility of government. In short, if the Labour Party decided to join the Cabinet, it should do so without reservation and should do whatever was possible to make it a success. Such an argument referred directly to the possible repetition of the events of 1982 that have already been described. To join again a Cabinet that might fall in a very short time would likely damage the party almost beyond repair.

In this case, the party congress shared the opinion of the leadership that the opportunity to govern should not be spurned. With a degree of consensus seldom found in the Labour Party, the congress voted unanimously to accept the proposed coalition agreement and join the new Cabinet. The choice for office had been made, and the following day the new government was installed by the queen.

Despite the somewhat different starting point, the events that followed during the ensuing months bore a remarkable resemblance to the events of the fall of 1981. Again, it quickly became clear that the financial position of the government was considerably poorer than had been apparent during the Cabinet formation period. Within the first few months of the new government, a series of disappointing financial figures came to light. Nevertheless, with its very clear policy concerns, the Labour Party could hardly not attempt to put forward new policy initiatives. Its commitment to the underprivileged in society was too great for it not to wish to make some attempt to present proposals to make societal improvements, even if these cost money. In 1981–2 it was the proposal for a job creation scheme that placed financial demands upon the government. This time it was the desire to attack the problems of the inner cities. Policy in this area was diverse and uncoordinated; what was needed was a coordinated set of policies to attack the problem from several angles simultaneously. The programme, which would be a joint effort of national and local governments, became known as *social rejuvenation*. Clearly, rejuvenation would cost money, and with the new financial problems, funds were becoming increasingly difficult to find. The parallel with 1981 is obvious; where could the funds for new Labour policies be found when the government was repeatedly faced with declining revenues? Cuts would have to be made just to bring expenditures and revenues more in line, let alone provide extra funds for carrying out Labour policies. Media observers began to cast a more sceptical eye on the program for social rejuvenation. Thus, within a matter of months, the image of the policy-versus-office dilemma began to loom for the Labour Party. Could or should the party stay in office if it was next to impossible to carry out desired policies?

NEW PROBLEMS AND DECLINING ELECTORAL SUPPORT

In January 1990 a new problem began to emerge for the Labour Party. At the beginning of the new year, tax reform measures passed under the previous government took effect. It began to appear that higher-income groups would benefit more than expected from the new measures, whereas lower-income groups, especially older persons on small pensions, would suffer losses. During the election campaign, the Labour Party had demanded that certain portions of the reform measures be rescinded, but in making the choice to participate in government, the demands had been dropped. Whether the announcements of the effects of tax reform were a cause or not, the Labour Party began to show losses in the polls at about this time.

On March 21, 1990, municipal elections were held. Since elections are held in all municipalities on the same day and since local issues have only limited impact upon voting behaviour, the results are often seen as a referendum on national politics, as were the provincial elections in 1982. The weakening position of the Labour Party became starkly visible as the party lost about 4 per cent of the vote when compared to the previous parliamentary elections.

With party electoral support withering, Labour ministers began the difficult negotiations over the new governmental budget. This was the first budget to be prepared solely by the new coalition. Labour and Christian Democrats differed over how much room was available for new policies, what the levels of budget cuts would have to be, and how these cuts were to be divided among the various departments. When the budget was presented in September 1990, not all problems had been solved, and it was announced that the Cabinet would present an interim report (*tussenbalans*) at the beginning of the following year.

Labour had high hopes for this interim report. After a period of uncertainty and inability to reach decisions, the party hoped to demonstrate that there was a social-democratic impact upon Cabinet policy. The interim report was scheduled for publication well in advance of the provincial elections on March 6, 1991, and it was hoped, even assumed, that this would help to reverse the party's downward trend in the polls. The election campaign was planned with this effect in mind. However, negotiations again took longer than anticipated, so the Cabinet had to decide whether to release the interim report just before or after the provincial elections. The measures to be taken would not be popular. An almost unheard-of 17 billion guilders would have to be cut from expenditures, and new revenues would come from hefty increases in prices for public transportation and housing rent.

By agreeing to such measures, Labour politicians hoped to show that they were willing to take drastic, yet necessary, measures in order to make it possible to carry out equally needed new policies, all with an eye toward potential electoral support. This formed part of the electoral strategy for the provincial elections, but although the plans were released before the elections, the strategy never really had a chance. The news media were dominated by coverage of the Gulf War, and whatever attention was given to the interim report concentrated on the increased revenues that the taxpayers would have to pay. Labour was placed on the defensive and was unable to paint a sufficiently positive picture of the benefits that could be expected.

The strategy failed, and the provincial elections on March 6 were a disaster for the Labour Party. The party fell from 31.9 per cent at the 1989 parliamentary elections to an historic low of only 20.4 per cent of the vote. The results were a clear indication of waning support, and thus weakened the party considerably both within the Cabinet and in Parliament. In the search for policy, votes, and office, the Labour Party seemed to be losing the battle on two fronts. The impact upon policy was insufficient to convince voters that there was a difference with the policies of the previous centre–right Cabinets.

Various political commentators pointed to previous instances in 1958, 1966, and 1982, when poor results at provincial elections led to the fall of the government within months. In such cases, the Labour Party seemed to have concluded that participation in office was the cause of electoral loss. This time, however, the leaders of the party hastened to discredit any such interpretation and declared that the poor results would have no implication for the relationship within the coalition. Party leader Kok announced that he was "very motivated" to continue, and although voters did not yet seem to understand governmental policy, there was no reason to change course. He compared himself to a marathon runner; all the pain would be worth it when the race was completed successfully. Such statements reiterated the commitment of the Labour Party to office holding as the means to influence policy, with votes as the long-term goal.

A NEW TEST

Although friends and foes felt that the Labour Party had just gone through the deepest possible valley, the party's office-seeking strategy would soon be put to an even greater test. In the spring of 1991, the parliamentary leader of the Christian Democrats demanded that measures be taken in the 1992 budget to limit the ever-increasing payments from governmental general revenues to the social insurance programs. Of particular concern was the continuing rise in claims for employment disability compensation. In the Netherlands, this insurance scheme provides for payment of 70 per cent of the last earned income. Since disability benefits lasted longer than unemployment benefits, workers threatened by possible unemployment sometimes took advantage of the relatively easy regulations to obtain disability compensation. This led to unexpectedly high numbers of recipients, and the problem of how to stop the rise in these numbers led to lengthy, difficult, and heated discussions within the Cabinet. In a joint press conference on July 15, Prime Minister Lubbers and Minister of Finance Kok announced the plans that the Cabinet had agreed upon. In the future, for disability payments for persons under age fifty, the length of time such payments could be received was to be limited. As part of the package, a proposal from 1981 that employees would not be compensated for the first few days of sickness was revived.

Although the parliamentary Labour Party initially declared its support for the proposals, a storm of protest followed. Just as in 1981, the trade union federations were enraged, withdrew their support for the Cabinet, and announced that strikes would be organized. Other traditional supporters of the Labour Party were astounded by the party's acceptance of such proposals.

The announcement could not have come at a more inopportune time for the Labour Party. In the middle of the summer, various top party leaders, including party chairman Marianne Sint, were on vacation and unavailable for comment. This fact in itself led to a flood of criticism in the media, and the party was left in a confused state. The party executive announced that it could not comment on the plans until the middle of August. However, this vacuum at the top did not stop the media from soliciting comments from within the party; with national leaders unavailable, regional leaders were only too eager to express their total rejection of the Cabinet proposals.

Within days, Kok realized that he had totally underestimated the reaction within his party and among party supporters. He now argued that the proposals should be softened for those persons who truly had no hope of reentering the workforce. Although such an amendment would revive tensions with the Cabinet, it was nevertheless insufficient to soothe his disappointed opponents. The genie was out of the bottle and was not about to go back in. Illustrative of the position of the Labour Party as a policy-oriented party is the fact that all attention and criticism were focused on the Labour ministers in the Cabinet and not on the minister most directly responsible for the proposals, the Christian Democratic minister of social affairs. Clearly, party members, voters, and the media saw it as the task of the Labour Party to preserve the pillars of the welfare state.

Disillusionment with the Labour Party could be seen in the opinion polls. According to a poll dated July 31, 1991, if new elections had been held, the Labour Party would have lost twenty-two of its forty-nine parliamentary seats; on August 8 a poll showed a loss of twenty-eight seats, which would have reduced the party to the fourth largest in the country. A substantial proportion of Labour supporters answered that they would vote for D66, now basking in opposition. The Labour Party's central office was flooded with membership cancellations. Some who did not resign founded a group called "Labour Again Socially Minded" in order to organize opposition to the proposals. The Labour Party executive decided to hold a special party congress on October 26 to discuss the proposals concerning employment disability compensation and to debate the future of all the areas involving social security and welfare.

On August 8, the Christian Democrats agreed to reopen discussions, but they made it clear that the margins for alterations in the proposals were quite small. Negotiations were made even more difficult by a new demand arising from the Christian Democratic parliamentary party. The parliamentary party leader demanded that for the following year, the provisions that welfare benefits would rise at the same rate as wages in the private sector must again be abandoned. Despite announcements that he "could not live" with such a proposal, Kok was unable to salvage this point in the Cabinet. In the view of many party supporters, he had suffered yet another defeat and was no longer a credible leader. The new compromise agreement on employment disability was also insufficient for many party members, and the trade unions were determined to continue the battle.

TRADE-OFFS

In terms of trade-offs, in the case of the employment disability question, there was a clear choice. The Labour ministers, however, had maneouvered themselves into an impossible position. No option was open that would not damage the party. A decision by the Labour Party ministers to withdraw support from the proposals would have brought about the fall of the government. Even if the electoral losses could be contained, the loss of face that had already been incurred could not be repaired. The alternative was to reach agreement on a package that was as good as possible under the circumstances (and, in the eyes of party leaders, better than what might come out of a centre–right Cabinet). Having accepted the position of minister of finance, Kok had little choice but to recognize that something had to be done about the rising costs of employment disability and other welfare state programs. Nevertheless, in accepting the proposals, the Labour ministers seriously underestimated the opposition that the proposals would generate. Continued support of the proposals, even in an altered form, would cost the party scores of voters. Even if in the long run losses could be kept to a minimum, in the short run a major split within the party was looming, as it was clear that a majority of party members opposed the governmental plans.

For party leader Kok, the options were even more sharply defined. If the Cabinet were to fall, he surely would not be the person to lead the party in a new campaign. He would hardly be credible as the defender of a party programme that completely rejected cuts in social security and welfare programs. Yet if he and the party stayed on, his position as party leader and vice-premier would be undermined considerably by the lack of confidence expressed within his own party. He seriously considered tendering his resignation but was kept from doing so by two party colleagues in the Cabinet. Their advice was to place his own position on the line by having the special congress meet earlier than planned and calling upon the congress to express a vote of confidence. Kok was finally convinced, and the congress was scheduled for September 1991.

Before the party congress, Kok addressed the members of the party via a personal letter. The question to be resolved by the congress was put simply and bluntly: "could Kok continue as leader of the party and could the party continue in the Cabinet?" There had to be clarity, he argued; "to leave any doubt would undermine the position of the party to govern." The congress was to vote on the disability proposals, but his own position was tied to support for the proposals. The vote was to be a written one, normally used only when voting on individuals.

During the three weeks preceding the congress, members of Parliament and national party executives attended tens of party meetings throughout the country. Kok was criticized heavily for coupling his own future with support for the proposals. Some members felt this was an intolerable form of blackmail. Whatever their feelings, however, the tactic succeeded. Many members were not at all pleased with the idea that by rejecting the proposals the party would force a cabinet crisis and lose its leader simultaneously. Since Kok had the support of most of the parliamentary party and the party executive, to reject the proposals would rob the party of virtually all its national leaders. Yielding to such pressures, 80 per cent of the party congress supported the employment disability proposals and stated their confidence in their party leader.

Thus, faced with one of the most crucial decisions in its existence, the party decided to remain in office. In an attempt to minimise the damage, a committee was appointed to develop views on future developments in social welfare. The report of this committee was adopted at a party congress in the spring of 1992, and further attacks on the social welfare system were rejected. Although this may have at least temporarily restored some semblance of unity within the party, not all the damage could be contained. After the September 1991 party congress, public opinion polls continued to show dramatic losses for the party; the number of party members fell from 97,000 to 77,000 in 1991, and some prominent members threatened to organize a new political party.

In contrast to 1982, the Labour Party decided in 1991 to remain in office. In doing so, it took a major gamble that, through this office-seeking strategy, it would be able to influence policy sufficiently to win votes in the long run. The results of the 1994 election reveal just how relative a concept such as winning can be. For months the Labour Party did badly in the polls. As late as January, a leading newspaper published an analysis that claimed that the party would gain no more than twenty seats. However, at about the same time, the CDA began to take an electoral nose dive that was unprecedented in Dutch politics, while the Labour Party began to rise slowly. When the election results were in, it became clear that the Labour Party had climbed from the depths and with thirty-seven seats actually became the largest party in Parliament. Although they had lost twelve seats when compared to the previous election, the CDA lost even more (twenty seats), and since the Labour Party's expectations had been so low, they actually felt like winners.

DISCUSSION

The two cases presented in this chapter dramatically illustrate the dilemma faced by the Dutch Labour Party. Based upon these case studies, it is possible to draw several conclusions relating to the position of the Dutch Labour Party in particular and to the question of the goals motivating political party behaviour in general. Regarding the Labour Party, seven points can be made:

1. These cases demonstrate without question the primary importance that the Labour Party attaches to public policy. Not only through its historical roots but also in its modern orientation, the primary goal of the party is to influence policy. In both cases, the Labour Party wished to introduce and implement new policies that led to conflict with its coalition partners. In 1981, Den Uyl was committed to creating new jobs to reduce the unacceptably high level of unemployment. In 1991, the party wished to protect important aspects of the social welfare state and to formulate programs to rejuvenate the inner cities. In both cases, funds were needed, so that these goals collided with Christian Democratic demands to cut both the governmental budget and the tax burden.

2. In the Dutch Labour Party, power traditionally has been highly decentralized and a strongly policy-minded membership has been committed to holding the party to its true course. As hypothesized in the theoretical framework of this book, this internal organization has had a major impact upon its choice of goals. In both of the cases, internal party organs and groups were important in influencing the choice of strategy.

The conflict in socialist parties between government and parliamentary party and between parliamentary party and party executives was observed in the seminal study by Robert Michels (1911). In these two case studies, we have seen that the parliamentary party played a relatively minor role. In 1981–2 there were rumblings, but no overt action was taken. In 1991, the party members in Parliament initially accepted the controversial proposals and again played no prominent role in the decision making.

This cannot, however, be said for the party executive. In 1981–2, the party chairman, Van den Berg, was one of the first to condemn his own ministers for their acceptance of the compromise proposals. By doing so, he brought the internal party conflict into the open and made a satisfactory settlement more difficult. However, if his goal was to preserve the purity of party policies, his action may be seen to have succeeded. In 1991 it was the holiday absence of party chairman Sint that aggravated the situation. Because of her absence, the party executive delayed taking a stand. This made it possible for regional leaders to take stands in opposition to the decisions taken by the party's ministers. Again, the internal conflict was out in the open, forcing the issue. As a result of the entire affair, the chairman resigned in the fall of 1991.

Party congresses play an important role in Labour Party decision making. In 1981 and 1991, congresses were asked to approve decisions taken by the party leadership. In 1981 party leader Den Uyl put his position on the line in order to force the party to accept a limited number of nuclear responsibilities within NATO. In 1991 his successor, Wim Kok, threatened to resign unless the party congress accepted his decisions on the employment disability compensation proposals. In both cases, these threats from office-seeking leaders were sufficient to pressure a policy-seeking party congress into accepting some form of compromise in order to participate in government.

Finally, rank-and-file members can influence the party to maintain its policy goals. The structure of the party allows members considerable influence through the choice of delegates to the party congress. Moreover, members can take a clear stand and protest party action by resigning their membership. In 1991 thousands of Labour Party members did so in the wake of the party decision to accept cuts in disability benefits.

3.   Voters can also influence the decisions of the party. As was argued earlier, votes are instrumental in achieving office, which is essential for influencing policy. The problem for the party is that any causal model involving the three goals would show arrows running in all directions. Votes are necessary in order to achieve policy, but good policies are necessary to obtain votes, and so on. Thus, whatever the policies proposed, and however great the desire to remain in office, electoral support remains crucial. Both in 1981 and in 1991, loss of support, as shown in the polls, put pressure on the party to consider its action.

Even more important than opinion polls are local and provincial elections. Coming at intervals between the parliamentary elections, they are generally seen as referenda on the popularity of the current government. Poor electoral results also lead to unrest in the party, in part because hundreds of municipal and provincial elected officials are dependent upon the results for their own positions. In both 1982 and 1991, the results of the provincial elections were disastrous for the Labour Party. In 1982 this seemed to have been an important factor in allowing the Cabinet to fall; in 1991 the party did not wish a repetition and emphasized that it would continue despite the poor results. In the difficult decision concerning which of the goals should take precedence, the party chose to follow a new strategy and continue, in the hope that successful policies would bring votes back.

4.   Although the relationship between political parties and other organizations within their segment of the population is not as tight as it once was, the traditional relationship between the Labour Party and the trade unions cannot be ignored. In recent years, the largest trade union federation has given substantial support to the election campaigns of the Labour Party and is still a natural, if watchful, ally. In both 1981–2 and 1991, the trade unions were strongly opposed to governmental policies. It often seems to be the case that they resent policies even more if they have been agreed upon by Labour Party cabinet members, even if the policies are the result of hard-fought compromise negotiations. The anger of the unions seems fuelled by their feeling of betrayal, even though policies of a centre–right Cabinet might be more abhorrent. Whatever the case, in both years, the unions have led the opposition to the party's decisions.

An ironic but perhaps poignant detail is that the labour leader of 1982, Wim Kok, was the Labour leader of 1991. Placed in a different situation and a different role, his answer was quite different, while the trade unions themselves were quite consistent in their opposition.

5.   This also illustrates the crucial role of the party leader. In both cases, the party leader was highly criticized within his own party. In 1981 this occurred both in the acceptance of nuclear responsibilities and in the financial proposals concerning health care and job creation. By placing his position on the line, Den Uyl was able to get the party congress to accept nuclear responsibilities. In the conflict surrounding health care, he did not take such action but allowed the crisis to develop. It is rumoured that high-level party officials considered removing Den Uyl from his leadership position, but no action was taken. Even after the Cabinet fell, he led the party at the new elections.

In 1991 there was also considerable talk that party leader Kok should be removed. Yet when he forced a confrontation with the party, with the consequence that the government would fall and a new leader would be necessary at the ensuing elections, the party fell into line. The conclusion from these cases is thus that if the party leader is willing to put his entire weight behind a decision, the party feels it has little choice but to accept. Despite the importance of party membership, coups within the Labour Party have been nonexistent.

6.   A factor affecting these and all other cases involving the Labour Party has been the degree of electoral support. Since its inception, the Labour Party and its predecessor have dreamed of obtaining an electoral majority. However, this did not happen when universal suffrage was granted. It did not happen after the attempted "breakthrough" following the Second World War. And it did not happen when electoral change took place during the 1960s. Even in combination with other parties, no progressive majority has been even close to emerging. The policy strategy remains too heavily influenced by this dream.

7.   Lacking such majority support, the Labour Party must join coalition governments in order to influence policy. The process of coalition formation was for decades firmly in the hands of the Christian Democrats. This was illustrated dramatically in 1991, when the Christian Democrats moved to prohibit D66 from participating in government. In order to join a coalition, the Labour Party had to be acceptable to the Christian Democrats. Any office-seeking strategy had to focus on not offending the Christian Democrats so much that they might look to the right.

These two case studies have illustrated the dilemmas political parties may face. Although three goals of political parties may be defined, it is probably impossible to maximize all three. Difficult choices must often be made, and many factors may influence both the possibilities and the choices. Such factors may be both external and internal to the party involved. All parties must operate within the environment of the political and party systems. Of crucial importance, then, is whether the party can hope to obtain a majority position. If so, a party may forgo short-term policy influence while waiting for the votes that produce the majority needed for office. Lacking the hope of a majority, all three goals must be balanced simultaneously. In a multiparty system in which coalition governments are necessary, policy compromises are always necessary in order to obtain office. And since any dilution of the party programme can lead to dissatisfaction among voters, the eternal dilemma for the party continues.

Internal party factors also influence the choices that a party must make. Since choices are difficult, decisions are not easily reached. The larger the number of persons involved, the more difficult the situation will be. In a party committed to internal party democracy and the participation of the members, the possibility for conflict becomes greater. The membership and the party elite may place different emphases upon the conflicting goals. A party elite is not only confronted with the need to achieve party policies, but is also likely to be more aware of what may affect the party vote and may have a personal stake in obtaining office.

How these external and internal factors affect the decisions taken may depend upon the particular situation. As has been illustrated in the two cases, politicians are often quite conscious of the need not to repeat previous mistakes. Although objectively the circumstances may seem to be quite similar, this desire may tip the balance in a new situation.

EPILOGUE

In the period following the second case study, and in fact since the initial draft of this chapter was written, many developments have occurred that relate to the choice of strategy within the Labour Party. In the aftermath of the events described, during which the party began to fall dramatically in the opinion polls, the climate of opinion, even among rank-and-file members, began to alter drastically. The strongest pessimists began to worry that the end of the party was nearing. This new climate of opinion, which included a feeling at all levels that something must be done to improve the party's vote-getting capacity, helped produce support for proposals to alter drastically the internal environment of the party. These changes were designed to reduce the strength of the amateurs within the party and place more influence in the hands of professionals. The obvious concern was that amateurs are too policy-oriented and insufficiently oriented to the needs of the party in seeking votes and office. Although party members are still obviously important, and although no one in the party wishes to eliminate discussion within the party, accountability had been weakened to a degree and decisions were no longer seen as binding upon the leadership. In general, it can be said that all changes were designed to strengthen the position of the party leader and the party chairman.

The importance of these changes was seen in the preparations for the 1994 parliamentary elections. The process for selecting names for the list of candidates was altered substantially, taking power away from the regional party organs and assigning it to the top leadership. A new party chairman, Felix Rottenberg, pushed hard for recruitment outside the usual internal channels. This led to a high percentage of newcomers on the list of candidates, with less emphasis upon party service as a criterion for selection. In the 1994 campaign, reliance upon amateurs from the local party chapters was reduced as professionals at the top organized and carried out the campaign. Even with the loss of twelve seats, the results of the election were so much better than had been predicted in the polls only a few months earlier that they strengthened those who had pushed for such changes.

The results of the 1994 election also dramatically altered the external environment in which the Labour Party (and all other major parties, for that matter) must function. With the coalition partners (Labour and Christian Democrats) losing a record total of thirty-two seats, and with substantial gains by the Liberals and D66, the four parties were more equal in strength than ever before. At the beginning of this chapter, the factors that made it possible for the Christian Democrats to control Cabinet formation since the introduction of universal suffrage in 1917 were explained. In 1994 these factors no longer held. With only thirty-four seats, the CDA could not form a coalition with either Labour or the Liberals that would hold a majority of parliamentary seats. In fact, no combination of only two parties could reach the crucial figure of seventy-six seats, so three parties would be necessary. The possibilities for coalitions were broadened when the Labour Party and the Liberals discontinued their policy of mutual exclusion. This opened up the possibility of formation of a Cabinet along a different dimension than the traditional socioeconomic left–right dimension. These changes in the political landscape meant that suddenly it was D66 rather than CDA that held the key position in the government formation process. Whichever dimension formed the basis for a coalition, D66 would be necessary. D66 had been formed with the expressed purpose of exploding the party system, including the stranglehold of the CDA on coalition formation. In addition, in 1994 D66 was especially piqued by the treatment it had received at the hands of the CDA in 1989 (see the earlier discussion). As a result, D66 had a strong preference for a coaltion with Labour and the Liberals. After some complicated negotiations this preference prevailed, and what had previously been unthinkable became fact. The coalition is called the *purple* coalition, combining socialist red with Liberal blue.

As the largest party, Labour could lay claim to the position of prime minister, and Wim Kok became the third Labour prime minister since the Second World War. The party has thereby clearly chosen to take office, since joining a coalition with the Liberals involved a definite risk for the party. In order to form the coalition, it was necessary to agree to compromises that might be seen as too liberal to the voters – for example, on monetary and budgetary policy, government expenditures for social programs, and privatization of sick leave compensation. During the first year, it was also not possible to maintain the coupling between wages and governmental benefits. All these measures were seen as necessary in order to promote job creation.

This time, somewhat in contrast with 1981 and 1991, the risk paid off. The economic situation improved substantially, and the *polder model* (cooperation of government, employers, and trade unions) began to receive attention around the world. Economic growth produced more jobs and additional revenues for the government. This eased the pressure on budgetary cuts and even provided some room for social policies.

In 1998 the Labour Party was finally able to turn policy and office into votes. The election campaign focussed on the economic success of the "purple" coalition and retention in office of Prime Minister Wim Kok. Although scientific analysis of the election is not yet completed, it seems clear that the solid economy contributed significantly to the electoral success of the Labour Party. The party raised its proportion of the vote from 24 to 29 per cent, gaining eight additional seats in the Second Chamber. Although one of the coalition partners, D66, lost ten seats, the Liberal Party gained seven seats for a total gain of five seats for the coalition. Having been rewarded by the voters, the coalition returned to office, again under the prime ministership of Wim Kok.

In addition to economic success, the popularity of Kok was a second major factor contributing to the electoral success. He enjoyed such support that, during the campaign, Liberal Party leader Bolkestein announced that even if his own party emerged after the election as the largest party, Kok could continue as prime minister. Much was made of the electoral "bonus" that the party achieved by holding the office of prime minister.

In 1996 the Labour Party took a step that in the future may reduce the possibility of the kind of internal party conflict noted in the two case studies previously examined. Despite protests by some party members about violation of party rules, a member of the Second Chamber of Parliament, Karen Adelmund, was elected as the party chairman. When these functions are combined the strength of the party membership is weakened, and since it has been the membership that has often been the most strongly policy oriented, this act can be viewed as raising the priority of office-seeking and lowering that of policy.

In conclusion, it can be stated that policy-seeking, at least in its purest form, has given way to office-seeking in the Labour Party. Vote-seeking in 1998 was based on economic policy and the office of Wim Kok. This strategy involves a calculated risk. In the short run, the Labour Party is absolved from making hard choices, as an uneasy balance between the three party goals has been achieved. However, economies have a tendency to move in cycles, and Wim Kok does not possess eternal life. Inevitably, a time will come when the party will be forced to seek a new balance. When that time arrives, the choice among party, office, and votes will again become difficult.

NOTE

1. As background material for this case study, the following sources have been consulted: Bosmans (1990), Dittrich, Cohen, and Rutgers (1983), and Toirkens (1988).

REFERENCES

Andeweg, Rudy B. (1982). *Dutch Voters Adrift. On Explanations of Electoral Change (1963–1977)*. Leiden: Diss.

Bewogen beweging (1988). Amsterdam: Internal document of the Labour Party.

Bosmans, J. (1990). *Staatkundige Vormgeving in Nederland. Deel II. De Tijd na 1940*. Assen: Van Gorcum.

Commissie C. (1987) *Politiek a la carte in plaats van politiek als dagschotel*. Amsterdam: Internal document of the Labour Party.

Daudt, Hans (1980). "De Ontwikkelingen van de Politieke Machtsverhoudingen in Nederland sinds 1945." In *Nederland na 1945, Beschouwingen over Ontwikkelingen en Beleid*, eds. G. A. Kooy, J. H. de Ru, and H. J. Scheffer. Deventer: Van Loghum Slaterus.

Dittrich, K., J. Cohen, and V. Rutgers (1983). *Het Einde van een Tijdperk. Verslag van de Kabinetsformaties 1981 en 1982*. Maastricht: University of Limburg.

Koole, Ruud A. (1987). "Uiterst Noodzaak en Partijpolitieke Eenwording. Over het Belang van Interne Partijverhoudingen bij Coalitievorming." In *Jaarboek Documentatiecentrum Nederlandse Politieke Partijen 1986* (pp. 99–117). Groningen: University of Groningen.

   (1992). *De Opkomst van de Moderne Kaderpartij. Veranderende Partijorganisatie in Nederland 1960–1990*. Utrecht: Het Spectrum.

Michels, Robert (1911). *Zur Soziologie des Parteiwesens in der Modernen Demokratie: Untersuchungen über die oligarchischen Tendenzen des Gruppenlebens*. Leipzig: Klinkhardt.

Schuivende Panelen: Continuïteit en Vernieuwing in de Sociaal-Democratie (1987). Amsterdam: Internal document of the Labour Party.

Toirkens, J. (1988). *Schijn en Werkelijkheid van het Bezuinigingsbeleid 1975–1986. Een Onderzoek naar de Besluitvorming over Bezuinigen in de Ministerraad en het Gedrag van Individuele Ministers*. Deventer: Kluwer.

6

PARTY BEHAVIOR IN A POLARIZED SYSTEM: THE ITALIAN COMMUNIST PARTY AND THE HISTORIC COMPROMISE

Roberto D'Alimonte

INTRODUCTION

On August 11, 1976, the Italian Communist Party (PCI) decided to abstain in the vote of confidence for the third Andreotti cabinet – a *monocolore* (single-party cabinet) of the Christian Democracy (DC) – thereby making possible the formation of the first government with Communist support since May 1947. This event took place a few weeks after the parliamentary elections (June 20), in which the party had gained a very significant electoral success (Table 6.1). In July 1977, after weeks of negotiations, the PCI signed an agreement for a "common policy program" with the DC, the Socialist Party (PSI), the Social Democratic Party (PSDI), the Republican Party (PRI), and the Liberal Party (PLI). In March 1978, the fourth Andreotti cabinet marked the official participation of the PCI in the parliamentary majority supporting the cabinet – again, a DC *monocolore* – along with DC, PSI, PSDI, and PRI. In January 1979 the PCI withdrew its support from Andreotti, forcing the cabinet to resign. A tripartite cabinet (DC–PRI–PSDI) – Andreotti's fifth – was formed with the PCI in opposition. The PCI has never again been in office.

This is, in brief, the history of the so-called governments of national solidarity. What makes this an interesting case of trade-offs between party goals is that the PCI until 1976 had constantly reaped the electoral benefits of being in opposition; yet, as it shifted from opposition to office, it immediately lost votes and continued to lose them until 1994 (Figure 6.1). My objective in this chapter is to examine the development of PCI choices, to provide a framework within

Table 6.1. *Parliamentary elections: Chamber of Deputies, 1968–1979 (percentage of valid votes)*

	1968	1972	1976	1979
Turnout	92.8	93.2	93.4	90.6
Valid votes	96.4	96.8	97.3	95.9
Blank votes	1.9	1.7	1.5	2.2
Null votes	1.7	1.5	1.2	1.9
DC	39.1	38.7	38.7	38.3
PCI	26.9	27.1	34.4	30.4
PSI	14.5[a]	9.6	9.6	9.8
PSDI	—[a]	5.1	3.4	3.8
PRI	2.0	2.9	3.1	3.0
PLI	5.8	3.9	1.3	1.9
MSI-DN	4.5	8.7	6.1	5.3
PPST	0.5	0.5	0.5	0.5
PSIUP	4.4	1.9		
PR			1.1	3.5
PDUP				1.4
DP			1.5	
Other	2.3	2.5	0.3	2.1

[a] PSI and PSDI joined to form the United Socialist Party (PSU).
Parties: DC, Christian Democracy; PCI, Italian Communist Party; PSI, Italian Socialist Party; PSDI, Italian Socialdemocratic Party; PRI, Italian Republican Party; PLI, Italian Liberal Party; MSI-DN, Italian Social Movement–National Right; PPST, South Tyrol People's Party; PSIUP, Italian Socialist Party of Proletarian Unity; PR, Radical Party; PDUP, Party of Proletarian Unity; DP, Proletarian Democracy.

which to explain why those choices, and not others, were made, and to draw from this case suggestions on how to refine Strøm's theoretical scheme for the analysis of party behavior in advanced parliamentary democracies (Strøm 1990b).

THE PCI AND THE ELUSIVE PURSUIT OF OFFICE

The elections of June 20, 1976, marked the peak of PCI electoral growth (Figure 6.1): the payoff of almost thirty years of opposition. Yet, the party chose to abandon a competitive position vis-à-vis its major adversary – the DC – and adopt instead a cooperative one.[1] Why?

The most immediate answer lies in the *historic compromise* strategy developed by the PCI leadership between 1971 and 1973. The strategy's ultimate goal

Figure 6.1 PCI/PDS electoral trend (Chamber of Deputies), 1946–96. The figure for 1948 is just an estimate since the party ran together with the PSI. The figures for 1992, 1994, and 1996 refer to the Democratic Party of the Left (PDS) that replaced the PCI in 1991. The figures for 1994 and 1996 are based on the votes the party received in the proportional arena.

was a government of broad democratic unity with the participation of the PCI, that is, a coalition government including both the PCI and the DC, along with the other popular forces in order to implement a progressive democracy. The alternative strategy for gaining office, a coalition of the left seeking to gain a majority, was discarded as ineffective and too risky. On this point, Berlinguer (1975: 633), the party secretary, was quite clear: "it would be completely illusory to think that, even if the parties and the political forces of the left succeeded in getting 51% of the votes and of the seats in Parliament (which would certainly be a great step forward in establishing a new equilibrium among the parties in Italy), this result could guarantee the survival and the functioning of a cabinet that were the expression of that 51%."[2]

The historic compromise was a strategy for gaining office in order to implement the policies of a progressive democracy. In this chapter, I show that for the PCI leaders, votes became less important than the pursuit of party alliances and government participation (office). Yet, it is difficult to cast PCI behavior as a conscious choice among conflicting objectives. Actually, PCI leaders saw no conflict and therefore no trade-off, at least in the short run, between votes and office/policies. Indeed, after the public announcement of the new strategy, the party had done consistently well at the polls during the period 1974–6. The PCI leaders attributed this performance to the historic compromise. As long as this causal linkage was accepted, no conflict was perceived between that strategy and the maximization of votes. This is clearly demonstrated by the available documentary evidence. A straightforward electoral strategy for gaining office was discarded because its very success would have been a mixed blessing, given the risk of polarizing the country.

Was this a correct interpretation? Was the electoral growth in 1976 a payoff for the historic compromise? Or were these additional votes given to the PCI because it still represented, or at least appeared to represent, the opposition and the alternative to the long incumbent DC? Clearly, if the correct answer is the first one, the strategy of the historic compromise involved no trade-off between the goal of maximizing votes and that of gaining office. In the second case, however, a potential conflict is inherent in that strategy. Pursuing office *could* cause a future loss of votes out of voter disappointment and disenchantment with a PCI more cooperative than competitive. I think that the PCI leaders did not anticipate a trade-off; they believed instead that the increasing legitimization, sought through the alliance with the DC, combined with the resources of office and the organizational strength of the party, would help it consolidate and even extend its electoral and political gains.

Three days after the elections of June 1976, the PCI directorate unanimously approved a document that clearly restated the party's strategy. The following July, the central committee of the party also approved it. The key question was the end of the *conventio ad excludendum*, the unwritten agreement among the democratic parties to keep the PCI out of government because of its alleged nondemocratic credentials. Gerardo Chiaromonte, a top party leader and the official speaker at the meeting, made this point very clear: "the bias against the PCI must end. Parliament must function correctly and democratically. It is necessary to form a government which, because of its structure, its membership, its program, may enjoy the largest possible support and may act decisively, with the speed that the situation requires."[3]

These official declarations suggest the following:

1. The PCI did not ask for the immediate formation of a cabinet with direct Communist participation. The party was very cautious in this regard, though this was clearly the most important goal. Office was seen as the outcome of a process that *for the benefit of the PCI itself* had to go through "intermediate steps."
2. As a result, the PCI's negotiating strategy can be summed up as a readiness to lend its support to a DC cabinet in exchange for the long-sought relegitimization offered by the end of the anti-Communist bias (the *conventio ad excludendum*) and for the allocation of key parliamentary positions to PCI members.

In sum, the PCI was willing to trade its opposition status (which had been until then a vote-maximizing position) for "a certificate of legitimacy" and a number of "offices" in Parliament that would give the PCI a more influential role. The exchange would be based not on "office" but on "offices": not the full participation in the cabinet, but the presidency of the House and the chairmanships of a number of parliamentary committees. In addition, but clearly a lower priority, the PCI requested that the new cabinet have a more appropriate structure: new members and a satisfactory program.

However, there is no evidence that, at this time, the PCI leadership framed its decision as a conflict between votes and office. No clear evidence existed to suggest that accommodation with the DC would entail in the short or long run a loss of support. The conventional wisdom in the party was the one stated by Chiaromonte (1986: 39): "we (leaders of the party) thought – and we had said it since the Bologna Congress in 1969 – that the political forces that would do more to get the country out of the crisis would be rewarded." This was the view at the top. The agreement, or at least the outward lack of disagreement, was such that no member of the party directorate demanded that the central committee itself make the final decision on whether to abstain on the vote of confidence for the third Andreotti cabinet. Within the party at large, doubts were real and widespread about the wisdom of this choice, in spite of the prestige enjoyed by the party leadership. Activists doubted not only the alliance with the DC, but also the decision to support a DC cabinet without being part of it.

We are left to wonder what would have happened if the PCI had tied its support of Andreotti to its participation in the cabinet. Most likely these demands would have led to new elections and a dramatic polarization of the country. This is precisely what the PCI leaders wanted to avoid. What we do know is that the flexibility of the PCI left the door open for a tentative collaboration with the DC.

The DC position was ambiguous. On the positive side, there was its relative success in the June elections. After all, it was still the largest party, and its percentage of the votes was exactly the same as in the previous election and within its normal range of fluctuation since 1968 (Table 6.1). On the negative side, the party had to reckon with the *unavailability* of most of its historical allies, particularly the PSI, to form or even just to support in Parliament another DC-led cabinet *without* some kind of agreement with the PCI. Even the highly respected leader of the traditionally moderate PRI – Ugo La Malfa senior – spoke of the historic compromise as "inescapable."

Given these party positions, no feasible coalition formula was available that excluded the PCI. As Table 6.2 shows, the center–left coalition (DC–PSI–PSDI–PRI) had 348 votes out of 630 in the Chamber of Deputies. Without the PSI, the coalition would have been far short of the majority, even including the votes of the South Tyrol People's Party (PPST), a moderate Catholic group traditionally close to the DC. Nor would a centrist coalition (DC–PSDI–PRI–PLI) have had a majority. As long as the PSI was excluded, any feasible coalition would have to include the PCI or the Italian Social Movement (MSI), the only party

Table 6.2. *Party seats in the Chamber of Deputies after the election of June 20, 1976*

Christian Democracy (DC)	262
Italian Communist Party (PCI)	228
Italian Socialist Party (PSI)	57
Italian Social Movement (MSI)	35
Italian Social Democratic Party (PSDI)	15
Italian Republican Party (PRI)	14
Proletarian Democracy (DP-PDUP)	6
Italian Liberal Party (PLI)	5
Radical Party (PR)	4
South Tyrol Peoples Party (PPST)	3
Other	1
Total	630

on the far right of the political spectrum. Since no coalition with the MSI was acceptable to the centrist parties, the PSI was the indispensable actor in any coalition with the DC that would exclude the PCI. Note, however, that the PSI was not pivotal in any other feasible coalition without the DC.[4]

Given the position of the PSI, the DC's range of choices was very limited: either some kind of arrangement with the PCI or new elections. The PCI's decision to accept a path to office based on "intermediate steps" made an agreement possible. Between August 6 and August 11, the third Andreotti cabinet – a DC *monocolore* – received its vote of confidence or – better – its vote of "no nonconfidence." In the Chamber of Deputies, out of 605 ballots cast, there were 258 votes in favor (the DC), 44 against (MSI, Radical Party, and Proletarian Democracy), and 303 abstentions (PCI, PSI, PRI, PSDI, PLI). The PCI abstention was crucial.

Before the vote of confidence, the DC had agreed to assign to the PCI a number of important offices, such as the presidency of the Chamber of Deputies and the chairmanships of a number of parliamentary committees (four in both chambers of Parliament). But there is no evidence that the composition of the cabinet and/or its policy program was negotiated with the PCI. Chiaromonte (1986: 33) states this explicitly: "I repeat: there was never, in any moment, a real negotiation between the DC and the parties that abstained and so allowed the parliamentary approval of the Andreotti government. There were contacts between the president of the council of ministers (Andreotti) and the parties: and particularly, there was a meeting with Berlinguer."[5]

The Andreotti cabinet did not please the PCI. Yet, the PCI supported it. The reasons were stated clearly by Berlinguer in his speech in the Chamber at the time of the vote of confidence. Though criticizing the oversized cabinet, its membership, and particularly the "vagueness of its policy program," he claimed that it represented a "new fact": without the PCI there would be no cabinet. "Everybody knows that if we (the PCI) vote against, the cabinet would fall immediately." For the PCI leadership, this public recognition amounted to the end of the anticommunist bias and therefore to a new legitimacy. This was, for the time being, sufficient compensation, and the party leaders never really considered any alternative course of action.

Another important reason behind the PCI decision to abstain on the Andreotti cabinet was related to its desire to help strengthen those groups inside the DC that were supporting Moro's strategy of collaboration with the PCI. According to this line of thinking, this was a necessary condition for gaining office. The problem, however, was that this outcome depended, in turn, on certain developments within the DC, namely, the strenghtening of its left wing (Moro–Zaccagnini).

This outcome depended, in turn, upon Moro's capacity to extract concessions from the PCI in order to please the more conservative groups within his party. Moro considered these concessions (on time, policies, and personnel) necessary for the DC's intraparty negotiations. However, they tended to weaken the PCI because they raised the costs of its strategy of accommodation and so made it more difficult to succeed. In other words, these concessions raised the vote–office trade-off. The greater the concessions, the more likely it was that the PCI would be perceived as subservient to the DC. This was hardly the kind of image that could gain the party votes and the enthusiasm of its rank and file. But the PCI at this time failed to perceive the true costs of this compromise.

Whether or not the PCI leadership fully recognized it (and in our opinion it did not), the plain fact is that in August 1976 the PCI gave up its "asset" as the opposition party par excellence to embark on what it defined "as a new political experiment." As a result, the view of the PCI, for the public and within the party itself, changed: though the party was not in the cabinet, it was seen as a government party. Future trade-offs resulted from this new image, as well as from the impact upon its old and new electorate of the policies it supported in Parliament from then on.

After August 1976 the game shifted from office to policies. Office remained the PCI's most important goal but, having accepted the decision to delay its access to office, the conflict with the DC focused on what policies to pass in the meantime. The office game became a policy game. But, in my opinion, for the PCI the policy game was internal to the office game and in a sense less salient. The PCI connected the two games by assuming that (1) policy *gains* could compensate for the delay in gaining office, and (2) policy *costs* could be kept under control and used as a bargaining tool for further legitimization and eventually full government participation. The majority of the DC, by contrast, aimed at keeping the two games separate: not to trade office participation for policy concessions. At least officially, the DC gave no indication that it would ultimately agree to accept the PCI in office. In the end, the crucial question was simply: how long would the PCI sit in the waiting room or, in the jargon of the day, how long would it remain in midstream?

SHIFTING GOALS: FROM OFFICE TO POLICIES

The policy game was complex and risky for the PCI due to two basic constraints: the precariousness of the economic situation and the escalation of terrorism. With regard to the latter, the party found itself in the position of having to support law-and-order measures that were unpopular among some of its *new* voters who considered them illiberal.

As to the economic constraint, the widespread belief, accepted also by the PCI, was that Italy in the summer of 1976 faced an economic and financial disaster that could only be avoided by a series of deflationary measures to control the price–wage spiral. This predicament posed a serious conflict between different PCI constituencies. Its traditional electorate expected the party's support for the government to bring about the long awaited structural reforms. These represented the core of the party's policy platform and its long-term strategic objective. Moderate parties and voters made up another constituency. They expected instead from the PCI restraint and "responsibility" (i.e., policy concessions) because of the difficult situation. In its quest for re-legitimization, the party felt it could not neglect these latter demands.

The PCI sought a way out of the dilemma by linking deflationary measures and structural reforms. It decided to support the former, provided that (1) the latter were also included in the agenda, and (2) the two kinds of policies were connected in such a way that the former would necessarily result in structural reforms. This was the basic meaning of the "policy of austerity," which became the party line between 1976 and 1977. This policy gained the grudging support of the unions' leadership, particularly the Confederazione Generale Italiana dei Lavoratori (Italian General Confederation of Labor) (CGIL), but it met with lingering opposition from the rank and file of the labor movement.

The problem for the PCI was that deflationary measures have immediate and visible costs, whereas structural reform policies produce benefits that are less visible and in any case deferred in time. They cannot be passed by executive decree; in addition, they are subject to a lengthy and uncertain implementation process through inefficient bureaucratic structures.[6] As a result, the linkage sought by the party was lost. Nor was the party's acceptance of deflationary measures compensated by office gains.

This basic situation did not change even after the so-called programmatic agreement signed in July 1977 by the PCI, DC, PSI, PSDI, PRI, and PLI, the same parties that had supported Andreotti or abstained the previous August. This agreement was a long shopping list of measures that the parties had negotiated as the agenda of the Andreotti cabinet. The document was divided into separate chapters, each dealing with a different set of issues: public order and security, economic policy, regions and local governments, schools and universities, information and national television, and appointments to public offices. As an introduction, there was a "political premise" that summarized the reasons why the parties had agreed to a common program that would be binding for the government. Following an explicit request by the DC, foreign policy remained outside the scope of the agreement. This document was approved by the Chamber of Deputies. No cabinet crisis marked, as the PCI initially had asked, the transition to this second phase of the third Andreotti cabinet. No changes occurred in the structure and composition of the cabinet.

The major difference between the two phases can be stated as follows: in the summer of 1976 the PCI had not negotiated the government program and had abstained on the vote of confidence; in the summer of 1977 the PCI did negotiate a common government program with the other parties and voted in favor in the Chamber of Deputies. So, what was the value of the programmatic agreement for the PCI? The answer is that it represented another intermediate step toward office. Berlinguer spoke of it in the Chamber as "a real step forward," as a "signal," as "an impulse in the direction of solidarity, responsibility and recomposition of the unitary spirit of the popular masses and of the nation," but he also added that "this process of overcoming the anticommunist bias has gone ahead slowly and sometime in contorted and strange ways, not always clear and declared. More progress has been achieved in the realization of agreements at the local and regional level. Now finally we have arrived at a public agreement at the national level among the top leadership of all the constitutional parties. . . . We are not yet at what we call the turning point, that is a cabinet coalition including the two parties of the working class movement. . . . In every phase of our talks with the parties, and in front of the country, we have reaffirmed that this is our principal goal" (Parliamentary Proceedings, Chamber of Deputies, Seventh Legislature, July 14, 1977).

These words show that the PCI considered the common program as another gain in legitimacy and therefore as another step toward office. However, the DC leadership was far from warranting such an interpretation. The DC (or, to be precise, the majority within the party) remained noncommittal on the future developments on which the entire PCI strategy rested. For the DC there was no connection between policies and office; for the PCI, instead, policy cooperation was a step toward cabinet participation.

Before the signing of the programmatic agreement, a few cities and provinces had held local elections in April 1977. This was the first significant electoral test after June 1976. The two most important cases were the provincial elections in Rovigo (in the North) and the communal elections in Castellammare di Stabia (near Naples). The results were mixed for the PCI: it did well in Rovigo but lost badly in Castellammare. The reaction within a large segment of the PCI rank and file was of great concern. Chiaromonte (1986: 76) refers to it as to "one more demonstration of the political uneasiness and of the nervousness existing in the party." Yet, the party leadership did not change its strategy.

The major risk perceived in the summer of 1977 was not a significant loss of support, but rather a failure to obtain the full implementation of the agreement signed in July.

THE EMERGING TRADE-OFF

In the winter of 1977–8 the situation became very difficult for the PCI. The escalation of terrorist activities, the increasing number of strikes, and the unions' statements and demonstrations in favor of a different economic policy (particularly the demonstration in Rome on December 2, 1977, by 100,000 workers in the mechanical industry) increased the cost of the PCI strategy.

At this time, the PCI leadership began to think in terms of an emerging trade-off between votes (support) and office/policies. The threat of a general strike called by the unions against the government accelerated the crisis of the Andreotti cabinet. In a television interview on December 15, Berlinguer explicitly demanded the formation of a cabinet with full Communist participation. The PSI and PRI supported his request. On January 16, 1978, Andreotti resigned. Three days later, the president of the Republic again gave him the mandate to form a new cabinet, which eventually occurred on March 11. Five days later, Moro was kidnapped by the Red Brigades.[7] The fourth Andreotti cabinet was still a cabinet *without* the Communists. The PCI, however, had become an official "member of the parliamentary majority of the government," and as such voted in favor of the motion of confidence, which was hastily approved in Parliament in the aftermath of Moro's kidnapping. The DC, PSI, PSDI, and PRI (but not the PLI) did the same.

The long duration of the cabinet crisis (almost two months) reflects the difficulties encountered. The deadlock between the PCI request to enter the cabinet and the DC refusal was resolved through another byzantine compromise that was more favorable to the DC. The game between the two remained basically a policy game, just as the DC wished. In the office dimension the PCI felt that it had taken one more step toward full cabinet participation, though being a member of the parliamentary majority clearly was not the same thing as being in office. The incremental gain over the previous arrangement was difficult to explain to members and sympathizers.

The PCI leaders rationalized it one more time as a gain in legitimacy and a promise that office at last would be the next step. Yet, the DC failed again to accommodate PCI demands on the structure and composition of the cabinet. Its size (too large) and its membership (the same personnel) were totally disappointing for the PCI. Its structure reflected the balancing of DC factional demands rather than the request of the PCI for a break with the past. When the cabinet was announced, the disappointment of the PCI leadership was so strong that, according to Chiaromonte and others, Berlinguer seriously entertained the idea of voting against it in Parliament (Chiaromonte 1986). Reportedly, only the need to show unity in light of the terrorist challenge convinced the PCI to make the decision it did.

I am skeptical about this interpretation. My guess is that the PCI would have voted in favor regardless. In the spring of 1978, the party leaders were still willing to trade time for policies and a marginal gain on the path to office. What eventually changed their view of this trade-off were events and evidence that emerged after March 1978: the position of the PSI, the results of the elections and referenda of May and June 1978, and the growing opposition within the party. At the end of this cycle of negative developments, policy disagreements became the pretext for the break, as they had previously been for cooperation. The basic point is that the probability of gaining office diminished, whereas the probability of losing support increased.

Under the pressure of unanticipated events, the PCI leadership came to the conclusion that an unfavorable trade-off existed between electoral support and office/policies. On January 26, 1979, Berlinguer announced his party's decision to leave the majority. Five days later, Andreotti resigned. At the same time, the PCI renewed its demand for office, making it clear that it was not negotiable. Specifically, the PCI proposed three solutions to the governmental crisis (see Chiaromonte 1986: 144): (1) that the DC would finally form a cabinet coalition with the PCI; (2) that, failing the previous option, a candidate outside the DC be given the mandate to form a coalition government with all the democratic parties in it; and (3) that, in case the DC refused to join such a cabinet, it at least would agree to give external support to a government formed on the basis of a program of national solidarity and with the largest possible base. None of these options was accepted by the DC; consequently, the PCI returned after two and a half years to opposition. At this point, however, another coalition formula became available: a revised version of the center–left.

I turn now to a closer look at the factors behind the PCI move. I have already discussed the position held by the PSI in the party system. Since the 1950s, a parliamentary majority without the PSI was either too weak, nonexistent, or politically nonviable. Therefore, the PSI refusal after the June 1976 elections to support, even from the outside, another government based on the center–left formula offered the DC no choice but to accept some kind of arrangement with the PCI or to call new elections. After the Moro affair, however, the position of the PSI changed. Actually, the first signs had appeared before March 1978, but only after that date did the PSI begin to differentiate its position from that of the PCI. At the end of this process a new strategy emerged: a renewed coalition with the DC and the other centrist parties without previous agreements with the PCI.

This change stemmed from the consolidation within the PSI of a new leadership and a new political strategy identified with Bettino Craxi, who had become party secretary in July 1976. This new PSI stance weakened the PCI's bargaining power and made it less likely that office could be achieved within a reasonable time span. This was even more the case given the effect of the new

Table 6.3. *Local elections, May 14, 1978: Comparison with parliamentary elections of June 20, 1976*

| | Chamber, June 1976 | | Local elections, May 1978 | |
| | Turnout 91.1% | | Turnout 89.2% | |
Party lists	Valid votes	%	Valid votes	%
DC	855.922	39.0	935.852	42.6
PCI	780.232	35.5	580.584	26.4
PSI	202.680	9.2	291.413	13.3
MSI-DN	155.313	7.1	98.290	4.5
PSDI	72.957	3.3	105.266	4.8
PLI	22.316	1.0	29.509	1.3
PRI	57.382	2.6	70.144	3.2
DP	30.373	1.4	12.568	0.6
PR	15.914	0.7	1.056	0.1
Others	4.224	0.2	74.635	3.2
Total	2.197.313	100.0	2.199.317	100.0

Note: The table includes all the communes that have voted using the proportional electoral system.
Source: Urbani 1979: 180.

position of the PSI on the balance of power within the DC. The left factions (the so-called area Zac) who were still interested in continuing Moro's policy of collaboration with the PCI lost influence vis-à-vis the moderate factions that, with increasing force, demanded the end of that policy.

A second important factor that helped change the PCI's perception of its trade-off was the outcome of the local elections of May 1978 and of the referenda the following month. Recall that the year before, local elections had provided the PCI with mixed (but still worrisome) evidence on its electoral performance. That test was limited, however, to a few towns. The test of May 1978 was more important since it involved about 4 million voters and 816 towns all over the country. Table 6.3 reports the results for all the communes with over 5,000 inhabitants where the proportional electoral system was used. The evidence is clear, particularly if we take into account the fact that in the June 1976 elections the results in these communes were very similar to those at the national level ($r = .96$). The losses for the PCI were very significant. They were also uniform throughout the country: the party lost votes between 1976 and 1978 in 97 percent of the communes where the elections were held in 1978 (Urbani 1979).

Two referenda held the following month provided additional negative signals. In this case, however, the evidence for the PCI was of a different kind. Italian voters were asked to decide whether they wanted to repeal two laws. One

Table 6.4. *Results of the referenda of June 11, 1978*

	Law on the public financing of political parties	"Reale Law"
Turnout	81.4	81.4
Blank ballots and null ballots	6.7	6.2
"No"	56.3	76.7
"Yes"	43.7	23.3

was on the public financing of political parties that had been approved almost unanimously by Parliament in 1974. The second law (called the Reale Law after the minister who proposed it) concerned public order and security, and consisted of a series of restrictive measures adopted in light of the escalation of political terrorism. This law had been approved in 1975 against the wishes of the PCI. Both referenda had been organized by the Radical Party. In spite of its previous stand, the PCI joined the DC, PSI, PRI, and the PSDI in asking its voters to vote in favor of both laws. Table 6.4 shows the results. They were surprising and, for the PCI, very disappointing and worrisome.

In the case of both laws, the option of repeal received far more votes than it should have according to the parliamentary strength of the parties that had campaigned in its favor. Obviously, party discipline had weakened. The PCI worried about this outcome more than the other parties did. The vote was read as a sign of the existence of a diffuse area of opposition that the PCI had failed to represent and that had been mobilized effectively by the Radicals. In short, being in opposition was paying off for the Radicals, particularly among the younger generations of voters, who were a potentially important market for the PCI and who had been a relevant source of support in the 1976 elections.

Here is one significant comment on the events of May–June 1978: "People looked at the comparison with the elections of two years before: and from this point of view the electoral performance of the PCI appeared extremely negative. The shock in the ranks of the Communist Party was widespread. There was among the militants, but also among the upper echelons of the party, a very strong emotional reaction, prompted also by the results of the referendum on the public financing of political parties, which had revealed a worrisome gap between the parties and a large sector of public opinion" (Chiaromonte 1986: 126).

The reaction in the ranks of the party can be understood better by looking at the data drawn from three surveys conducted between 1977 and 1980 to explore the relations between PCI members, militants, and leaders (Barbagli and Corbetta 1982; Barbagli, Corbetta, and Sechi 1979). The most interesting results are summarized in Table 6.5.

Table 6.5. *Attitudes and predictions regarding governmental formulas: Members (1978) and section secretaries of the PCI (1978 and 1980)*

	Members	Section secretaries	
	1978 %	1978 %	1980 %
Government considered "most adequate, most possible, most realistic"			
PCI-PSI-DC	31	20	22
Government of national unity	47	79	69
Government of the left	13	—	8
Government of the PCI alone	5	—	—
Dictatorship of the proletariat	1	—	—
No reply	3	1	1
Total	100	100	100
Government "preferred"			
PCI-PSI-DC	12	36	28
Government of national unity	10	12	10
Government of the left	31	27	45
Government of the PCI alone	37	4	2
Dictatorship of the proletariat	8	19	10
No reply	2	2	5
Total	100	100	100
Predictions of the position of the PCI in five years			
In coalition governments with the DC	50	72	35
In opposition	5	7	30
In a left government	37	10	17
Governing by itself	2	—	—
Clandestine (after a coup)	1	—	—
Other	—	5	5
No reply	5	6	12
Total	100	100	100
Number of cases	(431)	(205)	(205)

Source: Barbagli and Corbetta 1982: 217.

These data seem to show that the historic compromise, and particularly its implementation with the support given to Andreotti's third and fourth governments, was never completely accepted by the rank and file of the party. This resistance, as can be seen from Table 6.5, was stronger among the members (column 1) than among the militants (the section secretaries, columns 2 and 3): only 22 percent of the members preferred a government with the DC (i.e., PCI–PSI–DC or a government of national unity). Moreover, the resistance grew over time even among party secretaries: in 1980 only 38 percent of the section secretaries in the sample still preferred a government with the DC, as opposed to 48 percent in 1978. The authors of that study conclude that "with respect to the PCI's attitude towards the government of the 1976–8 period, it could be said that the position of the leadership and that of the ranks moved steadily apart after the formation of each government, to diminish clearly when the latter entered into crisis" (Barbagli and Corbetta 1982: 216).

I think that the top leadership of the PCI became more and more aware of the tensions existing within the party and of the costs that this implied. These costs are not to be understood as a threat to party unity, but more in terms of their negative consequences for the functioning of the party, the activism of the militants, and the party's capacity for initiative and mobilization (Lange 1980). All of this was also confirmed indirectly by the data on party membership. As Figure 6.2 shows, party membership had declined from 1953 to 1968 but then increased significantly from 1968 to 1976, only to decrease again as soon as the PCI decided to support the governments of national solidarity. This evidence was the more disturbing since the PCI's chances to succeed in its pursuit of office also rested on its capacity to maintain a strong party organization "with a presence in all the arenas of economic, social and political life; a presence that would have to serve to mediate between the demands of potential allies and the members, on the one hand, and the requirements of the party's strategy on the other" (Lange 1979: 701–2).

At the end of 1978 the PCI leadership concluded that the costs of supporting the Andreotti cabinet outweighed its benefits. These costs, as I have shown, are primarily to be measured in terms of a serious degeneration of the party's relations with its members, its older electoral constituencies, and its new potential voters. At the same time, the probability of gaining office in a coalition with the DC declined as a result of changing attitudes and strategies by the PSI and the DC. In this light, the decision to put an end to the collaboration with the DC can be interpreted both as a stop-loss move and as a shift in priorities. Votes became more important because office was more elusive. Indeed, the PCI did lose a significant number of votes in the parliamentary elections of 1979, but not as many as its leaders had feared and other observers had expected. The winner of those elections was the Radical Party, which was clearly identified with the referenda of 1978 and with adamant opposition to the historic compromise and the governments of national solidarity (Table 6.1).

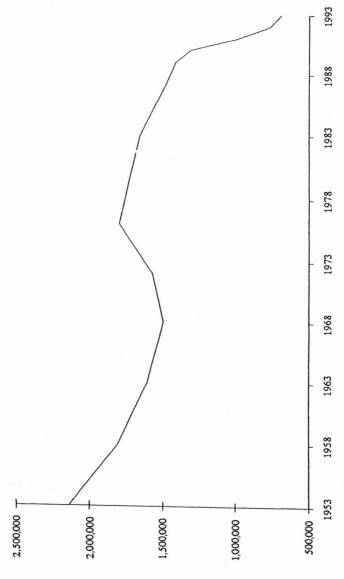

Figure 6.2 PCI/PDS membership trend (1953–93) (absolute values). After 1990 the figures refer to the PDS.

PCI CHOICES: A LEXICOGRAPHIC EXPLANATION

What has emerged in the preceding pages is not yet a satisfactory answer to the question with which I started: why did the PCI in 1973, in 1976, and again in 1978 choose a cooperative strategy instead of a competitive one? The question is not about goals, but about strategies. As I have shown, the dominant party goal in the period considered was office, or, it could also be said, legitimization through office. This goal, however, could have been achieved through different strategies. This point leads to a general argument: the calculus of trade-offs between party goals cannot be done separately from that of the electoral and coalitional strategies parties adopt. Hence, goals (and therefore trade-offs) cannot be analyzed independently of strategies. *Different strategies to pursue the same goal yield a different set of trade-offs.*

In the case of the PCI, the choice of office was linked with the choice of a cooperative strategy predicated on a coalitional alliance with the DC: the historic compromise. This was not the only conceivable strategy. The alternative option would have been the pursuit of office through a competitive strategy aimed at replacing, not joining, the major incumbent party. However, the choice of the latter (what Berlinguer himself labeled as the "51 percent strategy") would have required the PCI to redefine drastically its position within the party system.

The structure of the party system is the variable I examine in this final section. First, I treat the party system as an independent variable to show how its structure, and the PCI view of it, has shaped the available electoral and coalitional strategies. Second, I treat the party system as a dependent variable in order to argue that the range of available strategies could have been redefined by the PCI if it had decided to change its position in the system. Finally, I argue that the PCI choice not to redefine its position to the extent required to change the structure of the system was also based on a trade-off between office/votes/policies and the goal of maintaining certain features of the party identity – an *identity core* – in order to preserve party unity.

The party system is not a variable explicitly called for in Strøm's unified theory of party behavior, though some of the features of the party system are included in what Strøm (1990b) calls *institutional factors* (i.e., the distribution of bargaining power generated by a particular party system). I believe that the structure of the party system is an important independent determinant of party behavior. This structure is based on a number of factors. Here I consider specifically the dimensionality of the political space, the position of different parties and different sets of voters in the space, and the distance separating parties and voters.

Following Sartori's typology, the Italian party system has traditionally been included in the category of polarized pluralism (Sartori 1976). In the 1970s this model explained well the nature of party competition in Italy. The Sartorian model of polarized pluralism assumes *ideological distance* as the major explanatory factor. This distance is defined in terms of a unidimensional space of competition. The distance between extreme parties in this space is used to classify party systems as more or less polarized (Sani and Sartori 1983).[8]

The assumption of unidimensionality is misleading and unnecessarily restrictive. A different model of polarized pluralism can be developed based on the assumption of a multidimensional political space (D'Alimonte 1978). This model, which I call the *lexicographic model of polarized pluralism*, helps explain better not only PCI choices but also essential features of Italian electoral and coalitional politics. In my model, the political space within which Italian parties and voters made their choices was bounded by three dimensions: left–right, system–anti-system, and religion.[9] The first dimension needs no explanation. Its relevance in the Italian case is well documented (Barnes 1977; Mastropaolo and Slater 1987; Sani 1977b; Sani and Sartori 1983). The religious dimension is necessary to explain the connection between the DC and Catholic voters and the distance between lay and confessional parties.

The most important dimension is the second. This is the one that I use here in conjunction with the left–right continuum. The second dimension of Italian politics captures the perception that certain parties were not considered to be fully legitimate. Survey evidence about the popular image of Italian parties shows that the majority of the voters, as well as the moderate parties, have considered the PCI and the MSI different or distant, not only because of their positions on the left–right dimension, but also because of their degree of acceptance of the rules of the game. In other words, they were perceived in some ways as anti-system (Marradi 1978; Sani 1973, 1975b).[10] This distance, however, cannot be squeezed into a single dimension by "stretching" the left–right space (Sartori 1976: 343), nor it can be treated simply as a discontinuity of the political space.

If we combine the left–right dimension with the system–anti-system one, we have the political space shown in Figure 6.3. This space is actually split into two subspaces divided by the line LT, which represents a *legitimacy threshold*: parties perceived to be on this line were viewed as fully legitimate actors in the system, whereas parties below the line were seen as anti-system.

The position of the PCI in Figure 6.3 (as well as that of the DC) has been defined on the basis of the evidence on the popular image of the party (see Marradi 1978; Sani 1973; Sani and Sartori 1983). Specifically, this was the view of the PCI held by centrist voters and parties.[11] To be sure, the PCI was not considered as an anti-system party by *all* noncommunist parties and voters. There were certainly parties and voters that, though not sympathetic to the PCI, did not think of it as a nondemocratic party. However, there are two points that need to be stressed here: (1) the number of those holding a negative view of the PCI was high enough to make the Italian system polarized, and (2) even those noncommunist actors who did not believe the PCI was a threat to democracy were not willing to vote for or ally themselves with it without a general

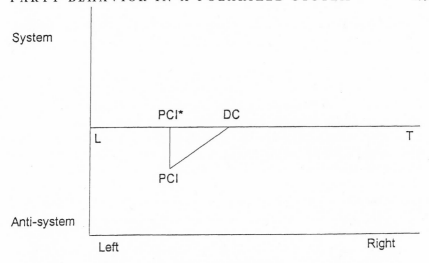

Figure 6.3 A simplified representation of the Italian political space in the 1970s.

consensus on its nature and its ultimate goals. This perception was not entirely subjective. In fact, in the 1970s, there were still enough elements of ambiguity in the PCI positions to substantiate the claim that the party had not yet completed its process of ideological revision.

In order to understand the behavior of the PCI during the 1970s, it is also important to ask whether the party viewed its position in the system as described in Figure 6.3. My answer is yes. Of course, this is not to say that the PCI considered itself as an anti-system party. It simply means that it considered the party system polarized. While it rejected strongly any notion that it was a nondemocratic party, it maintained a view of the system based exactly on that notion. This is why its choice of goals and strategies was profoundly influenced by that view.

To complete the model of polarized pluralism, it is necessary to specify analytically the behavior of the parties and voters whose spatial location is on the line LT. My hypothesis is that the voting and coalitional preferences of these actors were lexicographic. I specifically exclude a Euclidean type of preference.[12] Centrist voters and centrist parties would not consider voting for or allying themselves with the PCI, *no matter what the position of the PCI was on the left–right dimension,* unless the party was located on the legitimacy threshold.

There are two related and important implications of the lexicographic hypothesis: (1) the PCI could expect no gain, either in terms of votes or in terms of coalitional partners, by staying in the position shown in Figure 6.3; (2) as long as the PCI was perceived as anti-system, the party system would remain noncompetitive since centrist voters and parties would not switch their voting and coalitional choices in favor of the PCI and away from the DC, no matter how much they disliked the latter.

Given this structure of the party system, the PCI had the following strategic options:

1. Stay put in the political space; the party could choose to maintain fundamentally its ideological identity and its organizational pattern (democratic centralism) without seeking any form of positive integration in the system. I call this the *conservative strategy*; given the assumptions of the lexicographic model of polarized pluralism, this strategy was not compatible with the goal of maximizing office or votes.
2. Complete its process of ideological revision and move to any position on the legitimacy threshold (point PCI* in Figure 6.3); this strategy would remove the lexicographic factor and therefore would have been compatible with both office and vote maximization; I label this the *social democratic strategy*.
3. Gradually revise its ideological beliefs and its organizational pattern and move either along the PCI–PCI* path or the PCI–DC path (see Figure 6.3). Given the assumptions of the lexicographic model of polarized pluralism, this strategy would not have helped the PCI maximize office or votes unless we assume that the closer the PCI got to the legitimacy threshold, the more likely it would be that voters and parties would switch to Euclidean behavior; this strategy is close to the "via italiana al socialismo" (the Italian way to socialism), but I will call it here the *revisionist strategy* or, alternatively, the *mixed strategy*.

These options characterize the political history of the PCI. Since the Second World War the PCI has shifted from strategy 1 to strategy 3, only to adopt strategy 2 between 1989 and 1991 with its decision to transform itself into a new party, the Democratic Party of the Left (PDS) (see Ignazi 1992). More specifically, in the first years of the postwar period, the party chose to maintain a double image: that of a Marxist party willing to work within democratic institutions. Later on, it started to reconcile this fundamental ambiguity by revising elements of its ideology (the revisionist strategy). Only in 1991 did it complete its process of ideological revision.

Throughout this period, the party was excluded from government participation but was never really excluded from legislative influence (Cazzola 1972; Di Palma 1977). A number of institutional features of the Italian parliamentary system, along with the ambiguity intrinsic in what Di Palma (1977) has called the *uncertain compromise*, allowed the party to pursue a policy-making strategy successfully even from opposition. Among these features are the number, the role, and the working rules of standing committees; the freedom of individual members of Parliament to initiate legislation and to introduce amendments; and the widespread use of the secret ballot (Manzella 1992; Strøm 1990a). This institutional context has given the PCI a significant degree of "oppositional influence" (Strøm 1990a), and it has decreased its motivation to seek office.

In addition, this strategy has paid a handsome electoral dividend (Figure 6.1): from 1946 to 1972 the party gained 8.2 percent of the national vote (Chamber of Deputies). Actually, the electoral performance of the party during this period calls into question the validity of the lexicographic hypothesis. If this hypothesis were correct, the party *could not* have made electoral gains, and therefore the argument I have developed here would be invalid.

To reconcile PCI electoral trends with the lexicographic hypothesis, we have to look at *where* the PCI gained votes, that is, at the spatial location of the additional votes. Very clear evidence shows that these gains were made at the expense of the PSI. Throughout the postwar period and up to 1972, the correlation between PCI gains and PSI losses is significant.[13] Such evidence suggests that the electoral volatility that benefited the PCI was *within the Marxist–socialist bloc.* Within such a bloc, which corresponds to one of the two historical subcultures in the country, the lexicographic hypothesis did not apply. Socialist voters did not see the PCI in the same way as voters outside the Marxist–socialist bloc did. To falsify the lexicographic hypothesis at the electoral level, we have to look at *between-blocs volatility* (Bartolini and Mair 1990).[14] Here, however, the image of the PCI represented an insurmountable barrier.

The election of 1972 is very significant in supporting this argument. In spite of the very high level of social and political mobilization of the "hot fall,"[15] the PCI gained influence but not votes. Actually, it was the extreme right that benefited electorally, with the MSI scoring its greatest postwar success up to then (8.7 percent of the votes for the Chamber of Deputies). It is no coincidence that the following year, Berlinguer formally announced that the PCI was ready to assume "government responsibility" (office goal) through the historic compromise (cooperative strategy). The logic of strategic interparty behavior prevailed over a purely electoral calculus. Major gains in votes were considered unlikely, whereas the growth in bargaining power had been substantial. Under these conditions, the decision to seek office appeared reasonable.

So, the combination of the poor electoral performance of his party in 1972 and the threat of a conservative backlash pushed Berlinguer to redefine the party's goals. In 1973 office became a priority, both as a goal in itself and as a means to achieve other goals (full democratic legitimization, the consolidation of an antifascist bloc, the implementation of the so-called structural reforms). But the choice of the goal was closely intertwined with the choice of the strategy. What remains to be explained is why cooperation was chosen instead of competition.

As I have stressed before, Berlinguer was well aware that office could be pursued through two possible strategies, and he outlined them clearly in his writings for *Rinascita* (Berlinguer 1975). He discarded a competitive strategy on the ground that it would have polarized the country. This analysis was plausible, *given the position and the image of the PCI at that time*. But why not change the position?

The answer, in my opinion, lies in the conflict between the goal of reaching office through the social democratic strategy and the goal of maintaining the identity and unity of the party. Berlinguer explained this point retrospectively. On July 2, 1979, speaking to the central committee of the party, he responded to the critics of the historic compromise by denying once again the feasibility of the 51 percent strategy. According to him, such a strategy would have required accepting the PSI demands for a social democratic transformation of the PCI. "But if we moved in this direction," he said "the PCI would lose every trace of its intellectual and political autonomy, it would give up that very peculiarity which defines it as a party that wants to strive and does strive for the realization of socialism. . . . Socialdemocracies are one thing, and we are another, and so we have to remain: we have to develop, to be sure, our ideas, but always within a non-socialdemocratic, but communist framework" (Berlinguer 1979: 91).

These words reflect the bitterness of the recent break with the DC, but they also reveal a deep-seated problem within the party. The resistance to a social democratic transformtion was real and significant. We can assess its strength after the fact. When in 1991 the transformation did occur, the PCI split into two parties: the PDS and the Communist Refoundation (RC). In the first political elections after the split (1992), RC gained 5.6 percent of the votes in the Chamber, and in the 1994 elections it got 6.0 percent (Chamber, proportional votes).

Given this ideological constraint and the unwillingness of the leaders to remove it, the PCI decided to trade marginal/gradual changes on the system–anti-system dimension for office, but it refused to trade the total/sudden change of party identity for office.[16] The trade-off appeared to be between office and identity, but it was also between office and party unity. For Berlinguer, the way out of this unpalatable dilemma was the historic compromise. Whatever the other reasons for it, this compromise was instrumental in gaining office without having to face the changes required to remove the lexicographic factor. In other words, the party would be legitimized as a governmental party without having to give up its core identity, at least in the short run. The coalition with the DC would resolve the dilemma posed by the conflict between potentially irreconcilable goals.

To sum up, I have argued that the choice of goals by the PCI was influenced in 1973 by the following interdependent factors:

1. The lexicographic polarization of the party system.
2. The costs to the PCI in terms of party unity of the social democratic strategy.
3. The limited electoral competitiveness measured in interbloc volatility.

What happened after 1973 seemed to validate Berlinguer's strategy. I argue, however, that the PCI misread the changes to the party system. In my opinion, PCI behavior after 1973 is a textbook example of the failure to perceive party system changes and therefore to adapt party strategy accordingly.

Three events marked the electoral scene: the divorce referendum in 1974, the regional elections in 1975, and the parliamentary elections in 1976. The outcome of each was a success for the PCI. The PCI was the major party of the victorious prodivorce alignment; it won the elections in 1975, becoming the largest party in most metropolitan areas; and it gained 34.4 percent of the vote in the Chamber in 1976 compared to 27.1 percent in the previous parliamentary elections in 1972. What these events show is that electoral volatility had increased significantly in this period and that the PCI was a beneficiary of the increased competitiveness of the system. At this point it could have expected a shift in party goals (from office to votes) and consequently in party strategy (from cooperation to competition vis-à-vis the DC). This change, however, did not occur. But before I analyze why, it is necessary to take a closer look at the election of 1976.

Does the electoral success of the PCI mean that the structure of the party system had drastically changed? In my opinion, important changes had occurred in the electoral market, but the system still remained polarized to a significant degree: many voters still viewed the PCI as a party of dubious legitimacy. Yet, where did the new PCI voters come from? According to Giacomo Sani (1975a, 1977a, 1977b), two factors explain the PCI electoral growth: (1) the generational turnover that had benefited the party because of the greater presence of left-leaning voters among the younger generations and (2) the amount of vote switching from the moderate bloc to the PCI due to the new image of the PCI and the decline of the anticommunist bias.

This explanation is convincing.[17] However, there is a complementary hypothesis that needs to be taken into account. The system–anti-system dimension of Italian politics no longer worked as effectively as it had beforehand because another dimension had become salient for a segment of the voting population: the government–opposition cleavage. Certain voters seem to have based their electoral choices on the location of parties on this cleavage. This *incumbency factor* entered Italian politics in the mid-seventies. Since then, it has produced a fundamental restructuring of the party system and the underlying political space.[18]

The PCI in the pre-1976 period was the opposition party par excellence and could therefore capitalize on the anti-incumbent vote. The strategy of the historic compromise had not yet modified the popular perception of the PCI as the major antagonist of the DC. What I want to emphasize here is that this new dimension "compressed" the system–anti-system one to the point where certain voters switched to Euclidean behavior: they were willing to accept a trade-off between the two. The plausibility of this hypothesis is enhanced if we take into account that the changes in the PCI image in the mid-seventies had blurred its anti-system connotation given its proximity to the legitimacy threshold. Sani's data tend to support this hypothesis, though his analytical framework is different from mine.[19]

This development presented the PCI with an opportunity and a risk at the same time. The opportunity lay in the fact that the new dimensionality of the political space increased electoral volatility, and this, in turn, increased the potential payoff for an outright opposition strategy aimed at further maximizing votes. This option corresponds to one of the hypotheses on party behavior suggested by Strøm and Müller in Chapter 1 of this volume. The risk was connected to the unresolved question of the legitimization of the party. In spite of the electoral breakthrough in 1975–6, the PCI was well aware of the opposition its image still had among important segments of the Italian electorate, not to mention foreign actors. In other words, the PCI leadership recognized that the party system was still polarized. Therefore, it turned out to be more frightened by the risk than attracted by the opportunity. Under the new circumstances shown by the electoral results of 1975–6, we could have expected the PCI to reassess the historic compromise strategy developed in 1972–3 within a very different context. There is no evidence that any reassessment toke place. Why?

I think that the PCI leadership held to its previous decision for these reasons:

1. It considered the electoral gains to be a consequence of the strategic choice made. In other words, the gains were seen as a function of the historic compromise, not of other variables (the changed dimensionality of the political space), as I have suggested.
2. It was concerned about its own success. The strategy of the historic compromise became a self-fulfilling prophecy: the choice of this strategy was predicated exactly on the need to avoid a dramatic confrontation between left and right, but the very success of the PCI risked an exacerbation of tensions, fears, and a possible backlash against which the PCI saw no other remedy than to speed up the strategy of supporting DC-led cabinets to balance the centrifugal pulls of the party system.
3. It did not recognize the potential conflict between gaining office through cooperation with the DC, on the one hand, and the expectations of old and new party members and voters on the other. The failure to take into account the salience of the new dimension of Italian politics – the incumbency factor – has much to do with this oversight.
4. It did not want to face the hard choice of changing entirely the foundations of party ideology and party organization.

Whatever the merits of this explanation, the fact is that the PCI held to its office-seeking goal through a cooperative strategy. The rest of the story is described in the first part of this chapter. The follow-up is today's history.

CONCLUSION

The structure of the party system shapes party choices. Parties are not free to pursue whatever goal the leadership might prefer. The party system restricts these choices and influences the trade-offs among them. At the same time, it cannot be treated only as an exogenous variable. The party system itself is determined by the choices parties make.

The case I have analyzed here shows that Strøm's analysis of the factors that influence parties' choice of goals has to be extended beyond organizational and institutional determinants (which still are clearly quite relevant) to include *directly* the structure of the party system. Besides this, two other points seem relevant for refining what Strøm (1990b) calls a "unified theory of party behavior."

The first has to do with the question of party objectives. Policies, office, and votes don't exhaust the list of party goals. At least one more has to be added: the maintenance of party unity (Sjöblom 1968). In a very substantial sense, the hardest choice parties have to make are those that entail a threat to their survival. Very often these choices involve a drastic change in fundamental aspects of the party historical identity. This was clearly the case for the PCI.

The second point deals with party strategies. To what extent is it possible to distinguish between goals and strategies? Precisely what is the interrelationship between goals and strategies? In the case of two-party systems, the question is relatively simple. A party that wants to maximize its chance to gain office has to win enough votes and seats to control the executive. But in multiparty systems things are quite different. To gain office, parties may have more than one strategy. Here the logic of interparty strategic behavior, as Strøm (1990b) points out, is a crucial determinant. This is particularly true in party systems characterized by multidimensional political spaces, since the number of dimensions increases the strategic opportunities available. This is why the structure of the party system is an important variable in a theory of party behavior.

The case I have analyzed here exemplifies both points well. The real trade-off the PCI faced in the seventies was between two different strategies. Both could have gained the party office. The first, which I have labeled the social democratic strategy, required the transformation of the party and the elimination of the lexicographic factor. In this case, political legitimization would have been the result of internal changes in party identity and organization. This strategy would have transformed the party system to a nonpolarized, potentially competitive structure. The second strategy was the historic compromise. With this strategy, office would have been achieved through a grand coalition and a process of external legitimation (legitimation through the alliance with the DC). My argument is that the PCI leadership chose the latter strategy because the former entailed a trade-off between office and party unity.

However, another set of trade-offs, not clearly anticipated, was hidden in the strategy of the historic compromise. First, there was a trade-off between office/legitimation and policies. The pursuit of office, even in the awkward form inaugurated with the third Andreotti cabinet, was "paid" for with the support given to a set of moderate policies that were very unpopular with the major constituencies of the party. The structural reforms that the party demanded in return did not compensate for these costs. The second trade-off was between office and votes. New and potential voters alike were put off by a strategy based on the alliance with the DC. The PCI failed to capture the emergence of a new, distinctive cleavage in Italian politics: the government–opposition one. This cleavage had also a lexicographic nature: a subset of voters wanted to remove the incumbents from office, *no matter what*. They failed to grasp, or were not interested in, the intellectual subtleties of the historic compromise. The third trade-off was between office and party support. Party mobilization and party membership, as we have seen, increased before 1976 and declined soon afterward.

If this analysis is correct, it was not office per se that set the trade-offs the PCI faced. They were actually set by the decision to pursue office through a coalition with the major incumbent party. This decision was based on the objective of maintaining fundamental traits of the party's identity and avoiding major risks to party unity. This case, then, raises the following general point: the calculus of trade-offs between party goals cannot be done independently of the electoral and coalitional strategies parties choose. Different strategies to pursue the same goal may yield a different set of trade-offs. These strategies, in turn, also depend on the structure of the party system. In a given party system, each party has certain strategies that are a function of its position in the system, its relations with other parties, and the image other actors have of it. A party may or may not be able to change its position and influence its image. This capacity depends at least in part on its willingness to trade off internal objectives (i.e., identity/unity/mobilization) for external ones (i.e., office/votes/policy). This seems to us one of the lessons to be drawn from the behavior of the PCI in the seventies.

NOTES

1. In this context we define as competitive a type of behavior that aims to replace in government the major incumbent party (parties); a cooperative strategy, by contrast, is one based on seeking a coalitional agreement with the major incumbent party (parties) in order to govern together. From this definition, it follows that a party is competitive vis-à-vis another if it pursues a strategy such that both cannot simultaneously belong to a government coalition.
2. Among the articles written by Berlinguer on the historic compromise, the most important are those published in *Rinascita* (the weekly magazine of the

PCI) between September 28 and October 12, 1973. Here he systematically outlined the strategy of the party and its rationale. These articles can be found in the collection edited by A. Tato and published as *La questione comunista* (1975).

3. Chiaromonte (1986) is an important history of the period. There are a number of other relevant books on the historic compromise written by PCI leaders (Berlinguer 1979; Di Giulio and Rocco 1979; Napolitano 1979). On the same subject see also Hellman (1977), Tarrow (1981), La Palombara (1981), Gismondi (1986), and Vacca (1987).

4. After the 1976 election a majoritarian coalition in the House without the DC (and without the MSI) would have had to include PCI, PSI, PSDI, PRI, and at least one of these parties: PLI, PR, or DP-PDUP (see Table 6.2). Such a coalition was not feasible because of the unavailability of some of these parties, including the PCI.

5. Andreotti himself (1981) has given an account of the byzantine process that led to the formation of his Cabinet.

6. The problem was discussed by PCI leaders as "the policy of the two stages." For a thorough analysis, see Vacca (1987). The legislative output of the governments of national solidarity is examined in Cazzola (1982).

7. Aldo Moro was at the time the president of the DC (the secretary was Zaccagnini). He was the leading DC spokesperson of the policy of opening to the PCI and the architect of the compromise that made possible the formation of the fourth Andreotti Cabinet.

8. The concept is operationalized as "the distance between any two groups of partisans, as measured by the (absolute) difference between their mean self-locations divided by the theoretical maximum, which, on the left-right scale in question, is 9" (Sani and Sartori 1983: 321).

9. Even though I cannot discuss the role of religion in the Italian elections here, I feel that it must be treated as a separate dimension of the political space. It cannot be considered only as a domain of identification, as Sani and Sartori (1983) do. Though parties do not compete on the religious dimension, it affects the overall pattern of electoral competitiveness in the party system. The argument is fundamentally analogous to the one developed here regarding the system–anti-system dimension. For details see D'Alimonte (1987).

10. Based on a survey conducted in Italy in the mid-seventies on the mass images of the PCI and the DC, Marradi (1978: 103) concludes that the view of the PCI is characterized by a "perception of a position still not clear and satisfactory of that party on the issue of liberty (which instead is indicated by the respondents as the main, almost unique advantage, of the DC). Such perception in various shades is shown by one young respondent out of four and by one adult out of three. More than half of this group of respondents speaks in clear-cut terms and often through stereotypes of a totalitarian, dictatorial nature." This perception of the PCI is the basis of what we referred to earlier as the *conventio ad excludendum*, the pact among the democratic parties not to include the PCI in any government coalition.

11. I use the term center here in a loose sense to define the location of voters and parties between the PCI and the MSI, the two largest extreme parties on the left–right dimension. For a detailed analysis of the concept see Daalder (1984).

12. These concepts are used in voting models based on rational choice theory. For a formal, but not too technical explanation, see Enelow and Hinich (1984).

13. This is true particularly in northern and central Italy, where the socialist subculture was more embedded. See Galli (1968) and Tarrow (1967).

14. Interbloc volatility is the net electoral interchange occurring between blocs of parties in two consecutive elections. The parties are grouped in blocs according to some relevant characteristics. If we take class as such a characteristic in our case and group together the PCI, the PSI, and other, smaller left parties, we can see that the electoral size of this bloc did not change significantly in the period 1946–72. See also Martinotti (1978).

15. I refer to the period 1968–9. This period was characterized by an intense and sustained cycle of worker and student protests with a strong ideological component (see Tarrow 1989).

16. There is an interesting episode that helps us understand the difficulties and the hesitations of the PCI leadership in changing the identity of the party. Just before the elections of June 20, 1976, Berlinguer was interviewed by G. Pansa for the *Corriere della Sera*, at that time the most influential daily newspaper in Italy. In this interview, Berlinguer not only affirmed that he did not wish to see Italy out of NATO, but went on to say that he "felt more secure being on this side." When the interview was published in the PCI daily *L'Unità*, this statement did not appear – a clear example of different statements for different audiences.

17. Subsequent developments have not borne out Sani's hypothesis that the electoral changes of the mid-seventies would lead to the rise of the electoral hegemony of the left. Yet, his analysis of voting shifts remains valid. On this and related topics see also Martinotti (1978) and Barbagli, Corbetta, and Schadee (1990).

18. The relevance of this cleavage has become very clear since 1992 with the judicial investigations for political corruption involving many politicians, particularly those from the PSI and the DC (the two major governmental parties of the old system). The dramatic collapse of these two parties has coincided with the rise of new and old parties that have captured support precisely on the basis of their being perceived as "out of the system" (i.e., not connected to the old government establishment). I refer here to the winners of the parliamentary elections of March 1994: Forza Italia, Lega Nord, and Alleanza Nazionale–MSI.

19. This interpretation does not contradict our hypothesis that there were many voters in the mid-seventies who still perceived the PCI as anti-system. On this point see Marradi's (1978) data from the same period, cited previously. For this reason, I disagree with Leonardi (1978) when he says that the party system was no longer polarized and had in fact become deradicalized. Putting together Marradi's and Leonardi's data, my conclusion is that the PCI was successful in being perceived as a *more* moderate party on the left–right dimension, though not able to dispel the remaining ambiguity about its position on the issue of liberty (the second dimension). However, this move of the party toward the center may be one of the factors explaining the shift of some voters from lexicographic to Euclidean behavior.

REFERENCES

Andreotti, Giulio (1981). *Diari 1976–1979*. Milano: Rizzoli.

Barbagli, Marzio, Piergiorgio Corbetta, and Hans Schadee (1990). *Le elezioni in Italia*. Bologna: Il Mulino.

and Piergiorgio Corbetta (1982). "After the Historic Compromise: A Turning Point for the PCI." *European Journal of Political Research* 10, 3: 213–39.

Barbagli, Marzio, Piergiorgio Corbetta, and Salvatore Sechi (1979). *Dentro il PCI*. Quaderni dell'Istituto Cattaneo. Bologna: Il Mulino.

Barnes, Samuel H. (1977). *Representation in Italy. Institutionalized Tradition and Electoral Choice*. Chicago: University of Chicago Press.

Bartolini, Stefano and Peter Mair (1990). *Identity, Competition and Electoral Availability. The Stabilization of European Electorates 1885–1985*. Cambridge: Cambridge University Press.

Berlinguer, Enrico (1975). *La questione comunista*, Vol. 2. Roma: Editori Riuniti.

(1979). *La nostra lotta dalla opposizione verso il governo*. Roma: Editori Riuniti.

Cazzola, Franco (1972). "Consenso e opposizione nel parlamento italiano. Il ruolo del PCI dalla I alla IV legislatura." *Rivista Italiana di Scienza Politica* 2, 1: 71–96.

(1982). "La solidarietá nazionale dalla parte del Parlamento." *Laboratorio Politico* 2/3: 36–52.

Chiaromonte, Gerardo (1986). *Le scelte della solidarietá democratica. Cronache, ricordi e riflessioni sul triennio 1976–1979*. Roma: Editori Riuniti.

Daalder, Hans (1984). "In Search of the Center of European Party Systems." *American Political Science Review* 78, 1: 92–109.

D'Alimonte, Roberto (1978). "Competizione elettorale e rendimento politico: il caso italiano." *Rivista Italiana di Scienza Politica* 8, 3: 457–493.

(1987). "Competizione politica e sistemi di partito." In *Politica e economia* (pp. 47–67), ed. Giuliano Urbani. Milano: Franco Angeli.

Di Giulio, Fernando and E. Rocco (1979). *Un ministro ombra si confessa*. Milano: Rizzoli.

Di Palma, Giuseppe (1977). *Surviving without Governing*. Berkeley: University of California Press.

Enelow, James M. and Melvin J. Hinich (1984). *The Spatial Theory of Voting: An Introduction*. Cambridge: Cambridge University Press.

Galli, Giorgio (ed.). (1968). *Il comportamento elettorale in Italia*. Bologna: Il Mulino.

Gismondi, Arturo (1986). *Alle soglie del potere. Storia e cronaca della solidarietá nazionale: 1976–1979*. Milano: Sugarco Edizioni.

Ignazi, Piero (1992). *Dal PCI al PDS*. Bologna: Il Mulino.

Hellman, Stephen (1977). "The Longest Campaign: Communist Party Strategy and the Elections of 1976." In *Italy at the Polls, 1976* (pp. 155–82), ed. Howard R. Penniman. Washington, DC: American Enterprise Institute.

Lange, Peter (1979). "Il PCI e i possibili esiti della crisi italiana." In *La crisi italiana* (pp. 657–718), eds. Luigi Graziano and Sidney Tarrow. Torini: Einaudi.

(1980). "Crisis and Consent, Change and Compromise: Dilemmas of Italian Communism in the 1970s." In *Italy in Transition* (pp. 110–32), eds. Peter Lange and Sidney Tarrow. London: Frank Cass.

La Palombara, Joseph (1981). "Two Steps Forward, One Step Back: The PCI's Struggle for Legitimacy." In *Italy at the Polls, 1979* (pp. 104–40), ed. Howard R. Penniman. Washington, DC: American Enterprise Institute.

Leonardi, Roberto (1978). "Polarizzazione e convergenza nel sistema politico italiano." In *La politica nell'Italia che cambia* (pp. 299–319), eds. Alberto Martinelli and Gianfranco Pasquino. Milano: Feltrinelli.

Manzella, Andrea (1992). *Il Parlamento*. Bologna: Il Mulino.

Marradi, Alberto (1978). "Immagini di massa della DC e del PCI." In *La politica nell'Italia che cambia* (pp. 66–103), eds. Alberto Martinelli and Gianfranco Pasquino. Milano: Feltrinelli.

Martinotti, Guido (1978). "Le tendenze dell'elettorato italiano." In *La politica nell'Italia che cambia* (pp. 37–65), eds. Alberto Martinelli and Gianfranco Pasquino. Milano: Feltrinelli.

Mastropaolo, Alfio and Martin Slater (1987). "Italy 1946–1979: Ideological Distances and Party Movements." In *Ideology, Strategy and Party Change: Spatial Analyses of Post-War Election Programmes in 19 Democracies* (pp. 345–65), eds. Ian Budge, David Robertson, and Derek Hearl. Cambridge: Cambridge University Press.

Napolitano, Giorgio (1979). *In mezzo al guado*. Roma: Editori Riuniti.

Sani, Giacomo (1973). "La strategia del PCI e l'elettorato italiano." *Rivista Italiana di Scienza Politica* 3, 3: 531–79.

(1975a). "Ricambio elettorale e identificazioni partitiche: verso una egemonia delle sinistre?" *Rivista Italiana di Scienza Politica* 5, 3: 516–44.

(1975b). "Mass Constraints on Political Realignment: Perceptions of Anti-System Parties in Italy." *British Journal of Political Science* 6, 1: 1–31.

(1977a). "Le elezioni degli anni '70: Terremoto o evoluzione?" *Rivista Italiana di Scienza Politica* 6, 2: 261–88.

(1977b). "The Italian Electorate in the Mid-1970s: Beyond Tradition?" In *Italy at the Polls, 1976* (pp. 81–122), ed. Howard R. Penniman. Washington, DC: American Enterprise Institute.

and Giovanni Sartori (1983). "Polarization, Fragmentation and Competition in Western Democracies." In *Western European Party Systems: Continuity and Change* (pp. 307–40), eds. Hans Daalder and Peter Mair. London: Sage Publications.

Sartori, Giovanni (1976). *Parties and Party Systems. A Framework for Analysis*. Cambridge: Cambridge University Press.

Sjöblom, Gunnar (1968). *Party Strategies in a Multiparty System*. Lund: Studentlitteratur.

Strøm, Kaare (1990a). *Minority Governments and Majority Rule*. Cambridge: Cambridge University Press.

(1990b). "A Behavioral Theory of Competitive Political Parties." *American Journal of Political Science* 34, 2: 565–98.

Tarrow, Sidney (1967). *Peasant Communism in Southern Italy*. New Haven, CT: Yale University Press.

(1981). "Three Years of Italian Democracy." In *Italy at the Polls, 1979* (pp. 1–33), ed. Howard R. Penniman. Washington, DC: American Enterprise Institute.

(1989). *Democracy and Disorder*. Oxford: Clarendon Press.

Urbani, Giuliano (ed.) (1979). *1978: elezioni con sorpresa*. Torino: Quaderni di Biblioteca della Liberta.

Vacca, Giuseppe (1987). *Tra compromesso e solidarietá. La politica del PCI negli anni '70*. Roma: Editori Riuniti.

7

DECISION FOR OPPOSITION: THE AUSTRIAN SOCIALIST PARTY'S ABANDONMENT OF GOVERNMENT PARTICIPATION IN 1966

Wolfgang C. Müller

INTRODUCTION

The general election of 6 March 1966 changed Austrian politics. The People's Party (ÖVP) won eighty-five seats and an absolute majority, five seats more than the other parliamentary parties combined. The Socialist Party (SPÖ) lost two seats but still held seventy-four seats, while the Freedom Party (FPÖ) was reduced from eight to six seats (see Table 7.1). It was the first time since the election of 25 November 1945, that a party had been able to win a parliamentary majority. Until this point, Austria had been governed by the famous "black-red" coalition, which, after an initial all-party government, had been in charge since 1947. As a consequence of the 1966 election, the grand coalition was finally replaced by a single-party government of the ÖVP. This is exactly the result that would normally be expected from this kind of seat distribution, a "minimal winning" government. From this perspective, any lengthy discussion of government formation in party-political terms would seem superfluous. However, the actual process that led to this outcome was not that straightforward. For more than six weeks, ÖVP and SPÖ aimed at and negotiated in order to form a joint government again. Only when these negotiations failed did the ÖVP form the first single-party government in the post–World War II period.

This chapter deals with the unsuccessful coalition negotiations and the SPÖ's decision to reject the final offer of the ÖVP to form a joint government. To lose

Table 7.1. *Austrian parliamentary parties 1966–1970*

	1966 Election	
Party	Votes (in %)	Seats
People's Party (ÖVP)	48.30	85
Socialist Party (SPÖ)	42.60	74
Freedom Party (FPÖ)	5.40	6

government participation after having been used to it for more than twenty years certainly constitutes a critical situation for every party. It was even more so in the case of the SPÖ because of its traumatic interwar experience: after having lost its governmental status in 1920, the socialists had never been able to return to government; finally, the party and democracy were destroyed and the country experienced a civil war. Consequently, since 1945, the SPÖ leadership had been keen to maintain government participation. Over time the intraparty opposition to this government participation had almost disappeared, and the SPÖ had even normatively accepted the permanent grand coalition government as the most adequate form of democracy for Austria (Müller 1988).[1] Thus, the decision for opposition in 1966 was clearly a significant break in party history. In retrospect this becomes even more obvious since the party's opposition period allowed for its revival and introduced the "golden age" decade of the 1970s.

This decision fundamentally altered the political system, too. It meant a change from coalition to one-party government, a transformation of parliament, and, to a large extent, a replacement of consociational by competitive behavior (Gerlich 1987; Müller 1993). Although the end of the grand coalition did not cause civic unrest, as a majority of citizens had expected only a few years before it actually occurred (Blecha, Gmoser, and Kienzl 1964: 151–2), it remains one of the most important political turning points in the country's postwar history.

Despite its importance, the 1966 abandonment of the grand coalition has not received much academic attention.[2] The logic of the electoral result was so obvious that few observers have found it worthwhile to examine this case.[3] Thus, this chapter is based on original empirical research. Fortunately, I was able to get access to extremely valuable sources, including the minutes of the SPÖ's executive bodies and national congress, as well as interviews with some of the key actors.[4]

The period between the 1966 election and the formation of the first single-party government is without doubt an important episode in Austrian politics. And the events that led up to this outcome lend themselves to a fascinating report. However, I have selected this case to do more than tell an interesting story about Austrian party politics. It was because this case is suitable for examining the central theoretical question of this book: which goals do competitive political parties pursue, especially in situations of goal conflict? While different rational choice theorists have argued that parties pursue either votes or office or policy (see Laver and Schofield 1990), this book proceeds from a unified model of party behaviour (Strøm 1990). As laid out in Chapter 1 of this book, political parties pursue votes *and* office *and* policy. They try to maximise all three of these objectives whenever this is possible. However, there may be trade-offs between votes, office, and policy, and in certain situations, political parties have to choose between conflicting goals. The 1966 coalition negotiations in Austria were such a case. In this chapter I examine the coalition negotiations in order to learn about the objectives of the SPÖ. In the next section I reconstruct the political process and illuminate the objectives of the SPÖ. The final section attempts to explain the party's preference of one goal over the others and draws some general conclusions for a behavioral theory of political parties.

THE COALITION NEGOTIATIONS: PROCESS AND CONTENTS

Both SPÖ and ÖVP had fought the 1966 election with the pledge that the grand coalition should subsequently be renewed, though in a modified form. This position was not changed after the votes were counted, although this election had removed one of the binding elements of the grand coalition: the unability of either major party to win a majority on its own. Neither party had seen a coalition with the FPÖ as an acceptable alternative to the grand coalition. Consequently, both parties nominated negotiation teams of high-ranking party officials in the week following the election. The ÖVP nominated Josef Klaus, Hermann Withalm, and Alfred Maleta. The SPÖ nominated Bruno Pittermann, Bruno Kreisky, and Alfred Schachner-Blazizek (see Table 7.2).[5]

The federal president designated Klaus as chancellor. Klaus declared that he would try to form a grand coalition government and informed Pittermann of this fact. After an initial meeting of the two party chairmen, the negotiation teams met nine times from 18 to 23 March 1966. Then the designated chancellor reported to the federal president. On 31 March the SPÖ's Full Party Executive found the ÖVP's offer of government participation unacceptable. It therefore summoned an extraordinary party congress for 15 April in order to deal with this question. Before the SPÖ's congress, two more meetings of the negotiation teams of ÖVP and SPÖ were held, and the results of the negotiations were summed up by a subcommittee. The resulting report, the ÖVP stated, would be its final offer. The SPÖ's Full Party Executive judged this offer unacceptable, though there were considerable differences about the degree of unacceptability and the chances of improving this result in further negotiations, notwithstanding the ÖVP's claim that this report would constitute its final offer. As a compromise, the congress prepared a resolution stating the SPÖ's conditions for government participation. The party's strategy was hotly debated

Table 7.2. *Key actors in the 1966 inter- and intraparty negotiations*

Party and individual	Party positions	State and other positions
Socialist Party		
Bruno Pittermann	Party chairman	Vice Chancellor
Bruno Kreisky	Deputy party chairman	Foreign Minister
Alfred Schachner-Blazizek	Deputy party chairman	Deputy Governor of Styria
Karl Waldbrunner	Deputy party chairman	Second President of Parliament
Anton Benya	Member Inner Party Executive	President Trade Union Congress
People's Party		
Josef Klaus	Party chairman	Federal Chancellor
Hermann Withalm	General secretary	Leader of the parliamentary party
Alfred Maleta	Deputy party chairman; leader of the League of Workers and Employees	President of Parliament

at the party congress. The SPÖ was split on the crucial question of to participate in government or assume the role of opposition. Nevertheless, the congress accepted the resolution almost unanimously, thus leaving the final decision to the Full Party Executive. The negotiation teams or subgroups held further meetings on 17 and 18 April in which the ÖVP made final concessions. However, the SPÖ's Full Party Executive on 18 April decided, by a majority of thirty to ten, that these concessions did not meet the requirements set by the party congress. This result was communicated to the chairman of the ÖVP, who then, after formal involvement of the federal president, formed a single-party government. On 20 April 1966 the new government was inaugurated. For the first time since 1945 the SPÖ did not participate in the government but faced it as opposition.

How did this come about? What prevented the SPÖ from accepting the ÖVP's invitation to join the government? An answer to this question requires a closer examination of the unsuccessful negotiations: What did the SPÖ want to achieve, and in what ways did the ÖVP's offer fall short of fulfilling the SPÖ's demands?

Traditionally, coalition negotiations during the period of grand coalition government have focused on (1) the rules of the game for the new government concerning coalition decision making and determination, (2) the distribution of government and other offices, (3) the distribution of portfolios between the government members, and (4) the policies to be pursued (see Dreijmanis 1982). An analysis of the five coalition contracts between 1949 and 1962 displays a clear bias in favor of the extensive regulation of the rules of the game, while policies clearly got the least attention (Müller 1994). This is not to say that the parties were not interested in policies. Rather, it means that they preferred a procedural over a substantive programming of government activities.

All the coalition agreements prior to 1966 had completely bound the parties in parliament and had explicitly ruled out parliamentary activities by the coalition parties to which they had not agreed in advance. This included the life span of parliament itself: a breakdown of the coalition automatically led to the election of a new parliament. Since 1956 the ÖVP negotiators had been under intraparty pressure to soften these conditions of iron "coalition discipline" and, in particular, to be free to form legislative coalitions with the FPÖ on issues with which the SPÖ was not prepared to agree. Until 1966 they had never succeeded in this quest.

While a softening up of the coalition was a long-term desire of the ÖVP, its performance in the previous coalition negotiations of 1962–3 constituted a specific burden for the 1966 negotiations. In 1962–3 the ÖVP had not been able to transform its electoral gains (two seats) into an adequate improvement of its position within the government (as opposed to the SPÖ, which in 1959 had transformed an electoral gain of the same size into an additional government department). This, in turn, had led to the replacement of the ÖVP chief negotiator, Alfons Gorbach, as party chairman and federal chancellor by the much tougher Josef Klaus in 1964 (see Müller and Meth-Cohn 1991).

Let us now turn to the contents of the 1966 coalition negotiations. The final ÖVP offer meant, in terms of cabinet positions, the transfer of one ministerial post from the SPÖ to the ÖVP and one additional secretary of state[6] for the ÖVP (Table 7.3). Measured against the shifts in cabinet positions between the coalition parties after previous elections the ÖVP's claim was modest, even more so if one takes into account its failure to improve on this score in 1962 despite its relative electoral success (gaining extra votes and seats). Moreover, the ÖVP declared that it would recruit an independent expert rather than a party politician to the department of justice, which was the one the SPÖ would lose. Even the SPÖ recognized the modesty of the ÖVP's office claims: in internal deliberations, influential members of the Full Party Executive stated that the transfer of a second ministerial post (i.e., department) to the ÖVP would be acceptable and preferable to a reduction in the jurisdictions of the remaining SPÖ ministers (FPE, 31 March 1966). The additional secretary of state position for the ÖVP did not cause any headache in the SPÖ. Thus, as far as cabinet positions were concerned, the ÖVP's offer was absolutely acceptable to the SPÖ.

The distribution of portfolios, as envisaged by the ÖVP, caused more problems. Besides the department of justice, the ÖVP at the end of the negotiations still claimed a number of changes, which are summarized in Table 7.4. Most of these changes were seen as minor or otherwise acceptable. The crucial points were the transfer of police competences (jurisdiction) to the *Länder* and the reorganization of the nationalized industries. Accordingly, the SPÖ congress

Table 7.3. *The distribution of cabinet positions 1963–1966, and in the 1966 coalition negotiations*

Cabinet position	Grand coalition 1963–6	Final offer, 1966
Federal Chancellor	ÖVP	ÖVP
Vice Chancellor	SPÖ	SPÖ
Ministers		
Interior	SPÖ	SPÖ
Justice	SPÖ	ÖVP
Education	ÖVP	ÖVP
Social Administration	SPÖ	SPÖ
Finance	ÖVP	ÖVP
Agriculture	ÖVP	ÖVP
Commerce	ÖVP	ÖVP
Transportation	SPÖ	SPÖ
Defence	ÖVP	ÖVP
Foreign Affairs	SPÖ	SPÖ
Secretaries of state		
Interior	ÖVP	ÖVP
Justice	ÖVP	—
Commerce	SPÖ	SPÖ
Commerce	ÖVP	ÖVP
Defence	SPÖ	SPÖ
Federal Chancellory	—	ÖVP
Social Administration	—	ÖVP

resolution conditioned government participation on the jurisdictions of the SPÖ's departments not being reduced substantially. In the following negotiations the ÖVP made some concessions, which led the SPÖ's Inner Party Executive and its respective policy specialists to conclude that with respect to portfolio distribution the ÖVP had met the party congress resolution (FPE, 18 April 1966).

As in previous coalition negotiations, policies were not of paramount importance in 1966. However, there was one crucial point: the financing of investments for the railways and the postal service. According to the ÖVP plans, the current budgetary problems were to be solved by massive cuts in these investments. Despite some wavering, the ÖVP maintained this point during the first phase of the negotiations. Consequently, the fair distribution of investment funds among all departments became one of the three conditions for government participation put forward by the SPÖ party congress. In the following negotiations, the ÖVP gave in and agreed to provide extra investment funds

Table 7.4. *Reductions of the SPÖ's portfolios according to the ÖVP's final offer*

Department of Interior
Transfer of a substantial part of the police competences to the *Länder* (six of nine were governed by the ÖVP).
Transfer of the supervision of savings banks to an ÖVP department.
Abolishment of co-competences concerning the export of animals, thus leaving this competence in its entirety with an ÖVP department.
Transfer of the competence of fixing the customs for certain goods to an ÖVP department.

Department of Social Administration
Transfer of the funding of sports and nonschool education to the Department of Education. There a commission, whose composition is proportional to parliamentary party strengths, make the decisions.

Department of Transportation and Electricity
Transfer of the competence to appoint high-ranking civil servants in the railway and post administration to the cabinet.
Appointment of a deputy chairman of the railways coming from the ÖVP.
Transfer of the competences for broadcasting to the Federal Chancellory.
Appointment of an ÖVP majority in the boards of trustees of the electricity industry.

Nationalised Industries (vice chancellor)
Transfer of the nationalised industry from the vice chancellor to a holding company with a chairman from the SPÖ. A Socialist minister continues to be responsible for the nationalised industries. However, the ÖVP will hold the majority in the boards of trustees in the holding company and in almost all of the individual firms.

---

for the railways. The SPÖ's Inner Party Executive interpreted this concession as fulfillment of the party congress's condition, an interpretation that the Full Party Executive did not question.

Regarding the rules of the game for a new grand coalition, the SPÖ had from the outset of the negotiations accepted that the old inflexible pattern could not be maintained. They were ready to accept that the ÖVP could use its parliamentary majority to impose policies the SPÖ opposed. According to party chairman Pittermann, it was clear that it was no longer possible "to bind both parties in parliament to common resolutions; it was only natural to allow the ÖVP to use its parliamentary majority."[7] The only limitation was a vaguely formulated agreement on the "principles of cooperation," which required that in each case the two governing parties should strive for joint action both in the cabinet and in parliament. Any unilateral parliamentary activity should be conducted only after "intensive attempts" to arrive at a joint solution and after a time of negotiations "appropriate to the respective question." The ÖVP was further willing to guarantee that the distribution of portfolios would not be changed by its parliamentary majority during the period of the envisaged coalition government.

Thus the SPÖ was willing to accept that the ÖVP could not be prevented from using its parliamentary majority to renege on policy decisions. However, the SPÖ was very concerned about getting a guarantee for the life of the new government. It was clear to the party that the ÖVP could not be expected to accept the agreement of previous coalitions, that is, the coupling of the term of the coalition with that of the parliament. If they did, the SPÖ would have the chance to force new elections simply by leaving the government. Therefore, the SPÖ in the coalition negotiations aimed to get an explicit guarantee from the ÖVP to maintain the coalition at least for a shorter period, such as two years. However, the ÖVP negotiators were unwilling to comply with this request. They repeatedly let the SPÖ know that their party would not accept any agreement of this kind. The ÖVP also rejected the idea of having a secret agreement in the form of an exchange of letters between the leaders of the two parties, not intended for publication, as the SPÖ side informally suggested (Benya, PTP 1966: 103).

Yet, negotiators of both teams were willing to look for a functional equivalent to a formal agreement on a minimum term for the coalition. One possibility was constituted by the laws concerning the regulating of the economy (*Marktordnungsgesetze*), which are the legal basis for subsidies, mainly to farmers. According to the constitution, these laws would fall under the jurisdiction of the Austrian *Länder*. A qualified parliamentary majority is thus required to allow the parliament to intervene. Since (1) the farmers and other groups that benefit from these laws constitute core groups of the ÖVP, and since (2) this party alone was not in command of a qualified parliamentary majority, the laws concerning the regulation of the economy provided a starting point for such a functional equivalent.

Until 1966 these laws had a temporary character and regularly appeared on the political agenda at the beginning of each parliament. In 1966 the ÖVP at first demanded that these laws be renewed for an unlimited period of time. This, of course, was unacceptable to the SPÖ because it would have considerably reduced its negotiating power, not only for the coming government term but also beyond it. Then the ÖVP reduced its demand to four years and finally was willing to accept a renewal for a two- to two-and-a-half-year period. Two of the three SPÖ negotiators, Kreisky and Schachner-Blazizek, were willing to interpret this as a de facto guarantee by the ÖVP to maintain the coalition at least for two and a half years.[8] On the one hand, this was signalled – though not publicly stated – by the ÖVP negotiators.[9] On the other hand, the ÖVP would have been the more dependent on the SPÖ the closer the date to a further renewal of the respective laws; therefore, it seemed unlikely that the ÖVP would terminate the coalition just before these laws would expire. In defending his interpretation of the *Marktordnungsgesetze* function, Kreisky reminded his party that other countries have coalitions without a written contract and that "nothing is certain in politics" (PTP 1966: 45).

However, the ÖVP rejected any formal recognition of this interpretation. It was not prepared to guarantee the maintenance of the coalition, neither for the term of the respective laws nor even for the term of the budget. This unwillingness was based on the experience of stalemate coalition politics over the last half decade. The ÖVP feared that a formal guarantee of the coalition's term would encourage obstructive behaviour on the part of the SPÖ. The government then would fail to produce adequate policies and the ÖVP would face internal troubles and potential electoral punishment.

Before the party congress, some of the SPÖ leaders had believed that the ÖVP would be willing to improve its offer if the SPÖ demonstrated that it was not bluffing but indeed was willing to assume the opposition role if its conditions were not met.[10] For most party leaders, however, the party congress resolution stating the conditions for government participation was nothing more than an attempt to force the ÖVP to say "no" and therefore bear responsibility for the destruction of the grand coalition.[11] The resolution prepared for enactment at the party congress was a compromise between these two groups, but its wording already reflected the majority opinion within the party leadership. Consequently, the terms it set for a coalition left little room for interpretation. Government participation was declared acceptable only "if the Socialists have the guarantee that the government cooperation cannot be terminated unilaterally by the ÖVP at any date appropriate to it."

In the negotiations after the party congress the ÖVP made one concession concerning the term of the government. It offered to incorporate a passage in the government declaration stating that it was the firm will of both parties to implement the government program and to avoid any crisis. Consequently, the cooperation for the whole legislative period would seem assured. However, the ÖVP still refused to put this in any contractual form. In the internal deliberations of the SPÖ's executive bodies, it was Anton Benya who articulated the majority's position most clearly. He said that what the government statement had to say about the length of government cooperation

> sounds very good but you can't bank on it. . . . We will be responsible for the budgetary problems so we have to have a commitment for at least one year. The vague statements we are getting from a partner as unreliable as the ÖVP are . . . too little. (FPE, 18 April 1966)

The SPÖ's Inner Party Executive, by majority vote, interpreted this offer as still falling short of fulfilling the condition set by the party congress. By a thirty to ten majority the Full Party Executive arrived at the same conclusion.

This meant the end of the grand coalition. After having been in government for more than twenty years, the SPÖ had decided to reject the ÖVP's offer for further government participation. As I have shown, this decision was not made

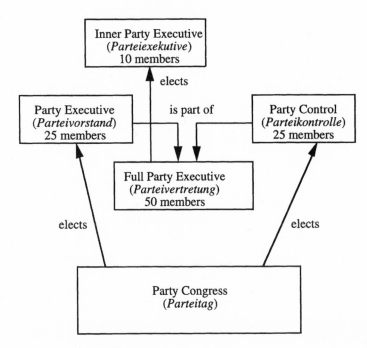

Figure 7.1 The SPÖ party structure in 1966.

because the ÖVP had offered too few cabinet positions. Nor were unfulfilled policy objectives decisive, either directly or indirectly (via the distribution of portfolios). On both counts an agreement with the ÖVP was finally achieved. What caused the SPÖ's decision for opposition was the disagreement over the rules of the game – more precisely, the unwillingness of the ÖVP to guarantee formally a minimum term for the coalition. How can these considerations be translated into the party objectives relevant to this book: office, policy, and votes? In the remainder of this section I provide an answer based on the minutes of the SPÖ Full Party Executive and party congress.

The majority of the SPÖ leadership expected the required government policies over the next one to two years after the 1966 election to be very unpopular. Already existing budgetary problems would require austerity policies; according to party chairman Pittermann, the 1966 budget "can't include any gifts, only reductions and cuts" (PTP 1966: 18). Moreover, an economic downturn was expected in the near future. Participation in the cabinet therefore would have meant accepting responsibility for all government actions (and possibly for the economic recession as well). This, of course, would have reduced the SPÖ's capacity to attract votes, both vis-à-vis the ÖVP and vis-à-vis the DFP.[12] Without a guarantee from the ÖVP that the coalition would be maintained for a certain period of time, government participation would have implied great risks for the SPÖ. The ÖVP, some party leaders expected, would pack all the unpopular decisions into the first budget and then, at a strategically convenient time, terminate the coalition. Deputy party chairperson Rosa Jochmann, for instance, assumed that

> the ÖVP definitively wants us in the government for the first few months to let us decide on all the unpleasant matters with them. (FPE, 18 April 1966)

Similarly, Grete Wondrack claimed that

> if we are in the government the ÖVP will give us everything that is unpopular and blame us during the next election. (FPE, 18 April 1966)

She and another member of the Full Party Executive, Josef Kratky, feared that the SPÖ would "lose face" because

> we would be responsible for lots of unpopular measures and would not be able to say anything about them in parliament.

Kratky also warned his party about the "insidiousness of the ÖVP." According to Waldbrunner, the ÖVP would use

> our team in government to drive a wedge between it and the party [or] would take every opportunity to show our ministers the door. (FPE, 18 April 1966)

Other members of the party leadership expected the ÖVP to postpone the termination of the coalition until the business cycle displayed an upward trend.[13] In either case the SPÖ would, in electoral terms, share the burdens but not the benefits of government. In this scenario, the ÖVP could then fight the next election with the slogan that economic prosperity had returned once the party governed alone and, on this basis, would claim a renewal of its majority. After the SPÖ left the government,

> the ÖVP would throw in a few electoral goodies and people would say that when the SPÖ's in the government things are bad, and when the ÖVP is on its own, things go well (Wondrack, FPE, 31 March 1966)

The SPÖ would then have alienated many of its core supporters by its government participation[14] but would not have been able to attract new voters by sharing the responsibility for the more popular policies in the second part of the government's term.

Besides these party leaders who speculated *à la baisse,* there were some who speculated *à la hausse* and opposed government participation on those grounds. They expected that the intraparty problems of the ÖVP, resulting from the factionalized party structure, would increase in a single-party government. Because of this and the foreseeable economic difficulties, the SPÖ would have a good chance to improve its position substantially in the 1970 election.[15] As central secretary, Leopold Gratz explicitly put it, being in opposition would mean "having a free hand for 1970." Thus, for all SPÖ leaders who were against government participation, *future votes* were the decisive objective.

It is also interesting to examine the arguments of the 25 per cent of the party leadership who wanted to accept the final offer of the ÖVP. None of them made reference to office per se, but almost all of them mentioned the policy and patronage capacity of the government positions the SPÖ would lose. Though he characterized the ÖVP offer as "extremely tough, more than tough," Schachner-Blazizek argued that

> the loss of ministries and power and other problems would hit us at least ten times harder or even more, if we reject this and go into opposition. (PTP 1966: 35)

Coalition proponents also argued that being in opposition would not automatically lead to a better electoral performance in the future. Four specific arguments were made. First, the government-controlled TV and the bourgeois press would not give much coverage to the SPÖ as an opposition party and would also display a qualitative bias against it. Schachner-Blazizek (PTP 1966: 36) reminded his party comrades that not even half of the SPÖ electorate reads SPÖ newspapers, and that television and radio would be

> in alien hands. We would not even see one of our ministers opening a bridge or at other official occasions.

Similarly, Kreisky (PTP 1966: 47) doubted that the SPÖ would ever find recognition in the "bourgeois press" as a serious opposition: "They will not publish our good speeches but rather our bad ones." Thus, the SPÖ's ability to communicate with the voters would be substantially reduced in opposition. Second, being chancellor of a single-party cabinet would not subject the ÖVP's leader, Klaus, to the kind of attrition he would face in a coalition government. If the SPÖ participated in government, Klaus's image as a strong leader would be damaged, thus improving the SPÖ's electoral chances (Kreisky, FPE, 18 April 1966).[16] Third, in a single-party government the ÖVP would for the first time have the chance to get credit for expansive welfare policies. In the future, therefore, the party could attract more voters from blue- and white-collar employees than in a coalition government.[17] Fourth, given the SPÖ's willingness to be a constructive opposition, it would be an error to believe that the opposition would bear no responsibility for government policies.[18] Thus, for instance, the SPÖ would have to vote for the *Marktordnungsgesetze* anyway.[19]

As these arguments show, the loss of office did not play a role in the arguments of those party leaders who wanted to maintain the grand coalition.[20] However, it is interesting to note that the majority of the incumbent government personnel preferred this option to opposition. Only Vice Chancellor Pittermann, Minister of Justice Christian Broda, and, to a lesser extent, Minister of Transport Otto Probst favoured an opposition role for their party. The picture becomes even more unambiguous when we focus not on positions held in the last grand coalition but on the anticipated positions of the members of the party leadership in a renewed grand coalition. While all of the incumbents who supported the maintenance of the coalition could expect to be renominated, this was not clear in the case of Probst,[21] it was very unlikely in the case of party chairman Pittermann,[22] and, due to the transfer of his department to the ÖVP, it was impossible in the case of Broda. To put it more bluntly, there was total consistency between positive personal incentives and the vote for maintaining government participation. This suggests that office was a relevant objective for those SPÖ leaders who would have been likely to benefit personally.

The majority of the fifty-person Full Party Executive did not have a direct career interest in the decision on government participation. More important, none of the three party leaders most responsible for the SPÖ's abandonment of government participation had any direct career interest. (They were party chairman Pittermann, his deputy Karl Waldbrunner, and the leader of the SPÖ trade unionists, Anton Benya.[23] As mentioned earlier, Pittermann would not have returned to government but would have taken the leadership of the parliamentary party. Waldbrunner was the second president of parliament, and Benya was president of the Austrian Trade Union Federation.)

TENTATIVE CONCLUSIONS FOR A BEHAVIOURAL THEORY OF POLITICAL PARTIES

Though the limits of a case study are obvious,[24] we can draw some general conclusions for a behavioural theory of political parties from the SPÖ's 1966 decision for opposition. As we have seen, the first objective of the SPÖ in the mid-1960s was votes rather than office or policy. Since votes have no intrinsic value, this means that the party was willing and able to postpone office and policy rewards into the future (Strøm 1990). I will now try to identify the most important institutional, organizational, and situational conditions that contributed to the SPÖ's vote-seeking behaviour. In doing so, I will examine a number of potential determinants discussed in Chapter 1 of this book and by Strøm (1990).

PARTY SYSTEM AND INSTITUTIONAL SETTING

For many party leaders the 1966 election indicated a qualitative change in the Austrian party system. For the first time in seventeen years (or, discounting the atypical 1945 election,[25] for the first time ever since full democratisation in 1918), one party had been able to win an absolute majority. Since party system fragmentation had constantly declined since 1949, first with the Communists' loss of parliamentary representation and further electoral decline, then with the gradual reduction in the size of the "Third Camp" (the League of Independents [1949–56] and FPÖ [since 1956]), this was not interpreted as an isolated event. As the former chairman of the Lower Austria party organization, Otto Tschadek (PTP 1966: 40), put it, there was a "trend toward a two-party system."[26]

> I don't know how long the FPÖ will still have seats in parliament. It looks like it is on its death bed. If we end up with only two parties, there'll be one with the majority and one with a minority.

A two-party system means that a party's capacity to pursue office and policy objectives depends first and foremost on its electoral strength. Thus, the decision to reject immediate office and policy advantages can be interpreted as an attempt to enhance the SPÖ's electoral chances. The decision was promoted by increased *electoral competitiveness* (as indicated by the 1966 election result) and by the fact that the *electoral system's distortion* did not constitute a major handicap for the SPÖ (as opposed to the smaller parties).

The change from government to opposition was also eased by the *legislative* and *governmental institutions*, which in policy terms favor governing parties less than those in most other democracies. The requirement of a qualified parliamentary majority, not only for constitutional amendments but also for a number of other decisions, provided some bargaining power for a big opposition party such as the SPÖ would be. This influence could be used to achieve a compromise on the particular issue under consideration or for logrolling. The limitation of party politics by corporatist institutions had the same effect: it allowed the SPÖ – via its trade unionists – to influence on policy decisions irrespective of their governmental participation (Müller 1985).[27]

PARTY ORGANIZATION

In the interparty negotiations the SPÖ acted as a unitary actor. Also, the party congress resolution stating the SPÖ's terms for further government participation was passed almost unanimously, and the party did not show any internal parliamentary divisions after the new government was inaugurated. Thus, it indeed came out of the grand coalition as a single bloc. In order to explain the SPÖ's decision to abandon government participation, however, we have to look "inside the black box" (Laver and Schofield 1990: 15). In our case, we can single out four organizational characteristics relevant for the SPÖ's vote-seeking strategy: the relatively *homogeneous social structure* of the SPÖ's supporters, the *low level of factionalization*, the *strong tradition of party discipline*, and the *dominance of nongovernmental career perspectives among the party leaders*. The SPÖ's relatively homogeneous support structure did not provide suitable target groups that the governing party could try to attract by strategically designing specific policies. Similarly, a low level of organizational factionalization limited the opportunity for a *divide et impera* strategy on the part of the government. The importance of this factor becomes particularly clear when we compare the SPÖ's opposition term with the ones of the highly factionalized ÖVP between 1970 and 1987. A tradition of tight party discipline allowed the party to speak with one voice and to develop and implement a coherent opposition strategy (Müller, Philipp, and Steininger 1992; Müller 1996).[28] As we have seen, the actual decision was also influenced by the dominance of nongovernmental career perspectives within the SPÖ's leadership body and, in particular, by some of the top leaders' lack of any ambition for government office. Thus, the individual rationales of the key players can help us understand intraparty politics (see Frohlich, Oppenheimer, and Young 1971).

SITUATION

Empirical studies often show that decisions depend on external circumstances that cannot, to any relevant degree, be influenced by the actor (see Farr 1985). The SPÖ's decision for opposition also seems to indicate that such situational aspects cannot be discounted when we look for explanations of the party's behaviour. In this case, the party's anticipation of economic developments was important: the expectation of an economic downturn was particularly relevant for the SPÖ's decision to avoid government responsibility.

This chapter has focused on the unsuccessful coalition negotiations between ÖVP and SPÖ in 1966 from the perspective of the SPÖ. I have sought to show which goals the party had and what accounted for its critical decision to give up government participation after more than twenty years. The available evidence on the negotiations and internal deliberations demonstrated that the SPÖ leaders indeed pursued all three goals assumed by the rational choice literature: office, policy, and votes. However, when it turned out that the party could not realize all its objectives, it became clear that votes were its central goal. This meant that party leaders were prepared to postpone policy and office rewards into the future. In the final section of this chapter, I have tried to extract the factors that accounted for the SPÖ's vote-seeking behavior. Some of them, in particular those concerning the party system and the institutional setting, are consistent with theoretical arguments already elaborated elsewhere in some detail (see Strøm 1990). With respect to these factors, the present case study can be seen as a theory-confirming one. As regards other factors and in particular the party organizational characteristics, however, this chapter can be regarded as a hypothesis-generating case study (see Lijphart 1971). In particular, I would suggest that parties are in a better position to, and therefore more likely to, postpone immediate office or policy rewards in order to win votes in the future if their support structure is homogeneous, their level of factionalization is low, and their capacity to maintain party discipline is high. The case of the SPÖ also suggests the hypothesis that parties are more likely to disregard office benefits the more the career perspectives of their leaders and, in particular, top leaders, are nongovernmental. My study confirms the fruitfulness of this book's approach to the study of goals and strategies of political parties.

NOTES

1. In the early 1960s there was an episode when the SPÖ discussed forming an alternative coalition with the FPÖ. Once the decision to maintain the grand coalition government had been made, its normative character had even been strengthened.
2. See, however, the contemporary record of Ornauer (1968), who had to restrict himself to published sources.
3. The most detailed study on the old grand coalition (Rauchensteiner 1987: 479ff), for instance, devotes only 3 of 577 pages to its abandonment.
4. Other sources were the parties' press releases, the media coverage, and the memoirs of some of the key participants (Klaus 1971: 154; Withalm 1973: 136–7; Kreisky 1988: 388–9).
5. On the main actors see the analytical biographies in Dachs, Gerlich, and Müller (1995).
6. According to the constitution, secretaries of state (*Staatssekretäre*) are not members of the cabinet, though they are present at its meetings. Secretaries of state are auxiliaries of the ministers and are entitled to stand in for their ministers in parliamentary meetings. Within the government departments, their competencies are very limited. In practice, those of them who served under a minister from the other governing party functioned as instruments of control and internal opposition.
7. Pittermann, PTP 1966: 25; see Schachner-Blazizek, PTP 1966: 30.
8. FPE, 14 April 1966 and 18 April 1966; PTP 1966: 45.
9. Party Chairman Pitterman's written summary of the ÖVP proposals; FPE, 14 April 1966; PTP 1966: 18; see Withalm 1966: 68.
10. Kreisky, FPE, 31 March 1966; Kreisky, PTP 1966: 44 and 116; Sebastian, PTP 1966: 104; Korp, PTP 1966: 104.
11. Pittermann, PTP 1966: 27; Tschadek, PTP 1966: 40; Benya, PTP 1966: 101; Häuser, PTP 1966: 112.
12. The DFP was a splinter party that had broken away from the SPÖ. It had a charismatic leader, Franz Olah, and had polled 3.3% of the vote in 1966.
13. The SPÖ's distrust in the nonbinding declarations of the ÖVP politicians about their willingness to maintain the coalition for the whole parliamentary term may astonish some observers, who know that much in Austrian politics is based on mutual understanding and gentlemen's agreements. However, first, this is generally more so in less competitive fields than in party politics. Second, the SPÖ generally distrusted the ÖVP leaders who had assumed power in the 1960s (as opposed to the men who had been in charge in the 1940s and 1950s). This attitude grew stronger in 1964, when the ÖVP leaders who had signed the coalition contract of 1963 on behalf of their party retired and the new leaders, still in charge in 1966, claimed that this coalition contract was not binding on them.

14. Many party functionaries in the party's executive bodies and the party congress expressed concern about the party's ability to maintain the loyalty of its core groups.
15. The SPÖ was right in expecting economic problems ahead. In 1967 Austria experienced the first economic recession since the upswing of the early 1950s (see Butschek 1985). The ÖVP's policies to counter these economic problems – a textbook case of an adequate economic strategy – proved to be very unpopular and substantially contributed to the electoral defeat of the ÖVP in 1970.
16. This indeed had happened in the case of the two predecessors of Klaus, Raab, and Gorbach, who suffered both physically and politically from the fights within the coalition.
17. Rösch, PTP 1966: 68; Staribacher, PTP 1966: 121.
18. Slavik, PTP 1966: 96; Sebastian, PTP 1966: 96.
19. At the party congress, Kreisky and another member of the Full Party Executive, Neugebauer, as well as many delegates, reminded the party of the setting up of a dictatorship by the ÖVP's predecessor in 1934. According to Kreisky (PTP 1966: 46), a single-party government of the ÖVP would threaten democracy in Austria, since their government representatives are "not good democrats." This interpretation was rejected by a representative of the Socialist Trade Unionists, Paul Blau (PTP 1966: 75–6). Since this argument was not used in the internal deliberations of the party executive bodies, it may well have been intended to generate support at the party congress rather than to constitute a serious issue.
20. Indeed, some of them did find it important to point out that this is not connected to their personal career ambitions; see Schachner-Blazizek (the probable vice chancellor in a renewed coalition), Kreisky, and Rösch, PTP 1966: 29, 44, and 79 and Kreisky, FPE, 14 April 1966.
21. Probst had not performed well as a minister. By his intransigence in a purely symbolic matter, the naming of a ship on Lake Constance, he had caused public uproar and civil unrest, the loss of possibly tens of thousands of votes for the SPÖ, and severe intraparty conflict between the national and some *Land* parties.
22. Pittermann would have been replaced in his position as vice chancellor by one of his two comrades in the SPÖ negotiation team, Kreisky or Schachner-Blazizek, who both wished to accept the ÖVP's final offer. (This was Pitterman's own preference [FPE, 14 April 1966], and it was confirmed by interviewees from both parties.) Ironically, Kreisky was the one who finally gained most from the decision for opposition, becoming the SPÖ's chairman in 1967 and chancellor in 1970 and maintaining both positions until 1983.
23. Karl Waldbrunner was not a major speech maker but rather the "grey eminence" of the party. Already on 24 March 1966 in the Party Executive he established the policy that "we can't risk constantly being threatened by the ÖVP with being kicked out of the government." During the decision-making process, he intervened with short but authoritative statements supporting the course that finally succeeded. And it was he who forcefully chaired the decisive meetings of the party executive bodies and who put the proposal to the Full Party Executive to reject the final offer of the ÖVP as falling short of the party congress resolution (Fischer 1993: 22–3). Anton Benya, as the president of the Trade Union Congress, one of the most important party leaders, intervened forcefully in the deliberations of the party congress and the executive bodies of the party.

24. See, however, Eckstein (1975), Yin (1984), George and McKeown (1985), and Fagin, Orum, and Sjoberg (1991).

25. In 1945 more than 500,000 former members of the Nazi Party were not allowed to vote; thus, the so-called Third Camp of Austrian politics, the German National one, was not represented, which allowed the ÖVP to win an absolute majority of seats.

26. Indeed, the Austrian party system of the 1960s was characterized by a very low level of fragmentation: according to the measures of Blondel (1968) and Rae (1971), the party system in 1966 had a two-party format (see Müller 1997).

27. However, it should be noted that the scope of corporatist policy making to a large extent is at the government's disposal. Thus, when the SPÖ made its decision, it was not clear what importance the corporatist institutions would actually have during the ÖVP's government term.

28. At first sight, this argument may not seem convincing. Before the 1966 election, the SPÖ had gone through a series of internal upheavals, including the expelling of one of its leaders, Franz Olah, who then contested the 1966 election with his own party (see note 12). And as we have seen, the SPÖ, and its leadership in particular had been split over the coalition question. However, after the decision was made, the leaders assured each other that they would now demonstrate unity and indeed did so to a remarkable extent. Despite another controversy over the party leadership in 1967 (Müller and Meth-Cohn 1991), the SPÖ remained a unitary actor in the parliamentary and electoral arenas.

SOURCES

Minutes of the SPÖ *Parteivorstand* (Party Executive, cited as PE) and the *Parteivertretung* (Full Party Executuve, cited as FPE), 24 March to 18 April 1966.
Österreich Jahrbuch 1966. Vienna: Bundespressedienst, 1967.
Protokoll. Ausserordentlicher Parteitag der Sozialistischen Partei Österreichs, 15 April 1966 (cited as PTP 1966).
SPÖ Bericht 1967.

REFERENCES

Blecha, Karl, Rupert Gmoser, and Heinz Kienzl (1964). *Der durchleuchtete Wähler.* Vienna: Europaverlag.

Blondel, Jean (1968). "Party Systems and Patterns of Government in Western Democracies." *Canadian Journal of Political Science* 1, 2: 180–203.

Butschek, Felix (1985). *Die österreichische Wirtschaft im 20. Jahrhundert.* Stuttgart: Gustav Fischer.

Dachs, Herbert, Peter Gerlich, and Wolfgang C. Müller (eds.) (1995). *Die Politiker.* Vienna: Manz.

Dreijmanis, John (1982). "Austria: The 'Black'-'Red' Coalitions." In *Government Coalitions in Western Democracies* (pp. 237–59), eds. Eric C. Browne and John Dreijmanis. New York: Longman.

Eckstein, Hary (1975). "Case Study and Theory in Political Science." In *Handbook of Political Science*, Vol. 7. (pp. 79–137), eds. Fred I. Greenstein and Nelson W. Polsby. Reading, MA: Addison-Wesley.

Fagin, Joe R., Anthony M. Orum, and Gideon Sjoberg (1991). *A Case for the Case Study*. Chapel Hill: University of North Carolina Press.

Farr, James (1985). "Situational Analysis: Explanation in Political Science." *Journal of Politics* 47, 4: 1085–1107.

Fischer, Heinz (1993). *Die Kreisky-Jahre 1967–1983*. Vienna: Löcker.

Frohlich, Norman, Joe A. Oppenheimer, and Oran R. Young (1971). *Political Leadership and Collective Goods*. Princeton, NJ: Princeton University Press.

George, Alexander L. and Timothy J. McKeown (1985). "Case Studies and Theories of Organizational Decison Making." *Advances in Information Processing in Organizations* 2: 21–58.

Gerlich, Peter (1987). "Consociationalism to Competition: The Austrian Party System since 1945." In *Party Systems in Denmark, Austria, Switzerland, the Netherlands and Belgium* (pp. 61–106), ed. Hans Daalder. London: Pinter.

Klaus, Josef (1971). *Macht und Ohnmacht in Österreich*. Vienna: Molden.

Kreisky, Bruno (1988). *Im Strom der Politik*. Vienna: Kremeyer & Scheriau.

Laver, Michael and Norman Schofield (1990). *Multiparty Government. The Politics of Coalition in Europe*. Oxford: Oxford University Press.

Lijphart, Arend (1971). "Comparative Politics and the Comparative Method." *American Political Science Review* 65, 3: 682–93.

Müller, Wolfgang C. (1985). "Die Rolle der Parteien bei Entstehung und Entwicklung der Sozialpartnerschaft." In *Sozialpartnerschaft in der Krise* (pp. 135–224), eds. Peter Gerlich, Edgar Grande, and Wolfgang C. Müller. Vienna: Böhlau.

    (1988). "SPÖ und große Koalition." In *Auf dem Weg zur Staatspartei. Zu Geschichte und Politik der SPÖ seit 1945* (pp. 23–46), eds. Peter Pelinka and Gerhard Steger. Vienna: Verlag für Gesellschaftskritik.

    (1993). "Executive-Legislative Relations in Austria: 1945–92." *Legislative Studies Quarterly* 18, 4: 467–94.

    (1994). "Koalitionsabkommen in der österreichischen Politik." *Zeitschrift für Parlamentsfragen* 25, 3: 347–53.

    (1996). "Die Organisation der SPÖ, 1945–1995." In *Die Organisation der österreichischen Sozialdemokratie, 1889–1995* (pp. 195–356), eds. Wolfgang Maderthaner and Wolfgang C. Müller. Vienna: Löcker.

    (1997) "Das Parteiensystem." In *Handbuch des politischen Systems Österreichs* (pp. 215–34), eds. Herbert Dachs, Peter Gerlich, Herbert Gottweis, Franz Horner, Helmut Kramer, Volkmar Lauber, Wolfgang C. Müller, and Emmerich Tálos. Vienna: Manz.

    and Delia Meth-Cohn (1991). "The Selection of Party Chairmen in Austria: A Study in Intra-Party Decision-Making." *European Journal of Political Research* 20, 1: 37–63.

    Wilfried Philipp, and Barbara Steininger (1992). "Wie oligarchisch sind Österreichs Parteien? Eine empirische Analyse, 1945–1992." *Österreichische Zeitschrift für Politikwissenschaft* 21, 2: 117–46.

Ornauer, Helmut G. (1968) "Der Verzicht auf das politische Gleichgewicht: Von der Koalition zur Opposition." In *Nationalratswahl 1966* (pp. 181–7), eds. Peter Gerlich, Georg Ress, and Rodney Stiefbold. Vienna: Jugend und Volk.

Rae, Douglas W. (1971). *The Political Consequences of Electoral Laws*. New Haven, CT: Yale University Press.

Rauchensteiner, Manfred (1987). *Die Zwei. Die Große Koalition in Österreich 1945– 1966*. Vienna: Österreichischer Bundesverlag.

Strøm, Kaare (1990). "A Behavioral Theory of Competitive Political Parties." *American Journal of Political Science* 34, 2: 565–98.

Withalm, Hermann (1966). "Folgerungen und Aufgaben." In *Die Wahl 1966* (pp. 65–80). Vienna: ÖVP.

(1973). *Aufzeichnungen*. Graz: Styria.

Yin, Robert K. (1984). *Case Study Research. Design and Methods*. Beverly Hills: Sage.

8

LEADERSHIP ACCOUNTABILITY AND BARGAINING FAILURE IN NORWAY: THE PRESTHUS DEBACLE

Kaare Strøm

INTRODUCTION

Party politics can be spectacular popular entertainment.[1] Regardless of whether they ultimately act out a tragedy or a comedy, party politicians occasionally grip the public's attention in powerful ways. Even the most prosaic of bills can at times set the stage for a parliamentary drama. Such was the case when the Norwegian parliament, the Storting, debated the government's farm bill in the hectic days of June 1987. I shall refer to these events as the *Presthus debacle*, in reference to Conservative leader Rolf Presthus, the man whose life was most severely affected by this dramatic fiasco of interparty bargaining.

This chapter analyzes the strange events that led to the Presthus debacle. These events are interesting for a number of reasons. First, the strategic moves that were made led to an outcome that none of the principal players preferred and few anticipated. Four parties explicitly committed to a change of government and collectively a legislative majority twice failed to oust a minority Labor government. The Presthus debacle shows that parties differ in the objectives they bring to coalition bargaining. In explaining such differences, we have to consider the constraints of within-party politics, and especially the consequences of different intraparty *delegation regimes*.

PRESTHUS AND THE EVENTS OF JUNE 1987

On Monday, June 8, 1987, Rolf Presthus was widely expected to become prime minister of Norway within a few short days. His Conservative Party had just agreed to join forces with the other two major nonsocialist parties, the Christian People's Party, and the Center Party, to bring down Gro Harlem Brundtland's Labor Party government on the farm bill it had brought before the Storting. The nonsocialist motion of no confidence (censure), which would be attached to the farm bill amendment, needed only the additional support of the right-wing Progress Party, which had repeatedly expressed its preference for a nonsocialist government. Well-informed observers estimated the likelihood of a change of government at 80 or 90 percent (Rommetvedt 1991: 198). Yet, on June 12, the Storting rejected two separate no confidence motions against the government. The nonsocialist majority of four parties, each explicitly committed to dislodging Brundtland's government, twice failed to agree on a simple vote to that end. Presthus's dream of becoming prime minister never materialized, and the nonsocialist parties were humiliated.

The Presthus debacle ended a lengthy effort by the Norwegian Conservative Party and its sometime allies to resurrect the nonsocialist coalition that had governed Norway from 1965 to 1971 and again between 1983 and 1986.[2] The Labor Party had dominated Norwegian party politics from the 1930s to the early 1980s. In 1981 the party decisively lost ground, and Kåre Willoch was able to form the first Norwegian single-party Conservative government in more than fifty years. In June 1983, Willoch's cabinet was expanded to include the Center Party and the Christian People's Party, thus acquiring for the first time a legislative majority. In May 1986, Willoch's coalition, which had been reduced to a minority government in the September 1985 election, resigned. Willoch's resignation followed his defeat on a bill to increase gasoline taxes to offset the precipitous decline in government revenues caused by falling oil prices. Gro Harlem Brundtland formed a precarious Labor minority government facing a nonsocialist legislative majority. Upon his resignation as prime minister, Willoch also passed the leadership of the Conservative Party to his hand-picked successor, Rolf Presthus, who had previously served as Willoch's finance minister.

Reconstruction of the bourgeois coalition became Presthus's chief concern.[3] As finance minister, he had distinguished himself as an effective facilitator of interparty compromise, and the Conservatives had elected him as their leader in large part for this reason. Since the Conservative Party was twice as large as its two potential partners combined, Presthus was also the designated prime ministerial candidate of the three coalitional parties: the Center Party, the Christian People's Party, and the Conservatives. His first opportunity to gain office arose during the finance debate in October 1986, following the budget presentation by Finance Minister Gunnar Berge. Yet, this so-called autumn hunting season failed to produce a change of government. On October 28 it became clear that the three coalitional parties had failed to reach a budget accord and that the Labor government therefore would survive. The breakdown of these negotiations immediately led to mutual blaming and name-calling by Conservative and Center Party representatives.

The next chance to defeat Brundtland arrived the following spring. During the spring session, there were two legislative opportunities for joint nonsocialist action: the revised national budget, which contained an agenda for long-term economic policies such as taxation, and the government's farm bill. During April and May 1987 the three parties began to coordinate their policies in these two areas amid extensive media speculation about the prospects for a change of government based on either issue. Such speculations were encouraged by leaders of all three parties, who issued optimistic, though duly ambiguous, public declarations.

As negotiations moved into a definitive phase in early June, the different designs of the three parties became more evident. Several different potential censure motions were discussed, and the Center Party and the Conservatives in particular had distinctly different preferences. One possibility was a general motion of no confidence that would specify no particular issue. The second and third options were no confidence motions attached to a farm bill amendment (insufficient farm support) or to a minority report on the revised national budget (excessive taxation). The Center Party, with its distinctly rural and agricultural constituency, clearly favored the farm bill option, whereas the Conservatives equally clearly preferred the third (the revised national budget).

The position of the Christian People's Party was less clear. On June 5, party leader Kjell Magne Bondevik expressed a weak preference for the option favored by the Conservatives. However, he seemed most concerned with maximizing the likelihood of passage. What bothered Bondevik was that since the three coalitional parties collectively controlled only 78 of the 157 seats in the Storting (see Table 8.1), they needed the two votes of the pivotal right-wing Progress Party. The six Socialist Left Party representatives had to be counted on to support the Labor government in any showdown with the bourgeois opposition.

Although the three coalitional parties needed the Progressive vote, they were not prepared to enter any binding agreement with a party many considered irresponsible and illegitimate. The question, therefore, was what sort of no confidence motion Carl I. Hagen, the Progress Party leader, would support without a quid pro quo. Hagen had explicitly supported a general no confidence motion. He could also be counted on to be sympathetic to a tax-based challenge to the Labor government, since tax relief was his party's principal policy concern. Higher farm subsidies, on the other hand, was hardly an issue for which the Progress Party was likely to muster any enthusiasm. If the no confidence vote was attached to this bill, Hagen would therefore be forced to choose

Table 8.1. *Norwegian parliamentary parties 1985–1989*

	1985 election	
Party	Votes (in %)	Seats
Labour (A)	40.80	71
Conservatives (H)	30.42	50
Christian People's Party (KRF)	8.26	16
Center Party (SP)	6.47	12
Socialist Left Party (SV)	5.46	6
Progress Party (FRP)	3.72	2

Note: Votes received on joint lists have been apportioned between the participating parties.
Source: Torp 1990.

between his preferences for a nonsocialist government versus lower farm spending.

Negotiations between the three coalitional parties increased in pace through June 8, as the end of the parliamentary session was rapidly approaching. After June 12, the Storting would be in recess for four months, with the September local and regional elections due before another opportunity for a parliamentary showdown would arise. It became clear that the Center Party would insist on attaching the no confidence motion to a farm bill amendment. The Center Party's insistence, which left no room for concessions to the Christian People's Party, the Conservatives, or the Progress Party, set the agenda for the battle over the Labor government's life. The Christian People's Party, which had few stakes in farm policy, quickly accepted the Center Party's policy demands. With the end of the spring session less than a week away, the national executive committee of the Conservative Party on June 8 eventually swallowed the Center Party's insistence on greater farm support as the key to a nonsocialist government. This agreement was cemented on July 10, when the three parties' members of the Agriculture Committee drafted a joint no confidence motion calling for higher farm subsidies.

The pivotal Progress Party decision came on June 11, the penultimate day of the Storting's spring session and the day before the parliamentary vote. Precisely at 7:30 P.M., Progress Party leader Carl I. Hagen held a press conference, which was broadcast live at the beginning of the prime time television news hour. Hagen's speech, in which he made it clear that the Progress Party would not topple Brundtland at the cost of a budget-busting farm bill, was an immense publicity hit. In chastising the other bourgeois parties for their irresponsibility and opportunism, Hagen managed to project fiscal and ethical integrity. And while he rejected the agricultural no confidence motion, Hagen explicitly committed his party to a *general* no confidence vote against Brundtland.

The next day the final act unfolded. Arne Alsåker Spilde, a Conservative member of the agriculture committee, formally introduced the no confidence motion. At about 9:30 P.M., the Storting defeated Spilde's motion by a vote of eighty to seventy-seven when the Progress Party and the Socialist Left cast their lots with the Labor government.[4] Approximately one hour later, the legislators faced a second no confidence motion, pressed by Conservative Jan P. Syse. Syse's motion expressly built on the joint financial statement of the three coalitional parties on the revised national budget. This motion was also supported by the Christian People's Party and allegedly was authored in large part by Kjell Magne Bondevik (*Dagbladet*, June 17, 1987). Yet, after a bitter debate, Syse's motion failed by a larger margin (eighty-nine to sixty-eight) than Spilde's (*Stortingstidende* 1986–7: 4082–4214). The Center Party voted against Syse's measure even though it was based on the party's own financial program. These defeats left the nonsocialist parties embarrassed and bitterly divided, and Socialist Left parliamentary leader Hanna Kvanmo gloated over "this historic moment: the burial of nonsocialist cooperation" (Rommetvedt 1991: 208).[5] Kvanmo was at least temporarily correct, since no further nonsocialist coalition would be attempted until after the September 1989 election.

The Presthus debacle also took a human toll. When the Storting finally took its summer recess at 2:30 A.M., Center Party Deputy Leader Anne Enger Lahnstein remained seated in the empty chamber, quietly weeping over the humiliations her party had suffered during the acrimonious debate. Yet the defeat was hardest on Rolf Presthus himself. More than anybody else, he had been the architect of nonsocialist cooperation, and as the bourgeois prime ministerial candidate, he would also have been its main beneficiary. The failure of Presthus's efforts quickly led to calls for his resignation as Conservative leader. In September the Conservatives suffered a staggering defeat in the local and regional elections, and Presthus immediately tendered his resignation. Four months later he was dead, felled by a massive heart attack.

COALITION BARGAINING

The Presthus debacle was a complex process with many players. Table 8.2 provides a list of the main protagonists. In order to make sense of the events that led to the events of June 1987, I use a game representation in which each of the critical parties is a player. The game between these parties can be divided into two subgames: an unstructured bargaining game up through June 10, which set the agenda for a subsequent, structured end game over the following two days.

Table 8.2. *Players in the Presthus debacle*

Party	Individual	Position
Labor (A)	Gunnar Berge	Finance minister
	Gro H. Brundtland	Prime minister
Conservatives (H)	Jo Benkow	President of the Storting
	Rolf Presthus	Party leader
	Arne A. Spilde	Member of Agricultural Committee
	Jan P. Syse	Parliamentary party leader
	Kåre I. Willoch	Former prime minister (1981–6)
Christian People's Party (KRF)	Kjell M. Bondevik	Party leader
Center Party (SP)	Ragnhild Q. Haarstad	Member of Hedmark guerrilla
	Johan J. Jakobsen	Party leader
	Anne E. Lahnstein	Deputy party leader
	Lars Velsand	Member of Hedmark guerrilla
Socialist Left Party (SV)	Hanna Kvanmo	Parliamentary party leader
Progress Party (FRP)	Carl I. Hagen	Party leader

Consider first the end game, as illustrated in Figure 8.1. The game tree in Figure 8.1 contains three decision nodes. These decision nodes represent choices faced by the various nonsocialist parties and the sequence in which they were confronted.[6] The branches lead from the starting node to four different outcomes (end nodes), identified by roman numerals. End node III represents the actual outcome. For simplicity, Figure 8.1 excludes parties whose moves were taken for granted by all players. Thus, it was common knowledge that Labor and the Socialist Left would vote against any no confidence motion, that the Christian People's Party would support any feasible motion, and that the Progressives would join any taxation-related or general motion pressed by the Conservatives. The parties in question had, in essence, precommitted themselves to these strategies. The agenda reconstructed in Figure 8.1 had been set by the previous bargaining between the three coalitional parties.

The sequence of moves is as follows. The Progress Party first decides whether to accept the farm bill amendment. If it does, the government is defeated (outcome I). If, on the other hand, the Progress Party rejects this no confidence motion, then Brundtland's fate depends on the further moves by the other bourgeois parties. The Conservatives have to decide, presumably after consultations with the Christian People's Party, whether or not to press their own motion of no confidence, based on the long-term economic program. If they do not, the game ends at outcome IV. If they do press the second no confidence motion, and assuming the support of the Christian People's Party and the Progressives, the Center Party subsequently has a second opportunity to

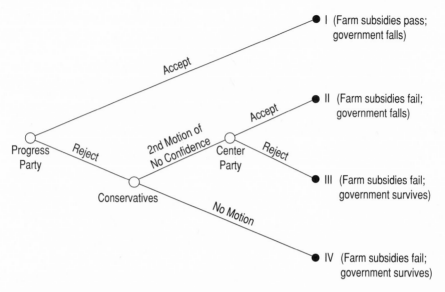

Figure 8.1 Extensive-form representation of the Presthus debacle end game.

dislodge Brundtland (outcome II). If the Center Party rejects the second (Syse) censure motion, however, the outcome is III.[7]

PARTY OBJECTIVES

In order to solve this game, we need to stipulate how each party evaluates the outcomes to which each of its choices may lead. It is clearly desirable to derive these preferences from some general assumptions about the motives ("objective functions") of the players, here the relevant Norwegian party leaders. For this purpose, we rely on three common and parsimonious models of competitive party behavior. These behavioral models, which are discussed in Chapter 1 of this volume, are (1) the office-seeking party, (2) the policy-seeking party, and (3) the vote-seeking party. These general models must be given concrete meaning in this Norwegian case. This is done by specifying the aspects of the various outcomes that are relevant to each party under each behavioral assumption. This specification is obviously a very tall order, and again, I simplify as much as possible.

POLICY PREFERENCES

If parties were pure policy seekers, then what was the critical aspect of the game outcome? As shown in Table 8.3, the only policy issue clearly riding on the June 1987 negotiations was agricultural policy. On June 6, Center Party leader

Table 8.3. *Properties of different bargaining outcomes*

Property	Outcome			
	I	II	III	IV
Government falls?	Y	Y	N	N
Farm subsidies pass?	Y	N	N	N
Coalition politics agree?	Y	Y	N	Y
Center Party policy – consistent?	Y	Y	N	Y

Johan J. Jakobsen had taken pains to stress that a potential nonsocialist government should not be expected to pursue significantly different general economic
policies from its predecessor (Rommetvedt 1991: 196). I hence assume that
policy-seeking parties vote according to their preferences on the farm issue, and
that they are indifferent between outcomes that are equivalent as far as farm
policy is concerned.[8] Only secondarily do other issues enter their calculations,
in the sense that if forced to vote on other issues (i.e., the long-term economic
program), parties prefer voting in accordance with their program to voting
against it.[9]

> *Assumption P1:* The Center Party prefers any outcome in which the govern-
> ment's farm bill fails to any outcome in which it passes. Thus, outcome
> I is preferred to all others. Secondarily, if forced to vote on its long-term
> economic program, the party prefers to support this motion rather than
> oppose it. Hence, the Center Party prefers outcome II to outcome III.
>
> *Assumption P2:* The Conservative Party and the Progress Party prefer any
> outcome in which the farm bill amendment fails to any outcome in
> which it passes. Thus, outcomes II through IV are preferred to outcome
> I.

OFFICE PREFERENCES

The implications of an office-seeking model are more straightforward. Under
these assumptions, the three potential coalition partners prefer office to opposition. The Progress Party, which would be without office under any circumstances, is assumed to be indifferent. I assume that Brundtland's resignation
would lead to the formation of a three-party bourgeois cabinet, and that she
would not resign voluntarily.

> *Assumption O1:* The Center Party and the Conservative Party prefer any out-
> come in which the Brundtland government must resign to any outcome

in which it is not forced to resign. Thus, these parties prefer outcomes I and II to all others.

Assumption O2: The Progress Party is indifferent between outcomes in which the Brundtland government must resign and outcomes in which it does not resign. Thus, this party is indifferent between all outcomes.

ELECTORAL PREFERENCES

Finally, assume that parties are motivated strictly by future electoral gain. We can distinguish between *individual* and *collective* electoral costs that parties may suffer as a consequence of their parliamentary behavior. Individual costs are associated with policy *inconsistency*, that is, with voting against party programs or previous commitments. Collective electoral costs are a more complex matter. The Norwegian electorate apparently contains a significant number of sophisticated nonsocialists whose first preference is a minor party such as the Progress Party or the Liberals. Yet, these voters may be induced to vote strategically for one of the three coalitional parties if and only if these parties jointly present a credible alternative to a Labor government. Otherwise, these individuals vote sincerely for the smaller party closer to their policy preferences. In other words, these voters can be persuaded to cast a *governmental*, rather than a *partisan*, vote if they believe that a governmental choice exists. The three coalitional parties therefore have a collective interest in enhancing their credibility as a potential government. Hence, they should avoid any behavior, such as overt policy disagreements, that detracts from this credibility. The Progress Party, on the other hand, should for electoral purposes seek to provoke precisely such conflict.

This interpretation is corroborated by the 1987 events. Polls taken immediately after the Presthus debacle showed marked declines for the Conservatives (from 30.2 percent to 27.1 percent) as well as the Center Party (from 5.9 percent to 5.2 percent). The Christian People's Party, which had been conciliatory throughout, registered a modest gain (from 8.1 percent to 8.4 percent). But the big winner was the Progress Party, which leaped from 5.1 percent to 7.1 percent (Rommetvedt 1987).[10] The Progress Party later continued to surge, reaching a stunning 12.3 percent of the national vote in the September regional elections, a result more than twice as strong as in any previous election.

Hence, the assumptions of the vote-seeking model are as follows:

Assumption V1: The Center Party prefers any outcome in which it does not vote against its previous policy to any outcome in which it does. It also prefers voting consistently with the other coalition parties to voting contrary to one or both of them. Consequently, the Center Party prefers all other outcomes to outcome III.

Assumption V2: The Progress Party prefers any outcome in which any subset of the Center Party, the Christian People's Party, and the Conservative

Party vote inconsistently with each other to any outcome in which they all vote consistently. Hence, outcome III is preferred to all others.

Assumption V3: The Conservative Party prefers voting consistently with the Center Party and the Christian People's Party to voting inconsistently with one or both of them. Hence, the Conservative Party prefers all other outcomes to outcome III.

THE PUZZLES

With these assumptions, we can apply simple, noncooperative game theory to solve the end game in Figure 8.1. Working back up the game tree, we find that outcome II is in Nash equilibrium under all three behavioral assumptions, as shown in Table 8.4. Outcome IV is also an equilibrium if we assume policy- or vote-seeking parties, whereas outcome I is an option if parties are assumed to be office seekers. The problem, of course, is that outcome II failed to materialize on June 12, 1987. The Center Party did *not* vote for Jan P. Syse's motion of no confidence. And the outcome that *did* result is the only one that is not an equilibrium under *any* of our behavioral models.

Three puzzles thus persist: (1) Why did the Progress Party oppose the farm bill amendment, even though it turned out to be the only feasible way to give Norway the nonsocialist government the party explicitly favored? (2) Why did the Conservatives support higher farm subsidies, even though this policy ran counter to their program and failed to win the party either office or votes? (3) And finally, why did the Center Party, after its farm bill amendment had been defeated, vote against a measure that would have put the party in government and prevented an acrimonious conflict with the other nonsocialists? The remainder of this chapter examines these questions in turn, exploring some additional considerations that could be incorporated in an extensive-form model. These considerations include interparty differences in objectives, incomplete information, and the effects of organizational arrangements that involve party leaders in simultaneous games with their respective followers, as well as with one another.

COMPLEX OBJECTIVES

Initially, we assumed that all parties had identical goals: policy, office, or votes. We later relaxed that assumption so as to permit lexicographic preferences. Still, however, we assumed that all parties had the same objective functions. In order to grasp the June 1987 events, however, we need to move beyond these simplifications and to consider (1) how different goals may be traded off against each other and (2) how parties differ in the weight they give to different objectives.

Let us examine the end game under the assumption that parties have objective functions that include office, policy, and votes. The goals can be traded

Table 8.4. *Equilibria according to party objectives*

	Outcome			
Party objective	I	II	III	IV
1. Office (O)	X	X	—	—
2. Policy (P)	—	X	—	X
3. Votes (V)	—	X	—	X
4. O > P	—	X	—	—
5. O > P	X	X	—	—
6. P > V	—	X	—	—
7. O > P > V	—	X	—	—

Note: X denotes a subgame perfect Nash equilibrium. Stipulations 4–7 assume lexicographic preferences.

off against each other, and parties may vary in their valuation of, for example, policy benefits vis-à-vis marginal votes. Only if we acknowledge such goal differences between parties can we have any hope of understanding the sequence of decisions that led to the Presthus debacle. How do we then, in turn, explain such differences in party preferences? Surely, *institutional explanations* will not do, since all three parties were operating within the same political arena. In this case, therefore, it is natural to consider differences in party organization.

PARTY ORGANIZATION AND LEADERSHIP

Party organizations, of course, have many facets, most of which cannot be examined here. Yet, decisions concerning cabinet formation and participation have the advantage that they directly involve only a small elite of party leaders. In such negotiations, party leaders act as *agents* for their respective parliamentary or extraparliamentary parties (their *principals*) in coalition bargaining. Because of variation in *delegation regimes*, different leaders may be variously constrained in these negotiations, and it is these patterns of delegation and constraint that can help us understand the puzzles of party behavior associated with the Presthus debacle. This analysis will disclose dramatic and consequential differences in intraparty delegation between the Center Party and the Conservatives. Bargaining outcomes may be severely affected by such constraints, and when bargaining fails, it may be because of the ways the hands of the bargaining parties are tied.

Most Norwegian parties have a similar organizational structure. At the national level, each party has a fairly standard set of organizational units. The national congress (*landsmøtet*), which normally meets in the spring, is the highest formal authority within the party. A partial exception must be made for the Conservative Party, in which such authority is not formally vested in the party congress (Heidar 1997). In practice, however, Conservative Party congresses perform much the same functions as those of every other party. Their lack of formal recognition as the highest party authority is an interesting reflection of the Conservatives' origins as the "internally created" party par excellence in Norwegian politics. The congress elects key officers and adopts various official policy documents.

Between party congresses, the leadership function is officially delegated to two party committees elected by the congress: the national council (*landsstyret*) and the central committee (*sentralstyret*).[11] The national council, which in large part consists of representatives from the provincial organizations, meets several times per year but is not in continuous activity. The central committee, which typically has between eight and twenty members, conducts the daily leadership of the party. From 1960 on, the structures of the party organizations have converged. All parties have, in fact, become mirror images of the Labor Party's structure.[12]

Identifying the party leader can be treacherous in Norway, since each political party has several positions of leadership and since the powers given to these offices vary. Norwegian parties have two top leadership positions: one associated with the extraparliamentary party organization and one with the parliamentary party. Each party's extraparliamentary organization has a chair (*formann* or *leder*) and typically two deputy chairs (*viseformann* or *nestleder*), all elected at the national party congress.

PARTY CHAIRS

In most parties, the chair is the effective organizational leader, though jurisdictions and responsibilities vary. The effective power of the various office holders obviously also varies with their personal leadership qualities and organizational resource base, issues I explore later. The Labor Party, though, is a clear example of a party in which the parliamentary leader has played a clearly minor role compared to the party chair. In the Conservative Party, on the other hand, there is a tradition of organizational subservience to the parliamentary party, and many Conservative chairs have essentially been *managers* rather than top-flight decision makers. Thus, Alv Kjøs (1954–62) and Sjur Lindebrække (1962–70) each served a long term as chair without in any way being the effective Conservative leader. Certainly, neither was ever considered for the prime ministership of the 1963 and 1965–71 coalitions in which the Conservatives participated. The smaller centrist parties, such as the Christian People's Party and the Center Party, have generally fallen between Labor and the Conservatives in these respects, though as some of these parties have had their parliamentary representation reduced, the locus of power seems to have shifted to the extraparliamentary party. Interestingly, the two parliamentary parties of postwar origin, the

Socialist Left Party and the Progress Party, have very strong extraparliamentary chairs despite their radically different political colorations.

PARLIAMENTARY LEADERS

The second leadership office is that of parliamentary leader. Each of the parties represented in the Storting (six in the 1985–9 term) has a parliamentary party organization separate from but linked to the regular party organization. The party caucus in the Storting is called the *Storting group* (*stortingsgruppe*) and is headed by the party's parliamentary leader (*parlamentarisk leder*). Each party, even if it consists of only one representative, constitutes a parliamentary group. If a group has only two members, then one of them acts as parliamentary leader. The parliamentary leader is the main spokesman for the party and therefore plays a vital role in interparty negotiations.

In some parties, the parliamentary leadership has traditionally been the effective leadership position. This is most clearly the case for the Conservative Party, whose prime ministers (John Lyng in 1963, and Kåre Willoch in 1981) have moved up from this rank rather than from the party chairmanship.[13] Yet, in the 1980s, power seems to have shifted decisively away from the Conservative parliamentary leader to the party chair, a trend noted by Heidar (1988: 29). Since Willoch's political retirement in 1986, the party chairs have been the Conservative Party's prime ministerial candidates, a phenomenon most clearly illustrated in 1991, when the effective leadership was vested in chair Karin Cecilie ("Kaci") Kullman Five rather than in parliamentary leader Anders Talleraas. In the Labor Party, on the other hand, the parliamentary leader has never been close to parity with the party chair. The Center Party, the Liberals, and especially the Christian People's Party have traditionally had strong parliamentary leaders, but the power relationship between the two top offices in these parties has been obscured by the frequent occupation of both offices by the same person.

Over the last three decades, the position of the parliamentary group has changed dramatically in several parties. The Conservative parliamentarians have lost their dominating position within the party's national council as the latter has been expanded through the addition of representatives from various ancillary organizations. Such provisions do not exist in any of the other nonsocialist parties, with the recent exception of the Progress Party.

LEADERSHIP SELECTION

Norwegian law treats political parties, in the main, as *private* organizations. Consequently, there are few binding regulations concerning such matters as their leadership selection processes. Indeed, the principle of nonintervention applies even to public party finance, as well as, with modifications, to candidate selection. Although there exists a *nomination law*, for example, it is not obligatory. General compliance is secured through positive financial inducements, as parties that follow prescribed procedures get some of their expenses covered by the government.

Party Chairs

Norwegian party chairs and deputy chairs are elected regularly by their respective party congresses (*landsmøtet*), which normally meet in the early months of the year. Some parties have annual congresses (Conservatives, Progress Party), whereas others (Christian People's Party, Center Party) meet only every other year, that is, in all election years (all odd-numbered years). The congress elects party chairs, deputy chairs, and other key organizational officers. These officers are typically elected for two-year terms, even in parties that have annual congresses. All elections are normally by simple majority, although few parties have very specific election rules. Though some serve ex officio, most congress delegates are elected by their respective province organizations. Demographically, they do not deviate greatly from the activists and other members who elect them (Heidar 1988). Formally, the selection process is therefore relatively *inclusive*. Well in advance of the congress, a nominating committee is appointed by the national council, or in some cases by the congress preceding the one where the election will take place. This nominating committee is the official body that seeks to find appropriate candidates for various national offices.

Parliamentary Leaders

The parliamentary leader in all parties is formally elected by the party's parliamentary caucus (*stortingsgruppe*). Typically, only the party's elected representatives enjoy voting rights in the caucus, though it is customary for other officials, such as cabinet members, undersecretaries of state, the party's general secretary, its parliamentary secretaries, and sometimes other leading party figures to have the right to attend and speak. Only in the Progress Party, however, do individuals who are not members of parliament have actual voting rights. In the Progress Party, the national council elects five members of the parliamentary caucus, a practice that illustrates its radical subordination of the parliamentary group to the extraparliamentary organization.

Despite their general similarities, the Center Party, the Conservatives, and the Progress Party thus present somewhat different organizational features. The Conservative Party traditionally has featured a strong parliamentary party accustomed to delegating critical decisions to its leader, whereas particularly in the Progress Party, the influence of the extraparliamentary leadership is stronger. More important, however, were the characteristics of the particular leaderships of 1987. Whereas Jakobsen and Hagen were entrenched leaders with almost ten years' tenure each, Presthus was still new and inexperienced. Even more critically, the Center and Progress leaders had a much firmer grip on their extraparliamentary parties (both were party chairs as well as parliamentary leaders). Yet, Hagen could dominate his parliamentary delegation of two (himself and a military officer used to taking orders) much more thoroughly than Jakobsen could.

THE INTRAPARTY GAMES

Let us now return to the decisions of the three critical parties, with an eye toward the constraints each leader faced within his own party.

THE CENTER PARTY: THROWING THE STEERING WHEEL OUT THE WINDOW

The greatest puzzle in the Presthus debacle is the behavior of the Center Party at the last decision node, where it faced no uncertainty. If he rejected the censure motion from the Conservatives and the Christian People's Party, Jakobsen's party would be left in opposition and susceptible to electoral repercussions. The farm bill amendment had already been lost. As costless office benefits were rejected and electoral liabilities accepted, the party seems deliberately to have made itself worse off.

Yet, this behavior was no accident. Immediately after Hagen's press conference, the Center Party declared its opposition to a potential censure motion based on the revised national budget. The party's executive council issued a similar proclamation the day *before* Hagen's press conference (Rommetvedt 1991: 206). At that time, Center Party representatives explained their apparently uncooperative behavior as a way to force the Progress Party to accept higher farm subsidies. If Hagen believed that the Center Party would support a second no confidence motion, they argued, he would have no incentive to accept higher farm spending. However, the Center Party's posturing was "cheap talk" rather than a credible threat. If ultimately forced to choose between outcomes II and III, the party would still have office as well as electoral incentives to vote *for* the no confidence motion. Hence, Hagen could confidently call the Center Party's bluff. Yet even before the final vote, neither Hagen nor the Conservative leaders apparently harbored much hope that Syse's no confidence motion would carry. Even the Labor Party taunted the Center Party during the debate, essentially daring the party to bring down the government.

The key to the Center Party's intransigence surely lies in intraparty constraints. Jakobsen's insistence on the farm bill measure was at least in part caused by the deep skepticism of two members of parliament, Ragnhild Q. Haarstad and Lars Velsand, about any coalition with the Conservatives. Haarstad and Velsand represented the so-called Hedmark guerrilla, a vocal and well-organized left-wing faction of the party.[14] Jakobsen, who himself favored a change of government, appears to have precommitted himself to this group in internal party negotiations. In the parliamentary caucus, Velsand on June 5 voted to accept the Labor Party's farm bill. His eventual support for a censure motion was expressly conditional on the farm bill amendment. A censure motion on any other basis was unacceptable (Thomassen 1991: 33–4).[15] Haarstad was even more intransigent and proceeded to vote against the party's own (technically, Spilde's) no confidence motion, a highly unusual occurrence in traditionally cohesive Norwegian parties.

Could Jakobsen have reneged on his commitment and thrown his weight behind the Syse no confidence motion anyway? Even if no formal mechanisms existed through which he could be held responsible for his precommitments, informal sanctions might well have been applied against Jakobsen in such an event. Besides, had he supported a second no confidence motion, a humiliating scenario might have ensued. The bourgeois majority in the Storting was so slender (eighty to seventy-seven) that it could tolerate only one defection, such as Haarstad's on the first censure vote. Had both Haarstad and Velsand opposed the Syse motion, it would have failed even with Progress Party support, and no one would have looked more ineffectual than Jakobsen.

Thus, the Hedmark guerrilla was in fact pivotal, and Jakobsen may therefore have preferred the seemingly irrational strategy leading to outcome III for internal party reasons. The nested games in which the Center Party leader was involved may account for his anomalous behavior (Tsebelis 1990). His impotence was caused by the pivotal parliamentary position of the Hedmark guerrilla. This small group of parliamentarians was able to impose strict ex ante controls on their leader's negotiations with the Conservatives. By allowing Jakobsen virtually no discretion in bargaining, the Center Party had essentially "thrown the steering wheel out the window." Such brinkmanship may have helped the party in bargaining with the Conservatives, but it came back to haunt the agrarians in the parliamentary debate on June 12.

One additional consideration may have been involved in the Center Party's decision. Quite possibly, Jakobsen did not think of himself as playing a one-shot game. If indeed he foresaw a series of interparty games, his concern may have been *reputation* (Kreps 1990; Calvert 1987). According to Rommetvedt (1991: 207), one Center Party parliamentarian remarked in retrospect that he would have preferred a different strategy. But once the party had insisted on the farm bill measure, it had to stick with it. Or in Rommetvedt's (1991: 210) words, "the party had tied itself so tightly to the mast that it could not vote for the general motion of no confidence without losing credibility at later junctures." Jakobsen thus became a victim of his own precommitment (Elster 1984).

THE CONSERVATIVE PARTY: INCOMPATIBLE INCENTIVES

Our next puzzle is the behavior of the Conservative Party. As much as the Progress Party won the June 1987 showdown, the Conservative Party was the loser. The party failed to dislodge Brundtland, poisoned its relationship with the Center Party, and suffered badly in the polls. After June 12 the political career of Rolf Presthus was effectively ruined. One could hardly imagine a less desirable outcome. Both critical Conservative decisions seem foolhardy in retrospect: acquiescence in the farm bill censure motion as well as the subsequent decision to press a second no confidence vote. Why on earth did the Conservatives go down this path to disaster?

The answer surely involves incomplete information concerning the Progress Party. Also, Presthus's dilemma directs our attention to the internal politics of the Conservative Party. The Conservatives clearly realized the risk that their acquiescence on the farm subsidy issue would be for naught if the Progress Party balked. Ideally, Presthus therefore wanted some guarantee of cooperation, either from the Progress Party or from the Center Party (concerning a potential second censure motion), before accepting this agenda. Unfortunately, any explicit agreement with the pariah Progress Party was ruled off limits by his two would-be coalition partners. Hence, the Conservatives repeatedly attempted to extract assurances from the Center Party that the latter would remain committed to bringing down Brundtland in a potential second round.[16] Parliamentary leader Jan P. Syse raised this issue during negotiations on June 7. But Jakobsen steadfastly refused to issue any such guarantee.

Given this uncertainty, the prospects seem to have been estimated differently by the various Conservative leaders. Former Prime Minister Kåre Willoch and Storting President Jo Benkow both opposed Presthus's course of action (Bakke 1990: 187; Rommetvedt 1991: 196; Willoch 1990: 404). And though he supported Presthus, parliamentary leader Jan P. Syse seems to have pressed more insistently for a guarantee from the Center Party.[17] Did these experienced parliamentarians estimate more correctly the probabilities that the Progress Party and the Center Party would make the choices necessary to propel Presthus into the prime ministership? Was Presthus a victim of wishful thinking?

Perhaps. But according to Thomassen (1991: 35), both Presthus and Syse recognized that the farm bill amendment was a huge gamble. Presthus apparently chose to accept big risks and to "swallow camels" in order to gain the prime ministership. He was willing to accept quite unpalatable policies and take substantial electoral risks in the hope of dislodging Brundtland. Rather than any personal idiosyncracy, however, this behavior reflected Presthus's "contract" with the Conservative Party and, more specifically, the incompatibility between his incentives as an individual and the interests of the party.

After only about a year as Conservative leader, Presthus's star had already begun to fade. Though he had been elected in large part because of his perceived skills in promoting nonsocialist cooperation, he had failed to deliver the bourgeois government for which many Conservatives were hoping. A consummate insider, Presthus also had not proven to be an inspiring opposition leader. He was hounded in the media for his failure in the "autumn hunting season," as well as for his awkward style. And in the Norwegian Conservative Party, as among tories elsewhere, nothing fails like failure. The party's biennial congress in Tromsø in early May 1987 made a change of government before the end of the spring session an explicit party goal, thus adding to the pressure on Presthus (Norvik 1990: 156; Thomassen 1991: 30–1; Willoch 1990: 403–4). Time was already running out for Presthus, and he knew it. Regaining executive office had been defined as his overriding concern, and there was little difference to him between the various outcomes short of this goal.

Thus, in considering the second censure motion, Presthus may not have attached much value to the *added* electoral liability of outcome III as compared to outcome IV. Either way, the party would remain in opposition and be electorally damaged. Presthus's leadership was also likely to come to an end. But if Presthus was thus essentially indifferent between outcomes III and IV, then any infinitesimal chance that the Center Party would "tremble" and support the Syse censure motion would lead Presthus down this path (Selten 1975). In fact, the negotiators from the Conservative Party and the Christian People's Party took care to maximize the costs to the Center Party of rejecting Syse's proposal (Rommetvedt 1991: 208).

The Conservative executive committee members may not have shared Presthus's preferences, but with customary deference they allowed him the rope by which he would come to his political demise. Presthus's gamble was approved by the party's executive committee, as well as by its parliamentary caucus. In fact, in the parliamentary caucus only three out of fifty members were opposed (Bakke 1990: 188; Norvik 1990: 158).[18] By tradition, the Conservative Party's control of its leaders has taken the form mainly of ex post accountability. And predictably, after his gamble failed, Presthus's leadership of the Conservative Party was doomed. While his complicity in the design to increase farm subsidies might have been forgiven, it was much more difficult to overlook the electoral damage he had inflicted. In other words, while Presthus might have been able to trade off policy goals with impunity, he could not get away with sacrificing the party's electorate.

THE PROGRESS PARTY: STUDIED AMBIGUITY

If both the Center Party and the Conservatives had insisted on their own no confidence motion, the parliamentary session would have ended without a change of government. In all other scenarios, however, the Progressive vote would decide Brundtland's fate. The preferences of the Progress Party were therefore critical to the calculations of the other parties. Though the Progress Party kept Norwegians in suspense about its intentions, one thing was perfectly clear. If the government's farm bill and the no confidence motion were separated, the Progressives would support both and thereby give the country a bourgeois cabinet without higher agricultural spending. Hagen had committed his party as early as May 29 (Rommetvedt 1991: 191), by declaring that the Progress Party would support a Conservative censure motion. As it turned out,

Hagen would not have the luxury of separating these two issues. Until June 11, however, he remained noncommittal concerning the farm bill amendment favored by the Center Party.

The private information the Progress Party had about its own preferences can be a source of considerable bargaining power. Carl I. Hagen exploited this advantage to the hilt, playing his cards extremely close to his chest. The public statements Hagen made prior to his dramatic press conference on June 11 were studiedly ambiguous. When it became increasingly clear that the farm bill would be the basis of the no confidence motion, Hagen tempered his enthusiasm for the bourgeois coalition. On June 6 he admitted to having doubts about the three-party coalition, citing internal differences and the lack of a clear policy alternative to the Labor government (Rommetvedt 1991: 196). Two days later he reiterated his opposition to increased agricultural transfers, yet the following day he told journalists that his party might well vote against the government's farm bill anyway.

In his equivocation, Hagen kept stressing the need to consult his party's national and regional officers, many of whom were known to oppose any policy compromise. And in Hagen's public justification of his final decision, the voice of his party's activists had a prominent place. Were Hagen's hands then tied by his organization, due, perhaps, to his party's commitment to reducing transfers to Norwegian agriculture? Not likely. Hagen's personal authority in his party was immense, and on a similar issue in 1985 he had, without serious repercussions, voted against his party's program in order to save Willoch. Hagen's deference to his party's officers was therefore probably more of a rationalization than a rationale.

Hagen possessed valuable private information about his party's preferences, which he could reveal at his discretion. As it turned out, Hagen precommitted himself to a Conservative-type no confidence measure but remained inscrutable concerning a potential farm-bill measure. Why did he make these choices? In all likelihood, Hagen's precommitment to no confidence on the revised national budget was designed to strengthen the Conservatives in their negotiations with the Center Party. Certainly, the Progressives shared with the Conservatives a preference for lower farm spending. But why did Hagen not further boost the bargaining power of the Conservatives by fully revealing his preference, that is, by clearly rejecting a farm bill amendment? The Progress Party, after all, had both electoral and policy incentives to vote against Spilde's censure motion. Yet, a threat to oppose this motion might not have been believed by the Center Party. After all, Hagen had an incentive to engage in cheap talk of this kind, regardless of his intentions. Alternatively, the Presthus debacle may have been Hagen's most preferred outcome if he placed sufficient value on the electoral damage the coalitional parties could inflict on themselves.

Hagen's electoral considerations were themselves probably something of a gamble. If he accepted increased farm subsidies, he stood to suffer a small but predictable loss of votes among his libertarian supporters. If, on the other hand, he made the much more dramatic gesture of opposing the bourgeois no confidence motion, the electoral fallout would be much more unpredictable. When the Socialist People's Party in a similar situation in 1963 brought down Einar Gerhardsen's Labor government, it suffered stinging losses among voters incensed at its complicity in the formation of Norway's first postwar bourgeois government. Hagen, however, gambled on his ability to frame the issues in such a way that he would appear the principled and responsible statesman rather than the traitor to the nonsocialist cause. Given the party's precarious electoral position, the Progressives could ill afford even a small but certain electoral setback. Even a drop of .5 percent in the national poll could deprive the party of its parliamentary representation. Better, then, to gamble at the high-stakes tables. His party's weakness among the voters made Hagen highly *risk-acceptant* over electoral outcomes and willing to take his case to the people. In this endeavor, he was amazingly successful, probably beyond his wildest imagination.

WHY PRESTHUS BLINKED

Having thus explored the seemingly irrational behavior of the Center Party and the Conservatives in the end game, we can now return to their preceding bargaining game. In game-theoretic terms, Jakobsen and Presthus were engaged in a form of "war of attrition," which is a version of the more familiar game of chicken stretched out in time. In such games, mutual insistence (or intransigence) is the most disastrous outcome for all players involved. In the Presthus bargaining game, the penalty for mutual intransigence would even rise dramatically at the end of the parliamentary session, when the opposition parties suddenly would have to wait four months and go through local elections before they had another shot at the government. As the end of the session approached, the incentives to acquiesce therefore rose dramatically. It was no surprise, therefore, that agreement on a censure motion was reached only two days before the summer recess.

This agreement obviously represented a major concession by the Conservatives, a concession that would turn into a humiliating rout. Clearly, Presthus blinked first. Initially, both the Center Party and the Conservatives had taken a tough bargaining stance. What accounts for the Center Party's success against the Conservatives in this game? Two factors seem plausible: (1) the credible constraints on Jakobsen versus the wide discretion given to Presthus and (2) the greater impatience (higher discount rate) of Presthus, due again to his personal incentives. Conservative leaders presumably knew of the resistance Jakobsen faced among the Hedmark guerrilla, as it was in the Center Party leader's interest to inform them that his hands were tied. Center Party negotiators, on the other hand, knew that Presthus had the latitude to make policy compromises and that he needed a quick fix. These circumstances eventually doomed the Conservatives in their negotiations.

Both Presthus and Jakobsen were thus constrained by their party organizations, but in radically different ways. Jakobsen was firmly policy-constrained ex ante and in reality had no choice but to oppose the Syse motion. Presthus enjoyed much more policy discretion but was constrained by his need to deliver office benefits. This contrast between the Center and Conservative parties reflects interesting organizational differences in delegation regimes. Presthus was constrained by his ex post *accountability* to his party. He was expected to produce office benefits at minimal electoral cost and knew that without results, he was eminently dispensable. Jakobsen, on the other hand, faced less obvious challenges to his leadership but was essentially powerless to make policy compromises.

CONCLUSIONS

This chapter has examined a dramatic and puzzling case of coalition bargaining failure in recent Norwegian history: the Presthus debacle of 1987. Whereas Hagen was seeking electoral gains and Jakobsen farm subsidies, Presthus was primarily concerned with office payoffs. Hagen's humiliation of Jakobsen, and especially of Presthus, demonstrates the value of private information. Finally, Jakobsen's case highlights the attractions and perils of precommitments.

With respect to intraparty decision making, the Presthus case offers us no happy medium between the Scylla of strict ex ante constraint (Jakobsen) and the Charybdis of lax ex post accountability (Presthus). Both the Conservatives and the Center Party featured delegation regimes ill suited to the bargaining situation in which they found themselves, and much of the responsibility for the Presthus debacle rests with these internal structures of Norwegian political parties.

Yet, even without misdelegation the bargaining situation faced by Presthus and his associates invited disaster. The most important peril lay in the impending summer recess. The closer the end of the session drew, the higher the stakes, until the flurry of frenzied activity in the last few days before the "guillotine" fell. Such frantic times have a way of producing ill-considered behavior, a phenomenon well known from congressional budget debates in the United States (Cox and Kernell 1991). Thus, time and structure are important keys to the dismal fate of Rolf Presthus and his would-be coalition partners. Given time, knowledge, and appropriate incentives, the story might have been a happier one for Presthus, Jakobsen, and Bondevik (and less triumphant for Hagen and Brundtland).

NOTES

1. I wish to thank the American-Scandinavian Foundation for its generous funding of this research through a King Olav V Fellowship. My thanks also to Paul R. Abramson, Scott Gates, John D. Huber, Arend Lijphart, Sharyn O'Halloran, Bjørn Erik Rasch, Steven S. Smith, Ruth M. Sylte, George Tsebelis, and especially Gary W. Cox for helpful comments on earlier drafts, and to Hilmar Rommetvedt for graciously making his personal notes and files available to me. I am solely responsible, of course, for all errors and interpretations.

2. The 1965–71 cabinet, headed by Per Borten of the Center Party, was a four-party coalition, whereas the 1983–6 government failed to include the Liberals (*Venstre*). The Liberals lost their parliamentary representation in 1985 and were therefore not a relevant party in the events described here.

3. In this chapter I use the terms *non-socialist* and *bourgeois* interchangeably. This usage is consistent with Norwegian convention and is neither derogatory nor indicative of a class-analytic perspective. In fact, the non-socialist parties frequently apply the label bourgeois (*borgerlig*) to themselves.

4. In addition, one member of the Center Party, Ragnhild Queseth Haarstad, voted against her party's position on this bill. After disposing of Spilde's no confidence motion, the Storting overwhelmingly, by a vote of 123 to 34, rejected a motion by Arent Henriksen of the Socialist Left party to increase agricultural appropriations.

5. Here as elsewhere, I am responsible for all translations from the Norwegian.

6. Note that this sequence corresponds to the order in which the parties had to make their actual decisions, and not to the formal voting procedure in the Storting.

7. It might seem that end node III could be followed by one or more additional no confidence motions. As the following argument shows, however, outcome III implies that no such motion would pass. Since we assume that there is an electoral cost to the coalitional parties to proposing divisive no confidence motions, any further agenda can be disregarded.

8. All preference relations are assumed to be *strict* unless otherwise indicated.

9. Note that this does not commit the Center Party or the Conservatives to prefer voting for its respective program to *not voting*. Hence, the Conservatives have no *policy* incentive to introduce the Syse motion.

10. In the case of both the pre-event and post-event polls, the figures referred to here represent the means of polls by several authoritative firms. The earlier figures are the averages of polls by Norsk Gallup, MMI, and Scan Fact. The later figures represent the means of polls by Norsk Gallup and Opinion. See Rommetvedt (1987) for details.

11. In the Conservative Party the equivalent of the national committee is called *sentralstyret* and the central committee *arbeidsutvalget*. The Christian People's Party, the Center Party, and the Progress Party reserve the latter label for a core subgroup of the central committee.

12. In the Conservative, Liberal, and Christian People's parties, there used to be only one national council, with an internal subcommittee. These parties introduced *two* committees in the early 1970s: a larger national council with representation

from the province organizations and a smaller executive committee, usually containing a subcommittee (Svåsand, Strøm, and Rasch 1997).

13. The third Conservative postwar prime minister, Jan P. Syse, held both the chairmanship and the parliamentary leadership concurrently when he took office in 1989.

14. The unofficial name of this faction alludes to the province of Hedmark, an agricultural area in east central Norway and the constituency of Ragnhild Q. Haarstad. The province is a traditional stronghold of the Center Party.

15. In his memoirs, Petter Thomassen (1991: 33) reports that the internal debate in the Center Party was so intense that Jakobsen wept when Velsand came around to supporting the Spilde no confidence motion. Thomassen is a leading Conservative who served as minister of industry in the Willoch cabinet (1985–6).

16. Bente Bakke, a Conservative maverick backbencher, reports that the need for a precommitment from the other coalitional parties was strongly felt within the Conservative parliamentary caucus. After the failed autumn hunting season the previous year, parliamentary leader Jan P. Syse had reportedly assured the members that no further assaults on the Brundtland government would be attempted without the binding agreement of both the Christian People's Party and the Center Party (Bakke 1990: 179–86).

17. Jan P. Syse later replaced Presthus as leader (chairman) of the Conservative Party. In October 1989 he became prime minister in charge of the same three-party coalition that Presthus had tried to establish. Syse's coalition, which was fragile from the very beginning, broke down after only one year in office.

18. The three skeptics were on the whole a prestigious group, however. They included Willoch, Benkow, and one backbencher.

REFERENCES

Aardal, Bernt and Henry Valen (1989). *Velgere, Partier og Politisk Avstand.* Oslo: Central Bureau of Statistics.

Bakke, Bente (1990). *På Bakerste Benk.* Oslo: Aschehoug.

Calvert, Randall L. (1987). "Reputation and Legislative Leadership." *Public Choice* 55, 1: 81–119.

Cox, Gary W. and Samuel Kernell (1991). "Conclusion." In *The Politics of Divided Government* (pp. 239–48), eds. Gary W. Cox and Samuel Kernell. Boulder, CO: Westview Press.

Dagbladet, June 17, 1987.

Elster, Jon (1984). *Ulysses and the Sirens.* Cambridge: Cambridge University Press.

Heidar, Knut (1988). *Partidemokrati på prøve.* Oslo: Universitetsforlaget.

(1997). "A 'New' Party Leadership?" In *Challenges to Political Parties: The Case of Norway,* (pp. 125–47), eds. Kaare Strøm and Lars Svåsand. Ann Arbor: University of Michigan Press.

Kreps, David M. (1990). "Corporate Culture and Economic Theory." In *Perspectives on Positive Political Economy* (pp. 90–143), eds. James E. Alt and Kenneth A. Shepsle. Cambridge: Cambridge University Press.

Norvik, Erling (1990). *Hiv Dokker i Kalosjan.* Oslo: J. W. Cappelen.

Rommetvedt, Hilmar (1987). "Velgerbevegelser i fire faser." *Folkets Framtid*, October 30.

(1991). "Partiavstand og partikoalisjoner." Unpublished dissertation, University of Bergen.

Selten, Reinhard (1975). "Reexamination of the Perfectness Concept for Equilibrium Points in Extensive Games." *International Journal of Game Theory* 4, 1: 25–55.

Stortingstidende 1986–7, pp. 4082–4214.

Svåsand, Lars G., Kaare Strøm, and Bjørn Erik Rasch (1997). "Change and Adaptation in Party Organizations." In *Challenges to Political Parties: The Case of Norway* (pp. 91–123), eds. Kaare Strøm and Lars Svåsand. Ann Arbor: Univeristy of Michigan Press.

Thomassen, Petter (1991). *En Regjerings Fall*. Oslo: J. W. Cappelen.

Torp, Olaf Chr. (1990). *Stortinget i navn og tall 1989–1993*. Oslo: Universitetsforlaget.

Tsebelis, George (1990). *Nested Games: Rational Choice in Comparative Politics*. Berkeley: University of California Press.

Willoch, Kåre I. (1990). *Statsminister*. Oslo: Chr. Schibsted.

9

THE WINNER TAKES ALL: THE FDP IN 1982–1983: MAXIMIZING VOTES, OFFICE, AND POLICY?

Thomas Poguntke

INTRODUCTION

Politics is about choice. It is therefore hardly surprising that political parties, still the central actor in most parliamentary democracies, frequently incur situations in which they need to make hard choices – choices between office, votes, and policies (Strøm 1990). Under specific conditions, however, parties may find themselves able to reach all three goals to a satisfactory degree, even if at the outset the strategy that allows them to do so may look risky. This chapter is concerned with such a case. The analysis of the developments that led to the breakup of the Social–Liberal coalition on 17 September 1982 shows that the FDP, conceptualized as a unitary actor, was confronted with a strategic choice in which most of the benefits in the end clearly lay with only one of the feasible courses of action, namely, the decision to leave the Social–Liberal coalition under Chancellor Helmut Schmidt and form a new government with the Christian Democratic parties. The subsequent account shows that the Free Democrats (FDP) was in a uniquely favourable position that ultimately allowed it to maximize office, votes, and, within limits, policy influence at the same time. Yet, this was a risky strategy ex ante, and the short-term costs could have been substantial, particularly if the party had been forced to face the electorate shortly after its defection.

There was a price, however, which demonstrates the importance of accounting for intraorganizational constraints: Party unity was severely disrupted, particularly among leadership circles. The party leaders responsible for this decision survived, but they were certainly bloodied. In addition, the FDP membership figures have never fully recovered from large-scale defections after the *Wende* (change of coalition partners), although this did not negatively affect the electoral performance of the FDP in the following decade (Poguntke with Boll 1992). The losses were mainly due to policy conflicts within the party. The majority faction within the FDP, which was primarily concerned with economic Liberalism, could hope to achieve more of its goals in a Christian–Liberal coalition. The Social–Liberals, however, who have always put strong emphasis on civil rights issues, were left deeply disaffected. Since such issues were only of secondary importance to the party majority, the party as a whole could maximize policies by changing the coalition, although this entailed the persistent alienation of sizable parts of the party's Social–Liberal activists and voters. It follows from this that the strategy involved considerable risks: The 5 percent hurdle of the West German electoral law could have guillotined the FDP out of federal existence because the inevitable loss of voters with a Social–Liberal orientation had to be compensated for by sufficient gains on the moderate right. It was not obvious that these voters would be forthcoming, particularly in the short run. Nevertheless, rather than having to choose between conflicting goals, the FDP could hope to maximize votes, office, and policy if it was prepared to incur a very high risk, that is, the possibility of losing representation in the Bundestag altogether.

In order to provide evidence for the preceding propositions, we first analyze the political context in which the FDP's decision had to be made. This provides us with the necessary information on the strategic situation of the FDP. Based on this information, it is possible to identify the options available to the party and to decide whether or not the trade-offs had been clear in advance. Finally, the actual strategic choice of the FDP is explained by its specific role in the West German party system, the logic of the electoral system, and the organizational characteristics of the party.

THE POLITICAL CONTEXT

The economic situation of the early 1980s caused serious strain on the government. The second oil shock and a prolonged recession had led to a deterioration of the labour market and a rapidly growing budget deficit in the early 1980s (*SPIEGEL*, 22/1981: 24ff.). Beginning in 1981, unemployment began to rise sharply. Whereas the average number of unemployed had been slightly under 900,000 in 1980, the monthly figures in 1982 indicated that the annual average was likely to be near the 2 million mark (Statistisches Bundesamt, 1989a: 88). In reaction to the gloomy domestic situation and to international pressures, the governing Social Democratic–Liberal coalition was increasingly torn between pacifying the trade unions and introducing austerity measures.

Not surprisingly, the Liberal part was easier to play in this situation. The FDP has always favoured the interests of the self-employed and the business community and began to demand significant cuts in social spending and substantial economic deregulation and privatization (Vorländer 1992: 284). The

Social Democrats (SPD), on the other hand, found Helmut Schmidt's course, which in some areas was more akin to Liberal than to SPD traditions, much more painful. When budget negotiations became highly contentious in the summer of 1981, Chancellor Schmidt followed a strategy that aimed at preventing the Liberals from leaving the coalition at almost any cost. As a result, battle lines were not always clearly drawn, and the Chancellor and his minister of finance, Hans Matthöfer, frequently sided with the Liberals in agreeing to new welfare cuts (*SPIEGEL*, 37/1981, 19ff.). In several instances, only rigidly enforced parliamentary voting discipline ensured a government majority in the Bundestag (Bickerich 1982).

When the economic crisis deepened in late 1981, the trade unions began to mobilize against the government when, contrary to the trade unions' demands, it did not embark on deficit spending in order to keep unemployment figures acceptably low (*SPIEGEL*, 47/1981: 19ff.). It was mainly the FDP that opposed such measures.

Arguably of similar weight, however, was the increasing reluctance of the New Politics-oriented wing of the SPD to support Helmut Schmidt's government policies. Two issues were particularly contentious during the late 1970s and early 1980s: nuclear power and the NATO decision to deploy new intermediate-range nuclear missiles in the Federal Republic. Both issues led to considerable dissent among lower-level SPD organizations. Similarly, although not on a comparative scale, the Liberals were ridden by internal conflict over these policies.

When nationwide protests against the construction of new nuclear power stations erupted in 1977, the federal party council (*Bundeshauptausschuß*) of the FDP called for a three-year moratorium on the construction of new plants. However, this decision was overruled by a pronuclear majority of the national party congress in autumn 1977. At the same time, several SPD *Land* organizations went antinuclear, and only Helmut Schmidt's authority forced the national party congress to rally to his flag and support the pronuclear course of his governing coalition (Poguntke 1988: 31ff.). Nevertheless, Erhard Eppler, the leader of the Baden-Württemberg *Land* party, took a leading role in mobilizing dissent inside the SPD. He turned the Baden-Württemberg SPD into the first ecologically oriented *Land* organization. Electorally, however, this strategy did not pay: The Baden-Württemberg SPD were heavily defeated in the 1980 *Land* election when the Green Party won representation in the *Land* parliament.

In addition, the foreign policy consensus, which had been one of the cornerstones of the Social–Liberal coalition, came into question as a result of the growing "nuclear pacifism" inside the SPD. By the end of 1981, it was less than certain that the SPD would rally to the chancellor's flag and continue to support the policy of the NATO twin-track decision. Substantial parts of the party had lost confidence in the willingness of the U.S. government to enter into serious negotiations with the Soviet Union in order to avoid deployment of new intermediate-range nuclear missiles in Western Europe (*SPIEGEL*, 2/1982:

19ff.) Consequently, it was becoming increasingly questionable whether the majority of the SPD would continue to support both parts of the twin-track decision, which involved the deployment of new nuclear missiles should negotiations between the Soviet Union and the United States fail. At the same time, the FDP remained, despite dissent among the lower ranks, supportive of both parts of the NATO decision, which meant another potential bone of contention between the coalition partners (*SPIEGEL*, 30/1982: 21–2.).

Although the conflict over social and economic policies was a catalyst for the eventual split between the coalition partners, it is necessary to emphasize that the coincidence of these two sets of political conflicts in the late 1970s and early 1980s proved to be particularly divisive for the SPD: The party was simultaneously divided over issues of the Old Politics and issues of the New Politics (Baker, Dalton, and Hildebrandt 1981; Dalton 1986). By and large, the Liberals were in a much more favourable position. Although there was a vociferous New Politics dissent inside the party, this faction was not of comparable in strength to the Green wing of the SPD. And, more important, there was very little disagreement over classic liberal themes like economic and civil rights policies.

ELECTORAL DEVELOPMENTS IN THE EARLY 1980s

Prior to the Baden-Württemberg election of 1980, the Greens had succeeded in overcoming the 5 per cent hurdle (threshold) only in the city-state of Bremen in 1979. Whereas this could still be regarded as an exceptional success due to the city's predominantly urban, highly educated middle-class population, the Baden-Württemberg result of 1980 was widely regarded as a decisive breakthrough for the Greens (Müller-Rommel and Poguntke 1992). Although the Baden-Württemberg Greens obtained their best results in university towns with a similarly favorable social structure, the result demonstrated that the new party was able to win sufficient support in a large *Land* with a much more heterogeneous social fabric.

The situation of the governing parties, particularly the SPD, was exacerbated by the growing tide of peace protest from 1981 on. When in October 1981 300,000 people gathered in Bonn to protest against the NATO twin-track decision, this signalled further tension between the New Politics–oriented wing of the Social Democrats and supporters of Chancellor Helmut Schmidt (Schmitt 1990: 13ff.) and a very favourable climate for Green electoral advance. In the early 1980s, the Greens were swept into several *Land* parliaments by the combined thrust of the peace and antinuclear movements, which reached unprecedented levels of extraparliamentary mobilization in the Federal Republic (Müller-Rommel 1985; Müller-Rommel and Poguntke 1992; Papadakis 1984; Roth 1985; Roth and Rucht 1987; Schmitt 1990).

Two other important factors created a favorable climate for the Greens by 1983: a financial scandal and an environmental crisis. The most severe financial scandal in the history of the Federal Republic, the so-called Flick affair, added much to the growing alienation from the established political parties. It became apparent that all Bundestag parties had been involved in illegal financial trans-actions in order to secure tax-free party funding through German industry and that many senior politicians had received large donations for their parties. Although no politician was convicted of corruption, the impression remained that a strong company could influence political decisions through its financial power (Kilz and Preuss 1983). Finally, the heated debate over the forest disease (*Waldsterben*), which culminated in 1982, made the severe and far-reaching consequences of the ecological crisis visible even to those parts of the population who had thus far tended to dismiss Green concerns as the immature obsessions of young intellectuals or alternative dropouts.

ELECTORAL INCENTIVES

The electoral success of the Greens (see Table 9.1) severely threatened the pivotal role of the FDP in the West German party system as it had evolved after an initial period of diffusion and a subsequent phase of one-party dominance (Smith 1982: 102ff.). Ever since the 1961 Bundestag elections, the FDP had been in a position to decide which of the two large parties was to govern – provided that the parties did not, as in 1966, join forces against the Liberals (see Table 9.2). After the negative experience with the 1966–9 Grand Coalition, however, which fuelled extraparliamentary protests against the alleged "power cartel" in Bonn, this option was reduced to a last resort in crisis situations. Consequently, another Grand Coalition was never seriously considered until the early 1990s.

The threatened position of the FDP in the early 1980s was amply demon-strated by three indicators: declining *Land* election results, declining participa-tion in *Land* governments, and declining figures in national opinion polls. The *Land* election results prior to the 1982 decision to leave the Social–Liberal coalition made it obvious that the Liberals were coming dangerously close to the fatal 5 per cent hurdle in several *Länder*. There was a general downward trend, which was interrupted only by the positive result of the elections in Lower Saxony (see Table 9.3). However, since the Liberals had not been repre-sented in the previous Lower Saxony *Land* parliament, this result could not be taken as an indicator of general electoral recovery, at least in the short run. On the contrary, it reflected a fairly stable pattern of West German *Land* electoral politics: Whenever the FDP fails to win seats in a *Land* parliament, it stands a good chance of being returned to the subsequent *Land* parliament because many voters wish to see the FDP represented and tend to dislike overall majorities.

In the early 1980s the number of *Land* governments with Liberal partici-pation declined (Figure 9.1). This resulted primarily from the surge of the

Table 9.1. *Green Party: Results in Land elections 1978–1982*

Date of election	Land	Percentage of vote	Change from previous election
4 July 1978	Hamburg	4.6[a]	
4 June 1978	Lower Saxony	3.9[b]	
18 March 1979	Berlin	3.7[c]	
18 March 1979	Rhineland-Palatinate	No participation	
29 April 1979	Schleswig-Holstein	2.4[d]	
7 Oct. 1979	Bremen	5.1[e]	
16 March 1980	Baden-Württemberg	5.3	
27 April 1980	Saarland	2.9	
11 May 1980	North Rhine-Westphalia	3.0	
10 May 1981	Berlin	7.2	+3.5
21 March 1982	Lower Saxony	6.5	+2.6
6 June 1982	Hamburg	7.7[f]	+3.1

[a] In 1978, three Green-alternative groups ran for the *Land* election (GLU: Grüne Liste Umweltschutz; AUD: Aktionsgemeinschaft Unabhängiger Deutscher; BWL: Bunte Liste–Wehrt Euch). These groups preceded the foundation of the Green-Alternative List of Hamburg, which acts as the Green *Land* Party.
[b] In 1978, the GLU participated in the *Land* elections. This party was an organizational forerunner of the Greens in Lower Saxony.
[c] In Berlin, the Alternative List acts as a Green *Land* Party.
[d] In 1979, the Grüne Liste Schleswig-Holstein (GLSH) ran at the elections.
[e] Bremer Grüne Liste (BGL).
[f] Grün-Alternative Liste (GAL).
Source: Statistisches Bundesamt 1989b.

Table 9.2. *Distribution of seats in the Bundestag, 1949–1982*

Year	Total	CDU/CSU	SPD	FDP	Other
1949	402	139	131	52	80
1953	487	243	151	48	45
1957	497	270	169	41	17
1961	499	242	190	67	—
1965	496	245	202	49	—
1969	496	242	224	30	—
1972	496	225	230	41	—
1976	496	243	214	39	—
1980	497	226	218	53	—
1983	498	244	193	34	27[a]

[a] Green Party.

Table 9.3. *FDP Land election results prior to September 1982*

Date of election	*Land*	Percentage of vote	Change from previous election
29 April 1979	Schleswig-Holstein	5.7	−1.4
7 October 1979	Bremen	10.7	−2.3
16 March 1980	Baden-Württemberg	8.3	+0.5
27 April 1980	Saarland	6.9	−0.5
11 May 1980	North Rhine-Westphalia	5.0	−1.7
10 May 1981	Berlin	5.6	−2.5
21 March 1982	Lower Saxony	5.9	+1.7
6 June 1982	Hamburg	4.9	+0.1

Source: Statistisches Bundesamt 1989b.

Greens, who took votes mainly from the Social Democrats. In addition, the Christian Democrats (CDU) benefited electorally from the growing dissatisfaction with the federal government. Furthermore, opinion polls indicated that a similar effect was imminent on the federal level: Due to substantial defections of former government supporters to the Green Party and the CDU, a Social–Liberal coalition was unlikely to win a majority of seats in the next Bundestag (Figures 9.2 and 9.3).

STRATEGIC OPTIONS OF THE FDP IN 1982

By 1982, continuation of the Social–Liberal coalition was clearly less than a promising strategy on all three important accounts: The party was already losing *votes* in *Land* elections, and as a consequence, it was losing office at the *Land* level. At the same time, governing with the SPD began to threaten the national electoral performance of the FDP. The prospects of remaining in *office* on the national level were becoming ever more gloomy as a result of SPD losses to the Green Party: A return of the Social–Liberal government to office after the regular 1984 Bundestag elections was highly unlikely, and a so-called traffic light coalition of Liberals, SPD, and Greens was clearly not feasible. In addition, the continuing agony of the Social–FDP coalition could have increased the danger of a Christian Democratic overall majority on the national level – hence precluding the possibility of the FDP joining a Christian–Liberal coalition.

Finally, since office is the precondition for realizing policy goals in the German political process, particularly for a small party, the FDP was also in danger of losing its influence on *policies*. In this context, it is important to emphasize the fact that German parties depend more on governmental incumbency than is the case in many other democracies. German politics is characterized by a pronounced orientation to majority governments. With very rare

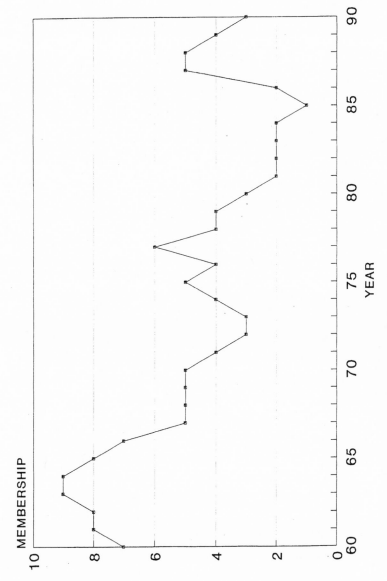

Figure 9.1 FDP membership Land governments 1960–90.

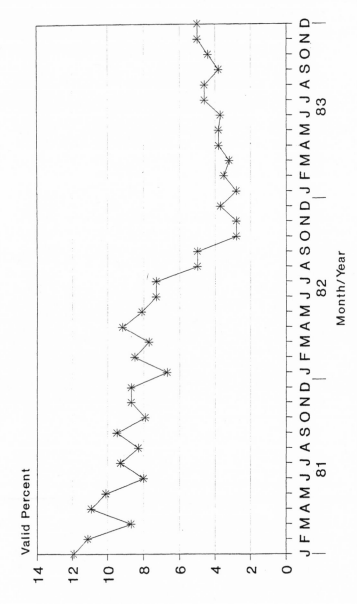

Figure 9.2 Voting intention: FDP, 1981–3. Source: Politbarometer.

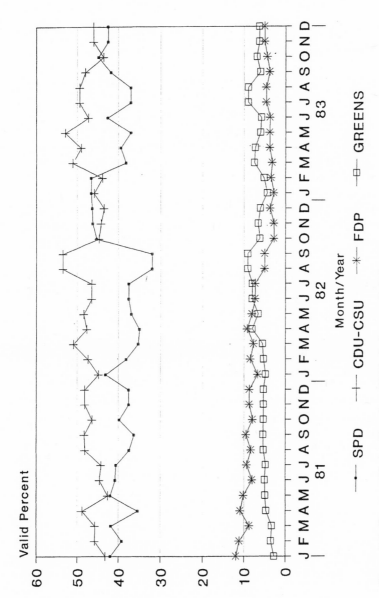

Valid Percent

60 50 40 30 20 10 0

Month/Year

JFMAMJJASOND JFMAMJJASOND JFMAMJJASOND
81   82   83

— SPD   —+— CDU-CSU   —*— FDP   —□— GREENS

Figure 9.3 Germany: Voting intention, 1981–3. Source: Politbarometer.

exceptions, minority governments have never lasted for more than transitory periods of a few weeks. This is partly because they are identified in the public mind with unstable circumstances – something that always evokes unfavourable memories of the Weimar experience. Moreover, this persistent trait of West German political culture is perpetuated by several constitutional and institutional arrangements that provide for stable majority governments (Wildenmann 1986: 87). Unlike some smaller democracies or Italy, Germany has no tradition of rule by parliament, and shifting majorities are conventionally regarded as indicating the imminent collapse of a governmental coalition. Hence, the voting discipline of members of parliament is strictly enforced by parliamentary leaders, sometimes up to the verge of unconstitutionality. Clearly, opposition parties can expect little, and unless a party believes in extraparliamentary politics, such as the former fundamentalist wing of the West German Greens (Poguntke 1993: 102ff.), office must be regarded as a virtual precondition for implementing policies.

The central importance of office for the pursuit of policy goals implies that a party that is trying to maximize policy goals must secure its survival in government beyond the next general election. As mentioned earlier, opinion polls clearly suggested that there was little hope for a Social–Liberal coalition to be returned with a majority in the next general election. However, even in this unlikely case, the FDP could not have expected to implement its own policies. As described earlier, the policy overlap between SPD and Liberals had been reduced considerably after thirteen years of coalition government. Major societal reforms had successfully been implemented, particularly in the early years of the Brandt government. A common strategy to address the growing economic problems of the 1980s, however, was hard to find. Basically, the FDP was confronted with the following options in 1982:

It could continue the coalition with the SPD until the end of the legislative term. The advantage of this choice would have been the maintenance of the party's credibility with the electorate, which had based its 1980 voting decision on the expectation of a stable Social–Liberal coalition. It was clear that changing the coalition partner at midterm would alienate a substantial number of Social–Liberal voters. Hence, the electoral survival of the FDP depended on the party's capacity to attract sufficient numbers of new Christian–Liberal voters – which could not be taken for granted. On the other hand, remaining in government with the SPD entailed liabilities in the form of policy compromises, likely electoral losses, and a substantial probability of being turned out of office in 1984.

The alternative strategy was to switch coalition allegiances to the CDU in midterm. Though this was risky, the most likely scenario was clearly more promising than the status quo. As mentioned already, there was a low probability of an office option with the SPD beyond the next election. On the policy level, the FDP could expect to realize more of its policy goals in a coalition with the CDU/CSU, although this would necessarily alienate a minority of committed Social–Liberal FDP members and voters. The electoral question was more complicated. Either way, the FDP was bound to lose votes (compared to the previous Bundestag election result). Continuation of the Social–Liberal coalition was a low-risk strategy insofar as it did not entail a high risk of falling below the 5 per cent hurdle. Leaving the coalition before the end of the legislative term, on the other hand, could have the advantage of preventing the CDU from using a campaign strategy aimed at an overall majority. Instead, it could encourage them to ensure a stable majority by "lending" votes to the FDP, thereby helping it to overcome the 5 per cent hurdle. However, the latter strategy was laden with considerable risk because it made the survival of the FDP dependent on tacit electoral support by the CDU and on the avoidance of an early election immediately after the collapse of the Social–Liberal coalition (see the later discussion.) It also rested on the ability of FDP leaders to survive and overcome internal party opposition.

If we want to understand why Liberal Party elites made the choice they did, we need to know their perception of the political situation. It was therefore not only highly indicative of the internal fractures of the coalition when a secret survey commissioned by the FDP was leaked in August 1981, which indicated that the FDP would be able to survive a change of coalition partners (*SPIEGEL*, 37/1981: 22). The prediction that the Liberals would remain safely above the 5 per cent hurdle also influenced the strategy of the party leadership. Of course, surveys need to be read with care, but it can safely be assumed that this one had two effects. First, it indicated that the party leadership had more room for manœuvre than it might have previously believed because a change of coalition partners appeared to be a viable alternative. And second, it limited the capacity of the SPD to resist Liberal pressures for a change in economic policies because it increased the Liberal potential for blackmail.

THE END OF THE COALITION IN 1982: FINDING THE RIGHT MOMENT

Apart from making the right decision, the actual orchestration of political moves is important. In our case, this meant that the FDP leadership had to find a convincing justification for leaving the coalition, identify a good moment to do so, and develop a strategy for the following months. There was an important part of the game that preceded the collapse of the coalition: The Liberals wanted to postpone a decisive move until a situation occurred that would allow them to shift the blame to the Social Democrats (*SPIEGEL*, 39/1981: 26). Ever since the FDP had broken its 1961 election pledge not to enter a government under

Chancellor Adenauer, the FDP was concerned with avoiding the electorally damaging allegation of being unreliable (Dittberner 1984: 1348; Wildernmann 1986: 91).

After the 1981 attempt to provoke a break had been stifled by the SPD's willingness to compromise even on essentials, and after a year of ambivalent leadership strategy regarding the continuation of the coalition, resistance from Left–Liberals was becoming more outspoken in the summer of 1982 (*SPIEGEL*, 32/1982: 23). As a result, the Liberal leadership could not leave the coalition during the budget negotiations that summer (*SPIEGEL*, 34/1982: 16; 36/1982: 21). There can be no doubt that it was substantially constrained by left-wing Liberals who wanted to prevent a change of coalition partners, at least until the regular election in autumn 1984. After all, the support of at least twenty-three Liberal members of Parliament was needed to establish a Christian–Liberal government and it was obviously not feasible to use such a risky strategy unless the bulk of the party leadership groups supported it. Consequently, the last year of the coalition was characterized by continued, at times ambivalent, moves of the FDP leadership aimed at undermining the common political base of the alliance. Obviously, the assumption was that a gradual deterioration of the "coalition climate" would serve to weaken intraparty support for a continuation of the Social–Liberal alliance (*SPIEGEL*, 38/1982: 21, 23).

In the end, the Hesse *Land* election of 26 September 1982 came to be regarded as a decisive date. This was because the Hesse Liberals had announced that they would change coalition partners after the election, even though the Hesse Social–Liberal coalition was working well (Vorländer 1992: 284f). Clearly, a good result for the Hesse FDP could legitimate a change in Bonn (*SPIEGEL*, 37/1982: 19ff.; 38/1982, 17ff.).

In this light, it is little more than a historic footnote that Helmut Schmidt, in the end, took the initiative and forced the Liberal ministers to resign from his cabinet. It is no question but that the Liberals provoked the breakup of the coalition. The final nail in the coffin was a memorandum from the minister of economics, Graf Lambsdorff, who demanded economic and social policies that were clearly unacceptable to the SPD (Vorländer 1992: 285). FDP leader Hans-Dietrich Genscher and his allies had hoped to determine the date of the break themselves, and for obvious reasons, they wanted to wait until the Hesse *Land* election gave them additional ammunition in the internal debate.

Helmut Schmidt's move was dictated by tactical considerations. The SPD wanted to clarify the responsibility for the failure of the coalition and launched a highly emotional campaign against the Liberals, accusing them of treason because they had not kept their election promise of 1980 when they committed themselves to the continuation of the Social–Liberal coalition (Bölling 1983; Süß 1986: 45ff.). In the short term, this campaign proved successful: In the *Land* elections of Hesse and Bavaria, held shortly after the dramatic events in Bonn, the FDP missed the 5 per cent hurdle by a clear margin. In addition, it created enormous pressure on the FDP and the CDU/CSU to agree to an early election and caused serious turmoil inside the FDP, which was deeply split over the legitimacy of leaving a coalition in midterm (*SPIEGEL*, 38/1982, 17ff.).

THE GAP BETWEEN LEGALITY AND LEGITIMACY

The preceding analysis suggests that changing coalition partners at midterm, though risky, was clearly the most promising strategy. In light of the electoral trends, any other behaviour would have entailed a high probability of losing office, and hence policy influence, without considerably brighter electoral prospects. Nevertheless, the event triggered an enormous row inside the party, as well as in the public as a whole. This can be explained by the established constitutional practice in the Federal Republic as it has evolved over the postwar period.

According to the constitution, the power of government formation rests unambiguously with the Bundestag – in conjunction with certain relatively limited powers of the president of the Republic. In practice, however, parties have developed a convention of announcing their coalition preference and their chancellor candidate before the election. As a result, Bundestag and Landtag elections have attained a quasi-plebiscitarian character where the electorate is in a position to decide directly on the preferred governmental coalition and the chancellor or prime minister (Ellwein and Hesse 1987: 270ff.). Consequently, any change of coalition partners during a legislative term, though perfectly constitutional, is widely perceived as illegitimate. In fact, the popular perception of the role of legislative elections has come to constrain the freedom of action of parliamentary parties.

The option to topple Helmut Schmidt's minority government through a constructive vote of no confidence, elect a CDU chancellor, and govern until the date of a regular election in autumn 1984 was therefore hardly feasible. Basically, it had only one advantage: Those FDP members of parliament with marginal placements on *Land* lists would probably be more willing to vote for a CDU chancellor because they would not be threatened by the imminent loss of their seats. Besides the problem of insufficient legitimation, a 1984 election would have increased the risk of electoral defeat for a new Christian–Liberal government. The government could not hope to solve the country's economic problems in less than two years. Hence, the election would almost certainly be held under very unfavourable economic conditions – but too late to blame the previous SDP chancellor for the problems.

An immediate election, on the other hand, was clearly against the interests of the FDP, which would almost certainly have missed the 5 per cent hurdle. However, the only constitutionally unproblematic possibility for an early election would have been a lost vote of confidence asked for by Chancellor Helmut Schmidt. In such a case, the Bundestag could be dissolved by the president of the Republic and an early election held. However, this would have necessitated an arrangement between the Bundestag parties. Since it was obviously not in the interest of the SPDs to allow the Liberals an easy way out of the coalition, they would have wanted the assurance of the CDU/CSU that in this case they would not just go ahead and elect another chancellor. Whereas CSU leader Franz-Josef Strauß favoured this solution, CDU leader Helmut Kohl had no interest in terminating the parliamentary existence of the FDP.

This disagreement can be explained by the problematic relation between the Christian sister parties CDU and CSU and their respective leaders, Franz-Josef Strauß and Helmut Kohl. Helmut Kohl had two reasons to favour the long-term survival of the FDP. On the one hand, it would help to limit the influence of the more right-wing Bavarian CSU, and particularly its controversial leader, Franz-Josef Strauß, a longtime foe of Kohl. On the other hand, it was obviously much riskier to campaign for an overall majority in an immediate general election, that is, for a Liberal result below the 5 per cent hurdle. After all, the size of a future Green parliamentary party was difficult to predict. Furthermore, Helmut Schmidt's considerable popularity, in conjunction with an emotional campaign against the "treacherous" FDP, could have helped the SPD to achieve a good result at the polls – probably good enough to prevent an alternative, CDU-led majority.

Hence, on balance, an election in the spring of 1983 was in the interest of both the CDU and the FDP. The date was before the prospective start of the deployment of new intermediate-range nuclear missiles in the autumn of 1983, which was bound to provoke considerable domestic protest. More important, however, it would give the FDP the necessary time to recover from the internal divisions caused by the change of coalition partners, and it would be sufficiently early to permit the new government to blame the previous coalition for the economic malaise.

Ironically, the previously mentioned gap between constitutional rules and constitutional practice compelled the newly elected Kohl government to seek popular legitimation through a method that was constitutionally highly questionable: Immediately after the new coalition had unanimously approved of the budget of the Kohl government, the coalition parties abstained from a vote of confidence initiated by Kohl in order to facilitate the dissolution of the Bundestag and a premature election in March 1983 (Ellwein and Hesse 1987: 306–7; Süß 1986: 44ff).

GAINS AND LOSSES

As a result of the popular disapproval of the Liberals' alleged disloyalty to their own election promises, the party suffered a dramatic decline in popular sympathy (see Figure 9.4). As already mentioned, the party was heavily defeated in the *Land* elections following September 1982. The FDP also remained firmly

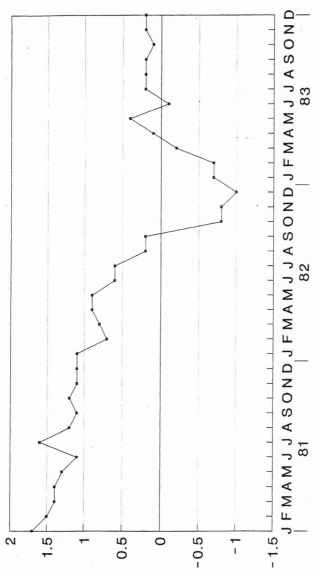

Figure 9.4 Evaluation of FDP, 1981–3. Mean of 10-point scale (range, +5 to −5). Source: Politbarometer.

below the fatal 5 per cent threshold in national election surveys throughout 1983 (see Figure 9.2). Nevertheless, the actual electoral costs were substantially lower federally. Although the party lost 3.6 per cent of the popular vote, it was safely returned to the Bundestag with 7 per cent. Compared to what the party could have expected to reach two years later, that is, after the continuation of a Social–Liberal coalition, the result was evidently not an electoral defeat. It is obvious that a successful "split vote" campaign, which was at least tolerated by the CDU, had helped the FDP to win substantially more votes than predicted by opinion polls. The proportion of split votes reached unprecedented levels in the 1983 elections: Only 29.1 per cent of those who cast their decisive second vote for the FDP gave their first vote to a Liberal constituency candidate, whereas 58.7 per cent supported Christian Democratic candidates (Vorländer 1992: 317).

It would be erroneous, however, to conclude from the preceding discussion of policy conflicts between the SPD and FDP that a potential Christian–Liberal coalition was entirely unproblematic from a Liberal perspective. The classic policy area of civil liberties had always been highly contentious between the Liberal minister for the interior, Gerhard Baum, who had followed a pronouncedly liberal course, and the right wing of the CDU and CSU, which argued for an expansion of state powers to fight crime and terrorism. Consistently – and not unexpectedly – the FDP had to concede substantial policy sacrifices in this area. In addition, the FDP had to accept the Christian–Social hard-liner, Friedrich Zimmermann, who had always been the preferred Liberal bogeyman when it came to demonstrating political differences between the FDP and CSU, as the new minister of the interior (*SPIEGEL*, 39/1982: 12ff.). Even economic policy goals could not be realized fully because the trade union wing of the CDU wanted to prevent the alienation of the Christian Democratic working-class voters. Nevertheless, it was clear that this would be much easier than in the previous coalition (*SPIEGEL*, 40/192, 20ff.). The incomes of self-employed persons consistently increased at a much higher rate during the 1980s than those of employees.

THE FDP: VIABLE ONLY AS A GOVERNING PARTY (?)

The foregoing discussion has been based on the assumption that remaining in the Social–Liberal coalition, with its likelihood of a subsequent period in opposition, was hardly a desirable alternative for the FDP. Clearly, this proposition needs justification. As already mentioned, the FDP has, for most of the Federal Republic's history, occupied a pivotal position in the party system. Largely lacking clearly defined linkages to organized interests and specific social groups, the party has justified its existence from a system-functional perspective by moderating its respective coalition partner and preventing unpopular overall majorities of one of the large parties (Schiller 1977). Unlike the situation of many small parties on the fringe of the political spectrum, office is hardly an electoral liability for the FDP (Strøm 1990). Since the party defines itself mainly as a centrist corrective to its respective coalition partner, it has not much independent identity to sacrifice. Furthermore, as a small party, the FDP can largely evade the problem that governing parties have their reliability more severely tested than that of opposition parties (Strøm 1990). By embarking on a strategy of opposition in government, that is, of limited conflict with the major governing party, the FDP can frequently hope to deflect popular discontent to its allies (Vorländer 1992: 270). This strategy is reflected by the electoral profile of the party. In 1983, only 45.7 per cent of its voters identified with the FDP, whereas 22.1 per cent of the Liberal vote came from committed CDU supporters. Another indicator of the comparatively small size of independent FDP support is the previously mentioned considerable split voting. Consistently, the party had its worst-ever election result after three years in opposition against the Grand Coalition between 1966 and 1969 – a strategic situation that, in principle, should have worked to the benefit of the sole opposition party in parliament (see Table 9.2)!

However, there is an inherent contradiction between the system-functional role and the constitutional practice that requires popular legitimation of changing coalition partners. Precisely because the FDP lacks sufficient independent identity, it is evaluated by the electorate primarily for its performance as opposition in government. Consequently, performance in an obsolete coalition is hardly a good asset for fighting an election. Once the coalition with the SPD had become unworkable, it was essential for the FDP to fight the next election as part of the new coalition. Obviously, the party had a vital interest in delaying an early election as much as possible, knowing that popular excitement is transient and likely to recede once the population has become familiar with a new political constellation. However, the preceding analysis has shown that the Liberal leadership had to take substantial risks. Although the FDP had probably obtained a clear commitment on behalf of the CDU leader, Helmut Kohl, that immediate elections would be avoided, FDP leaders could not know whether Kohl's position would be strong enough to resist pressures from the CSU under Franz-Josef Strauß and his many supporters within the CDU.

The 1983 Bundestag election result seems to suggest that the eventual choice of the FDP leadership meant that it was prepared to accept substantial short-term electoral costs in exchange for long-term consolidation (see Table 9.2). However, in the age of regular opinion surveys, previous election results are no longer a relevant benchmark of electoral performance. No doubt, parties make strategic moves based on current ratings in opinion polls and the opportunities of improving their situation. From this perspective, the FDP had to choose between highly likely electoral decline alongside the SPD and a promising but risky strategy for recovery.

This does not necessarily mean that the FDP would have been in danger of failing to obtain 5 per cent of the popular vote had it remained loyal to the Schmidt government until the regular election. But the party faced a high likelihood of losing any option for office. There was clearly little hope for a 1984 Social–Liberal majority. And the chances for an overall CDU majority would have been substantial had the country lived another two years under a decaying Social–Liberal coalition. Yet, the political weight of a party like the FDP in the West German context depended primarily on its ability to be pivotal in parliament. In order to do so, it needed to overcome the 5 per cent hurdle, whereas its number of seats was, in most cases, of secondary importance. Hence, electoral costs were tolerable as long as they did not endanger the parliamentary survival of the party. The federal structure of the German political system meant that the FDP had to pay a real electoral price only on the *Land* level, where it lost all seats in the *Land* parliaments of Hesse and Bavaria in autumn 1982.

The system-functional self-definition of the FDP is substantially eased by its Janus-faced character. The party has always lived with a precarious internal balance between national-economic and social Liberalism. Inevitably, a change of coalition partners coincides with a shifting balance between these currents. When the Social–Liberal coalition was formed in 1969, this resulted in an erosion of the right wing of the party, whereas 1982 made many prominent Left–Liberals leave. Obviously, such manœuvres are substantially eased by the fact that the FDP is no mass membership party. Compared to its share of the vote and its prominent role in national and *Land* governments, the party has always had few members (Poguntke with Boll 1992: 332) – and hence little extraparliamentary life. Most decisive political moves have been initiated by the federal parliamentary party and the federal leadership throughout its history (Kirchner and Broughton 1988: 68; Vorländer 1992: 312).

It is therefore questionable whether the previously mentioned retreat of the FDP from its long-standing commitment to civil liberties represented a real policy sacrifice. After all, the decision of party leadership to favor policy goals in economics and foreign relations brought about a simultaneous partial change of the character of the party. Hence, when the internal balance of power shifted substantially to the right, the number of party members and voters who considered CSU-inspired civil liberties policies as an important policy sacrifice decreased considerably. This is not to say that the party's centre–right faction was opposed to civil rights policies. Most of them just considered them as secondary. From this perspective, the strategic move of the FDP in 1982 required only a secondary policy compromise. Bearing this necessary qualification in mind, it can therefore be argued that as a result of the party's specific role as a governing party par excellence, and the reluctance of the CDU under Helmut Kohl to risk an electoral strategy aimed at achieving an absolute majority, the FDP in the end was able to capitalize on all three goals: policy, votes, and office.

REFERENCES

Baker, Kendall L., Russell J. Dalton, and Kai Hildebrandt (1981). *Germany Transformed. Political Culture and the New Politics*. Cambridge, MA: Harvard University Press.

Bickerich, Wolfram (1982) "Reformen rückwärts. Die Gesellschaftspolitik der sozialliberalen Koalition." In *Die 13 Jahre. Bilanz der sozialliberalen Koalition*, (pp. 45–64), ed. Wolfram Bickerich. Reinbek: Rowohlt.

Bölling, Klaus (1983). *Die letzten 30 Tage des Kanzlers Helmut Schmidt. Ein Tagebuch*. Reinbek: Rowohlt.

Dalton, Russell J. (1986). "Wertwandel oder Wertwende. Die Neue Politik und Parteienpolarisierung." In *Wahlen und politischer Prozeß*, (pp. 427–54), eds. Hans-Dieter Klingemann and Max Kaase. Opladen: Westdeutscher Verlag.

Dittberner, Jürgen (1984). "Die Freie Demokratische Partei." In *Parteien-Handbuch: die Parteien der Bundesrepublik Deutschland 1945–1980*, Vol. 2 (pp. 1311–81), ed. Richard Stöss. Opladen: Westdeutscher Verlag.

Ellwein, Thomas and Joachim Jens Hesse (1987). *Das Regierungssystem der Bundesrepublik Deutschland*, 6th edition. Opladen: Westdeutscher Verlag.

Kilz, Hans Werner and Joachim Preuss (1983). *Flick. Die gekaufte Republik*. Reinbek: Rowohlt.

Kirchner, Emil and David Broughton (1988). "The FDP in the Federal Republic of Germany: The Requirements of Survival and Success." In *Liberal Parties in Western Europe* (pp. 62–92), ed. Emil J. Kirchner. Cambridge: Cambridge University Press.

Müller-Rommel, Ferdinand (1985). "New Social Movements and Smaller Parties: A Comparative Perspective." *West European Politics* 8, 1: 41–54.

and Thomas Poguntke (1992). "Die Grünen." In *Die Parteien der Bundesrepublik Deutschland*, 2nd edition (pp. 319–61), eds. Alf Mintzel and Heinrich Oberreuter. Bonn: Bundeszentrale für politische Bildung.

Papadakis, Elim (1984). *The Green Movement in West Germany*. London: Croom Helm.

Poguntke, Thomas (1988). "Technikakzeptanz und politisches System: Die politischen Auswirkungen der Diskussion um die Kernenergie in Frankreich, Großbritannien, Italien, Japan, der Bundesrepublik und den USA." Research Unit for Societal Developments, Working Paper No. 10/88.

(1993). *Alternative Politics: The German Green Party*. Edinburgh: Edinburgh University Press.

with Berhard Boll (1992). "Germany." In *Party Organizations: A Data Handbook* (pp. 317–88), eds. Richard S. Katz and Peter Mair. London: Sage.

Roth, Roland (1985). "Neue soziale Bewegungen in der politischen Kultur der Bundesrepublik – eine vorläufige Skizze." In *Neue soziale Bewegungen in Westeuropa und den USA* (pp. 20–82), ed. Karl-Werner Brand. Frankfurt: Campus.

Roth, Roland and Dieter Rucht (eds.) (1987). *Neue Soziale Bewegungen in der Bundesrepublik Deutschland*. Bonn: Bundeszentrale für politische Bildung.

Schiller, Theo (1977). "Wird die FDP eine Partei?" In *Auf dem Weg zum Einparteienstaat* (pp. 122–49), ed. Wolf-Dieter Narr. Opladen: Westdeutscher Verlag.

Schmitt, Rüdiger (1990). *Die Friedensbewegung in der Bundesrepublik Deutschland*. Opladen: Westdeutscher Verlag.

Smith, Gordon (1982). *Democracy in Western Germany*. 2nd edition. London: Heinemann.

Statistisches Bundesamt (ed.) (1989a). *Datenreport 1989*. Bonn: Bundeszentrale für politische Bildung.

(1989b). *Bevölkerung und Erwerbstätigkeit. Fachserie 1. Sonderheft 40 Jahre Wahlen in der Bundesrepublik*. Stuttgart: Metzler-Poeschel.

Strøm, Kaare (1990). "A Behavioral Theory of Competitive Political Parties." *American Journal of Political Science* 34, 2: 565–98.

Süß, Werner (1986). "Wahl und Führungswechsel. Politik zwischen Legitimation und Elitekonsens. Zum Bonner Machtwechsel 1982/83." In *Wahlen und politischer Prozeß* (pp. 39–86), eds. Hans-Dieter Klingemann and Max Kaase. Opladen: Westdeutscher Verlag.

Vorländer, Hans (1992). "Die FDP zwischen Erfolg und Existenzgefährdung." In *Parteien in der Bundesrepublik Deutschland*, (pp. 266–318 eds. Alf Mintzel and Heinrich Oberreuter, 2nd edition. Bonn: Bundeszentrale für politische Bildung.

Wildenmann, Rudolf (1986). "Ludwig Erhard und Helmut Schmidt, die charismatischen Verlierer." In *Wahlen und politischer Prozeß* (pp. 88–107), eds. Hans-Dieter Klingemann and Max Kaase. Opladen: Westdeutscher Verlag.

10

TRADE-OFFS IN SWEDISH CONSTITUTIONAL DESIGN: THE MONARCHY UNDER CHALLENGE

Torbjörn Bergman

INTRODUCTION*

In Sweden, the head of state (the monarch) no longer takes part in the process of government formation. It is the speaker of the Riksdag who appoints a candidate for prime minister.[1] This candidate must be approved by the Riksdag. He or she is approved unless more than half of all members of parliament vote against the candidate. This constitutional rule was designed in the early 1970s. In this chapter I explain why the Swedish parties removed the monarch from the process of government formation and, for that matter, from most other formal functions and powers. At the heart of the explanation lie choices based on multiple goals in multiple arenas.

I focus on the parties' evaluations of available choices.[2] The Social Democratic Party programme calls for an elected head of state (a republic). I discuss only briefly the Social Democrats' decision not to propose a republic. More interesting is the Social Democrats' decision to propose a modified form of monarchy. I also briefly present the positions of two other parties involved in the constitutional bargaining, the Centre and Liberal Parties.[3] Of particular interest is the Conservatives' decision to accept a modified form of monarchy. This is given the most attention.

The outline of this chapter is as follows. In the next section I present the context in which the four parties reached a compromise. In the third section I present the content of the compromise and the events surrounding it. In the fourth section I explain in more detail why the Social Democrats proposed a modified form of monarchy. In the fifth section I discuss the calculations of the

Centre and Liberal Parties. In the sixth section I explain the choice made by the
Conservative Party. In the final section I summarize and discuss the findings.

POLITICAL AND INSTITUTIONAL
BACKGROUND

In order to explain how and why the compromise was reached, it is helpful to
consider the context in which the trade-offs were decided. The compromise on
the monarch's powers was reached after almost twenty years of constitutional
deliberations. The existing constitution, dating from 1809, was based on power
sharing between the monarch and the parliament (see, for example, Lewin
1992). Over time, however, a stable parliamentary democracy developed without
corresponding changes being written into the constitution. This discrepancy
between the written constitution and constitutional practice helped put the
issue of constitutional reforms on the political agenda (Holmberg 1972).

Another reason behind the push for constitutional reforms was that the
opposition parties, chiefly the Liberal Party, wanted to alter the constitution to
make it easier to unseat the Social Democrats. Not surprisingly, the Social
Democrats were less interested in such constitutional changes (von Sydow 1989).

In 1954 the four parties agreed to form a commission on constitutional
reforms. The commission was formally appointed by the government. In this
commission, *Författningsutredningen* (FU), representatives of the four parties de-
liberated for nine years without reaching an agreement acceptable to all. Many
of the commission's proposals were controversial, and in 1966 the government
appointed another four-party commission to work out a compromise. The second
commission, *Grundlagberedningen* (GLB), first worked out the details of a partial
agreement between the four parties.

In the 1970 elections, the two-chamber Riksdag was replaced by a one-
chamber Riksdag. The constitutional reform also included a change in the
electoral system to ensure stricter proportionality and a national threshold of 4
per cent for representation in the Riksdag. The old constitution had helped
facilitate stable control of the government by the largest party, the Social
Democratic Party (von Sydow 1989). The institutional changes of the early
1970s made a change of government more likely (Holmberg 1976; Johansson,
interview, 1990; Stjernquist 1978). The commission's expert study on comparative government formation, published in 1970 (SOU 1970: 16), gave the
parties further incentive to settle the issue of the powers of the king and in
particular the rules of government formation (Hermerén, interview, 1991).

Interparty relations is another important part of the context in which the
compromise was reached. In 1971, the Social Democrats (163 seats) had to rely
on the consent of the Communist Party (17 seats) to remain in power. With a
combined total of 170 seats, the three nonsocialist parties as a group were larger
than the Social Democrats. However, these three parties had a history of dis-

unity. For one thing, the Centre Party had joined the Social Democrats in a government coalition for six years between 1951 and 1957. In the 1960s, the Conservative Party was often held at arm's length by the Centre and Liberal Parties on the grounds that it was too far to the right on the political spectrum. However, in November 1971, shortly after the constitutional compromise had been reached, the three nonsocialist parties presented for the first time a joint program on economic affairs. This program, designed to combat unemployment, was presented by the leaders of the three parties at a joint press conference.

This newfound unity had been helped by the fact that all three parties changed leaders between 1969 and 1971. The election of new party leaders is important for two reasons. For one thing, the new leaders made determined efforts to increase intra-bloc cooperation (Hadenius 1990: 132; Hylén 1991: 178). The new Conservative Party leader, Gösta Bohman, was one of the chief architects of this newfound unity. He believed that removal of the Social Democrats from power and the Conservative Party's hope of gaining influence over national policies rested on the nonsocialist parties' ability to cooperate (Möller 1986: 98–120).

The election of new leaders was also important because none of the new nonsocialist party leaders had been directly involved in the discussions on constitutional design. Thus, for all three parties, the party's representative in the commission on constitutional reform was probably more informed about the institutional bargaining than the new party leader.

Another contextual factor was the Swedish political-administrative culture at the time (late 1960s, early 1970s). During this period the Swedish method of decision making was famous for its emphasis on deliberation and for thorough, lengthy treatment of political issues in government-appointed commissions. The Swedish political-administrative culture was also known for its emphasis on compromise and consensus (Sannerstedt 1987, 1989; von Sydow 1989). In the words of Anton (1980: 158):

> No image of modern Swedish politics is more widely celebrated than that of the rational, pragmatic Swede, studying problems carefully, consulting widely, and devising solutions that reflect centuries of practice at the art of compromise.

The way in which the constitutional issues were dealt with closely follows this standard description of the Swedish decision-making process. From the beginning, the parties held opposing positions on many issues, including the monarchy, the electoral system, and the structure of the Riksdag. But there was also consensus that a new constitution ought to be based on an agreement among all four major parties and that it ought to be able to win broad acceptance (Johansson, interview, 1990; Johansson, letter, 1991; Ruin 1983, 1988; Stjernquist 1978; Stjernquist, interview, 1990). If anything, this attitude grew stronger over time (Hermerén 1987; Johansson 1976). The norm was probably strengthened by the commission's conferences, in which the members worked in secluded and relaxing environments. This helped facilitate an almost ecumenical relationship between the members of the commission. It is also likely that the advanced age of many of the members might have helped produce a compromise. They wanted to get the job finished (Gadd, interview 1991a; Holmberg 1976).

A final but also very important feature of the context was the dominant ideas of the era in which the constitutional debate took place. On the one hand, the aging king was a very popular person, which made attacks on the monarchy as a whole quite difficult. On the other hand, there was a sentiment of leftist radicalism in the late 1960s and early 1970s that helped facilitate a large-scale constitutional reform that curtailed the formal powers of the monarchy. Among others, Gunnar Myrdal (1982: 107–11) has argued that the new constitution is a product of an era in which large-scale political reforms were seen as the natural way to make policy (see also Sterzel 1983).

THE COMPROMISE IN TOREKOV

In this section I present the content of the compromise and the events surrounding it. Beginning with the Social Democrats, I then go on to explain how the parties reached their particular decisions.

The new rules are part of the Swedish constitution that went into effect on 1 January, 1975. The former constitution from 1809 gave the king the formal power to appoint the government. The king also formally presided over government decision making, appointed high civil servants, and could dissolve the Riksdag. In his position as the head of state, he was the supreme commander of the military. The new constitution stripped him of these formal powers. While he was still the head of state, the new constitution only allowed him to open new sessions of the Riksdag, have occasional symbolic meetings with the government, and chair an advisory board on foreign affairs.[4]

The new rules were first agreed upon by representatives of the four major parties in August 1971, when the second commission (GLB) and its assistants and experts met in Torekov, a small town in southern Sweden. At a meeting in the spring of 1971 the Centre Party representative, Sten Wahlund, had proposed a compromise according to which the speaker would propose candidates for prime minister. The king would have only ceremonial functions: he would chair the government meetings at which high civil servants were appointed, and he would chair the advisory board on foreign affairs. At the time, no final agreement was reached; instead, the discussions continued (GLB, 5 March 1971; Wentz, interview, 1993; Wentz, letter, 1993).

Initially, very little progress was made at Torekov. Then, in a matter of two days, the commission members agreed on a compromise. According to Mr. Gadd (interview, 1991a), a Social Democrat and the youngest member of the commission, the Social Democratic chair (Valter Åman) first agreed with the representative for the Centre Party that the king should chair government meetings at which high civil servants were appointed. When Åman presented this proposal to his party colleagues, they simply refused. Twenty years later, Mr. Gadd recollects being surprised at his older colleagues' firm stand. They would simply not allow the king to chair any meeting at which the government made decisions. Thus, Åman had to go back to Wahlund and explain that the deal was off. After further deliberation, Åman came back to the Social Democratic group and said that the Centre Party's representative had decided to accept that the king be removed from all involvement in government decision making. The representative from the Liberal Party went along with the proposal shortly thereafter.

Three parties had now agreed, and it was up to the Conservatives to oppose or accept the proposal. Allan Hernelius from the Conservative Party accepted on the condition that the king be kept informed by the prime minister on government affairs (Gadd, interview, 1991a).[5] Thus, the members of the commission had reached a compromise. But why did the Social Democrats agree to keep the monarchy? And why did the Conservative Party agree to remove the monarch from important symbolic functions such as government formation and government decision making? The reasons behind the compromise are now explained.

THE SOCIAL DEMOCRATIC PROPOSAL

By the early 1970s, the Social Democratic Party had officially been in favour of replacing the monarchy with an elected head of state (a republic) for sixty years (since 1911). Since this party was by far the largest and had been in government for the entire post–World War II period, the continued existence of the monarchy was a source of some embarrassment for the party leadership.

Within the Social Democratic leadership almost everyone was, *in principle*, in favour of a republican form of government. However, there was little intrinsic interest in the issue of a monarchy versus a republic (Erlander 1982; Ruin 1986; Stjernquist 1971; Westerståhl 1976). After all, the powers of the monarch were largely symbolic and inconsequential. Rather, it was because of its potential as an electorally salient and decisive issue that it was seen as important. The Social Democratic leadership knew, as did the leaders of all parties, that Swedish voters were overwhelmingly in favour of the monarchy.

Tage Erlander, the Social Democratic Party leader from 1946 to 1969, took the position that the only way the party could bring up the issue of a republic was with a clear argument about why this would make representative democracy stronger and more effective. Without such an argument, he did not want to bring up the issue, particularly not when, he argued, polls showed that about 80 per cent of Swedish youth favoured the monarchy. The issue would obscure all others, and unless the Social Democrats wanted to lose the next election, it was an impossible proposal (SAP-PS, 1966, 1969).[6]

At the same time, however, the republic was part of the party program.

Activists within the party kept reminding the leadership about this fact (Eriksson 1985: 168–85). Thus, the Social Democratic leadership was faced with a dilemma: proposing a republican constitution was out of the question, but doing nothing about the king's powers could lead to internal protests and disunity. Above all, the leadership wanted to prevent the loss of internal cohesion. The Social Democratic Party leaders during the years of constitutional deliberation, Tage Erlander and Olof Palme, both held internal cohesion to be one of the main (if not the main) responsibilities of a party leader. To them, intraparty cohesion was a prerequisite for success in terms of other goals (see, for example, Elmbrant 1989; Erlander 1982; Ruin 1986).

The Social Democratic leadership also faced criticism from outside the party. Even if a majority of the Swedes supported the monarchy, a number of influential intellectuals did not.

One of the most influential critics was Herbert Tingsten, a liberal political science professor and former editor of Sweden's largest morning paper (*Dagens Nyheter*). Tingsten criticized the first commission (FU) on the grounds that it proposed that the king should appoint government ministers, have the authority to refuse to submit government proposals to the Riksdag, and be able to refuse government requests to dissolve the Riksdag. According to the commission, this would ensure the king a position in which he could help strengthen parliamentary democracy (SOU 1963: 17; see also Nyman 1981 and Tingsten 1964).

Tingsten (1964) criticized the idea that the king could strengthen representative democracy. On the issue of government formation, he argued that it was possible simply to let the parliament elect a prime minister. Or, if this was found to be unsuitable because of the obvious risk of tactical voting, the right to appoint the prime minister could be given to someone else. Tingsten (1964: 34) suggested that the responsibility for government formation should be given to someone elected to office – the speaker. Tingsten's ideas were highly influential (Ruin 1990; Sterzel 1983; Stjernquist 1971).

Other intellectuals joined in. For example, Professor Pär-Erik Back and Gunnar Fredriksson (1966), political editor of the largest Social Democratic newspaper (*Aftonbladet*), proposed that the constitution be reformed in two steps. In the first, the king would be stripped of all his political power. In the second, the monarchy would be replaced by a republic. The prime minister would at first be appointed by the speaker, and later this responsibility would be transferred to the president. This was also in line with ideas proposed in 1963 by three young, influential Social Democrats (Andersson, Carlsson, and Gustafsson 1963).

In 1969, at the party congress at which he resigned, Erlander articulated the specifics of the Social Democratic solution. He wanted the commission (GLB) to create rules that gave primacy to parliamentary democracy, regardless of whether the head of state was a king or a president. Two issues were, he argued, particularly important. The first was that the king be formally removed from government decision making. The second was that he be removed from the process of government formation. This would ensure a constitution that could work equally well under a monarch or a president. Erlander also stated that he believed it possible to come to an agreement with the other parties about giving the speaker the right to appoint the prime minister. With this strategy, he argued, the Social Democrats would not have to jeopardize the upcoming (1970) election. The Congress accepted the Erlander proposal (SAP-Congress 1969: 335–44).

In contrast to an electoral struggle over the issue of a republic, the Social Democrats did not have to fear the consequences of proposing a modified monarchy. By choosing to propose a modified form of monarchy, they also avoided giving the impression of doing nothing about their promise of a republic. Instead they could argue that they were moving forward on the issue and thereby deflect both internal and external criticism.

The Social Democratic leadership's acceptance of the compromise met little opposition within the party. Radical activists could see it as a step towards a republic (see, for example, Nancy Eriksson in *Riksdagens protokoll* 1973, Nr 111: 186). Others could see it as a more permanent solution. One who held the latter view was the commission's chairman. At a press briefing immediately after the compromise at Torekov, Åman began by declaring that the issue of republic and monarchy was now solved: Sweden was going to continue to be a monarchy (SDS, 21 August 1971). The other Social Democrats insisted that the issue of a republic or a monarchy had not really been dealt with. What they had done was to establish the proper powers of the head of state. In their view, the new constitution would work regardless of whether the head of state was a king or a president.

The most important critique came from the closely affiliated blue-collar trade union association (the Landsorganisationen, LO). With reference to the compromise in Torekov, the Congress of the LO argued in favour of abolishing the monarchy (LO-Congress 1971: 1122–7). However, the normally very influential LO was basically ignored (Gadd, interview, 1991b). In the late fall of 1971, the Social Democratic members of the commission presented the compromise to the Advisory Council (*Förtroenderådet*) of the party's parliamentary group. No one challenged the compromise. Only minor issues covering formation rules were discussed outside of the scope of the compromise (SAP-RGF, 1971). On the advice of the party leader (Palme), the next Social Democratic congress also accepted the compromise (SAP-Congress 1972: 989–1013). In the end, in its proposal to the Riksdag, the Social Democratic government stated that the continued existence of the monarchy was necessary if the new constitution was to gain sufficient support in the parliament and among the general public (Prop. 1973: 90: 171–2).

In sum, the Social Democrats had not been able to fulfil the promise of their party program. However, in spite of the unfulfilled promise of a republic, the Social Democratic leadership was rather pleased. They had been able to frame the constitutional reforms as a codification of parliamentary democracy and as a move in the right direction. This way they could satisfy proponents of a republic without having to fight for a republic in the next election (see also Ruin 1986: 253).

THE CENTRE AND LIBERAL PARTIES

The Centre and Liberal parties accepted the commission's proposal without much debate. The decision was not particularly difficult for either of them. In 1968 the Centre Party and the Liberal Party jointly declared that the king should not have power to influence government formation or Swedish politics (*Mittensamverkan* 68). This can be seen as an attempt by these parties to remain uncommitted on the issue of the powers of the king (Dahlén, interview, 1992). Evidently, the two parties were aware that on this issue they were in a pivotal position between the two major opponents (Brändström, interview, 1991; Hermerén, interview, 1991).

It was significant that both the Centre and Liberal parties had supporters in favour of a republic as well as ones who favoured the status quo (Fiskesjö 1973: 42). There was strong sentiment in favour of a republic in the youth wings of both parties. Bohman (1984: 51), the Conservative Party leader in the early 1970s, argues that this gave the two parties an incentive to try to keep the issue off the political agenda. Thus, internal cohesion was an important motive behind their willingness to reach a compromise. In terms of their other goals, they did not expect a compromise on the issue of a modified monarchy to have much consequence.

The compromise probably went a bit further than some of the party members wanted. They would have preferred the head of state to retain more symbolic functions. However, within the Centre Party, the party's representatives on the commission never received any critique of the compromise (Fiskesjö, interview, 1992). The Centre Party has a congress every year. There was not one single motion on the powers of the monarch during the period 1970–4 (C-Congresses 1970–4). The Liberal Party's parliamentary group debated constitutional issues such as the organization of the Riksdag and a Bill of Rights but not the powers of the monarch (FP-RG, 3 March 1970, 12 April 1973). The party viewed the removal of the monarch from political decision-making to be correct in principle (Molin, interview, 1991). There had also been broad and lengthy consultations on constitutional issues within the party. These consultations involved not only the party leadership but also liberal political scientists and political editors. Partly because of these broad consultations, the constitutional issues did not, as was the case in the Conservative Party, cause internal disagreement after the compromise (Dahlén, interview, 1992).

THE CONSERVATIVE DECISION

The constitutional design agreed upon in Torekov was not what the Conservative Party leader wanted. The Conservative Party fully supported the supremacy of parliamentary democracy. At the same time, however, it seemed natural to most Conservatives that the Swedish monarch (like other heads of state) would participate in the proceedings of representative democracy. This would, the Conservatives believed, ensure his position as a symbol of national unity. Should the party accept a modified monarchy?

Fighting a proposal for a modified monarchy would not provide the same significant gains as would a fight against a proposed republic. Instead, the Conservatives had a choice between two different strategies. One strategy was to oppose the compromise solution. With such a strategy, the Conservative Party could hope to benefit electorally (in 1973) from a campaign in which they fought a Social Democratic "attack" on the monarchy. This would separate the Conservative Party somewhat from the other two nonsocialist parties on the issue, but probably not in a way that would make a three-party government impossible. Thus, through moderate vote gains, opposing the compromise could be a way to increase the possibility of getting into government and thereby also to increase influence in other important policy areas. While some members would perhaps argue that the party should accept the compromise to ensure the continued existence of the monarchy, most Conservatives would probably have welcomed an electoral struggle with the Social Democrats on this issue. It was unlikely that the Social Democrats would abandon the compromise that they had reached with the other two parties if the Conservative Party rejected it. Without the support of these parties, the Social Democrats would not propose a republic. Seen in this light, the fact that the Conservative Party agreed to accept the compromise and chose another strategy is puzzling.

Immediately after the compromise, Professor Tingsten offered one part of the explanation (GHT, 3 September 1971). According to him, the Social Democrats did not want to jeopardize their slim electoral margin by pushing the issue of a republic. The Conservative Party, Tingsten believed, had agreed in order to avoid a controversy with the other nonsocialist parties. Disunity among the three parties on such an electorally salient issue would decrease their chances of unseating the Social Democrats in the next election. The desire to avoid disunity among the nonsocialist opposition parties is one reason behind the Conservative choice of strategy. However, two other important reasons are the motives of the Conservative representative (Hernelius) himself and the intraparty considerations of the party leader (Bohman).

What happened was that the new party leader initially wanted to choose strategy I (oppose) but ended up supporting strategy II (accept). In his memoirs, Gösta Bohman (1984) mentions that in the summer of 1971 Hernelius informed him about the commission's (GLB) deliberations. From this discussion, Bohman concluded that the commission was not going to reach an agreement. His party was going to take the position that the monarch should keep some of his ceremonial powers – especially the right to sign important laws and the right to formally appoint high civil servants. Bohman strongly agreed; he did not want a compromise on these issues. Bohman and Hernelius also agreed to discuss the issue with the Advisory Council (*Förtroenderådet*) of the party's parliamentary group. This meeting took place in the beginning of August 1971. The party leader could not attend, but it was reported to him that the Council had agreed with Hernelius's proposals.

Shortly before the commission met in Torekov, Bohman called a press conference and declared that the Conservative Party was ready for a political fight. The Social Democrats were not going to be able to abolish the monarchy "without anyone noticing" (Bohman 1984, 51; Exp., 4 August 1971, author's translation). When, through the news, Bohman found out that Hernelius had agreed to a compromise, he claims to have been taken by surprise. When he asked Hernelius about the compromise, Hernelius answered that he had acted in accordance with the will of the Advisory Council.

Some aspects of Bohman's historical account are puzzling. First, the chair of the meeting at which Hernelius reported about the commission's discussions stresses both that no decision was made at the meeting and that, when she learned about the extent of the compromise, she strongly opposed it (Kristensson, interview, 1991). Second, when asked about whether party representatives had contacts with their parties during the meeting in Torekov, the commission's chief secretary (Erik Holmberg) said that he believed they all had such contacts (Holmberg, interview, 1990; see also Stjernquist 1978: 363). Third, in the summer of 1972, after having been criticized for the compromise, Hernelius wrote an open letter to Per Unckel, the chairman of the Conservatives' youth wing. In the letter, Hernelius (letter, 1972) refuted the claim that he alone had agreed to the compromise. In 1970 he had informed the Conservative group in the Riksdag. In August 1971 he had discussed the issue with the group's Advisory Council. He had often informed the party leaders. In fact, he stated, while in Torekov, he had twice talked on the phone with the party leader (Bohman) and had gotten his approval for the compromise.

In the letter, Hernelius defended the content of the compromise. He pointed out that the instructions for the commission (GLB) in 1966 had been discussed by the leaders of all four major parties. These instructions called for a constitution in which the head of state had a symbolic role. Only the Conservative leader, at that time Yngve Holmberg, had raised objections when the Social Democratic government included the issue of a monarchy or a republic as one to be discussed (see also Svensson 1970: 111–112). Hernelius also stressed that with the compromise the Social Democrats had agreed to keep the king as the head of state and that the speaker's candidate for prime minister would be approved by the Riksdag.

It is probable that Bohman was more informed and involved than he remembered when he wrote his memoirs more than ten years later, but it is also likely that he was not fully informed about the extent of the compromise. Bohman (letter, 1992) insists that Hernelius acted independently of his wishes. The fact that Bohman announced at a press conference just before the meeting in Torekov that his party was ready for a fight on the issue supports his assertion.

A general presupposition on his part in favour of opposition against any Social Democratic proposal can perhaps also be counted in support of this conclusion (on this presupposition, see Adelsohn 1987: 263).

Accepting Bohman's claims that he was not fully informed and had not approved the compromise in advance raises the question of why Hernelius agreed. One important reason was probably that Hernelius personally saw this as a way to secure the monarchy and prevent a republic (a point stressed by Gadd, interview, 1991b; Hermerén, interview, 1990; Kristensson, interview, 1991). He believed that if he did not agree, the monarchy would remain under challenge from the Social Democrats. In addition, if he did not agree to the compromise, the other three parties could work out a proposal that, from his point of view, was even worse than the one he accepted.

It has also been argued that Hernelius had personal reasons for agreeing to a compromise. The argument is that he wanted to settle the issue and be known as one of the men who created the Swedish constitution (Lidbom 1982). This indicates the relevance of the fact (mentioned earlier) that many commission members were old and had been working on the issue for quite some time. They were determined to get the job done. Another reason for Hernelius's acceptance might have been that the chairman, Åman, had impressive mediating skills (Brändström, interview, 1991; Holmberg 1976). Åman (1982: 177; Åman, interview 1991) stressed to Hernelius that his party alone had not agreed and that the issue was no longer one of republic or monarchy but concerned a modified form of monarchy. Perhaps this helped convince Hernelius. According to some commentators, the sun and the baths could also have helped forge congeniality (Johansson, interview, 1990; *Riksdagens protokoll* 1973, Nr 110: 64; Stjernquist, interview, 1990). And, as alluded to earlier, the strong Swedish belief that it is desirable to have broad agreements on constitutional affairs might have helped create a bargaining environment that facilitated a compromise.

As Hernelius had already agreed, and as this had been made public, Bohman decided to accept the compromise as well. Once Hernelius had accepted the compromise, the expected gains of opposition changed dramatically. Had Bohman chosen to distance himself from the compromise, he would have caused a split in the party leadership and among the nonsocialist opposition parties. Hernelius had high status within the party. There had also been consultations on the issue of the compromise within the party. Though Hernelius had gone further than the party leader had wanted, to accuse him of having made a mistake would have led to at least a moderate loss of internal cohesion. To distance the Conservative Party from the compromise would also have been tantamount to distancing the party from an agreement it had accepted together with the two other nonsocialist parties. As nonsocialist cooperation was essential for the party's ability to gain government positions and to influence policies, to reject the compromise now could have led to at least a small negative effect in terms of both of these goals. For the party leader, a potential for a small gain in terms of votes did not balance the negative consequences of rejecting the compromise.

By accepting the compromise, Bohman removed the issue from his electoral agenda. Since all four parties now agreed, he would not be able to use opposition against the Social Democrats on this issue to gain votes in the next electoral campaign. However, by accepting a compromise that the other two nonsocialist parties already had accepted, he facilitated cooperation among the nonsocialist parties. The three parties' joint position on constitutional design could be referred to as a show of their ability to cooperate. Within Bohman's own party, however, accepting a compromise that changed the symbolic role of the monarch could turn out to be a problem. But compared to the alternative, which was to blame Hernelius, internal cohesion could be promoted by stressing that the Social Democrats had agreed to keep the monarchy.

When the compromise was made public, Bohman welcomed it as a bargaining success for the Conservative Party. Bohman declared that, thanks to the Conservatives, the Social Democrats had been forced to give in and keep the monarchy. He also stressed that the king was going to continue to have some ceremonial functions (SvD, 21 August 1971a). The immediate reaction of other Conservatives was fairly positive. The continued existence of the monarchy was greeted with satisfaction (see, for example, BT, 21 August 1971; SvD, 21 August 1971b). In spite of the initially positive reaction, however, the compromise turned out to be a problem for the party leadership. By early 1972 the initial satisfaction within the party had begun to fade. By the time the commission's written report was published (SOU 1972: 15), there was growing opposition within the party.

In September 1972 the Conservative Party held a party congress. At the previous party congress, Bohman had defeated the former party leader, Yngve Holmberg, in an open struggle for the party leadership. Bohman was now a popular and unchallenged leader of the Conservative Party. The only major debate and challenge to the leadership came on the issue of the Torekov compromise. In no fewer than ten different motions, party activists and subnational party organizations argued that the Conservative Party should distance itself from the compromise (M-Congress, 1972). Though the debate was intense, the party leader managed to win the issue. A speech by Bohman was especially important. He gave three basic reasons why the Conservative Party should stick with the compromise (DN, 16 September 1972; Exp., 18 September 1972; SvD, 17 September 1972).

1. The compromise at least ensured the continued existence of the monarchy, whereas a renewed debate and a political struggle could lead to a worse outcome – a republic.

2. The Social Democrats would campaign against the Conservative Party as being untrustworthy if it backed down on the compromise.

3. Withdrawal from the compromise would hurt the credibility of the party leadership. This could only benefit the Social Democrats.

The party supported Bohman and rejected proposals to withdraw from the compromise. However, the congress also gave the party leadership the task of advancing the Conservative position within the framework of the compromise. And in spite of the decision of the congress, the debate within the party continued until the new constitution was passed by the Riksdag (Bohman 1984). One of the Conservatives most critical to the compromise recalls that one important argument used by the party leader in the internal debate was that an agreement had been reached and that breaking it would publicly embarrass both Hernelius and Yngve Holmberg, the former party leader. After all, the argument was, Holmberg was the one who had agreed to the commission and its instructions in the first place (Strindberg, interview, 1991).

After the compromise, six meetings were held among the party leaders to discuss the proposal (Broomé & Eklundh 1976). There the Conservative Party won some concessions. For instance, the monarch would continue to enjoy immunity from prosecution, and he was given the highest military rank but no formal power (Bohman 1984; Broomé & Eklundh 1976; Orrhede, interview, 1993; Prop. 1973: 90, 113: 174–5). However, among other party leaders there was a strong desire to finally settle the issue, and the Conservative Party leader was unable to alter the compromise radically (Dahlén, interview, 1992). The debate within the Conservative Party and growing public opinion against the new constitution had very little effect on the rules agreed on in Torekov (Johansson 1976).

In the final Riksdag vote, one conservative voted against the new constitution and two abstained. The rest of the Conservatives voted in favour (DN, 28 February 1974; *Riksdagens protokoll* 1974, Nr 30: 139).

CONCLUSION

The compromise on the powers of the Swedish head of state was reached in a particular context. One important feature of this context was an era of leftist ideas and large-scale political reforms. Another important feature was that the four Swedish parties all embraced the norm that broad consensus on constitutional affairs was desirable. The Conservative Party's attempt to be accepted by the Centre and Liberal parties as a partner on equal terms was a third. By creating favourable conditions, this context facilitated a compromise at this particular point in time. However, by itself the context does not explain why the compromise was reached or the specific content of the compromise. To explain this, it is necessary to consider the parties' multiple goals in multiple arenas.

The Social Democratic and Conservative parties had to make important choices. For the Social Democratic leadership, their evaluation of the consequences of pursuing the official policy goal of making Sweden a republic was highly negative. In the early 1970s electoral competition was fierce, and the leadership considered a republic to be a mostly symbolic issue. With the electorate heavily in favour of a monarchy, the party could expect to lose votes by proposing a republic. Because the Social Democrats had only a slim electoral margin over the three opposition parties on the right, the loss of these votes would probably also mean losing government portfolios. A loss of government positions, would, in turn, reduce the party's ability to implement other policies of more intrinsic value to the party. This is why the party leadership chose not to propose a republic.

One possible alternative would have been simply to codify existing constitutional practice. However, doing nothing about the formal powers of the monarch would open the party leadership to criticism from more radical party members. This could result in a loss of intraparty cohesion and thereby a potential loss of votes. Doing nothing would also result in criticism from other supporters of a republic outside the party. This too could cause a loss of votes.

In promoting the removal of the monarch's formal powers, the leadership sought to prevent the loss of internal cohesion and the risk of losing votes. Stripping the king of his powers had the great advantage of satisfying critics within the party without risking a loss of electoral support. It was also easier to defend against criticism from radical voices outside the party. This was the basis for the Social Democrats' tough attitude in bargaining with other parties.

For the two parties in the middle, accepting the compromise did not constitute much of a problem. The compromise probably went a bit further than they wanted. They would have preferred the head of state to retain more of his symbolic functions. At the same time, however, their policy position on the issue was close to that of the Social Democrats. In keeping with its history of cooperation with other political blocs, it was the Centre Party that first broke the deadlock and sided with the Social Democrats. With the continuation of the monarchy, and with removal of the king from the proceedings of representative democracy, the leadership of the Centre Party could satisfy both the probable majority in the party who favoured the monarchy and the more radical, often younger members who favoured a republic. When the Centre Party agreed to the compromise, the Liberal Party had to choose between siding with the Centre Party or with the Conservatives. At the time, not least given the recent history of disunity with the Conservative Party, the choice was easy. By siding with the Centre Party, the Liberal Party avoided the internal discord and quite possibly the loss of votes that siding with the Conservatives could have meant.

For the Conservative Party, the trade-off was much more difficult. Activists did not want the monarch to be removed from all the proceedings of representative democracy. Moreover, the party leader expected that an electoral campaign in which the party defended the status of the monarchy would increase the party's share of the electoral vote. Thus, by accepting the compromise, the Conservative leader accepted a constitutional design that he did not want and gave up on a policy issue that he believed would win the party votes.

One reason for accepting the compromise was that this ensured the continued existence of the monarchy. This was probably of particular importance for the party's representative, Hernelius. However, given that the Conservatives knew that the electorate was heavily in favour of the monarchy, this was hardly the most important reason the Conservative Party accepted the compromise. With the possible exception of Hernelius, very few Conservatives expected the Social Democrats to actually propose a republican constitution. In fact, had Hernelius not chosen to agree to the compromise it is likely that the Conservative Party leader would have opposed the compromise.[7]

The pursuit of nonsocialist unity was one important reason behind the Conservative decision to accept the compromise. The Conservatives did not want to jeopardize nonsocialist cooperation and the possibility of a joint three-party majority in the 1973 election. By agreeing to the compromise, the party avoided giving the impression that the three parties could not agree on an issue as fundamental as the Swedish constitution. An even more important reason was that Hernelius, a leading party representative, wanted the compromise and agreed to it. Rather than oppose Hernelius, the party leader decided in favour of party cohesion and supported him.

When it was first made public, Bohman had greeted the compromise as a bargaining success for his party. After having endorsed the compromise publicly, withdrawing would, in effect, be tantamount to saying that the party leadership had been wrong in supporting it in the first place. This would not look good for a party that had just recovered from an internal struggle over the party leadership. It would also be an embarrassment for both Hernelius and Bohman. The credibility of the party leadership was saved when the party as a whole accepted the compromise.

Having chosen *not* to give priority to the preferred policy (important symbolic powers for the monarch) or to vote-maximise on this issue, the Conservative Party sought changes within the framework of the compromise. In so doing, the party was successful on issues such as the king's immunity and military rank. This enabled the party leadership to reduce some of the criticism from party activists.

In the case of the constitutional compromise, there are some important similarities in the way that the parties reached their decisions. One such similarity is that when it was not possible for the party leaders to achieve all of their goals simultaneously, both the Social Democrats and the Conservatives discounted an official policy position in favour of the pursuit of other goals. This could be seen as evidence that both the Social Democratic and Conservative parties gave priority to their vote- and office-seeking goals. However, another reasonable interpretation is that the leaders of both parties had traded off a programmatic policy issue in favour of potential gains in their ability to influence other policies. For the Social Democrats, the official policy issue (a republic) was of little or no value to the party leadership, and the trade-off was readily made. For many Conservatives, accepting the compromise was at least to some extent against their sincere position on the issue. But they too traded off the particular policy issue for a mix of policy-, vote-, and office-seeking concerns.

Further similarities were found in intraparty considerations. For the leaders of both the Social Democratic and Conservative parties, intraparty considerations were an important determinant of party behaviour. The Social Democrats, to satisfy party radicals, were determined to get policy concessions from the other parties in order to compensate for their initial trade-off (i.e., no republic). The desire to avoid a split within the party leadership was another very important motive behind the behaviour of the Conservative Party. Another similarity was that when a policy was (at least potentially) salient on the electoral agenda, the parties worried a great deal about the reactions of the electorate. Most important was to avoid losing votes on the issue. This, rather than an aspiration to win votes, was the bottom line for the parties when they faced tough trade-offs.

The most important general findings can now be summed up: When the parties faced hard choices among their multiple goals, (1) their positions on particular policy issues were traded off for both office and electoral reasons but also to increase their ability to pursue other policies; (2) in such situations, the parties worried more about not losing votes than about winning votes, (3) internal cohesion was an important motive behind (external) party behaviour; and (4) the parties, and the Conservative Party in particular, included interparty considerations (nonsocialist cooperation) in the evaluation of different alternatives.

In contrast, there is little evidence that the hard choices were directly shaped by party organizations, institutional structures, and the like. For instance, widespread consultations on constitutional issues of the kind that existed within the Liberal and Social Democratic Parties were lacking in the Centre and Conservative parties. However, this did not shape the reception of the compromise among party activists the same way. Both of the latter parties accepted the compromise, but only in the Conservative Party did the issue become a problem for the leadership. Instead, the analysis indicates that if and when party leaders are faced with very hard choices on issues that have the potential to become electorally salient and thereby are also of potential importance for their office- and policy-seeking goals, the motivational basis for their behaviour is very important. It might be that, in such instances, their decisions are shaped more by goal-seeking than by organizational and institutional arrangements. But neither goal-seeking nor context should be neglected when an important decision is analyzed.

NOTES

*Earlier I published on this topic in *Statsvetenskaplig Tidskrift*. I gratefully acknowledge the permission granted by the editors to use that article (vol. 95, 1992, 209–33) as the basis for this chapter.

1. In translation, the relevant Article (6:2) of the constitution (Instrument of Government) reads:

   When a Prime Minister is to be appointed, the Speaker shall summon for consultation one or more representatives from each party group in the Riksdag. The Speaker shall confer with the Deputy Speakers and shall then submit a proposal to the Riksdag.

   The Riksdag shall proceed to vote on the proposal, no later than the fourth day thereafter, without preparation in committee. If more than half of the members of the Riksdag vote against the proposal, it is rejected. In all other circumstances it is approved (Constitutional Documents of Sweden 1990: 47).

   Formally, the Prime Minister appoints the other government ministers.

2. The data come from written accounts and from party minutes. I have also interviewed a number of politicians, legal experts, and political scientists who were involved in writing the new constitution. I have shared a draft of this chapter with those I interviewed. Many of them, on the basis of the draft, agreed to a second, complementary interview or provided me with written comments.

3. A fifth party, the Communist Party, was represented in the Riksdag but was not invited to take part in the deliberations on the new constitution. Also, note that neither the king (who died in 1973) nor the crown prince is reported to have been involved with the issue of constitutional design in the late 1960s and early 1970s. The constitutional design was a matter decided by the four parties. Of course, this does not completely preclude informal contact on a personal level before or after the compromise. For example, a Social Democratic minister argues that when in 1966 the issue of a republic was on the parliamentary agenda, the party leader (Erlander) comforted the king on the issue (Lindström 1970: 297).

4. Until 1980 the monarch had to be male. From 1980 on, females of the royal family were also allowed to inherit the throne.

5. The chief secretary (Holmberg, interview, 1991) and the chairman (Åman, interview, 1991) do not dispute Gadd's account of the events.

6. The leadership's dual position on the issue is further exemplified by the fact that in 1968, Erlander stated that one of the tasks of the commission was to consider whether Sweden ought to be a republic or a monarchy (*Riksdagens protokoll* 1968 II, Nr 34).

7. For a different interpretation of Bohman's intentions, see Von Sydow (1995).

SOURCES

UNPUBLISHED SOURCES

Åman, Valter (1991). Interview conducted on telephone by the author on 30 October.
Bohman, Gösta (1992). Letter to the author dated 17 June.

Brändström, Dan (1991). Interview conducted by the author on 1 November.
C-Congresses (1970–1974). *Centerpartiet: Protokoll från partistämmor 1970, 1971, 1972, 1973 och 1974.*
Dahlén, Olle (1992). Interview conducted by the author on 8 May.
Fiskesjö, Bertil (1992). Interview conducted by the author on 8 April.
FP-RG, 3 March (1970). *Folkpartiets riksdagsgrupp, Protokoll.*
12 April (1973). *Folkpartiets riksdagsgrupp, Protokoll.*
Gadd, Arne (1991a). Interview conducted by the author on 7 January.
(1991b). Interview conducted on telephone by the author on 23 October.
GLB (1971). "Protokoll." *Grundlagberedningen,* 5 March.
Hermerén, Henrik (1990). Interview conducted by the author on 12 December.
(1991). Interview conducted by the author on 1 October.
Hernelius, Allan (1972). Letter to Per Unckel dated 26 July.
Holmberg, Erik (1990). Interview conducted by the author on 21 December.
(1991). Interview conducted on telephone by the author on 6 October.
Johansson, Hilding (1990). Interview conducted by the author on 10 December.
(1991). Letter to the author dated 18 November.
Kristensson, Astrid (1991). Interview conducted by the author on 6 November.
LO-Congress (1971). *Landsorganisationen i Sverige. Kongressprotokoll.* Del 2: 1122–7.
M-Congress (1972). *Handlingar till den ordinarie partistämman i Västerås den 14–17 september.*
Molin, Björn (1991). Interview conducted by the author on 4 January.
Orrhede, Björn (1993). Interview conducted by the author on 8 December.
SAP-Congress (1969). *Sveriges Socialdemokratiska Arbetareparti, Protokoll, 24:e kongressen,* Vol. 1: 335–344.
(1972). *Sveriges Socialdemokratiska Arbetareparti, Protokoll, 25:e kongressen,* Vol. 2: 989–1013.
SAP-PS (1966). *Sveriges Socialdemokratiska Arbetareparti, Partistyrelsens Protokoll,* 1 October.
(1969). *Sveriges Socialdemokratiska Arbetareparti, Partistyrelsens Protokoll,* 17 June.
SAP-RGF (1971). *Protokoll förda vid sammanträde med socialdemokratiska riksdagsgruppens förtroenderåd,* 11 October; 20 October; 2 November.
Stjernquist, Nils (1990). Interview conducted by the author on 5 December.
Strindberg, Per-Olof (1991). Interview conducted by the author on 15 November.
Wentz, Nils O. (1993). Interview conducted on telephone by the author on 17 March.
(1993). Letter to the author dated 25 March.

PUBLISHED SOURCES (NEWSPAPERS)

BT (1971). "Enighet om monarkin." *Borås Tidning* (BT), 21 August.
DN (1972). "Moderatkupp i kungafrågan." *Dagens Nyheter* (DN), 16 September.
"Hermansson pressad på demokratin, Solzjenitsyns utvisning fördömdes." *Dagens Nyheter* (DN), 28 February.
Exp. (1971). "När Bohman i strid skulle draga." *Expressen* (Exp.), 4 August.

(1972). "När kungen kom på tal tvingades Bohman ta i. . . ." *Expressen* (Exp.),
18 September.
GHT (1971). "Herbert Tingsten om grundlagsberedningen: Piruetter kring majes-
tätet." *Göteborgs Handels och Sjöfarts Tidning* (GHT), 3 September.
SDS (1971). "Har Sverige monarki?" *Sydsvenska Dagbladet* (SDS), 21 August.
SvD (1971a). "Regeringen går oss till mötes." *Svenska Dagbladet* (SvD), 21 August.
(1971b). "Moderniserad monarki." *Svenska Dagbladet* (SvD), 21 August.
(1972). "M-stämman bryter inte kompromissen." *Svenska Dagbladet* (SvD), 17
September.

OFFICIAL DOCUMENTS

Constitutional Documents of Sweden (1990). Stockholm: The Swedish Riksdag.
Prop. 1973: 90. *Kungl. Maj:ts proposition nr 90 år 1973*. Stockholm: Riksdagen.
Riksdagens protokoll 1968 II, Nr 34. 31 October. Stockholm: Riksdagen.
Riksdagens protokoll 1973, Nr 110. 5 June. Stockholm: Riksdagen.
Riksdagens protokoll 1973, Nr 111. 5 June. Stockholm: Riksdagen.
Riksdagens protokoll 1974, Nr 30. 27 February. Stockholm: Riksdagen.
SOU 1963: 17. Författningsutredningen. *Del 2. Motiv*. Stockholm: Statens Offentliga
Utredningar.
1970: 16. Grundlagberedningen. *Riksdagsgrupperna-Regeringsbildningen*. Stock-
holm: Statens Offentliga Utredningar.
1972: 15. Grundlagberedningen. *Ny regeringsform, Ny riksdagsordning*. Stock-
holm: Statens Offentliga Utredningar.

REFERENCES

Adelsohn, Ulf (1987). *Partiledare: Dagbok 1981–1986*. Stockholm: Gedins förlag.
Åman, Valter (1982). *Repor i färgen*. Stockholm: Timo Förlag.
Andersson, Leif, Ingvar Carlsson, and Agne Gustafsson (1963). *Författningsreform–nytt
alternativ*. Stockholm: Tidens förlag.
Anton, Thomas J. (1980). *Administered Politics: Elite Political Culture in Sweden*. Boston:
Martinus Nijhoff.
Back, Pär-Erik and Gunnar Fredriksson (1966). *Republiken Sverige*. Stockholm: Bok-
förlaget Prisma.
Bohman, Gösta (1984). *Maktskifte*. Stockholm: Bonniers.
Broomé, Bo and Claes Eklundh (1976). "Propositionsarbetet." *Statsvetenskaplig Tid-
skrift* 79: 23–6.
Elmbrant, Björn (1989). *Palme*. Stockholm: Författarförlaget Fischer & Rye.
Eriksson, Nancy (1985). *Nancy Eriksson minns*. Stockholm: Bonniers.
Erlander, Tage (1982). *1960-talet*. Stockholm: Tidens Förlag.
Fiskesjö, Bertil (1973). "Monarki eller Republik?" In *Modern Demokrati: Problem och
debattfrågor*, 5th edition (pp. 23–53), ed. Pär-Erik Back. Lund: Gleerups.

Hadenius, Stig (1990). *Swedish Politics During the 20th Century*. Stockholm: Swedish Institute.

Hermerén, Henrik (1987). "Författning och politik: Nåragra aspekter på regeringsbildning i Sverige." In *Statsvetenskapens mångfald: Festskrift till Nils Stjernquist*, (pp. 105–12), ed. Lars Göran Stenelo. Lund: Lund University Press.

Holmberg, Erik (1972). "Grundlagberedningens förslag till ny RF och ny RO." *Statsvetenskaplig Tidskrift* 75: 189–208.

—— (1976). "NY RF, ny RO." *Statsvetenskaplig Tidskrift* 79: 19–22.

Hylén, Jan (1991). *Fosterlandet Främst?*. Stockholm: Norstedts Juridikförlag.

Johansson, Hilding (1976). "Grundlagsfrågan i riksdagen–några avsnitt." *Statsvetenskaplig Tidskrift* 79: 27–31.

Lewin, Leif (1992). *Ideologi och strategi: Svensk politik under 100 år*. Stockholm: Norstedts.

Lidbom, Carl (1982). *Reformist*. Stockholm: Tidens Förlag.

Lindström, Ulla (1970). *Och regeringen satt kvar! Ur min politiska dagbok 1960–1967*. Stockholm: Bonniers.

Mittensamverkan 68 (1968). "Gemensamt politiskt handlingsprogram för centerpartiet och folkpartiet." Stockholm: Folkpartiets och centerpartiets samarbetsdelegation.

Myrdal, Gunnar (1982). *Hur styrs landet?* Stockholm: Rabén & Sjögren.

Möller, Tommy (1986). *Borgerlig Samverkan*. Uppsala: Diskurs.

Nyman, Olle (1981). *Parlamentariskt regeringssätt*. Stockholm: BonnierFakta.

Ruin, Olof (1983). "Svensk politisk stil: att komma överens och tänka efter före." In *Land i olag: Samhällsorganisation under omprövning*, (pp. 31–44), eds. Lennart Arvedson, Ingemund Hägg, and Bengt Rydén. Stockholm: SN&S.

—— (1986). *I välfärdsstatens tjänst: Tage Erlander 1946–1968*. Stockholm: Tidens Förlag.

—— (1988). "Sweden: The New Constitution (1974) and the Tradition of Consensual Politics." In *Constitutions in Democratic Politics*, (pp. 309–27), ed. Vernon Bogdanor. Aldershot: Gower.

—— (1990). "Statsministerämbetet: från Louis De Geer till Ingvar Carlsson." In *Att styra riket*, (pp. 92–133), Departementshistoriekommittén. Stockholm: Allmänna Förlaget.

Sannerstedt, Anders (1987). "Teorier om det svenska samförståndet." In *Statsvetenskapens mångfald: Festskrift till Nils Stjernquist*, (pp. 243–54), ed. Lars Göran Stenelo. Lund: Lund University Press.

—— (1989). "Forskning om författningsreformer." *Statsvetenskaplig Tidskrift* 92: 304–12.

Sterzel, Fredrik (1983). *Parlamentarismen i författningen*. Stockholm: P A Norstedt & Söners förlag.

Stjernquist, Nils (1971). "Grundlagberedningskompromiss i statschefsfrågan." *Statsvetenskaplig Tidskrift* 74: 377–9.

—— (1978). "Tillkomsten av Sveriges nya regeringsform." *Tidskrift utgiven av Juridiska Föreningen i Finland* 114: 339–70.

Svensson, Sven (1970). *Enkammarriksdag*. Stockholm: Almqvist & Wiksell.

Tingsten, Herbert (1964). *Skall kungamakten stärkas?* Stockholm: Bokförlaget Aldus/Bonniers.

Von Sydow, Björn (1989). *Vägen till enkammarriksdagen.* Stockholm: Tidens Förlag.
  (1995). "Torbjorn Bergman: Constitutional Rules and Party Goals in Coalition
  Formation." *Statsvetenskaplig Tidskrift* 98: 489–95.
Westerståhl, Jörgen (1976). "Författningsutredningen." *Statsvetenskaplig Tidskrift* 79:
  2–11.

11

PARLIAMENTARY RULES AND PARTY BEHAVIOR DURING MINORITY GOVERNMENT IN FRANCE[1]

John D. Huber

In May 1988, François Mitterrand was reelected as president of France, and he immediately exercised his right to dissolve the National Assembly and call for a new legislative election. As Table 11.1 shows, after the election, Mitterrand's Socialist Party held 275 of the 577 seats in the National Assembly. Two conservative parties, the Gaullists (RPR, 130 seats) and the Union pour la Démocratie Française (UDF) (90 seats), together held 220 seats. The Communists held twenty-five seats, and for the first time since the 1973 election, forty-one deputies formed a Center group (the Union du Centre, UDC) independent of the UDF. Since the election failed to return a majority for either the Socialist Party or the coalition on the right, the Socialists formed the first minority government in the history of the Fifth Republic, with Michel Rocard as prime minister.

The formation of the Rocard minority government raised speculation about the role that the French National Assembly might begin to play in French legislative politics. Until 1988, the French government had been able to use the numerous constitutional procedures to limit sharply the legislative role of parliament (see, e.g., Andrews 1982, Frears 1981, and Keeler 1993; in French see Masclet 1982 and Parodi 1972). However, given its minority status, it was not clear whether the Rocard government could use the wide range of institutional procedures at its disposal to limit the opposition's role in policymaking, or if the government would find it necessary to make policy concessions to the opposition in order to pass legislation.

After the adoption of the national budget in the fall of 1988, many observers believed that the government's minority status would indeed force the government to make significant policy concessions to the opposition and would therefore lead to a historic revitalization of the National Assembly's role in French policy-

Table 11.1. *Composition of the French National Assembly in June 1988*

Party[a]	Seats[b]	Percentage of seats
Communists (PCF)	25	4.3
Socialists (PS)	275	47.7
Center (UDC)	41	7.1
Union for French Democracy (UDF)	90	15.6
Gaullists (RPR)	130	22.5
Other	16	2.8
Total	577	100

[a] The parties are listed according to their left-right ideology, with the leftmost party listed first and the rightmost party listed last.
[b] Includes members and "apparentes" (affiliated deputies).
Source: Maus 1988: 120.

making. The budget debate was marked by a spirit of cooperation and conciliation. The government avoided using many of the institutional mechanisms available to it for limiting changes to its bill by the National Assembly. Large policy concessions were granted to the opposition parties, as well as to the Socialist group in parliament. In the end, deputies from the Socialist and opposition parties publicly praised the government for entering into a serious and constructive dialogue on substantive policy questions.

But one year later, with the same basic policy questions at issue, the budget debate unfolded completely differently. The government negotiated no important concessions with the opposition parties, and it used many of the institutional procedures available to it to prevent substantive policy changes by the National Assembly. The deputies of the opposition parties were harshly critical of the government for its unwillingness to enter into serious policy negotiations and for its use of institutional force. Ultimately, the budget was adopted using the confidence vote procedure, which permits the government to link the fate of a bill to the outcome of a vote on a motion of censure. The obvious question is: Given that the political actors, the political institutions, and the political issues were the same across the two years, why was the 1988 budget debate marked by policy negotiation and compromise between the government and the National Assembly while the 1989 budget debate was marked by a lack of negotiation and compromise and by widespread use of restrictive procedures, including the confidence vote procedure?

This chapter uses the puzzle that emerges from the 1988 and 1989 budget debates to examine how French parties make hard choices. During minority government, the confidence vote procedure often forces French parties to make trade-offs between electoral, office-seeking, and policy objectives. If the government invokes the confidence vote procedure on a bill, for example, the opposition parties must choose between censuring the government and accepting an undesirable policy outcome. Similarly, on each bill, the government must decide on the types of policy concessions it is willing to make in order to avoid using the confidence vote procedure. Drawing on seventeen private interviews that I conducted with the key participants in the 1988 and 1989 budget debates,[2] I argue that when French parties face difficult trade-offs, they almost invariably choose to pursue strategies aimed at achieving long-term electoral objectives. During the budget debates, however, French parties seemed to believe that future electoral success was linked less to short-term policy outcomes than to the types of signals sent to voters during the *process* of obtaining these outcomes. Institutional arrangements that shape the policymaking process therefore play a central role in shaping the choices made by French parties. Indeed, since parties with different organizational structures seem to pursue the same objectives, it appears that French constitutional arrangements are more important in determining party choices than are the internal organizational features of French parties.

This chapter has three main sections. In the first section I describe how the confidence vote procedure shapes the strategic options available to French parties. In the second section I examine the motivations and tactics of the Communists, the Center, and the Socialists in the 1988 and 1989 budget debates. Finally, I conclude by discussing how French electoral and legislative institutional arrangements orient French parties toward a particular type of vote-seeking behavior.

THE ROLE OF THE CONFIDENCE VOTE PROCEDURE IN SHAPING PARTY CHOICES IN FRANCE

The confidence vote procedure, found in Article 49.3 of the Constitution, permits the government to "engage its responsibility" – that is, to link the fate of a bill to a censure vote in the National Assembly. When the government invokes the confidence vote procedure, there is no vote on the bill itself. Instead, all debate ceases immediately, and if a motion of censure is not introduced and voted within a specified time limit, the bill is considered as adopted in the form designated by the government. The confidence vote procedure, then, forces the National Assembly to choose between voting a censure motion and accepting a policy package proposed by the government.[3]

The government's decision on whether or not to invoke Article 49.3 during a minority government has direct consequences for the achievement of office-holding, policy, and electoral objectives by the parties in government and opposition. For the parties in the government, if at least one pivotal opposition party (i.e., a party that can ensure that the government is not defeated on a censure vote) bears positive costs of censuring the government (i.e., values the government's continued existence in office), then the confidence vote procedure makes it possible to obtain policy outcomes that would be unobtainable without the procedure. We should expect, of course, that at least one such pivotal party exists because if this were not the case, then the opposition parties would simply submit and vote a motion of censure.[4]

The decision to use the procedure to obtain policy goals may, however, create trade-offs with respect to office- and vote-seeking objectives. When the government invokes the procedure, its control over office is jeopardized because the opposition can submit and vote a motion of censure. If the government is uncertain about the specific policy proposals that will lead the opposition to vote a censure motion, then the decision to invoke the procedure directly affects the government parties' ability to hold on to the reins of power. During minority government, this uncertainty may be especially important because although a pivotal party can have positive censure costs, the government may not know the precise policy sacrifices that the pivotal party will accept before deciding to censure the government. Hence, use of the procedure to obtain particular policy outcomes may have direct implications for the achievement of office-holding (or office-retaining) objectives.[5]

Perhaps more important, the decision to use the confidence vote procedure to achieve particular policy outcomes will often have negative electoral implications, even if the policies achieved with the procedure are viewed as instrumental to electoral success. Invoking the confidence vote procedure is electorally costly to the parties in government because the procedure invites the most "political" act in the life of a legislature – a motion of censure. The deputies I interviewed stressed that when the confidence vote procedure is invoked, a signal is sent to the voters that the government is divided and weak, that it cannot gain a majority for its policies, and that it is running roughshod over the directly elected representatives of the voters. One deputy stated that "[Article] 49.3 embarrasses the government because it gives the impression that there is not a majority in the country – that there is no direction and that the prime minister has become authoritarian." Similarly, the assistant to the prime minister charged with negotiating policy concessions with the opposition parties said, "[Using Article] 49.3 is not a sign of force but rather an admission of failure. . . . It shows that our bill is not sufficiently good to pass on its own merits." Consequently, in deciding whether or not to invoke the confidence vote procedure, the parties in government may face difficult trade-offs between achieving desired policy outcomes, achieving electoral success, and retaining control over the powers associated with being in office. The degree to which procedural choice entails these trade-offs depends largely on the actual electoral costs associated with invoking the confidence vote procedure.

The confidence vote procedure also forces opposition parties to make choices between different party objectives. If the procedure is invoked, opposition parties are given an opportunity to censure the government and hence to gain office. If they refuse to censure the government, they generally must accept a policy that is worse than the status quo, or at least that is worse than the policy that would be passed by a majority vote in the National Assembly. Similarly, if the government bears the electoral costs of using the procedure, the opposition must decide whether or not to use these costs to extract policy concessions. The model in Huber (1996a; see also Huber 1997) indicates that if an opposition party does not have strong electoral incentives to distinguish its policy position from that of the government, then the opposition party and the government should reach agreement on a policy that can be adopted without resort to the confidence vote procedure. But if the opposition party has strong "position-taking" incentives – that is, strong incentives to distinguish its position from that of the government – then the opposition should support a bill in parliament that is known to be unacceptable to the government, forcing the use of the confidence vote procedure.

Given the trade-offs that the confidence vote procedure creates for both the government and the opposition parties, how should we expect French parties to behave during minority government? One factor influencing the final policy outcome of the bargaining process is the costs to the pivotal opposition parties of throwing the government out of office. The higher these costs, the better the final policy that the government can achieve using a confidence vote procedure (because the government can propose any policy that is preferred by the pivotal opposition party to the alternative of bringing down the government).

Censure costs, however, should not affect whether we actually observe the use of the confidence vote procedure. Instead, the government's procedural decision should turn largely on the magnitude of the government's electoral costs of using Article 49.3. If these electoral costs are large, then a vote-seeking government may prefer to make policy concessions rather than to bear the electoral costs of using the procedure. If these costs are small, then the government may choose to use the procedure.

The government's procedural decision, of course, will also be conditioned by the behavior of the opposition. Opposition parties, in situations where the government bears large electoral costs of using the procedure, must weigh whether or not to obtain the best possible policy outcome or to be rigid and uncompromising, forcing the government to bear the electoral costs of using the procedure (at the expense of obtaining a more favorable policy). The decision between these options will depend on the extent to which parties can link the attainment of policy concessions from the government to electoral success. In situations where the government bears little or no electoral costs of using the procedure, opposition parties have little opportunity either to extract policy concessions or to force the government to bear heavy electoral costs. The opposition parties must decide in this case between censuring the government and choosing another position-taking strategy (such as strong public criticism of government policy) aimed at maximizing long-term electoral success.

The behavior of the parties, then, depends largely on the magnitude of the government's electoral costs of using the confidence vote procedure and on the ability of opposition parties to link policy outcomes to electoral success. I focus on these two factors in order to explain the choices made by the parties in the 1988 and 1989 budget debates.

THE FRENCH BUDGET DEBATES IN 1988 AND 1989

The Socialist minority government in 1988 and 1989 had two parties with which it could negotiate concessions in order to obtain support for its bills: the Communists to the left and the Center to the right. It is important to note that in 1988, the costs to both the Center and the Communists of throwing the government out of office were very large. Consequently, if the Socialists wanted to use the confidence vote procedure to obtain particular policies, either for instrumental electoral reasons or to satisfy their desire for good policy, they were in an excellent position to do so.

The costs to opposition parties of censuring the government are based on expectations about what will happen if the government falls. In France, if the government falls, either a new government can form or the president of the Republic can dissolve the National Assembly and call for new elections.[6] In 1988, however, the only choice following a dissolution would have been to form a new government because President Mitterrand had dissolved the legislature in May 1988, and the Constitution prevents the president from dissolving the National Assembly more than once per year.

The costs of censuring the government were very large for the Communists in the fall of 1988 because the Communists obtained only 11.9 percent of the vote on the first ballot in the June 1988 legislative elections, and they ended up with only twenty-five seats, their lowest total during the Fifth Republic. Given their poor electoral showing, and given that the Socialists had made it clear that they would not form a new government with the Communists, censuring the government could only have made the Communists' position worse. Moreover, censuring the government would have jeopardized the electoral alliances that remained between many Communists and Socialists at the local level. These electoral alliances were especially salient to the Communists during the fall of 1988 because nationwide municipal elections were scheduled for the spring of 1989.

The costs to the Center of censuring the government were high in 1988 because of the Center's justification for forming an autonomous parliamentary group following the June 1988 legislative elections. From 1978 to 1988, the Center deputies had been part of the UDF group in parliament, and in 1988 the Center deputies were elected as part of the UDF in an electoral alliance with the RPR. It was therefore necessary for the Center to justify its formation as an autonomous group. The central *public* justification given by the Center was a commitment to practicing a new style of opposition, called *constructive*. A constructive opposition would not be rigid and intransigent in all encounters with the government, but rather would negotiate with the government to improve final policy outcomes. Given that it publicly justified its existence by stating that it would attempt to negotiate constructively with the government in order to improve the content of bills, it would have been costly to the Center to be inflexible in its bargaining positions or to threaten to censure the government. One Center deputy stated quite candidly: "We were obligated to negotiate with the government in 1988."

Although the formation of the Center parliamentary group was publicly linked to the idea of a constructive opposition, the reasons given in interviews were linked almost exclusively to *electoral* considerations that had nothing to do with the active pursuit of policy concessions from the Socialists. The main electoral consideration was to achieve the increased public exposure that comes with the autonomy of a separate group in parliament. As a separate group, the Center deputies can make speeches in the National Assembly on their own behalf and are not identified in the media as members of the UDF. In addition, an autonomous group gives the Center an opportunity to have its own presidential candidate. Given the increased *personalization* of politics in France, the Center deputies argued that without their own presidential candidate, they were handicapped at all levels vis-à-vis the other parties.

Although the high costs to the Communists and the Center of throwing the government out of office made it possible for the government to use Article 49.3 to obtain a very favorable final policy outcome in 1988, the government did not use this procedure. One reason that the government avoided Article 49.3 was that a pivotal opposition party, the Center, clearly did not have strong position-taking incentives and thus was willing and able to work constructively with the government to reach a policy compromise. Another reason was the government's perception that there would be large electoral costs associated with using the procedure in 1988. This is due in part to the fact that Prime Minister Rocard wanted to demonstrate his political capacity and political independence to French voters. In particular, he wanted to prove that he had the skill to deal with a new and difficult political situation – minority government – without relying on the confidence vote procedure and without allying himself with any particular opposition party. One Socialist deputy explained: "We wanted to show – and this was psychologically very strong – that the minority situation would not block us or force us to make political compromises. Rocard wanted to show that he could take control of the situation and was not weakened by the fact that he did not have a majority." The Socialists argued that the government could prove its strength by governing effectively without "resort to institutional force."

The Socialist government also believed it was important to demonstrate to voters that the Socialists were not dependent exclusively on either the Communists or the Center. Traditionally, the Socialists and the Communists had cooperated closely during legislative elections under France's two-round electoral law, and the two parties formed a coalition government in 1981, despite the fact that the Socialists had won a majority of the seats in the National Assembly. In 1988, President Mitterrand's presidential campaign stressed a new "openness" of the Socialists toward the political center, and during the legislative elections, the Socialists made it clear to voters that they did not intend to form a coalition with the Communists. The electoral outcome of a minority government, however, made it difficult for the Socialists to demonstrate that they were, in fact, not dependent on the Communists. The assistant to the prime minister who was responsible for negotiating concessions with the opposition explained that the government wanted to use the 1988 budget debates to show its ability to do its work without the "failure" of the confidence vote procedure and without allying itself with the Communists. The Socialists calculated that to avoid appearing dependent exclusively on the Communists or the Center, it would be necessary to obtain the public support – through abstentions – of both the Center and the Communists on the budget.

The "stereo abstention," explained the government negotiator, was a crucial part of the government's strategy:

> It was very important for us to demonstrate that we weren't dependent on anyone. It was very important. It was our first budget, and it was the first vote that was at once politically difficult and important. We could have used Article 49.3, but we wanted to show that we could do our work without it – to show in the clearest manner possible that the survival of the government and the adoption of its bills won't depend solely on the good will of either the Communists or the Center. We wanted to show that the Socialists were not prisoners to either the Communists or the Center.

The Rocard government, then, made significant policy concessions to both the Communists and the Center in order to avoid the perceived electoral costs of failing to do so (and invoking the confidence vote procedure to pass the budget).

To see how these perceived electoral costs of using Article 49.3 affected bargaining strategies, it is necessary to consider the actual process used by the parties for negotiating policy agreements. The negotiations between the government and the Center on the first part of the budget (the vote on "receipts"), where the government was able to achieve the abstention of both the Center and the Communists, provide a general illustration of how this negotiation process unfolded in 1988. At the end of the debate, the Center spokesman pointed to five government policy concessions that led the Center to support the bill by abstaining on the final vote: (1) a decrease in the rate of the value-added tax (VAT) on luxury items from 33 1/3 to 28 percent; (2) a decrease in the *taxe professionnelle*, a tax paid by businesses; (3) an increase in academic scholarships; (4) an increase in renters' assistance (APL, or *aide personalisé de logement*); and (5) promises regarding future examination of taxes on undeveloped property.

The concession on the luxury VAT was the most important policy concession in terms of budgetary cost – more than 3.5 billion francs. The demand for a VAT reduction came from a Center amendment that was rejected by the Finance Committee. The amendment was attached to Article 6 of the budget, which proposed to decrease the "minor" VAT from 7.5 to 5 percent. When Article 6 came into debate, the government reserved it and all amendments using Article 95.4 of the Rules of the National Assembly (which permits the government to reserve articles and/or amendments, later establishing the moment at which they will be debated and voted). The government called for consideration of Article 6 near the conclusion of the debate on the first part of the budget, and at this time it introduced its own amendment reducing the VAT on luxury items from 33 1/3 to 28 percent. The Center voluntarily withdrew its amendment and the government amendment was adopted, as was Article 6.

The VAT example illustrates three institutional advantages the government enjoys over the parliamentary groups in amending bills. First, the government can use its right to reserve the vote and debate on specific articles to control the order in which certain parts of bills are considered on the floor of the National Assembly. Hence, if the government faces difficulties in the National Assembly on particular articles of its bills, it can stop the debate and move the negotiation process out of the public eye. Second, deputy amendments but not government amendments must be considered by the relevant standing committee (see Article 44 of the Constitution and Article 99.5 of the Rules of the National Assembly). It is therefore easier for the government than for parliamentary parties to offer amendments once a bill has been reported out of committee for consideration in the National Assembly. Third, deputy amendments must include a *gage* (a specific statement of how these funds will be replaced). Article 40 of the Constitution states that National Assembly amendments cannot have the net effect of decreasing public resources or increasing expenditures. Consequently, if one part of a National Assembly amendment calls for a decrease in funds (such as the Center's VAT amendment), another part must include a gage that specifies how these funds will be replaced. In the case of the VAT amendment, for example, the Center's proposed gage included an increase in the minor VAT to 7 percent and an increase in taxes on alcohol and tobacco. Often the government will amend National Assembly amendments by suppressing the gage, but if the government chooses instead to introduce its own amendment, then the National Assembly must choose between its own gaged amendment and the ungaged amendment of the government. In practice, Article 40 does not seem to affect significantly the policymaking role of parliament. It does, however, give the government control over *distributing* credit for policy proposals.

The other concessions to the Center and the Communists were made in a similar fashion. Opposition amendments were generally rejected or not considered in committee, were reserved on the floor without debate, and were withdrawn without being voted. Hence, the major concessions to the opposition were made without adoption of opposition proposals, but rather by adoption of

Socialist measures introduced after debate on the budget had begun in the National Assembly. At this time, the government, using its right to reserve votes, order the agenda, and amend its own bill, apparently made the concessions necessary for the Center and the Communists to abstain on the first part of the bill. How, then, were these concessions negotiated?

The key to the government's obtaining the support of both the Communists and the Center on the first part of the budget was secret bargaining sessions between the leaders of the opposition parties and representatives of the government after debate on the budget had begun. To understand specifically how these negotiations were accomplished, consider again the case of the Center party. The details of this strategy were described in an interview with one of the Center's leading participants in the budget debates:

> There was, first, a – no one has written about this in the press because until now I've been very discreet, but it's part of history – there was a position taken by [Center Deputy Raymond] Barre in the corridor. We exited from debate in the National Assembly and two or three Center deputies were discussing the budget with Barre. At this moment . . . [Socialist Finance Minister] Pierre Bérégovoy passed, simply to go to the toilet – there is the truth – and naturally he offered handshakes all around, and when he offered his hand to Barre, Barre said, "Listen, it's clear what's necessary to improve your budget – that is to lower the rate of the VAT from thirty-three to twenty-eight percent." And Bérégovoy said, "Yes, that's a possibility, that's an idea that must be kept in mind." After that I resumed negotiations with the government – something I've never said before. I had negotiations with Bérégovoy head to head in the room reserved for the government at the National Assembly. And I said to Bérégovoy, "That's not enough. We want more." He asked me "What do you want?" I said, "We will abstain on the first part [of the budget] if we get a decrease in the *taxe professionnelle* of a half a point." Then we want a few other things, among them the student scholarships, but I can't say exactly right now. . . . Later in some new conversations with his cabinet, I said, you must give. . . . 400 million for the scholarships and an increase in the APL . . . but especially the scholarships. And the government said, "Okay."

Why was secrecy such an important element of the policy negotiation process? For both the Socialists and the Center, the answer lies in electoral preoccupations having little to do with the nature of final budgetary policies. The Center wanted to have its cake and eat it too. They chose secret negotiations because they feared that overt cooperation with the government "would have had, psychologically, some very bad effects" with public opinion. More precisely, although the Center believed that the idea of a constructive opposition was the "only way the Center could justify its existence in the eyes of the public," they also believed that the actual practice of a constructive opposition carried with it very real electoral risks. It was one thing, they argued, to make public declarations to the effect that the Center had formed to pursue good policy. It was quite another thing to actually pursue such policies by crawling into bed with the enemy Socialists and hammering out the details of policy concessions. In addition, public cooperation with the Socialists could jeopardize the electoral alliance with the UDF and the RPR. For the Center, then, although the formation of an autonomous group was driven by electoral considerations, the public justification for the autonomous group obligated the Center to undertake negotiations with potential electoral costs. Secret negotiations were perceived to be the best strategy for keeping these costs in check.

The government also adopted the strategy of secrecy for electoral reasons. The government wanted to maintain the public appearance that the Socialists were unified, and it feared that negotiations with the Center would alienate certain Socialist deputies. One Socialist member of the Finance Committee summarized the government's dilemma:

> It was not evident that we could make the Socialist group accept the principle of obtaining, through concessions, the vote, through abstention, of the Center group. Historically, without exception, the Center deputies were allied with the right against us in virtually every district. . . . Now if these talks would have been in the public eye for a moment, we would have seen some incredible problems at the heart of the Socialist party related to the turn of the party toward the right.

An additional and related electoral benefit of secret negotiations was that they made it possible to obtain at the same time the abstention of the Communists and the Center, which, as noted earlier, was viewed as essential for establishing a public image of legislative independence.

The reactions of the opposition parties to the way in which the 1988 budget negotiations unfolded illustrate the parties' preoccupation with electoral considerations that seem unrelated to the nature of short-term policy outcomes. The Center deputy who had held a secret closed-door meeting with the finance minister described his personal reaction:

> Here is where the government made the error: it announced the increase in the scholarships and the aid to low-income renters, and the Communists stood up and said, "Thank you, Mr. Minister, for making that concession to us." Thus, the government had sold the scholarships and the renters aid to the Communists and to the Center at the same time! I was literally furious. I said in the corridor, "That doesn't satisfy us. You can't sell the same concession to two different groups." . . . We felt that in no case when the government made concessions to us could they also make concessions to the Communists.

Both the Center and the Communists argued that the government could play its cards either to the left or to the right, but in playing its cards in both directions, it compromised both the Center and the Communists, damaging long-range opportunities for further negotiations. That is, each party believed there would be negative electoral utility associated with sharing credit for the policy concessions with the other party. The Center deputies, in particular, were so furious that the government negotiator tried to calm them down by using his sense of humor:

> Both the Communists and the Center were upset when the vote occurred. Especially the Center when they saw that the Communists abstained. There was even a scene the night of the vote at the National Assembly where [some of the] Center deputies bawled me out. They cursed me, told me it was disgusting. Accused me of dealing behind their back. They were crazy with anger. When I saw how mad they were, how much they were bawling me out, I said, "Listen, I want to tell you something. Me, I'm Jewish. What have the Jews said for two thousand years? To sell something that I have to someone who wants it – that isn't commerce. Commerce, that's to sell something I don't have to someone who doesn't want to buy it. Now, to sell something I don't have to two persons at the same time who don't want to buy it – that's no longer commerce, that's art." They looked at me absolutely stupefied, and eventually they laughed, and from the moment they relaxed a bit after considering my provocative little story, I was able to explain seriously that I had simply done my job. It wasn't an insult to them.

The angry reaction of the Center deputies to the unfolding of the budget debates illustrates both the priority French parties placed on electoral considerations during the two budget debates and the parties' perception that electoral gain need not be linked to short-term policy outcomes. The Center was clearly less concerned with the policy outcome itself than with the political costs and benefits associated with obtaining policy concessions. In fact, both the Center and the Communists obtained exactly the policy concessions they desired, yet they were dissatisfied because they believed that the public perceptions linked to obtaining these concessions would be negative. Indeed, this dissatisfaction was strongest with respect to the renters' assistance and the scholarship aid, two concessions that were small in budgetary cost but large in political capital.

THE 1989 BUDGET NEGOTIATION PROCESS

The weak link between policy goals and party choices during the 1988 and 1989 budget debates is obvious in the Center's description of the factors affecting its negotiating strategies in 1989. The Center deputies stated that the Center decided not to enter constructive negotiations with the government for reasons entirely unrelated to policy considerations. One Center deputy, for example, stated outright:

> The decision to be more rigid on the 1989 budget had nothing to do with the content of the budget. The vote on the budget was simply a means for affirming our position in the opposition. It's not the content of the budget because, in my opinion, the content of the budget was even better than the content of the budget for 1988.

Another Center deputy on the Finance Committee was equally frank:

> Deputies from all parties were in agreement in the Finance Committee [in
> 1989]. Even often the Communists. I was struck by the debate in committee
> because I had nothing to say. I'm sorry, but I was in complete agreement
> with the Socialists. I applauded. But we voted against the bill. What we
> and all parties do in public has nothing to do with the facts.

The government's tactic of negotiating at once with the Communists and
the Center led both parties to be very rigid in their negotiations with the
government during the 1990 budget debates. The Center made it known in
advance that it would not support the budget. It strengthened its ties with its
allies on the right by forming various organizations intended to orchestrate
parliamentary strategies. The Center group also demanded many policy changes
that could never have been accepted by the Socialist government, including
large tax breaks for big business, unaffordable reductions in the medium VAT,
and, most important, reprivatization of French industries. The Communists,
like the Center, were also much more rigid in 1989 than in 1988. They
announced in advance that they would not support the budget, and they made
policy proposals that could never be accepted by the Socialists. For instance, the
Communists insisted on a huge increase in the *impôt de solidarité sur la fortune* (a
wealth tax) paid by the richest individuals in France; they submitted sixty-four
amendments attempting to link the *taxe d'habitation* (a per habitant tax on
living dwellings and an issue on which they received a concession in 1988) to
revenues; and they insisted that the *dotation globale de fonctionnment* (the formula
for distributing state money to local governments) continue to be determined
by VAT revenues, even though major changes in the VAT were necessary
because of European integration.

The increased rigidity of the two opposition parties was attributable not
only to the events in 1988, but also to exogenous political events that occurred
between the fall of 1988 and the fall of 1989. The event that led the Center to
believe that the voters were rejecting the effort to practice constructive opposition was the June 1989 European Parliament election. The European election
results were described as a "cold shower" – a "real disappointment." The Center
list received 8 percent of the vote when 12 percent was anticipated. The reaction
of the Center party, a Center leader explained, was that "certain deputies
thought [the electoral result] was a sanction by the voters against our autonomous attitude within the opposition and against our method of practice in the
opposition. They thought it was necessary to retreat a bit."

Like the Center, the Communists were prompted by exogenous political
factors to be more rigid in their relationship with the Socialists in 1989. One
important consideration was an increase in the level of social protest across the
two years. One Communist deputy explained:

> The strikes at the Finance Ministry, a strong movement at the PTT [Postes,
> Télécommunications et Télédiffusion], a movement among the teachers, and

a strike at Peugeot – these are very strong indices showing popular discontent. In setting our position, we integrate the degree of consciousness and mobility of the social movement. We take the temperature of the social movement to know how far we can go. We haven't voted a motion of censure yet, but we might.

In addition, after the municipal elections in the spring of 1989, in which alliances were negotiated district by district, increasing uncertainty about the benefits of the electoral alliance with the Socialists contributed to the increased rigidity by the Communists in the 1989 budget debates. Another Communist deputy explained:

It's difficult to say if the alliance will continue. . . . There are more and more divisions between the Socialists and the Communists. And the voters, especially the Socialist supporters but also the Communist supporters, are voting less and less in the confines of the alliance. Why have an alliance like that? Why do it?

In 1989, then, several exogenous political events, plus the 1988 "learning experience" that there can be negative electoral utility associated with the effort to obtain policy concessions, led both the Center and the Communists to refuse to negotiate with the government. Instead, the Center and the Communists both made uncompromising proposals to signal to the voters that each party represented an alternative to the Socialists.

In addition, the Socialist deputies pointed to exogenous political events that affected the government's electoral costs of using the confidence vote procedure by affecting the internal unity of the Socialist Party. In the interviews, the deputies stressed the importance of presenting an image of a unified party to the voters. If the government party (or coalition) is divided, then the confidence vote procedure can be invoked to protect the government party from undesirable debate, undesirable amendment activity, and undesirable votes on bills. In 1989, the Socialist Party was internally divided for several reasons. First, there was a division between centrist factions of the party (led by Prime Minister Michel Rocard) and more leftist factions due primarily to the negative reaction of many Socialist deputies to the government's negotiations with the Center in 1988. Leftist factions associated these negotiations with a repositioning of the party to the right and blamed this repositioning for poor success in by-elections. Similarly, disappointing returns in many districts in the May 1989 municipal elections gave an increased voice to militants who called for a repositioning of the party to the left.

Second, and more important, there were the effects of the preparation for the 1990 Party Congress in Rennes, where party militants were to choose a new first secretary of the party. The competition to become first secretary was marked primarily by a conflict between three individuals – the minister of education, the president of the National Assembly, and the president of the Socialist parliamentary group. This competition affected the preparation of the 1989 budget, as the three candidates began to oppose each other with the objective of moving the party to the left. One Socialist deputy believed that the divisions created by this competition were themselves sufficient to drive the government to use the confidence vote procedure in 1989:

> [T]he Socialists were very divided [in the fall of 1989] because of the approach of the Congress at Rennes. Therefore the government reduced its willingness to negotiate the budget, to enter into a real reflection of its content with its own group. That made it even that much more difficult to negotiate with the other groups. I said at the beginning of September in 1989 to my friends in the government that we'd have 49.3 right away because we were in such deep trouble to find a compromise with the Socialist group that it would be almost impossible to consider discussions with the other groups.

The competition to become first secretary of the party also affected the unfolding of the budget debates on the floor of the National Assembly in 1989. The budget negotiator knew that the Center and the Communists would vote against the budget, so he negotiated with individuals rather than with parties. He found the votes he needed among eight Center deputies who were close to Barre. However, when the president of the Socialist group saw that the Communists would vote against the budget no matter what happened, he became angry and told the government, "We cannot pass the budget against the Communists and with the votes of the right." The president of the Socialist group did not seem concerned about the nature of the actual policy concessions, which were measures necessary to prepare France for European integration, but rather about the image associated with voting the budget with the Center. On the night of the vote, he put extraordinary pressure on the government to use the confidence vote procedure. The assistant to the prime minister explained:

> [The President of the Socialist Group] didn't stop saying "49.3"; he kept calling the Elysée [Palace] every two minutes. [He] was so excited . . . that it was possible that for several Socialist deputies he would forget to turn the key [on the proxy vote]. He was really vehement. [He wanted] to maximize his chance to be first secretary . . . and was convinced that to pass the budget with the Center would have damaged his chances. . . . Finally, there was such pressure from [him] . . . that I said to the Center deputies, "We've really thought it out and [the president of the Socialist group] is so against voting the budget that you should go ahead and stick with your group and we'll use 49.3."

So in 1989, Rocard was able to find (in secret) several Center deputies who (verbally) promised to support the budget. But for Rocard, the events surrounding the 1988 budget debates, and, most important, the competition associated with the election of a first secretary at the annual Party Congress, made adoption of the budget with the votes of these centrists politically costly. Thus, to demonstrate the Socialists' independence of the center, Rocard used the confidence vote procedure to adopt the budget.

INSTITUTIONAL ARRANGEMENTS AND PARTY CHOICES IN FRANCE

The analysis of the 1988 and 1989 budget debates suggests that although French parties seemed concerned primarily with electoral objectives, future electoral success was often believed to be linked less to the nature of final policy outcomes themselves than to the messages sent to the voters during the process of obtaining these outcomes. Two incidents in particular suggest that during the 1988 and 1989 budget debates, final policy outcomes were not foremost on the minds of French vote-seeking parties. First, the Center and the Communists achieved all the policy concessions that they demanded in 1988 but were angry and dissatisfied because credit for obtaining the concessions was shared. Hence, both parties refused to enter into serious policy negotiations in 1989. Second, the Socialists made *unnecessary* policy concessions to avoid the electoral costs of Article 49.3 in 1988, and then in 1989 they obtained the necessary votes for its budget but still used Article 49.3 to avoid contributing to the image of a divided party.

It is, of course, very important not to exaggerate the extent to which French parties are indifferent to policy outcomes. Clearly, voters judge parties based on their policy positions, and the French parties must concern themselves with the nature of final policy outcomes (Converse and Pierce 1986). Nevertheless, the sequence of events that unfolded in the 1988 and 1989 budget debates leads us to ask: Why were the French parties so extreme in their pursuit of votes, and why did the pursuit of votes sometimes seem divorced from the pursuit of policies that might have been instrumental to obtaining votes?

Although party organization has not been my focus, it seems worth noting that we are unlikely to find answers to these questions in the organizational features of French parties. To see this, consider the differences in the organization of the three parties analyzed in this chapter.[7] The Communists are a highly structured party, with a centralized decision-making apparatus that demands extraordinary discipline and that marginalizes or expels critics of party leadership and party policy. The Socialists, on the other hand, are famous for their high level of intraparty pluralism. In fact, different "currents" of opinion have a formal status in the party. These factions compete for support from party members, and party leadership and policy are determined democratically by the members during the biennial party congresses. Finally, the Center is the least structured of the three parties. Since the early 1970s, the party has gone through more or less continuous change and mutation, with the dissolution of the Mouvement des radicaux de gauche (MRG), formation of the Centre Social

Democrats (CDS), participation in the UDF from 1978 to 1988, and departure from the UDF in 1988. Because these three parties are organized so differently, it is doubtful that internal organizational structure can explain the similarities in their vote-seeking choices.

Instead, two related institutional factors offer insight into the answers to these questions. The first concerns French legislative institutions, which permit the government not only to limit the extent to which opposition parties can affect policy outcomes, but also to control public perceptions of credit and blame for these outcomes. Although it was widely recognized during periods of majority government that office-holding was a prerequisite for policy influence, scholars believed that this situation would change with the disappearance of a progovernmental majority (see, e.g., Wright 1983: 127; see also Andrews 1982, Frears 1981, and Duverger, 1987). The predicted change, however, did not materialize, and the most important reason is that as long as no party is willing to censure the government, the confidence vote procedure permits the government to pass bills that are worse than the status quo for a majority in the National Assembly. Indeed, during the first three years of minority government, the Socialists used the confidence vote procedure almost as many times as it had been used in the history of the Fifth Republic, making it a central element in French politics and policymaking on numerous pieces of important legislation.

But the confidence vote procedure is not the only procedure that shapes the opportunities for opposition policy influence. Analysis of the budget debates shows that the government can use its control over the agenda and its right to amend its own bills in the National Assembly to control public perceptions of responsibility for policy outcomes. This was especially important during the negotiation of policy concessions in 1988. In addition, the government can use a procedure called the *package vote (vote bloqué)* to group selectively articles and amendments, excluding those to which it is opposed (see Article 44.3 of the Constitution). Under this procedure, the parliament must vote either to accept or reject the government's package. The package vote was used on numerous occasions during the 1989 budget debates to limit changes to the budget by the opposition parties; like the confidence vote procedure, it has been used frequently during minority government (Huber 1992, 1996b; Keeler 1991). French legislative institutions, then, make it difficult, even during minority government, for opposition parties to link the pursuit of policy objectives to electoral success. These difficulties explain to a large extent the different behavior observed by French parties during the 1988 and 1989 budget debates.

France's restrictive legislative institutions, however, only partly explain the choices made by French parties during the budget debates. To arrive at a more complete understanding, it is also necessary to consider the effects of French electoral institutions. France's two-round, single-member district, plurality electoral law generally ties the outcomes of elections to the formation of government coalitions by requiring parties to form electoral alliances that cooperate during second-round balloting. When alliance partners win control of parliament, all parties in the alliance usually form a government together, even if one of the parties wins a majority of the seats. In 1968, for example, the Gaullists won a majority in parliament but nevertheless included the other parties on the right in the government coalition, and in 1981, the Socialists won a majority but nevertheless included the Communists in the government coalition.

Historically, the two-stage electoral process has polarized French parties into two opposite camps. Although each party has competed with the other parties in its camp in order to maximize its position within the camp, this competition has necessarily unfolded without jeopardizing the maintenance of the camp itself. The maintenance of a camp is important not only because it has provided the best strategy for entering the government, but also because French voters have perceived the party system as involving two competing camps. Hence, when casting a ballot, the French voter has traditionally been able to estimate accurately how a vote for a particular party will affect the coalition formation game and hence affect final policy outcomes. The interparty cooperation necessary in two-stage electoral competition therefore has created vote-seeking strategies consisting of sending consistent signals to voters about which parties are on which side.[8] The 1988 and 1989 budget debate stories illustrate how these historical alliance patterns shaped, in contrasting fashion, the behavior of the Center and the Socialists.

The ultimate strategy adopted by the Center focused on the maintenance of the traditional conservative electoral alliance. The Center deputies suggested in the interviews that the advent of minority government created an initial impulse among some deputies to attempt to play the same pivotal role played by the Free Democrats in Germany, forming coalitions on the left or the right. That is, minority government presented an opportunity to break away from the traditional alliance. But following the poor performance in the European elections in 1989, the Center learned that there were serious electoral problems with the "constructive" strategy. The party therefore reaffirmed its position in the alliance with the other parties on the right. One Center deputy stated:

> The European elections showed us that it is very difficult to live alone – that the alliances are necessary to live, to last. . . . The maintenance of the alliances prepares us for the next election. The closer we get to these elections, the more difficult it is for us to separate ourselves in the vote on bills from our allies, the UDF and the RPR.

The deputies argued that the electoral success of the opposition parties depends on the extent to which the parties in the opposition can present themselves as a clear *alternative* to the party or coalition in power. A leader of the Center stated:

> In French politics, you must be clear and simple, you must explain to the voters which side you are on and who is on the other side. You can't be in the middle.

The Center, then, learned the importance of maintaining an electoral alliance that represented a clear alternative to the government. Since alliances were viewed as necessary to enter office, and since entering office was necessary to affect policy, the focus on seeking votes by maintaining an alliance is perfectly reasonable. It also highlights the difference between short-term and long-term party objectives. Although the Center passed up opportunities to influence policy in the short term, the decision was based on the belief that such a strategy would increase the probability of future control over office and, consequently, over future policy outcomes. Hence, in stating that the French parties seemed to believe that future electoral success was linked less to policy outcomes than to the signals sent to the voters during the process of obtaining these outcomes, it is important to distinguish between long-term and short-term policy concerns of the parties.

Like the Center, the Socialists, as noted earlier, also viewed the advent of minority government as an opportunity to change the traditional configuration of electoral competition. But unlike the Center, after adopting a strategy of independence in 1988, the Socialists did not return to the traditional leftist alliance. By continually striving for an image of independence in the early 1990s, the Socialists were seriously flirting with the idea of ending the period of cooperation with the electorally unpopular Communists. Interestingly, however, the Socialists never closed the book on their cooperation with the Communists. After losing power in the 1993 legislative elections, the Socialists engineered a surprise win in 1997. Following that victory, they formed a coalition government with the Communists (and several Green parties).

In conclusion, the analysis of the 1988 and 1989 budget debates suggests that French legislative and electoral institutions focus the attention of French parties on vote-seeking behavior. At the same time, the difficulties that French opposition parties have in linking policy pursuits to electoral success, and the ability of the government to use institutional structures to shape perceptions of alliances, suggest that the behavior of French parties is often inconsistent with the model of vote-seeking parties proposed by Downs (1957). In the Downsian framework, parties care only about attracting the votes necessary to obtain power, and policy is the only convertible vote-buying currency. Rational party behavior therefore consists simply of advocating and adopting the policies that will attract the largest number of voters. The difficulty with this model is that it ignores the roadblocks parties often face in linking policy pursuits to electoral success (Denzau, Riker, and Shepsle 1985). That is, the Downsian conception of vote-seeking parties fails to consider that party behavior consists not only of "position taking," but also of "credit claiming" for implementing particular policies (Mayhew 1974). If a party's role in implementing a policy is unclear to voters, then it will be difficult for the party to translate its policymaking role into electoral success. Therefore, the extent to which parties can pursue votes by pursuing policies will depend on the extent to which it is clear to voters where responsibility for policy outcomes lies.[9] The degree to which vote-seeking parties are Downsian, then, depends on the ways in which institutional arrangements shape voters' perceptions of the policymaking process.

NOTES

1. This chapter is based in large part on (Huber 1996b, ch. 6), to which the reader is referred for a more extensive treatment of the issues discussed here.
2. The interviews were with deputies from each of the five parties, as well as with the assistant to the prime minister charged with negotiating concessions with the parties in parliament. The interview targets were selected using the public records of the debates to determine which deputies played key roles in the budget process. The interviews were tape-recorded with the understanding that the interviewees would remain anonymous.
3. For a formal model of how the confidence vote procedure shapes party strategies, see Huber (1996a). For a discussion of this model in the French context, see Huber (1996b, ch. 5).
4. Strøm (1990) provides an excellent explanation for why political parties might prefer to remain in opposition during minority government.
5. Huber (1997) uses an incomplete information model of the confidence vote procedure to analyze the circumstances under which such procedures can lead to inefficient government terminations.
6. Unlike the situation in many parliamentary democracies, the prime minister in France cannot call for the dissolution of the legislature.
7. My discussion of French party organization relies on Bell and Criddle (1988), Ehrmann and Schain (1992, chap. 7), Frears (1991), and Ysmal (1989).
8. For analyses of the ways in which French electoral laws shape interparty cooperation and competition in France, see Tsebelis (1990, ch. 7), Converse and Pierce (1986, part II), and Rochon and Pierce (1985).
9. For a comparative discussion of how institutional arrangements shape clarity of responsibility for policy outcomes, see Powell (nd, 1989).

REFERENCES

Andrews, William G. (1982). *Presidential Government in Gaullist France*. Albany: SUNY Press.

Bell, David S. and Byron Criddle (1988). *The French Socialist Party: The Emergence of Party Government*. Second edition. London: Clarendon Press.

Converse, Philip E. and Roy Pierce (1986). *Political Representation in France*. Cambridge, MA: Harvard University Press.

Denzau, Arthur, William Riker, and Kenneth Shepsle (1985). "Farquharson and Fenno: Sophisticated Voting and Home Style." *American Political Science Review* 79, 4: 1117–34.

Downs, Anthony (1957). *An Economic Theory of Democracy*. New York: Harper & Row.

Duverger, Maurice (1987). *La cohabitation des français*. Paris: PUF.

Ehrmann, Henry W. and Martin A. Schain (1992). *Politics in France*. Fifth edition. New York: HarperCollins.

Frears, John R. (1981). "Parliament in the Fifth Republic." In *The Impact of the Fifth Republic on France* (pp. 47–68), eds. William Andrews and Stanley Hoffmann. Albany: SUNY Press.

—— (1991). *Parties and Voters in France*. London: Hurst & Company.

Huber, John D. (1992). "The Role of Restrictive Legislative Institutions in France and the United States." *American Political Science Review* 86, 3: 675–87.

—— (1996a). *Rationalizing Parliament: Legislative Institutions and Party Politics in France*. New York: Cambridge University Press.

—— (1996b). "The Vote of Confidence in Parliamentary Democracies." *American Political Science Review* 90, 2: 269–82.

—— (1997). "Political Uncertainty and Bargaining Failure in Parliamentary Democracies." Typescript. University of Michigan, Ann Arbor.

Keeler, John T. S. (1993). "Patterns of Policymaking in the French Fifth Republic: Strong Governments, Cycles of Reform and Political Malaise." In *Ideas and Ideals: Essays in Honor of Stanley Hoffmann* (pp. 200–19), eds. Linda Miller and Michael Smith. Boulder, CO: Westview Press.

Masclet, Jean-Claude (1982). *Un député: Pour quoi faire?* Paris: Presses Universitaires de France.

Maus, Didier (1988). *Les grandes textes de la pratique institutionnelle de la Vᵉ République*. Paris: La Documentation Française.

Mayhew, David (1974). *Congress: The Electoral Connection*. New Haven, CT: Yale University Press.

Parodi, Jean-Luc (1972). *Les rapports entre le legislatif et l'executif sous la Cinquième République 1958–62*. Paris: Presses de la fondation nationale des sciences politiques.

Powell, G. Bingham, Jr. (1989). "Constitutional Design and Citizen Electoral Control." *Journal of Theoretical Politics* 1, 2: 107–30.

—— (n.d.). *Elections as Instruments of Democracy*. Unpublished book manuscript.

Rochon, Thomas R. and Roy Pierce (1985). "Coalitions as Rivalries: French Socialists and Communists, 1967–78." *Comparative Politics* 17, 4: 437–51.

Strøm, Kaare (1990). *Minority Government and Majority Rule*. New York: Cambridge University Press.

Tsebelis, George (1990). *Nested Games: Rational Choice in Comparative Politics*. Berkeley: University of California Press.

Wright, Vincent (1983). *The Government and Politics in France*. New York: Holmes & Reiter.

Ysmal, Colette (1989). *Les partis politiques sous la Vᵉ République*. Paris: Montchrestien.

12

CONCLUSIONS: PARTY BEHAVIOR AND REPRESENTATIVE DEMOCRACY

Wolfgang C. Müller and Kaare Strøm

If political science is both the study of public decisions and a dismal science (along with economics), it is because public decisions are often inherently difficult and unpleasant. Public life often presents decision makers with unwelcome trade-offs, with choices they would rather not have to make. This volume has examined the decisions of Western European party leaders in a variety of situations of goal conflict. Clearly, these choices induced a great deal of agony, they were often controversial, and they may have caused a fair amount of regret. In many cases, they may have puzzled the immediate observer and called for an explanation.

This book has examined a number of such hard and critical choices. In each of these cases, as outside observers, and sometimes with the considerable benefit of hindsight, we can identify the objective dilemmas faced by parties considering, for example, government participation, coalition termination, or constitutional reform. Such analytical efforts are helpful, but they still leave us at some distance from the world of party leaders themselves. And such descriptions are themselves of limited value if they do not help us understand the situation in anything like the framework adopted by the relevant actors in the parties themselves.

Political parties are by no means all alike, nor are the choices their leaders make. Hence, generalization about their behavior is an endeavor fraught with difficulties. While the behavior of political parties has always been of central importance to political scientists, the progression of our understanding of these matters has sometimes been slow. Thus, the literature on decision making in political parties has largely fallen into two separate traditions: (1) radically stylized formal models, beginning with (and abstracting from) Downs (1957), and

(2) an intensively empirical literature, which has often failed to aspire to general validity. Cross-fertilization between these traditions has been too scarce.

A middle road between these extremes has much to offer, particularly if it can draw on some of the lessons of both. The main purpose of the essays in this volume has been to present such a project and demonstrate its viability. Thus, we offer a conception of political parties as organizations driven by the pursuit of three different goals: office, policy, and votes. Each of these objectives, we suggest, can be pursued instrumentally (as a means toward some other end), and two of them, office and policy, may be ends in themselves (intrinsic pursuits). However, parties are not always in the blissful situation of pursuing all these goals simultaneously and independently. Sometimes goal conflicts occur, trade-offs exist, and hard choices have to be made. When they do, party leaders may need to make hard choices between their objectives, and it is such choices that the contributors to this volume have set out to explore.

Chapter 1 presented an analytical framework within which such trade-offs and choices can be understood. That has been the tool kit with which the various contributors have sought to understand and explain their respective cases. The purpose of this chapter is to survey and assess their efforts and thereby to evaluate the tools they have used. The utility of our framework, then, depends on the answers we can give to four critical questions:

(1) Can we confidently ascribe goal conflicts and trade-offs to these cases of critical party leadership decision making?
(2) If so, is there any evidence that these goal conflicts and trade-off functions were recognized and acted upon by the leaders of these parties?
(3) If so, can we identify any differences in the weights given to the various considerations across players, parties, or policies?
(4) If such differences exist, is there any way to explain this variation in party behavior?

In the pages that follow, we address these issues in order. Our answers, in turn, will provide the basis for a more fundamental reassessment of the role of political parties in representative democracy.

IDENTIFYING GOAL CONFLICT

The first question, about whether we can identify significant cases of goal conflict, can be confidently answered in the affirmative. In all but one of the cases discussed in this volume, we can identify an unambiguous goal conflict facing political parties. Of course, this may not seem like much of a claim given the fact that we selected these cases expressly because a priori we had reason to believe that we would indeed be able to identify such dilemmas. Yet, we might have been wrong, or different investigators might have come to different conclusions. At a minimum, our exercise demonstrates the applicability of the conceptual framework within which we seek to understand the behavior of political parties.

What forms do these conflicts and trade-offs most commonly take? Our cases offer a wide variety of goal conflicts. They can be divided into three general categories. One common situation in which such dilemmas arise is where electoral considerations conflict with either or both of the other objectives: policy and office. In the Danish case, for example, the electoral liabilities of holding executive office tempered the willingness of several parties to enter coalitions that surely would have given them both policy influence and perquisites unavailable to oppositions. The Social Democrats seem to have felt this conflict very acutely in the mid-1970s. Similarly, Müller has shown that the Austrian Socialists' sacrifice of both office and policy influence brought the electoral gains they predicted. Their socialist brethren in the Netherlands and Ireland have faced remarkably similar dilemmas. The German FDP constitutes a deviant case because it eventually managed to satisfy all three objectives. However, this was possible only under considerable risk. In less favorable circumstances, the FDP may well have found itself in the position of having traded off votes for office and, in a worst-case scenario, may even have been relegated to opposition status in the longer run. The electoral costs of policy and office might well have been high.

A second common type of goal conflict is where parties face stark choices between their policy commitments, on the one hand, and their present or future (via elections) prospects of holding office on the other. For the Swedish Social Democrats, for example, the abolition of the monarchy was a feasible policy goal, but one that could easily have cost the party critical electoral support and thereby control of the government. Likewise, the Italian Communists eventually found that the policy influence they gained through cooperation with the Christian Democrats in the Historic Compromise came at a significant electoral cost and brought them no closer to control of the government. In the end, they despaired of the electoral costs of this strategy.

Finally, there are cases in which the control of office has been available only to the detriment of both the party's electoral fortunes and its policy agenda. Rolf Presthus's ill-fated attempt to capture the Norwegian government for the Conservatives is one such case. Even if Presthus's gamble had paid off, the Conservatives would have been saddled with an undesirable farm policy, and there is every reason to believe that many of their supporters would have balked at this compromise. The situation facing the Dutch Labor Party in 1991 represents a similar case. The price of continued coalition with the Christian Democrats was a more restrictive disability benefits policy, as well as, as it turned out, a disastrous and precipitous fall in the opinion polls. By the time of the 1991 provincial elections, about a third of its electorate had been lost. Both cases are horror stories concerning the costs of office pursuit.

Some contributors have identified goal conflicts that transcend the theoretical framework of this book. Following Sjöblom (1968), D'Alimonte identifies "party identity" as a major concern of the PCI. Similarly, Marsh and Mitchell point to the self-perception of the Fianna Fáil as "more than a party and unlike any others." However, it is possible, to a large extent, to translate party identity in a meaningful way into more familiar analytical categories. As we argue in Chapter 1, party identity or unity may simply be a shorthand for future electoral considerations. Such rhetoric is typically more palatable to the party faithful than is electoral opportunism, though the behavioral consequences may be the same. Since we believe in analytical simplicity, we opt for this shorthand. The fruits of our reductionism are an analysis that is more parsimonious and more compatible with existing rational choice explanations of party behavior.

Goal conflicts thus come in a multitude of forms, and the compatibility of the several objectives varies from one case to the next. For any one objective, we can identify situations in which it conflicts with one or both of the others, and apparently the trade-offs can be more or less steep. In some cases, the price of office may be very high; in others more moderate, and similarly for the other goods. Of course, it is also possible for all goals to be mutually compatible, but such cases hardly make for exciting studies of party decision making. To the extent that we can identify goal conflicts, we can then go on to describe the trade-offs made by the relevant parties and characterize their behavior through "as if" stipulations.

GOAL PERCEPTION AND STRATEGIC BEHAVIOR

A more intriguing and challenging question than whether conflicts exist is whether the principal party actors perceive any goal conflicts and trade-offs of the kinds we have described. Do party leaders recognize, for example, that office may have an electoral price or vice versa? This, of course, is where careful historical case studies yield particular payoffs, since politicians are often reluctant to voice such perceptions in public. Though the contributors to this volume have availed themselves of different data and methods, they have collectively presented us with impressive evidence that political party leaders often engage in calculations in which conflicts between office, policy, and electoral objectives are explicitly recognized and acted upon. In their conversations with the author, Huber's French parliamentarians are amazingly frank in their admission that electoral concerns often overrode their professed policy goals. Through his unprecedented access to party minutes, Müller presents striking evidence of strategic calculations within the Austrian Socialist Party. Quite evidently, the party's leaders went through sophisticated estimations of the ramifications of each of their options for future policies and elections. Even forecasts of economic developments entered into their calculations.

Through similarly careful scrutiny of archival and interview data, Bergman demonstrates how the leadership behavior of the Swedish Social Democrats in designing a new constitution was conditioned by their perception of a trade-off between electoral goals and their republican sympathies. Not all of our contributors have been able to draw on equally revealing evidence or equally frank politicians, but their inferences generally point in the same direction. Share, for example, shows that the Spanish Socialists recognized that their policy goals carried a price tag denominated in electoral fortunes and the prospects of holding office, and he illuminates the process by which the Socialist leadership became progressively less willing to pay this price. In sum, there can be little doubt that the analytical categories we have adopted are ones that closely reflect the perceived reality of many party leaders.

GOAL PRIORITIES

We have established the applicability of our conceptual apparatus to political party decision making and reconstructed major party decisions within this framework. The latter task has been accomplished in ways that would be recognizable to the relevant party leaders themselves. A natural result of this exercise is to characterize the goal priorities (or objective functions) of the parties in question. Indeed, some of the contributors have given pride of place to such descriptions. Huber, for example, characterizes French political parties in the late 1980s as extreme vote seekers, whose attainment of policy objectives in large part is evaluated only as a means toward electoral success. Marsh and Mitchell paint a picture of Irish parties, especially the Fianna Fáil, which is similar to Huber's characterization of their French opposite numbers. The Dutch Labor Party, on the other hand, is primarily a policy-seeking organization, according to Hillebrand and Irwin. Strøm shows how Norway's policy-seeking Center Party coexisted with a vote-seeking Progress Party, as well as with the office-seeking Conservatives.

Sometimes the preferences of party leaders are less clear-cut. Elklit provides a more conditional portrait of the Danish parties in the 1970s and 1980s. Although policy concerns seem to be their primary goals, these considerations are tempered by a view toward elections as well as toward the perks of office per se. The author further distinguishes the more policy-oriented Social Democrats from the more office-seeking bourgeois parties. In Share's analysis of the Spanish Socialists, the significant difference is not between different parties in the same situation, but rather between the same party at different times. In other words, here is a study of a party's development from a policy-seeking organization to one whose primary concern is control of the reins of government for its own sake. Interestingly, this has happened to a party in a newly redemocratized state, and the transformation is amazingly swift. Is this process perhaps a natural or even an inevitable consequence of the institutionalization of political parties, as Panebianco (1988) would argue?

Table 12.1. *Summary of party behaviors*

Country	Party	Period	Policy pursuit	Office pursuit	Vote pursuit
Ireland	Labour	1981–6	High	Low	Moderate
	Fine Gael	1987–9	High	Low	Low
	Fianna Fáil	1989	Low	High	Low
Denmark	Social Democrats	1973	Moderate	Low	High
	Liberals	1973	Moderate	High	Low
	Social Democrats	1975	Moderate	Low	High
	Liberals	1975	Moderate	High	Low
	Social Democrats	1982	Moderate	High	Low
	Social Liberals	1982	High	Low	Low
	Social Liberals	1988	Moderate	High	Low
Spain	Socialist	1975–8	High	Moderate	Low
	Socialist	1982	Low	High	Moderate
Netherlands	Labor	1981–2	High	Moderate	Low
	Labor	1989–4	Moderate	High	Low
Italy	Communists	1976–9	Moderate	High	Low
Austria	Social Democrats	1966	Low	Low	High
Norway	Conservatives	1987	Low	High	Low
	Center	1987	High	Low	Low
	Progress	1987	Moderate	Low	High
Germany	Free Democrats	1982	Moderate	High	High
Sweden	Social Democrats	1971–4	Low	High	Moderate
	Conservatives	1971–4	Low	High	Moderate
France	Center	1988–9	Low	Moderate	High
	Communists	1988–9	Low	Low	High
	Socialist	1988–9	Low	Moderate	High

Table 12.1 summarizes the goal priorities of the various parties in our study, as reflected in their behavior. In summarizing the observations of our contributors, we have classified the weight given to policy, office, and electoral pursuits as "high," "moderate," or "low." It is, of course, difficult to make direct comparisons of party behaviors across countries and situational contexts. Yet, our various contributors clearly spell out some quite distinct behavioral patterns, which we have attempted to capture here. The table shows that policy pursuit seems have been given high priority in six cases, office in twelve, and votes in eight. On the other hand, policy ranks low in priority in nine cases, office similarly in nine, and votes in thirteen. Does this mean that parties generally give higher priority to their office objectives than to their electoral concerns? Such a conclusion would be premature at best. For one thing, there is no natural metric by which these priorities can be measured, and the trade-offs between different objectives vary widely, depending on the context. Moreover,

our cases are in no way a representative sample even of competitive European parties. Note, for example, that this sample includes seven Danish cases and only one German one. Instead of trying to reach such global generalizations about the importance of different goal priorities, we would like to examine simpler and more partial relationships between organizations, institutions, and goal priorities. On this basis, we may be able to draw more discriminating lessons concerning the conditions most likely to facilitate vote-seeking, office-seeking, or policy-seeking party behavior. The next section will address that issue.

EXPLAINING GOAL PRIORITIES

Given the diversity of goal priorities that our case studies have revealed in party leadership behavior, we would like to identify some systematic explanatory factors. In Chapter 1, we suggested that differences in goal priorities could be the result of the following factors: (1) institutional determinants, such as the electoral system, (2) properties of the party system, such as competitiveness or the number of spatial dimensions, (3) organizational features of the parties, especially such constraints on the leadership as factions or rules that give members and activists an effective say in party decision making, and, finally, (4) exogenous or endogenous situational factors, such as the state of the national or international economy, the personal characteristics of party leaders, the events that precipitated the situation in question, and so on. In this section, we examine the evidence concerning each of these effects. In Chapter 1, we subsumed items (1) and (2) under the same institutional rubric. Here, however, we shall distinguish between direct institutional effects (item 1) and those indirect institutional (and other) effects that operate through the party system (item 2).

INSTITUTIONAL DETERMINANTS

There are, prima facie, many plausible ways in which institutions could influence the goal priorities of political party leaders. Several important factors, such as the magnitude and distribution of the spoils of government, the decision-making structure within and between the legislative and executive branches of government, and the rewards of size embedded in the electoral system, have been reviewed in Chapter 1. One problem with such variables, of course, is that they rarely vary within countries. Hence, case studies of a single country typically do not capture any significant variation in the independent variables. Cross-national studies could, of course, alleviate these problems, but we are rarely in the enviable situation of having enough cases to control for the large number of institutional differences even between very similar states. We can therefore rarely establish precisely which institutional differences most effectively account for variation in party leadership behavior. Yet, the case studies provide enough evidence to demonstrate the relevance of institutions and to suggest some specific ways in which institutions influence party leadership behavior.

PUBLIC PARTY FINANCE

A multitude of institutional features may affect party leadership behavior, as discussed in Chapter 1. One of these concerns the effects of public party finance. According to the argument we developed in Chapter 1, public party finance should tend to make party leaders more autonomous vis-à-vis their followers and thus reduce their incentive to engage in policy-seeking behavior. In other words, it should lessen the policy constraints party leaders are willing to adopt in order to secure the support of their activists.

The impact of public party finance on party behavior has been discussed elsewhere at some length (Strøm 1990a). Since the behavioral effects of party finance are largely indirect, most of the contributors to this volume have not taken up the issue separately. While it is not altogether straightforward to measure the relative generosity of such subsidy schemes, it seems clear that Germany, Austria, and the Scandinavian countries rank high in such government profligacy, whereas Ireland and Italy, for example, rank considerably lower. We would therefore expect parties in the latter countries to show a greater inclination toward policy pursuit. While it is hardly simple to make such assessments, the hypothesis seems to fly in the face of conventional accounts of these various systems. Irish and Italian party leaders do not seem particularly policy constrained in comparative terms. Nor do Scandinavian leaders seem especially shielded from such pressures. Yet, it is difficult to know what weight to attribute to public subvention schemes in making such comparisons.

Spain is the only case in which our volume speaks directly and forcefully to the issue of public party finance effects, and quite understandably so. While for all other parties public party finance either has not been an important source of revenue or, in most cases, has been one of several important financial sources, the PSOE depends entirely on this kind of income. Consequently, the Spanish case is of paradigmatic importance for the impact of public party finance on party behavior. As Share demonstrates, the relative importance of public party finance greatly promoted the PSOE's strategy to stress votes and office at the expense of policy, and thus led to the transformation of the party. In general terms, the less a party depends on resources provided by the party organization, the more it will seek votes or office.

REGIME EFFECTS

Chapter 1 discussed the process by which political institutions convert votes into legislative representation, and further into executive representation and control of office and policy benefits. We can refer to the institutional framework in which these processes take place as the *political regime*. And, as we pointed out in the introduction, a variety of regime characteristics should be expected to influence the goal priorities of party leaders through their effects of this conversion process. Unfortunately, many of these institutional determinants are difficult to capture in adequate operational measures. It is difficult to find measures that are both valid (i.e, they capture the theoretical content of variables that in some cases may not be common in the literature) and reliable (i.e., they are not highly dependent on subjective judgments that may vary from person to person). Due to these problems, any systematic account of such institutional effects therefore has to simplify drastically.

Electoral Institutions

The electoral system is the first stage in the conversion of votes into the types of benefits that party leaders intrinsically desire. In Chapter 1, we argued that the less predictable the conversion of votes into seats, the less fervently we would expect to see party leaders chasing votes. One problem we encounter in putting this proposition to a test is that there simply is not that much variation in the independent variable among the cases in our study. Indeed, most of our countries have high-magnitude proportional representation systems, in which the incentives for vote-seeking should be high. Nonetheless, there are at least partial exceptions. Ireland uses the single transferable vote with relatively small districts (three to five members). France, at the time of Huber's study, had (and still retains) a double-ballot majority-plurality system. Spain has an unusually low district magnitude in a single-tier system. We might therefore expect parties in these countries to score lower in electoral pursuits than others. The evidence produced by our contributors suggests that while this expectation may hold true in Ireland and Spain, it does not seem to do so in France. Of course, we should keep in mind that these kinds of cross-national comparisons are very problematic, and that we have not attempted to control for any of the other factors that are likely to affect parties' goal priorities.

Legislative Institutions

The next stage in the conversion of a party's electoral assets takes place in the legislative arena. As we noted in Chapter 1, the critical question here is how faithfully legislative representation is transformed into bargaining power. This conversion depends partly on characteristics of the party system, as we shall discuss. It is also affected by various agenda powers that impinge on coalition bargaining, notably the discretionary power of the head of state in this process. The more important such discretionary powers and constraints, the less prominent vote-seeking behavior should be. Again, the countries in our study do not exhibit great variation in legislative institutions. Few of them impose serious constraints on coalition bargaining, and only in France and Italy have presidents traditionally exercised much influence on this process. Again, France defies our expectation that parties under such circumstances should place less emphasis on vote-seeking. The Italian Communists, on the other hand, are consistent with this expectation, but keep in mind that D'Alimonte's study covers only one party under highly unusual circumstances.

Governmental Institutions

Finally, the conversion of votes into office and policy benefits depends on executive (governmental) institutions. Conventionally, we often assume that the parties that control the executive branch monopolize both policy and office payoffs. However, in reality, parties not represented in government often have a significant policy impact and may even share in office payoffs. Some institutional arrangements favor governing parties more than others, and we can characterize different polities as having different systemic *office benefit differentials* and *policy influence differentials* – different modal distributions of office and policy influence between government and opposition. The office and policy benefit differentials, respectively, refer to the ex ante expectations among party leaders concerning the allocation of these goods. These differentials are at least partly captured in the distinction between *Westminster* (majoritarian) systems (Lijphart 1984), in which the incumbent parties tend to monopolize both office and policy benefits, and *consensus* (Lijphart 1984) or *inclusionary* (Strøm 1990b) systems, in which policy influence may be gained without control of the executive branch. Of the ten countries covered in this book, some have strong features of consensus or inclusionary democracy (Austria, Sweden, Norway, and Denmark), thus allowing opposition parties potential policy influence. Others, such as Spain, France, Ireland, and Germany, lean more toward the Westminster model.[1]

Ceteris paribus, parties operating under Westminster-type executive institutions should display a greater concern for office than those operating under consensual or inclusionary government institutions. Due to the complexity of the factors affecting party goals, we cannot expect a very good fit between institutional features and party behavior. However, a reasonable correlation between the character of governmental institutions and party behavior nonetheless seems to obtain. In Spain and Germany, the parties in our case studies can without qualification be described as office-seeking. According to Marsh and Mitchell, this is also the case for the two major Irish parties, except in the case of Fine Gael's Tallaght Strategy. The French case, however, is less supportive, as Huber stresses the parties' electoral pursuits. In the low-differential countries (see the earlier discussion), the picture is even less clear, as most of the relevant case studies stress the differences in goal priorities *between* parties in the same country. In sum, there may be some support for the expected effects of governmental institutions, but the record is clearly mixed.

Institutions and the Visibility of Party Impact on Policy

If parties pursue policies for purely instrumental reasons, that is, to win elections, as Downs (1957: 28) assumes, they need to make the electorate aware not only of what these policies are, but also of which party sponsors them.

Parties that pursue policies for intrinsic reasons, but also hope thereby to attract votes, basically face the same situation. Of course, not all policies are popular. Parties governing alone will try to attract attention to policies that are popular with their constituencies and to hide the more unpopular ones. In coalition governments the situation is likely to be more complex: what is popular with the constituency of one party may be highly unpopular with those of other parties. All coalition parties may want to claim credit for some coalition policies but blame their partners for others (Mayhew 1974: 52–61). The design of political institutions can render the control by specific parties over different policy areas more or less obvious, for example, if cabinet portfolio assignments entail strong agenda powers (see Laver and Shepsle 1994, 1996). The more obvious these lines of responsibility, the more confidently voters may assign credit or blame. Our case studies demonstrate that such effects can have an impact on party behavior.

As Poguntke shows, the German FDP has no problem communicating its distinct effects on government policy to the electorate. Its considerable political success in the post–World War II period is based exactly on the party's capacity to moderate the policies of either the CDU/CSU or the SPD in specific ways. This contrasts with the situation of the Irish Labour Party. As Marsh and Mitchell note, Labour's successes in the coalition with Fine Gael went largely unnoticed or benefited the coalition as a whole rather than Labour.

What accounts for this difference? In institutional terms, there seems to be a different conception of *collective cabinet responsibility*. The Irish Labour Party was completely bound by this doctrine and could neither take credit for its proposals nor blame its coalition partner for policies unpopular with Labour's potential electorate. The FDP, in contrast, had no problem indicating to the electorate what part of government policy carried its imprint. While both countries allow cabinet decision making by majority rule, the FDP apparently benefits from a less strict interpretation of collective responsibility. Granted, this differential success in credit claiming reflects not only variations in collective cabinet responsibility, but also differences in the bargaining power of the two parties. While the Labour Party, if it wanted to be in power, had no choice but to coalesce with Fine Gael, the FDP was able to choose between the CDU/CSU and the SPD. Yet, these examples show that the more government institutions allow parties to display their distinctive impact on government policy, the more attractive government office is.

Recall also the French case and consider the *parliamentary rules of procedure*. As Huber shows, these rules provide the government with an opportunity to distribute credit for policy proposals. Indeed, the Socialist government did its best to hide its concessions to the centrist opposition in order to avoid conflict with its own deputies and leftist party activists. Interestingly, the invisibility of the Center's impact also served the interests of the Center itself. By hiding its direct impact on government policy, it could avoid alienating bourgeois voters and political allies. Thus, the case of the French Center shows that fuzzy lines of responsibility can occasionally be an electoral asset, specifically when the object is blame avoidance rather than credit claiming.

PARTY SYSTEM DETERMINANTS

The party system is another potential source of variation in goal priorities among political parties. Party systems are an intermediary context of party decision making. On the one hand they are shaped by electoral and legislative institutions. On the other hand, they form part of the environment that impinges on the strategic decisions of the leaders of individual parties. Our case studies illustrate three party system effects on party behavior: (1) the number of parties, (2) the spatial location of the particular party within the party system, and (3) the competitiveness of the party system.

THE NUMBER OF PARTIES

With respect to the number of parties, the crucial distinction is between two-party and multiparty systems. In a two-party system, according to Sartori, "the existence of third parties does not prevent the two major parties from governing alone", that is, "coalitions are unnecessary" (Sartori 1976: 186, 195). In such party systems, winning office requires maximizing votes (or, more precisely, maximizing seats; see Robertson 1976). Thus we expect the contenders in competitive two-party systems to be vote maximizers.

Our case studies support this reasoning. In Austria, the Socialist Party leaders in 1966 concluded that the party system had become duopolistic and that holding office in the future would depend upon the party's capacity to maximize its electoral support. Consequently, the party turned down the offer of immediate office benefits and gave priority to winning votes in a medium-term time perspective. In France, the two-bloc system of competing party alliances has a similar effect. As Huber shows, perceived electoral costs and benefits are the major determinants of the parties' parliamentary behavior. Similarly, in Spain, maximizing votes and winning office have gone hand in hand for the Socialists. Due to their position in policy space and the fragmentation of the opposition, however, the connection between vote maximization and winning office weakened in the second half of the 1980s. Poguntke's study of the FDP's decision on the *Wende* in West Germany allows us to adopt the perspective of a party that would be deprived of its chances for office if the party system became duopolistic. Consequently, in 1982 the FDP was very careful not to force the CDU/CSU to campaign for a majority of its own.

SPATIAL POSITIONS

While in two-party systems there is a monotonic and predictable relationship between the electoral strength of parties and their bargaining power, in multiparty systems this need not be the case. Our case studies support theoretical considerations elaborated elsewhere (Strøm 1990a: 583–6; Strøm, Budge, and Laver 1994). They clearly indicate that certain parties face hard choices more often than others. The location of a particular party in policy space has a clear effect on its opportunity sets. Pivotal parties have a better chance of maximizing their office *and* policy goals. The German FDP is a case in point. Between 1949 and 1998 it was only twice excluded from the government, and its share of cabinet portfolios has always been substantially greater than its electoral strength. Moreover, it has always occupied some of the most prestigious and important government positions. Another example is the Christian Democrats in the Netherlands. Because of their pivotal position, they (or their Catholic predecessors) participated in all postwar cabinets until 1994. The French Center cannot play a similar role due to institutional differences, in particular the majoritarian electoral system. Parties located toward the extremes of the party spectrum are less likely to realize their office or policy ambitions. The Dutch Labor Party, for example, has, according to many observers, been included in the government only as a last resort, and in Italy the Communists (now the Democratic Party of the Left) did not manage to gain government representation between 1947 and 1996.

ELECTORAL COMPETITIVENESS

Electoral competitiveness refers to the aggregate uncertainty of electoral contests as perceived by party leaders. Specifically, competitiveness is the degree to which they ex ante expect electoral results to vary across the set of feasible policy positions. The more electoral outcomes hinge on policy positions, the more competitive the election. Our expectations concerning electoral competitiveness are obvious and straightforward: the greater the competitiveness, the more party leaders value votes. While there is no fully satisfactory empirical measure of competitiveness, we can at least draw on a set of conventional quantitative measures (see Strøm 1989). If we focus on electoral volatility, for example, we have clear evidence of secular as well as cross-national variation (Pedersen 1979). Denmark and the Netherlands have in recent decades experienced particularly high levels of volatility. As Elklit and Irwin and Hillebrand show, these trends are indeed associated with highly vote-oriented party leaderships. Conversely, parties in low-volatility contexts should sacrifice votes particularly readily. D'Alimonte's analysis of the Italian Christian Democrats suggests that this may indeed be so.

ORGANIZATIONAL DETERMINANTS

While political institutions provide a host of sometimes conflicting incentives for party leaders, the story does not end there. The goal priorities of party leaders are affected not only by these external circumstances in which they operate, but also by the organizational properties of their own parties. Our case studies have sought to examine such organizational sources of variation in goal priorities between parties. Building on the insights of our contributors, in this section we discuss three such sets of organizational determinants: (1) the impact of party activists and members, (2) the role of factions, and (3) the incentive structure of party leaders.

THE IMPACT OF THE MASS MEMBERSHIP ORGANIZATION

The mass organization of a party may affect critical party decisions in two broad ways: directly or indirectly. In the direct way, party members and activists influence party decision making via the formal mechanisms of intraparty democracy. In doing so, they may constrain the party's leading representatives to follow a clearly defined policy course, or they may rule out certain strategies by imposing demands on their leaders under the threat of dismissal or defection. The indirect impact of the party's mass organization rests in the power of party members and activists to "vote with their feet." Similarly, even if party activists retain their memberships, they may withhold their supply of cheap labor. To the extent that the party depends on membership fees and activist labor (e.g., canvassing), party leaders will likely try to anticipate the reactions of their rank and file to their strategies and avoid negative reactions that would undermine the party's resource base. However, while these factors determine the influence belonging to the party's rank and file, they do not a priori establish which goals will be stressed as a result. If we distinguish between ideological (policy-motivated) and nonideological activists (McLean 1982), we expect the former to press for policy, while the latter will push the party toward the goal of assuming governmental office.

Our case studies show the relevance of these considerations. The Irish Labour Party is the most clear-cut example of the direct impact of party organization. According to the 1977 organizational arrangement, the party leader has to submit the results of coalition negotiations to a special conference for a final decision. Since this conference is dominated by party activists who are strongly policy motivated, the Labour Party has to stress its policy concerns during coalition negotiations. As Marsh and Mitchell show, this went so far that in 1981 both negotiating parties, the leaders of Labour and Fine Gael, were concerned to meet the demands of the Labour activists. The Dutch Labor Party is in a similar situation insofar as it also has a militant party cadre pushing for policy. Moreover, the decentralization of the party organization and the separation of the offices of party leader and party chairman provide an organizational structure that is favorable for processing the rank and file's demands. In order to preempt criticism from the rank and file in 1981 and 1991, special party congresses were held to approve the decisions taken by the leadership and to commit the activists to the party's decision.

Elklit notes that, within the Danish Social Democrats, the party organization likewise has more de facto influence than in the two major bourgeois parties. This has led to the former party's greater focus on policy matters. In Sweden, as Bergman shows, it was the Conservative rank and file that pressed for greater policy concern and, albeit ultimately unsuccessfully, forced the party leadership to engage in further negotiations over these demands.

Like the Irish and Dutch labor parties, the Austrian Socialists consulted a special party congress concerning their decision about government participation in 1966. Yet, this was largely a formal matter, probably more a strategy for the Socialist leaders in their game with the People's Party leaders than a genuine intraparty decision-making mechanism. Despite the differences within the party leadership, the party congress had been presented only with a draft of a resolution unanimously decided on by the party leaders. Although the latter differed in their interpretation of this resolution, they did not want the party congress to decide this question. The SPÖ leaders maintained a united front vis-à-vis the public; the congress delegates voted as they were expected to vote. A similar case of largely unconstrained party leaders is the German FDP. According to Kirchner and Broughton (1988: 68), vital decisions such as the change of coalition in 1982, "are taken and implemented and they are then justified and legitimated *afterwards* at party congresses called, in effect, to acknowledge a *fait accompli.*"

A nice contrast to the Social Democrats of Ireland and the Netherlands can be found in their Spanish brethren. In the post-1979 period, the PSOE provides a particularly good example of a party organization with no influence on the policies of the party leadership, a textbook example of the "iron law of oligarchy" (Michels 1962). An extremely majoritarian party constitution and the dependence on the leadership on a majority of party activists (as paid party officials, holders of public offices, or beneficiaries of the spoils of office) provided ideal preconditions for unconstrained office-seeking behavior on the part of the party leaders. The Irish and the Spanish cases offer fascinating *developmental* perspectives. While the Irish Labour Party in the 1970s became more participatory, the Spanish Socialists a few years later moved to a more oligarchical party structure. Both developments were related to the office ambitions of the respective parties' leaders, and both had consequences for future party priorities. In the Labour Party, the downward delegation of the decision on whether or not to participate in government was an attempt to hold the party together after its experience of participating in the 1973–7 coalition, which had failed to provide the policy gains for which the activists had been waiting. For the future, this meant that policy would figure more prominently among the party's goals. In contrast, the Spanish Socialists concentrated intraparty power in the hands of the party leaders as a consequence of their 1979 electoral defeat, which was seen as having been caused by the PSOE's radical policy proposals. This party reform pushed policy concerns into the background, which allowed the PSOE to focus on winning votes and office in the 1982 elections and holding on to power since then.

Let us now turn to the more indirect impact of the party organization through the provision of vital resources. Where these are provided by the party organization, party leaders have to anticipate its reactions, so as not to jeopardize the flow of vital resources. The Italian Communists seem to constitute a case of extreme leadership dependence on the organization, probably beyond its importance in providing scarce resources. According to D'Alimonte, "party identity," that is, the consistent loyalty of members and voters, was the crucial issue. In order to maintain this loyalty, the PCI leaders chose the historic compromise strategy rather than the breakthrough strategy. They gave it up when it turned out that this halfhearted strategy could not even ensure party loyalty among members and activists. In our general scheme, *party identity* might be a shorthand for the services and support provided by activists, which, in turn, may be a means toward future electoral success.

Other examples of party leaders' dependence on the provision of resources include the Dutch and Irish labor parties, which in the Dutch case depends also on the trade unions (Koole 1989). At the other end of the continuum, we find the German FDP and the Spanish Socialists. Thanks to generous public funding and, in the case of the FDP, large donations from the business community, the leaders of neither party depend on their respective organizations to provide the required resources. Thus the FDP could afford to have a substantial number of party members and activists "vote with their feet," as happened after the *Wende*.

FACTIONS

Factionalism can be another major organizational constraint on party leaders. Unlike the impact of the mass organization, which rests in the activists' capacity to impose their will on the leaders via formal intraparty decisions or – indirectly – by their threat of desertion, the power of factions rests in their capacity to influence the implementation of party strategy, for example, via the behavior of MPs.[2] Members of party factions may not feel bound by the decision of the party's central decision-making body, be that the party executive or the parliamentary party. Rather, their behavior is determined by the interests of organizational subgroups, whose goals may differ from those of the party as a whole. The existence of such factions undermines the party's capacity to act as a unitary actor (Laver and Schofield 1990: 19–22). Either a factionalized party adopts a strategy that satisfies all factions, and thus is the party's lowest common denominator (Müller and Steininger 1994), or it faces difficulties in implementing its strategies. Both scenarios represent severe constraints on party leaders.

Three of our case studies throw some light on this aspect of party behavior. As Strøm shows, the apparently irrational behavior of the Norwegian Center Party was caused by the existence of a faction, the "Hedmark guerrilla," with goal priorities distinct from those of the party at large. Thus, in coalition bargaining with the other nonsocialist parties, the Center leadership was engaged in "nested games" (Tsebelis 1990) and could not select the optimal strategy in the *interparty* game. The high level of factionalization of the French

Socialists (Cole 1989) played a similar role in the party's 1989 decision to resort to the guillotine rather than accept the support of some Center deputies for its budget. As Huber argues, the use of the guillotine could, on the one hand, protect the party from undesirable debate, amendment activity, and votes on bills from its various factions. On the other hand, it enabled the parliamentary leader to enhance his appeal to the leftist factions in the upcoming leadership contest. Compromising the budget with the right would have jeopardized his electoral prospects.

Comparing the Austrian Socialists' experience in opposition with the subsequent one of the People's Party, Müller argues that the *absence* of factionalism in the Socialist Party was important for the party's decision to reject immediate office and policy benefits in order to win future elections. Though the Austrian case contrasts with the previous two in associating puzzling behavior with the *lack* of factions, the basic lesson is the same: factions imply constraints. In Norway and France, such constraints resulted in behavior that might not have served the interests of the party as a whole. In the Austrian case, a unitary organization allowed the Socialists to adopt a longer time horizon than parties frequently do.

THE INCENTIVE STRUCTURE OF PARTY LEADERS

Incentives also work at the top. Share reminds us that for decades Socialist Party leaders had had nothing to expect but prosecution under the franquist regime. In a democracy, party leaders are those most likely to benefit from office. It has therefore often been assumed that party leaders will value office more highly than other strata of the party do. Indeed, our case studies confirm that party leaders place a heavy emphasis on office, and it may only be fair to conclude that this is the single most important determinant of party leadership behavior (see the next section). Again, it is fascinating to consider the experience of the Spanish Socialist Party (PSOE), which within a few years went through a development that in other parties has taken decades (though they have not always arrived at the same result). As Share points out, the radical reorientation of the party from policy to office benefits went hand in hand with a replacement of party leaders recruited from the ranks of policy-seeking activists by technocrats and with the recruitment of non-Socialists to government offices.

The case studies also show, however, that it is worthwhile to examine the incentive structures of party leaders in more detail and to consider the implications for their individual careers. Three case studies demonstrate that the evaluation of party strategy from the perspective of individual leaders can help us a great deal in explaining party behavior. Knowing the price of failure in his party, and realizing that this might be his last chance to win office, the leader of the Norwegian Conservatives, Rolf Presthus, made extremely risky decisions that eventually led to disaster. Had he not been caught in this personal incentive structure, Presthus might have waited for a better chance to assume office, to the great potential benefit of his party. Elsewhere, the dominance of nongovernmental career perspectives among the top leaders of the Austrian Socialists led the party to reject office, although the price of taking office might well have been acceptable to others. And as we have seen, this battle for the party leadership had consequences for the French Socialists' legislative behavior.

SITUATIONAL DETERMINANTS

Organizational, institutional, and party system determinants may not fully explain party behavior. Indeed, the same party may under identical institutions adopt different strategies in different situations. Our case studies give some examples of the relevance of *situational* determinants of various sorts. These are relatively short-term conditions that affect the calculus of the relevant party leaders. Situational factors may be endogenous (subject to the actions of the party leaders themselves) or exogenous (beyond their control). They may be more or less easily anticipated in advance.

EXOGENOUS DETERMINANTS

Our cases afford several examples of exogenous situational factors that heavily affected the decisions of party leaders, such as the state of the economy. Anticipated economic problems, for example, were important reasons for the Austrian and Danish Social Democrats to avoid office (and hence blame) in 1966 and 1973, respectively. While under more favorable circumstances they would have tried hard to win governmental office, in the face of economic adversity they were ready to postpone office benefits in order to enjoy likely electoral gains in the future. It seems that the Spanish Socialists were at least partially guided by less opportunistic reasons when they modified their radical policy proposals. Because of the threat to democratic consolidation, they accepted the rules of political compromise rather than contribute to a new left–right polarization. Once elected to governmental office, the PSOE again reacted to the situation. In the context of an international sea change in economic policies, it quickly forgot about the Keynesian program on which it was elected and began to implement policies more in line with the emergent paradigm of neoliberalism.

The case of the Dutch Labor Party is also instructive for the impact of situational factors. Due to its weak bargaining position in the party system, the Dutch Labor Party has not had much choice as to the conditions under which it has been able to assume executive office. In recent decades, it has been invited to join in government only under unpleasant economic conditions. This has affected party behavior. Since, under the given circumstances, incumbency always caused unsatisfactory party performance, both in policy terms and electorally, the Dutch Labor Party was induced to give a relatively low priority to its office goals.

This Dutch example highlights a problem of which party leaders are well aware. The problem is that achieving their various goals depends on much more than their own designs and decisions. Actual goal attainment is obviously more likely in some situations than in others. Situational factors are greatly varied and notoriously ill-suited for generalization. Yet, we are nevertheless confident in singling out one critical and general situational factor: the state and prospects of the economy. Political parties clearly tend to value office more highly under favorable economic conditions than in times of crisis. While office benefits are much the same in good and bad times alike, policy and electoral rewards obviously are not. Potential conflicts between office and other pursuits will therefore tend to be particularly sharp under economic adversity or other crises. If economic recession is around the corner, parties are more likely to postpone office and policy benefits.

The Spanish and Dutch cases are hardly extraordinary. In France, the Communists' decision not to participate in budget negotiations in 1988 were in large part triggered by strikes and other expressions of popular discontent. For the German Free Democrats, the gloomy economic situation, with unemployment rising and projected to go still higher, was a major impetus toward a change of coalition partners. The sudden rise in prominence of the environmental issue contributed to the same effect, since it undermined the electoral support of the SPD and stimulated a surge in the support of the Greens. The Irish Fine Gael faced financial strictures of a more local variety. As Marsh and Mitchell point out, the party's empty coffers were among the causes of its Tallaght Strategy.

The Italian Communists, for their part, gambled on government participation in a situation in which the country faced an "economic and financial disaster," as Roberto D'Alimonte points out. While the weak economy was one of the background factors that helped the Communists enter a situation in which their participation in government seemed possible, it also made their attempt to capitalize on this opportunity more costly. The situation deteriorated for the Communists during the period in which they were approaching the DC because of circumstances that were at least partly outside their control, such as terrorist activities, strikes, and other forms of social unrest. In this sense, the predicament of the PCI is reminiscent of that of the Dutch Labor Party.

ENDOGENOUS FACTORS

But the economy is by no means the only source of situational constraints on the choices of party leaders. Nor are such factors always beyond the control of the parties themselves. In many situations, party leaders may be constrained by endogenous constraints, by choices and precommitments from their past. The framers of the Swedish constitution, for example, were constrained by the fact that they were negotiating "in the shadow" of an elderly and highly respected king, whose popularity prevented republicans from making proposals that they would have otherwise wanted to offer. The fact that all three nonsocialist parties had changed their leaders within two years of the negotiations also facilitated compromise during these negotiations. The new leaders were all more favorably predisposed toward nonsocialist cooperation than their predecessors had been. In addition, one of the Conservative negotiators, Allan Hernelius, was an elderly delegate who may have been more concerned about securing his own place in history, as "one of the men who crafted the Swedish constitution," than about mounting a steadfast defense of the Conservative Party's position on the monarchy. For all of these reasons, Bergman argues, the negotiating parties were more willing to compromise on their policy positions than they might otherwise have been. On the other hand, in France the upcoming congress of the Socialist Party made its leaders less likely to engage in compromises with the opposition than might have been the case under different circumstances.

BARGAINING COMPLEXITY

Our introductory discussion suggested that bargaining complexity may be among the situational factors that shape the critical decisions of party leaders. The greater this complexity, the more easily party leaders may miscalculate, and the more risk averse they may tend to be. In France in 1988, uncertainties resulted more from the novelty of the minority government situation and the secretiveness of the Socialist government than from the number of parties in the negotiations. The bargaining parties (Socialist and Center) had no previous record of cooperation. As Huber shows, the Socialist government courted parties both on its right (Center) and on its left (Communists) and in the process compromised both opposition parties. While in this case the Center was prepared to take risks in cooperating with the Socialists, the experience was on the whole not a happy one. Consequently, the Center in 1989 refused further cooperation due to its experiences the previous year and its expectation of an electoral fallout.

In Italy, the PCI and the DC did not have much of a record of collaboration. As a consequence, the PCI leadership misread the DC's willingness to engage in coalition politics. In this case, their inexperience may have led them to overestimate the chances of success. As discussed earlier, exogenous events soon further dimmed the PCI's prospects. When the costs of the historic compromise became visible, the PCI leadership became much more risk averse and decided against a "social democratic" strategy.

Denmark seems to have an uncommonly high degree of bargaining complexity in many of the situations described by Elklit, but perhaps most notably after the "earthquake" 1973 election and again in 1975. In both cases, the coalition negotiations could well be described as chaotic, both because of the number of parties involved and because of the internal disagreements that wracked some of them, including the Social Democrats. The most discernible effect of these complexities was the formation of numerically very weak governments. It is difficult to draw general lessons from these and other cases in which the bargaining situation was clearly complex. While one might expect such circumstances to induce caution among party leaders, it is not obvious that such an inference could be drawn from the cases we have examined.

INITIAL ENDOWMENTS

One situational factor that may easily affect strategies of party leaders is their initial endowments of votes, office, and policy benefits. Broadly speaking, we would expect that the less a given party has enjoyed of a particular good, the more it is likely to value that type of payoff. In Sweden, for example, the nonsocialist parties, and particularly the Liberals and Conservatives, had been out of office for so long that it was desperately important for them to position themselves well for the upcoming elections. In 1971, they had for the first time presented a joint program on economic affairs. The new Conservative leader, Gösta Bohman, was especially eager to cement an alliance with the Liberals and the Center Party. The situation of office deprivation no doubt contributed to the policy compromises that the nonsocialist parties, and the Conservatives specifically, were willing to make.

The French Center was keenly aware of its initial electoral endowment in resisting compromise with the Socialists in 1989 and 1990. French party leaders were well aware of the peculiar effects of two-bloc electoral competition under the majority runoff electoral system. Under this system, parties are forced into two electoral alliances, in which competition takes place both within and between blocs. The Center had learned from the 1989 European elections that a compromise strategy with the Socialist government did not sit well with voters committed to a nonsocialist bloc, and that the party ran a clear risk of losing its standing among voters in that bloc.

In Germany, it is even more evident that the 5 percent barrier had a profound impact on the FDP's strategy toward its larger competitors. The closer the party to this critical figure, the more overwhelmingly electoral considerations loomed in the decisions of FDP leaders. The Irish Labour Party experienced a similar fate in its 1980s coalition with Fine Gael. The party's projected electoral losses became so severe that they threatened to bring the party down to a critical level at which its very survival was threatened under the small-magnitude STV system. Eventually, this prompted the party leadership to force a dissolution of the coalition that had governed Ireland for much of the 1970s and 1980s.

These latter cases best illustrate the importance of initial endowments. When a party's realization of some goal, such as electoral support, is threatened to some extreme degree, the party may be willing to take unprecedented, costly steps to protect it. And as the "endowment" of expected electoral support becomes more plentiful, its relative value goes down.

PARTY DECISION MAKING

The previous sections have discussed the effects of various factors on the goal priorities that party leaders have set. So far, however, we have ignored the ways in which these results have come about. What can our case studies tell us about the *process* of party decision making? How orderly are such processes, and to what extent do they substantially deviate from the stylized notions with which we have operated so far? Is the decision-making environment either so anarchic or so constraining as to make a mockery of our preconceptions of strategic behavior?

OLIGARCHY AND THE IMPORTANCE OF LEADERSHIP

Probably the most striking general feature of party decision making is the importance of the party leader. In many of our cases, individual leaders committed their parties to behavior that otherwise would not have been likely to occur. At first glance, at least, our contributors seem to confirm many of Michels's (1962) fears concerning the inevitability of oligarchy. The most spectacular example is the Spanish Socialists. Felipe González' threat to resign presented his party with the choice "Felipe or chaos" and led it to accept serious policy sacrifices. Specifically, the PSOE accepted a reversal of its NATO policy and a U-turn in economic policy. Similarly, the Irish and Dutch labor leaders, O'Leary and Den Uyl, respectively, staked their personal leadership on getting their proposals accepted, and thus traded off the security of office for policy gains. In Ireland, the personal office ambitions of Fianna Fáil leader Charles Haughey led the party to give up its core value of "no coalition" and to accept the second-best result. Similarly, Presthus's personal ambitions saddled the Norwegian Conservatives with considerable policy sacrifices and electoral risks for the dubious opportunity of winning governmental office.

In a less spectacular manner, the Social Democratic and Conservative party leaders in Sweden managed to convince their parties to accept policies that fell short of their policy desires but promoted their chances of winning office. Similarly, Fine Gael's Tallaght Strategy (i.e., the attempt to attract votes by supporting the government) was singlehandedly engineered by party leader Alan Dukes. Danish party leaders seem to have acted without much constraint; the personal office ambitions of bourgeois party leaders have been critical to the party strategies pursued, and even the leader of the more policy-oriented Social Democrats, Anker Jørgensen, had critical personal stakes in the game. In several parties, party decision making was more collective in style, although power remained in the hands of a few people. Even if the party's mass organization was consulted, this often did not remove the decision from the leaders. Examples include the 1966 party congress resolution of the Austrian SPÖ and the post facto party congress legitimization of the 1982 decisions to change coalition partners already taken by the leaders of the German FDP.

It is more difficult to establish how often critical party decisions are determined by the personal interests of the party leaders rather than by the organizational interests of the party. This obviously was the case in the Norwegian and the last of the Irish cases, with Presthus and Haughey playing their personal cards rather than those of their respective parties. Similarly, the leader of the French Socialists' parliamentary party gave priority to his ambitions for party leadership over the electoral prospects of his party. Although they were unsuccessful, the same might be said about the office ambitions of a minority of the leaders of the Austrian Socialists. There also was a considerable gap in goal priorities between the party organizations and their leaders in those cases in which the latter resorted to blackmailing the former by threatening to resign. In other cases, party leaders have been able to convince their followers of the merits of their proposals, so that overt exercises of power have been avoided.

CONSTRAINTS

Although the discretion of party leaders is considerable, it is by no means unlimited. Such discretion is, for example, quite often constrained by precommitments intended to shape the bargaining situation to the party's advantage. Thus, a firm commitment to exclude coalitions with certain parties or not to compromise on specific policies may improve the party's electoral prospects. When it comes to government formation or policy compromises, the party leaders then find their hands tied. Our case studies demonstrate the relevance of precommitments in at least two respects.

First, precommitments are the focus of intraparty controversy. Knowing that many crucial decisions are made by the party leaders without consulting the rank and file, party activists quite often try to exercise their influence via precommitments, while party leaders do their best to avoid such constraints. A case in point is the 1982 struggle in the Irish Labour Party between party leaders who wanted a positive, or at least neutral, position on future coalescence with Fine Gael, and their adversaries, who wanted to rule out any further coalition a priori.

Second, precommitments are important for interparty negotiations. The 1981 coalition formation between Fine Gael and Labour shows how party leaders successfully adapted their precommitments (about the introduction of a wealth tax) to the requirements of the coalition at which they were aiming. However, not all party leaders are that flexible in their goals and skillful in their adaptation, and not all have the requisite leeway for doing so. In 1977, for instance, the Dutch Labor Party's precommitment that a number of points in the party program could not be compromised caused the failure of coalition bargaining. Similarly, the Norwegian Center Party's precommitment not to support a vote of no confidence based on the national budget caused the failure of the bourgeois parties to remove the Social Democrats from power. As Strøm argues, this precommitment and the consequent behavior may well have enhanced the credibility of the party and thus helped to maximize its gains in future interparty negotiations.

MISPERCEPTIONS

Not all the strategies developed by political parties in the case studies proved successful. Since party competition is, to a large extent, a zero sum game, this is not astonishing. There must be winners *and* losers. Who will win and who will lose depends upon many factors; the ability of party leaders to analyze the situation and to make the right strategic choices figures prominently. What interests us here is what role misinformation and misperception have in the making of hard choices.

The case studies in this book include some clear-cut cases of misperception on the part of party leaders. D'Alimonte, for example, refers to the PCI's historic compromise strategy as "a textbook example of the failure to perceive party system changes and therefore to adapt party strategy accordingly." The Communist leaders mistakenly considered their 1976 electoral gain to be a consequence of the first steps of the historic compromise strategy, rather than seeing it as a result of being the opposition party par excellence, a position to be increasingly undermined by the party's strategic choices. Similarly, Fine Gael leader Dukes had false hopes concerning the electoral viability of the Tallaght Strategy of backing the government's harsh economic policies without receiving much of a quid pro quo. The two episodes in the history of the Dutch Labor Party featured in the chapter by Hillebrand and Irwin can be read from the same perspective. In both cases, not only did the party believe that it could attract new voters through traditional means (i.e., the social policy initiatives it could launch in government), it also wanted to attract another segment of the electorate by disproving the belief that it was a "spendthrift." All of these parties eventually paid a high electoral price for their failure to calculate voter reactions.

In other cases, party leaders may misperceive the intentions of other politicians, with equally dire consequences. The Norwegian Conservative leader, Rolf Presthus, was not able to predict the moves of the Progress Party (and possibly those of the Center Party) and ended up inflicting a complete debacle on his party. On the other hand, parties also occasionally succeed in spite of ex ante misgivings on the part of their leaders. Thus, although the Austrian Socialists' decision to abandon government participation in 1966 led to an unprecedented series of successes in the 1970s and thus proved right, it is important to keep in mind that several distinguished leaders, including future party chairman

Bruno Kreisky, read the situation quite differently and felt considerable apprehension about the prospects.

Under what conditions, then, are party leaders most likely to be victims of wishful thinking? Though we are not in the position to answer this question definitively, a few comments seem justified. The Norwegian and Irish cases of misperception feature a party leader very inexperienced in hardball party politics. This, however, cannot be said of the Italian Communists, who were headed by the seasoned Enrico Berlinguer, or about the Dutch Labor Party, the leaders of which also had plentiful experience. What the Irish, Dutch, and Italian cases have in common is an assumption by party leaders that the voters would value "responsible" behavior in the national interest, even if it implied a deviation from the party's ideal policy position.

REPRESENTATIVE DEMOCRACY

Political parties face a multitude of demands on their behavior, and their leaders often find themselves facing trade-offs and making compromises between different demands and objectives. The case studies in this book have highlighted some of the factors that influence such decisions. We have also seen how party leaders can sometimes be led astray in their efforts to secure policy, votes, or office benefits for themselves and their parties. But while the organizational or human aspects of these situations may be fascinating in their own right, our main interest here is in the *political* ramifications of party behavior. Political parties are the main vehicles by which political officials in representative democracy can be held accountable by the citizens. The behavior of such organizations is therefore of direct relevance to the confidence we can have in representative institutions.

Representative democracy, according to Held (1987: 4), is "a system of rule embracing elected 'officers' who undertake to 'represent' the interests and/or views of citizens within the framework of law." In political systems that do not allow face-to-face contacts with citizens, and under the condition of increasing division of labor and complexity of politics, citizens have to delegate political decision making to elected officials. According to the mainstream of modern democratic theory, political parties play a crucial role in this process of delegation and hence are the principal instruments of democratic mass politics (Sartori 1987: 148). As David Robertson (1976: 1) puts it, "To talk, today, about democracy, is to talk about a system of competing political parties." Modern democratic theory does not agree, however, about the precise role political parties should play. For the sake of simplicity, we can distinguish two models. In the first one, the parties' contribution to democracy rests entirely on interparty competition. The second model similarly requires interparty competition but also stresses the importance of intraparty participation for democracy.

Democracy as Interparty Competition. In this model, parties serve democracy by offering teams of leaders to "produce government." Political participation by citizens is restricted to popular elections in which they choose one team of leaders, or perhaps simply have the opportunity to remove incumbent political leaders from office. This is the Schumpeterian (1942) model of democracy. In order to get elected, party leaders offer programs that are to be implemented once elected. As Riker (1982: 216) puts it, "In a democracy, the function of a politician is to find an issue on which he or she can win, for thereby a politician expresses some part of the values of the electorate. Political opportunism is not evil, therefore, but is instead the engine of democracy."

Democracy as Intraparty Participation. This second model requires parties not only to compete but also to be internally democratic organizations rather than simply "teams of leaders." Their existence extends the citizens' opportunities for political participation. As members and supporters, they can determine the parties' election programs. It has been argued that such participation will make it less likely that unspecific and ambiguous statements take the place of concrete policies in the programs presented to the voters (Ware 1987). Representative democracy consists of both intra- and interparty democracy, but in this model the emphasis is on the former.

In multiparty systems the voter is hardly in a position to determine who will govern on the basis of which program. These questions are largely left to interparty negotiations after the elections. If the activists and members hold their leaders accountable on a permanent basis, however, they can influence even these decisions, as well as the positions the party adopts vis-à-vis issues that arise between elections. Yet, constraints on party leaders need not produce policies more favored by members. Political leaders may be more in tune with their rank and file than middle-level activists are. Intraparty democracy therefore requires a careful weighting of the powers of different groups within the party. Whatever these institutional arrangements, political parties in this model are first and foremost vehicles for the representation of the preferences of their supporters. Empirical approximations of this model are Powell's *representational parliamentary systems* and Lijphart's *consensus democracies* (Powell 1982: 222–5; Lijphart 1984).

In the first (Schumpeterian) model, political parties fulfill their function to the extent that they are efficient vote seekers. In the second model, political parties should be either policy seekers or office seekers, depending on what their members want. Goal conflicts may arise between party members and ordinary voters; since voters will not be rewarded in terms of office, they will want their respective parties to act as policy seekers. Depending on both the scope of party organization and the volume of office benefits, the same kind of conflict may arise between rank-and-file party members and activists or between activists and leaders. The case studies have provided us with detailed accounts and explanations of party behavior. What are the implications of our findings for the role of political parties as mechanisms of mass representation? Although the number of cases is small, they represent critical decisions that may well give us a better understanding of political parties than a much greater number of day-to-day decisions would provide. Moreover, many authors committed to the second model of party democracy tend to see intraparty participation mainly in relation to such critical decisions.

Some of our results have similar implications for both models of representative democracy. In both models, political parties are likely to fail at their democratic task if their leaders act on misperceptions of the situation facing them. Examples of such behavior have been provided in the previous section. The more pervasive misperception is, and the greater the discrepancy between perception and reality, the less reliable parties become as vehicles of representative democracy. Eventually, however, effective interparty democracy should in itself constrain misperception. Parties whose leaders consistently are out of touch with reality (i.e., who hold inaccurate beliefs about the preferences of voters, activists, or other party leaders) will eventually be driven out of the electoral market.

About half of the parties covered in the case studies used a strategy of vote maximization and hence fulfill the democratic functions of political parties as prescribed by the model of democracy as *interparty competition*. A little less than half of the parties gave priority to office considerations, and only for three parties – the Norwegian Center Party and the Irish and Dutch Labor parties – can we identify policy as the main objective. In the cases where policy figured first among the parties' priorities, this was due either to constraints placed on party leaders by activists or – in the Norwegian case – to factionalism that would have prevented the implementation of a strategy other than policy-seeking. In those cases where the parties acted as office seekers, the leaders were largely unconstrained and thus could heed their own preferences (Riker 1962). The fact that gaining electoral support was the single most important goal of many parties can be read as empirical support for the democratic function of political parties via electoral competition. Within the model of democracy as interparty competition, however, the influence of party activists and the relative autonomy of party leaders – as expressed by giving priority to office rather than to votes – must be viewed as distortions of the democratic function of parties.

Let us now turn to the model of democracy as *intraparty participation*. Democratic intraparty decision making, involving party members and activists, occurred only in a few cases (the Dutch and Irish Labor parties). However, as we have pointed out, even unconstrained party leaders may act as faithful representatives of their rank and file. Unfortunately, in many cases we do not have information on the actual preferences of party members and activists. Nevertheless, the predominance of office pursuits vis-à-vis policy in several nonsocialist parties in countries without extensive spoils systems, such as Denmark, Norway, and Sweden, indicates that party leaders have substantial discretionary authority. In most cases, intraparty participation should probably be viewed *realistically* as a constraint on party leaders rather than as a mechanism for active participation by the rank and file in actual decision making.

Our discussion has generally presupposed that party activists are primarily motivated by policy concerns. However, two case studies demonstrate that even party activists may have preferences other than policy. In the case of the Spanish Socialists, the party leaders' desire for office was matched by the party activists' demands for the spoils flowing from office. The PCI constitutes a sharp contrast: as D'Alimonte has shown, its rank and file favored a vote-seeking strategy.

On balance, there is scant comfort for those who favor the participatory model of party democracy in its hard-core version. This vision of democracy rests on the rank and file's active involvement in important party decisions, and it seems best approximated in parties that combine the desire for sweeping social change with the unreserved acceptance of democracy and long stints of opposition. The number of parties in which intraparty mechanisms significantly constrain party leaders is certainly much higher. There is hardly any party that does not impose at least *some* constraints on its leaders.

ARE PARTIES RESPONSIVE?

Responsiveness means that decision makers are attentive to citizens' demands, respond to them, and consider these demands in policy formulation. At the very least, decision makers "must take these demands seriously and publicly argue why they accept, transform or reject them" (Sjöblom 1988: 189). Parties can be responsive to the electorate (or, more precisely, to their potential voters) or to the activists and members. In the remainder of this section, we briefly ask whether demands from voters and/or activists had an impact on party strategy. We are particularly interested in whether party strategies were altered in response to demands from voters or activists.

Let us start with intraparty responsiveness. The Swedish Conservatives and the Dutch Labour Party in 1991 proved responsive to dissatisfied party activists by trying to improve the bargains struck with other parties. However, both parties did so only within the limits defined by the electoral or office considerations of their leaders. According to our evidence, parties respond much more often to their (potential) voters. The German FDP reacted to declining *Land* election results and opinion polls, which brought the party dangerously close to the 5 percent hurdle, by changing its coalition partner. The Dutch Labor Party in 1982 responded to a decline in the polls and defeats in local and provincial elections by withdrawing from government. In France, the Center Party changed its strategy after an unsatisfactory result in the 1989 European Parliament election, and the Communists responded in a similar manner to an increase in social protest. The Irish Labour Party in 1986 proved responsive by leaving the coalition with the Fine Gael after its electoral commission identified government participation as the "single biggest cause of the party's decline" in the polls. The PCI responded to defeats in the referenda and local elections of 1978 by giving up the historic compromise strategy. The Spanish Socialists responded to electoral defeat in 1977 and 1979 by adjusting their program according to the electoral requirements identified by opinion surveys.

Judging from this evidence, it seems that parties are more responsive to the electorate than to their members and activists. This tendency should encourage proponents of Schumpeterian democracy more than those who champion intra-party participation. The overall responsiveness of political parties is difficult to assess. Yet, parties are reasonably responsive and probably more so than other political organizations or institutions. Though far from playing the role pre-scribed for political parties by democratic theory, in reality they remain the most important mechanism we have for containing political power and allowing widespread participation.

CONCLUSION

Despite the many proclamations of the decline of political parties, they remain the most important organizations in representative democracy. Interest in their organization, functions, and behavior remains deservedly high. Students of po-litical parties fall into a number of distinct camps. Some see parties as rational, disciplined, and competitive. Others stress their heterogeneity, their inclusive-ness, or the accidental nature of their decision-making process. Each facet of the many faces of political parties, in turn, has its normative proponents and detractors.

Political parties have been the subject of a family of formal models, as well as of a large body of often solid and informative empirical work. However, the two research traditions have not always been as fruitfully engaged with one another as one might have hoped. This book has suggested how the sharpest and most parsimonious conceptions of political parties can fruitfully illuminate the study of party decision making. Our approach has been to incorporate some of their analytical tools and their powerful ideas into a broader framework in which party leadership behavior can be understood. This is a book about trade-offs, and our approach in itself implies some important ones. While we have been able to discuss a broad range of goal conflicts and behaviors, and to motivate expectations concerning institutional and organizational effects, we do not have a rigorous deductive model. The main advantages of our framework are its generality and the fact that it builds on the most powerful theories of party behavior. These advantages allow us to study party behavior broadly and yet to be cumulative (Sjöblom 1977). We hope that some of the more tentative inferences we have drawn here will stimulate more intensive theoretical and empirical scholarship. In that sense, our foremost ambition is to set a research agenda. Our hope is that the ten case studies in this volume demonstrate that the notions of parties as seekers of office, votes, or policy can enhance our understanding of these democratic organizations.

NOTES

1. Our classification differs somewhat from Lijphart's (1984), since we are interested only in a subset of the variables that define his ideal types, namely, those having to do with the distribution of power between and within legislative and executive branches at the national level. Italy and the Netherlands are borderline cases for our purposes.
2. The literature offers various definitions of faction (see, e.g., Belloni and Beller 1978; Sartori 1976). Obviously, much of what goes on in mass party organizations is due to organized subgroups. Our focus here is narrower in that the factions discussed in this section display a very high degree of autonomy.

REFERENCES

Belloni, Frank P. and Dennis C. Beller (eds.) (1978). *Faction Politics: Political Parties and Factionalism in Comparative Perspective*. Santa Barbara, CA: ABC-Clio.

Cole, Alistair M. (1989). "Factionalism, the French Socialist Party and the Fifth Republic: An Explanation of Intra-Party Divisions." *European Journal of Political Research* 17, 1: 77–94.

Downs, Anthony (1957). *An Economic Theory of Democracy*. New York: Harper & Row.

Held, David (1987). *Models of Democracy*. Cambridge: Polity Press.

Kirchner, Emil and David Broughton (1988). "The FDP in the Federal Republic of Germany: the Requirements of Survival and Success." In *Liberal Parties in Western Europe* (pp. 62–92), ed. Emil Kirchner. Cambridge: Cambridge University Press.

Koole, Ruud. (1989). "The "Modesty" of Dutch Party Finance." In *Comparative Political Finance in the 1980s* (pp. 200–19), ed. Herbert Alexander. Cambridge: Cambridge University Press.

Laver, Michael J. and Norman Schofield (1990). *Multiparty Government. The Politics of Coalition Government in Europe*. Oxford: Oxford University Press.

    and Kenneth A. Shepsle (eds.) (1994). *Cabinet Ministers and Parliamentary Government*. Cambridge: Cambridge University Press.

    (1996). *Making and Breaking Governments*. Cambridge: Cambridge University Press.

Lijphart, Arend (1984). *Democracies*. New Haven, CT: Yale University Press.

Mayhew, David R. (1974). *Congress: The Electoral Connection*. New Haven, CT: Yale University Press.

McLean, Iain (1982). *Dealing in Votes*. New York: St. Martin's Press.

Michels, Robert (1962). *Political Parties*. New York: Free Press.

Müller, Wolfgang C. and Barbara Steininger (1994). "Party Organization and Party Competitiveness: The Case of the Austrian People's Party." *European Journal of Political Research* 26, 1: 1–29.

Panebianco, Angelo (1988). *Political Parties: Organization and Power*. Cambridge: Cambridge University Press.

Pedersen, Mogens (1979). "The Dynamics of European Party Systems: Changing Patterns of Electoral Volatility." *European Journal of Political Research* 7, 1: 1–26.

Powell, G. Bingham, Jr. (1982). *Contemporary Democracies*. Cambridge, MA: Harvard University Press.

Riker, William H. (1962). *The Theory of Political Coalitions*. New Haven, CT: Yale University Press.

——— (1982). *Liberalism Against Populism*. San Francisco: W. H. Freeman.

Robertson, David (1976). *A Theory of Party Competition*. London: John Wiley.

Sartori, Giovanni (1976). *Parties and Party Systems*. Volume 1. Cambridge: Cambridge University Press.

——— (1987). *The Theory of Democracy Revisited*. Chatham, NJ: Chatham House.

Schumpeter, Joseph A. (1942). *Capitalism, Socialism, and Democracy*. New York: Harper and Brothers.

Sjöblom, Gunnar (1968). *Party Strategies in a Multiparty System*. Lund: Studentlitteratur.

——— (1977). "The Cumulation Problem in Political Science." *European Journal of Political Research* 5, 1: 1–32.

——— (1988). "Some Democratic Regime Norms and Their Relations." In *Legitimacy and Democracy*, (pp. 181–201), eds. Dag Ancker, Hanno Nurmi, and Matti Wiberg. Helsinki: Finnish Political Science Association.

Strøm, Kaare (1989). "Inter-Party Competition in Advanced Democracies." *Journal of Theoretical Politics* 1, 3: 277–300.

——— (1990a). "A Behavioral Theory of Competitive Political Parties." *American Journal of Political Science* 34, 2: 565–98.

——— Ian Budge, and Michael J. Laver (1994). "Constraints on Cabinet Formation in Parliamentary Democracies." *American Journal of Political Science* 38, 2: 303–35.

Tsebelis, George (1990). *Nested Games: Rational Choice in Comparative Politics*. Berkeley: University of California Press.

Ware, Alan (1987). *Citizens, Parties and the State: A Reappraisal*. Cambridge: Polity Press.

INDEX